CAMBRIDGE
Primary English

Teacher's Resource 3

Kathrine Hume

CAMBRIDGE
UNIVERSITY PRESS

University Printing House, Cambridge CB2 8BS, United Kingdom

One Liberty Plaza, 20th Floor, New York, NY 10006, USA

477 Williamstown Road, Port Melbourne, VIC 3207, Australia

314–321, 3rd Floor, Plot 3, Splendor Forum, Jasola District Centre, New Delhi – 110025, India

103 Penang Road, #05–06/07, Visioncrest Commercial, Singapore 238467

Cambridge University Press is part of the University of Cambridge.

It furthers the University's mission by disseminating knowledge in the pursuit of education, learning and research at the highest international levels of excellence.

www.cambridge.org
Information on this title: www.cambridge.org/9781108876100

First published 2015
Second edition 2021

20 19 8 17 16 15 14 13 12 11 10 9 8 7 6 5 4 3 2

Printed in Great Britain by CPI Group (UK) Ltd, Croydon CR0 4YY

A catalogue record for this publication is available from the British Library

ISBN 978-1-108-87610-0 Paperback with Digital Access

Additional resources for this publication at www.cambridge.org/go

....

....

〉 Contents

Digital resources

The following items are available on Cambridge GO. For more information on how to access and use your digital resource, please see inside front cover.

Active learning

Assessment for Learning

Developing learner language skills

Differentiation

Improving learning through questioning

Language awareness

Metacognition

Skills for Life

Letter for parents – Introducing the Cambridge Primary and Lower Secondary resources

Lesson plan template

Curriculum framework correlation

Scheme of work

Audio files

Diagnostic check and answers

Mid-point test and answers

End-of-year test and answers

Answers to Learner's Book activities

Answers to Workbook activities

Glossary

You can download the following resources for each unit:

Differentiated worksheets and answers

Language worksheets and answers

End-of-unit tests and answers

> Acknowledgements

The authors and publishers acknowledge the following sources of copyright material and are grateful for the permissions granted. While every effort has been made, it has not always been possible to identify the sources of all the material used, or to trace all copyright holders. If any omissions are brought to our notice, we will be happy to include the appropriate acknowledgements on reprinting.

Excerpts have been taken from *Approaches to learning and teaching* series, courtesy of Cambridge University Press and Cambridge Assessment International Education.

Unit 1 Excerpt from *Matilda* by Roald Dahl, text copyright 1988 by Roald Dahl. Used by permission of David Higham Associates and Viking Children's Books, an imprint of Penguin Young Readers Group, a division of Penguin Random House LLC. All rights reserved; Excerpt from *Danny The Champion of the World* by Roald Dahl, illustrated by Quentin Blake, copyright 1975 by Roald Dahl. Used by permission of David Higham Associates and Puffin, an imprint of Penguin Young Readers Group, a division of Penguin Random House LLC. All rights reserved; Excerpt from *Charlie and the Chocolate Factory* by Roald Dahl, text copyright 1964 by Roald Dahl. Used by permission of David Higham Associates and Puffin, an imprint of Penguin Young Readers Group, a division of Penguin Random House LLC. All rights reserved; Excerpts from *The Enormous Crocodile* by Roald Dahl, copyright 1978 by Roald Dahl. Used by permission of David Higham Associates and Puffin, an imprint of Penguin Young Readers Group, a division of Penguin Random House LLC. All rights reserved; **Unit 3** 'Dancing Poinciana' by Telecine Turner; 'Hurricane' from *Earth Magic* written by Dionne Brand is used by permission of Kids Can Press Ltd., Toronto. Text Copyright 1979, 2006 Dionne Brand; 'Cat Haiku' by Kobayashi Issa; *Coral Reef* written by Clare Bevan is used by the permission of the author; **Unit 4** 'Bear and Fire' S.E Schlosser and AmericanFolklore.net. Copyright 2014. All rights reserved; Extracts from *Sinbad and the Roc* by Ian Whybrow, illustrated by Nick Schon, Cambridge Reading Adventures, Cambridge University Press, used by kind permission of the author; **Unit 6** Extract from *Four Clever Brothers* by Lynne Rickards, illustrated by Galia Bernstein © Cambridge University Press and UCL Institute of Education, 2017; **Unit 7** Extract and illustrations from *Alfie Small: Pirates and Dragons* and *Alfie Small: Ug and the Dinosaurs* by Nick Ward, copyright copyright by Nick Ward 2010, published by David Fickling Books 2012. Reprinted by permission of Penguin Books Limited; Extract from Who's A Clever Girl, Then? copyright © Rose Impey 1993 reproduced by kind permission of Rose Impey c/o Caroline Sheldon Literary Agency Ltd; Extracts from *Dragon Boy* by Pippa Goodhart, illustrated by Martin Ursell, Reprinted by permission of HarperCollins Publishers Ltd, copyright 2003 Pippa Goodhart and Martin Ursell; **Unit 8** *Caribbean Islands* by Alice Harman, Wayland. Reproduced by permission of Wayland, an imprint of Hachette Children's Books; **Unit 9** 'Wordspinning' by John Foster from *The Works*, reproduced by permission of author; 'Starter' from *Smile, Please* by Tony Bradman. Reproduced by permission of The Agency (London) Ltd. Copyright Tony Bradman, 1986, First published by Viking; 'Kite' by June Crebbin, originally in *The Crocodile is Coming*, June Crebbin, Walker Books 2005; The Elephant, The Scorpion and The Lion by Hilaire Belloc from Complete Verse by Hilaire Belloc reprinted by permission of Peters Fraser & Dunlop on behalf of the Estate of Hilaire Belloc; **Tests** Excerpt and Illustrations from *1000 Things to Make and Do* by Fiona Watt, Published by Usborne Publishing Ltd., London. © 2011, 2009, 2007 Usborne Publishing Ltd. Reprinted with the permission of Usborne Publishing Ltd; Excerpt(s) from *JAMES AND THE GIANT PEACH* by Roald Dahl, text copyright © 1961 by Roald Dahl. Used by permission of Puffin, an imprint of Penguin Young Readers Group, a division of Penguin Random House LLC. All rights reserved & David Higham Associates Ltd; Excerpt from *Dragon in the Cupboard* (Usborne Young Puzzle Adventures) by Karen Dolby, Published by Usborne Publishing Ltd., London. © 1995 Usborne Publishing Ltd. Reprinted with the permission of Usborne Publishing Ltd.

Cover image by Pablo Gallego (Beehive Illustration)

> Introduction

Welcome to the new edition of our Cambridge Primary English series.

Since its launch, the series has been used by teachers and learners in more than 100 countries for teaching the Cambridge Primary English curriculum framework.

This exciting new edition has been designed by talking to Primary English teachers all over the world. We have worked hard to understand your needs and challenges, and then carefully designed and tested the best ways of meeting them.

As a result of this research, we've made some important changes to the series. This Teacher's Resource has been carefully redesigned to make it easier for you to plan and teach the course.

The series now includes digital editions of the Learner's Books and Workbooks. This Teacher's Resource also offers additional materials available to download from Cambridge GO. (For more information on how to access and use your digital resource, please see inside front cover.)

The series uses the most successful teaching approaches, like active learning and metacognition, and this Teacher's Resource gives you full guidance on how to integrate them into your classroom.

Formative assessment opportunities help you to get to know your learners better, with clear learning intentions and success criteria as well as an array of assessment techniques, including advice on self- and peer assessment.

Clear, consistent differentiation ensures that all learners are able to progress in the course with tiered activities, differentiated worksheets and advice about supporting learners' different needs.

All our resources include extra language support to enable teaching and learning in English. They help learners build core English skills with vocabulary and grammar support, as well as additional language worksheets.

We hope you enjoy using this course.

Eddie Rippeth

Head of Primary and Lower Secondary Publishing, Cambridge University Press

> About the authors

Kathrine Hume

Kathrine Hume has been involved in primary-school education in the UK for 40 years, as both a teacher and headteacher. Her experience has been in mainstream and special education, within rural and city schools. As a headteacher, much of her work involved encouraging and developing trainee and recently qualified teachers.

Kathrine joined Cambridge University Press as an author following her retirement as a headteacher.

Sarah Lindsay

Sarah Lindsay started her educational career as a primary school teacher in the UK. She then moved into authoring educational material, full-time, for primary-school aged children; this she has done for the last 20 years, writing for international markets. For 12 years she has been a school governor.

Among many projects she has been involved with, Sarah was a lead author on the *Cambridge Grammar and Writing Skills* series.

Kate Ruttle

Kate Ruttle has been a primary-school teacher in the UK for over 30 years. She has been involved in educational publishing for over 25 years and has worked on a wide range of resources for teaching literacy as well as for supporting learners with special educational needs.

She has contributed to the development of the Cambridge International curriculum for English as a First Language as well as producing resources linked to the curriculum.

> How to use this series

All of the components in the series are designed to work together.

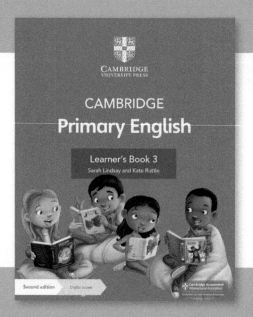

The Learner's Book is designed for learners to use in class with guidance from the teacher. It offers complete coverage of the curriculum framework. A variety of investigations, activities, questions and images motivate learners and help them to develop the necessary skills. Each unit contains opportunities for formative assessment, differentiation and reflection so you can support your learners' needs and help them progress.

A digital version of the Learner's Book is included with the print version and is available separately. It includes simple tools for learners to use in class or for self-study.

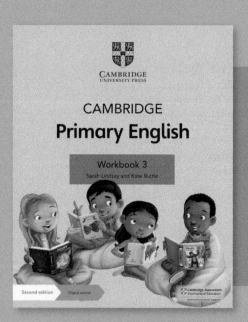

The skills-focused write-in Workbook provides further practice of all the topics in the Learner's Book and is ideal for use in class or as homework. A three-tier, scaffolded approach to skills development promotes visible progress and enables independent learning, ensuring that every learner is supported. Teachers can assign learners questions from one or more tiers for each exercise, or learners can progress through each of the tiers in the exercise.

A digital version of the Workbook is included with the print version.

The Teacher's Resource is the foundation of this series and you'll find everything you need to deliver the course in here, including suggestions for differentiation, formative assessment and language support, teaching ideas, answers, diagnostic checks and extra worksheets. Each Teacher's Resource includes:

- A **print book** with detailed teaching notes for each topic

- **Digital access** with all the material from the book in digital form plus editable planning documents, extra guidance, worksheets and more.

A letter to parents, explaining the course, is available to download from Cambridge GO (as part of this Teacher's Resource).

> How to use this Teacher's Resource

This Teacher's Resource contains both general guidance and teaching notes that help you to deliver the content in our Cambridge Primary English resources. Some of the material is provided as downloadable files, available on **Cambridge GO**. (For more information about how to access and use your digital resource, please see inside front cover.) See the Contents page for details of all the material available to you, both in this book and through Cambridge GO.

Teaching notes

This book provides **teaching notes** for each unit of the Learner's Book and Workbook. Each set of teaching notes contains the following features to help you deliver the unit.

The **Unit plan** summarises the topics covered in each unit, including the number of learning hours recommended for each topic, an outline of the learning content and the Cambridge resources that can be used to deliver the topics.

Session	Approximate number of learning hours	Outline of learning content	Resources
1.1 Setting the scene	1	Identify what a setting is, explore and talk about different settings, and write sentences to describe settings.	Learner's Book Session 1.1 Workbook Session 1.1

The **Background knowledge** feature outlines specific skills, resources, grammar and subject knowledge that you can familiarise yourself with in order to help you teach the unit content effectively.

Learners' prior knowledge can be informally assessed through the **Getting started** feature in the Learner's Book.

The **Teaching skills focus** feature covers a teaching skill and suggests how to implement it in each unit.

BACKGROUND KNOWLEDGE

It would be useful to have some familiarity with Roald Dahl's stories, in particular: *Matilda, Charlie and the Chocolate Factory, Danny the Champion of the World* and *The Enormous Crocodile*. Try to use one of Roald Dahl's books as a class story.

TEACHING SKILLS FOCUS

As with all skills, metacognition skills need to be taught. Ask yourself: *How often do I show learners that I am thinking?*

Reflecting the Learner's Book, each unit consists of multiple sessions. A session covers a learning topic.

At the start of each session, the **Learning plan** table includes the learning objectives, learning intentions and success criteria that are covered in the section.

It can be helpful to share learning intentions and success criteria with your learners at the start of a lesson so that they can begin to take responsibility for their own learning.

LEARNING PLAN		
Learning objectives	**Learning intentions**	**Success criteria**
3Rv.01, 3Rv.04, 3Rg.01	• Explore different settings for stories.	• Learners can explore different settings for stories.

There are often **common misconceptions** associated with particular learning topics. These are listed, along with suggestions for identifying evidence of the misconceptions in your class and suggestions for how to overcome them.

Misconception	How to identify	How to overcome
Adjectives can be added after the noun without using a verb (e.g. *There are flowers colourful*).	When learners describe a setting (note the word class order).	Give learners several simple sentences containing an adjective. Cut each sentence into individual words. Ask learners to put the sentences in order. You could give each word to a different learner so that they have to physically put themselves in order.

For each topic, there is a selection of **starter ideas**, **main teaching ideas** and **plenary ideas**. You can pick out individual ideas and mix and match them depending on the needs of your class. The activities include suggestions for how they can be differentiated or used for assessment. **Homework ideas** are also provided.

Starter idea

Talk about a picture (10 minutes)

Resources: Learner's Book, Session 1.1: Getting started

Description: Ask learners to talk in groups about what they can see in the pictures in the Learner's Book. Ask each group to focus on one of the settings and note down words they could use to describe it. Ask each group to share their words and write them on the board.

1 Talk about places (10 minutes)

Learning intention: To describe different settings shown in photographs.

Resources: Learner's Book, Session 1.1, Activity 1; Session 1.1: Getting started

Description: Ask learners to look at the photographs. Elicit the names of the places (*a market, a beach, a wood/park/jungle, a fairground*). Ask learners to work in pairs to talk about the photos using the questions as prompts.

The **Language support** feature highlights specific vocabulary and uses of English throughout the unit that learners might not have encountered before, or may struggle with. It contains suggestions on how to approach these with your class and helpful examples to help them better understand.

LANGUAGE SUPPORT

Help learners to remember and use their phonics while reading these poems. For those who need more practice, use games. For example, ask learners to stamp on a cup / jump over a letter grapheme written on a card and placed in front of them / leap up from their seat when they hear a specific sound.

The **Cross-curricular links** feature provides suggestions for linking to other subject areas.

CROSS-CURRICULAR LINKS

Science: As an introduction to solids, liquids and gases, learners could classify and describe materials with adjectives based on their properties (e.g. dull, shiny, hard, soft, transparent, opaque).

Digital resources to download

This Teacher's Resource includes a range of digital materials that you can download from Cambridge GO. (For more information about how to access and use your digital resource, please see inside front cover.) This icon ⬇ indicates material that is available from Cambridge GO.

Helpful documents for planning include:

- **Letter for parents – Introducing the Cambridge Primary and Lower Secondary resources:** a template letter for parents, introducing the Cambridge Primary English resources.
- **Lesson plan template:** a Word document that you can use for planning your lessons.
- **Curriculum framework correlation:** a table showing how the Cambridge Primary English resources map to the Cambridge Primary English curriculum framework.
- **Scheme of work:** a suggested scheme of work that you can use to plan teaching throughout the year.

Each unit includes:

- **Differentiated worksheets:** these worksheets are provided in variations that cater for different abilities. Worksheets labelled 'A' are intended to support less confident learners, while worksheets labelled 'C' are designed to challenge more confident learners. Answer sheets are provided.
- **Language worksheets:** these worksheets provide language support. Answers sheets are provided.
- **End-of-unit tests:** these provide quick checks of learners' understanding of the concepts covered in the unit. Answers are provided. Advice on using these tests formatively is given in the Assessment for Learning section of this Teacher's Resource.

Additionally, the Teacher's Resource includes:

- **Diagnostic check and answers:** a test to use at the beginning of the year to discover the level that learners are working at. The results of this test can inform your planning.
- **Mid-point test and answers:** a test to use after learners have studied half the units in the Learner's Book. You can use this test to check whether there are areas that you need to go over again.
- **End-of-year test and answers:** a test to use after learners have studied all units in the Learner's Book. You can use this test to check whether there are areas that you need to go over again, and to help inform your planning for the next year.
- **Answers to Learner's Book activities**
- **Answers to Workbook activities**
- **Glossary**

In addition, you can find more detailed information about teaching approaches.

🎧 **Audio** is available for download from Cambridge GO (as part of this Teacher's Resource and as part of the digital resources for the Learner's Book and Workbook).

> CAMBRIDGE PRIMARY ENGLISH 3 WORKSHEET 1.4: SEQUENCING EVENTS FROM *THE ENORMOUS CROCODILE*

Name _____ Date _____

Worksheet 1.4: Sequencing events from *The Enormous Crocodile*

Place each of these events from *The Enormous Crocodile* on the story mountain.

| A Enormous Crocodile leaves the river saying he has secret plans and clever tricks to catch a child to eat. | B Enormous Crocodile tries out his secret plans and clever tricks. | The elephant grabs Enormous Crocodile by the tail and swings him round and round. When he lets go Enormous Crocodile flies in to space and is never seen again. |

Enormous Crocodile meets other jungle animals. He tells them his plan to eat a child. None of them like his idea, they all like the children in the town.

happens [ ]

> CAMBRIDGE PRIMARY ENGLISH 3 WORKSHEET 1.5: THINKING OF IDEAS FOR A STORY

Name _____ Date _____

Worksheet 1.5: Thinking of ideas for a story

…n get some ideas for a new story by looking carefully at a story you already know.
…bout the order of events in *The Enormous Crocodile*.
…the events to make a new story.

	Order of events	New story
…ous Crocodile tells …g One he is going …little child for	**Introduction** Introduce the main character and main idea.	
…Crocodile …river saying he …lans and …to catch a	**Beginning/problem** Explain what's going to happen in the story.	
…codile …ngle …f them his …. None …ea, they …in the	**Development** Someone says the main character can't do something.	
…tries	**Exciting part**	

> CAMBRIDGE PRIMARY ENGLISH 3 WORKSHEET 1.3: DIALOGUE IN STORIES

Name _____ Date _____

Worksheet 1.3: Dialogue in stories

Read the story.

Vihaan and his sister, Ananya, …

'Hurry up, Vihaan,' called Anan… looking at now?'

Vihaan was staring into one of… could see Vihaan was in a wor…

Ananya headed back and sho… arm. 'We're going to be late!'

'But look, Ananya,' said Viha…

Ananya looked in the shop … it would be the start of this … more delicious than ever an… hungry!

'I hope mum makes some b… and it has little pieces of si…

Ananya took another look … murmured, licking her lips… crystallised fruits at the f…

'I think that's Agra Ka Pe… asked, pointing to anoth… wonderful?'

But Ananya was alread… Vihaan, running after h…

'Come on then, hungry…

Cambridge Primary English…

> CAMBRIDGE PRIMARY ENGLISH 3 WORKSHEET 1.2: CHANGING ADJECTIVES

Name _____ Date _____

Worksheet 1.2: Changing adjectives

Roald Dahl liked to paint very clear pictures of the characters in his stories. He liked his readers to know how special a character was. In *Charlie and the Chocolate Factory* he used lots of adjectives to describe Mr Wonka.

Sometimes he used words to emphasise a characteristic, such as 'extraordinary little man' or 'marvellously bright eyes'.

Look at the words in Box A.

Box A

| incredibly revoltingly dangerously …intingly disgustingly fabulously … |

Now look at the pairs of words in Box B.

Box B

| small box yellow jelly beautiful … scary spider fie… |

Choose a word from Box A to match with one … Write a sentence using these words.

Now do this again with other words from bo…

_____

_____

_____

_____

Cambridge Primary English…

> CAMBRIDGE PRIMARY ENGLISH 3 WORKSHEET 1.1: ORDERING ADJECTIVES

Name _____ Date _____

Worksheet 1.1: Ordering adjectives

Read these sentence pairs. Tick (✔) the sentence where the adjectives are in the correct place. Then write the correct sentence underneath. The first one has been done for you.

> In English, when you use an adjective next to a noun, you always put the adjective in front.

Miss Honey's cottage had windows two. ✔ ☐ Miss Honey's cottage had two windows. ☐

Miss Honey's cottage had two windows.

In the corner was a tiny little bed. ☐ In the corner was a bed tiny little. ☐

_____

The hyenas two chased the giraffe. ☐ The two hyenas chased the giraffe. ☐

_____

Dak had a big smile on his face. ☐ Dak had a smile big on his face. ☐

_____

1

> About the curriculum framework

The information in this section is based on the Cambridge Primary English curriculum framework (0058) from 2020. You should always refer to the appropriate curriculum framework document for the year of your learners' assessment to confirm the details and for more information. Visit www.cambridgeinternational.org/primary to find out more.

The Cambridge Primary English curriculum has been designed to help learners to become confident communicators. They will learn to apply reading, writing, speaking and listening skills in everyday situations, as well as develop a broad vocabulary and an understanding of grammar and language. Through this curriculum, learners will develop evaluation skills, learn to appreciate texts from different cultures and learn to write for different audiences and purposes.

The Cambridge Primary English curriculum framework is split into three strands: reading, writing, and speaking and listening. For more information, visit the Cambridge Assessment International Education website.

A curriculum framework correlation document (mapping the Cambridge Primary English resources to the learning objectives) and scheme of work are available to download from Cambridge GO (as part of this Teacher's Resource).

> About the assessment

Information about the assessment of the Cambridge International Primary English curriculum framework is available on the Cambridge Assessment International Education website: **www.cambridgeinternational.org/primary**

> Approaches to learning and teaching

The following are the teaching approaches underpinning our course content and how we understand and define them.

Active learning

Active learning is a teaching approach that places learner learning at its centre. It focuses on how learners learn, not just on what they learn. We, as teachers, need to encourage learners to 'think hard', rather than passively receive information. Active learning encourages learners to take responsibility for their learning and supports them in becoming independent and confident learners in school and beyond.

Assessment for Learning

Assessment for Learning (AfL) is a teaching approach that generates feedback, which can be used to improve learners' performance. Learners become more involved in the learning process and, from this, gain confidence in what they are expected to learn and to what standard. We, as teachers, gain insights into a learner's level of understanding of a particular concept or topic, which helps to inform how we support their progression.

Differentiation

Differentiation is usually presented as a teaching approach where teachers think of learners as individuals and learning as a personalised process. Whilst precise definitions can vary, typically the core aim of differentiation is viewed as ensuring that all learners, no matter their ability, interest or context, make progress towards their learning intentions. It is about using different approaches and appreciating the differences in learners to help them make progress. Teachers therefore need to be responsive, and willing and able to adapt their teaching to meet the needs of their learners.

Language awareness

For all learners, regardless of whether they are learning through their first language or an additional language, language is a vehicle for learning. It is through language that learners access the learning intentions of a lesson and communicate their ideas. It is our responsibility, as teachers, to ensure that language doesn't present a barrier to learning.

Metacognition

Metacognition describes the processes involved when learners plan, monitor, evaluate and make changes to their own learning behaviours. These processes help learners to think about their own learning more explicitly and ensure that they are able to meet a learning goal that they have identified themselves or that we, as teachers, have set.

Skills for Life

How do we prepare learners to succeed in a fast-changing world? To collaborate with people from around the globe? To create innovation as technology increasingly takes over routine work? To use advanced thinking skills in the face of more complex challenges? To show resilience in the face of constant change? At Cambridge, we are responding to educators who have asked for a way to understand how all these different approaches to life skills and competencies relate to their teaching. We have grouped these skills into six main Areas of Competency that can be incorporated into teaching, and have examined the different stages of the learning journey and how these competencies vary across each stage.

These six key areas are:

- Creativity – finding new ways of doing things, and solutions to problems
- Collaboration – the ability to work well with others
- Communication – speaking and presenting confidently and participating effectively in meetings
- Critical thinking – evaluating what is heard or read, and linking ideas constructively
- Learning to learn – developing the skills to learn more effectively
- Social responsibilities – contributing to social groups, and being able to talk to and work with people from other cultures.

Cambridge learner and teacher attributes

This course helps develop the following Cambridge learner and teacher attributes.

Cambridge learners	Cambridge teachers
Confident in working with information and ideas – their own and those of others.	**Confident** in teaching their subject and engaging each learner in learning.
Responsible for themselves, responsive to and respectful of others.	**Responsible** for themselves, responsive to and respectful of others.
Reflective as learners, developing their ability to learn.	**Reflective** as learners themselves, developing their practice.
Innovative and equipped for new and future challenges.	**Innovative** and equipped for new and future challenges.
Engaged intellectually and socially, ready to make a difference.	**Engaged** intellectually, professionally and socially, ready to make a difference.

Reproduced from Developing the Cambridge learner attributes *with permission from Cambridge Assessment International Education.*

More information about these approaches to learning and teaching is available to download from Cambridge GO (as part of this Teacher's Resource).

Approaches to learning and teaching English

In this new edition of Cambridge Primary English we offer an integrated approach to language skills (speaking, listening, reading and writing). This means that in each English lesson you can expect a focus on learning objectives from each strand of the curriculum framework. Each Learner's Book contains nine units: two long units and one shorter unit per 10-week term. Each long unit of 12 sessions has been designed to be delivered over four weeks, with three lessons per week, plus a revision session. If your timing is different we hope the materials are flexible enough for you to be able to fit them to your requirements. The shorter units of six sessions are intended to be delivered over two weeks, plus a revision unit. The units per term may be taught in any order with progression being built in per term, rather than unit-by-unit, to add further flexibility for the use of the programme and to allow for more cross-curricular matching.

Listening and speaking are a focus for effective communication, but also underpin reading and writing skills too. We consolidate and develop the sub-strands including: making yourself understood; showing understanding; group work and discussion; performance; and reflection and evaluation. We have included additional listening activities in this edition and there is enhanced support for developing listening and speaking skills in authentic and exciting contexts. Audio tracks actively promote good pronunciation of English and you will find recordings of all the texts from the Learner's Book in this Teacher's Resource.

Across each stage for reading and writing we introduce a wide range of fiction and non-fiction texts including fiction genres, poetry and non-fiction text-types for different purposes. There is a broad selection of authentic texts from around the world, which have been included to promote reading for pleasure as well as an understanding of meaning and the conventions and features of different types of writing.

For reading and writing we orchestrate rich coverage of each sub-strand and are still mindful to integrate listening, speaking, reading and writing skills as follows:

Word structure (phonics and spelling): We assume schools have followed a systematic phonics programme with decodable reading books and that increasingly learners are encouraged to enjoy and explore texts with less restricted word choice. We believe that phonics knowledge is a strong basis for reading and spelling, and that learners need to be both taught and have time to explore spelling patterns, rules and exceptions. By actively focusing the learners' attention on activities and useful rules in the context of the lesson, this course aims to improve the average spelling age in your classroom. Phonic workbooks are provided for Stage 1 and may be of some use for learners who need further or repeated practice in basic phonics at Stage 2.

The downloadable spelling lists in this Teacher's Resource are a supplement to the spelling activities at the back of the Learner's Book. Embedded throughout the notes are **Spelling links**; these are intended to suggest opportunities at which the indicated spelling areas can be looked at in greater detail.

There are three spelling spreads included at the back of each Learner's Book. Each spread contains specific spelling activities to address some of the spelling objectives in a systematic way to ensure complete coverage of all the objectives. They can be used at the teacher's discretion as part of a wider session or as part of a dedicated spelling session. The answers to the spelling activities are included at the end of this Teacher's Resource.

A suggested spelling session format

- **SAY the word and SEE the word.** Introduce words both orally and visually so the children see each word and hear the sound simultaneously to develop auditory perception. Use flash cards, words appearing on a screen or written on the board.

- **PLAY with the word.** They write it in the air or on their desk with a finger, mime it to a partner, write it on a slate or paper and hold it up, do visual memory activities with a partner: look at a word, close eyes and spell it. These activities provide immediate feedback and develop visual memory. Clap the sounds to demonstrate how the word is broken into syllables. Let the children find their own associations to help them remember words e.g. *ear* in h*ear* or *ache* in head*ache*.

- **ANALYSE the word.** Spelling rules can be helpful here to explain how words are built up, why letters move, how sounds change from one word to another and how patterns fit into words.

- **USE the word – make up a sentence.** Activities are provided in the Learner's Book but you can add to these by playing spelling games. Younger children enjoy spelling 'snap' or 'bingo'; older children might enjoy a spelling challenge/ladder or a competition that involves winners.

- **LEARN the word.** They commit the word to memory while writing it out in a wordbook or personal spelling notebook. Tests or assessments need not be repetitive weekly activities but learners do need incentive to internalise the spelling of words and to see they are making progress.

Vocabulary and language: We provide multiple experiences and strategies for securing vocabulary, including saying a word and then writing it, exploring context, grammatical features and a word's relationship to other words (word families, prefixes, suffixes etc.). We also explore texts with learners to reflect on writers' choices of vocabulary and language. In the final sessions of each unit we then innovate on the text vocabulary or language to apply learning and try out new found skills and knowledge.

Practical ideas for the classroom

Words and spellings need to be highlighted and enriched at every opportunity in the classroom.

1 Encourage personal word books or cards: include words covered in spelling sessions and ones they look up in the dictionary. At the back, suggest learners develop a bank of words they would like to use (especially powerful, descriptive or unusual words). Word meanings can also be included. Some children may benefit by using colours or underlining/ highlighting to identify tricky bits or root words.

2 Have a classroom display of aspirational words or themed words around a topic (any learning area).

3 Have plenty of large spelling resources – online and print dictionaries, thesauruses, etc.

4 Set up spelling buddies as a first line of check if a dictionary or thesaurus does not help.

5 Play word games such as word dominoes or phonic pairs on a set of cards as a memory game.

6 Highlight and discuss word origins and have a merit system for anyone with interesting words or word information to share.

7 Display lists of words with similar sounds or letter patterns (either at the start, middle or end) – write the words large in the handwriting taught at the school joined up if appropriate to stimulate visual and kinaesthetic knowledge.

8 Have an interactive word list of interesting words, or words that match a spelling rule or word pattern being focused on. Add to it whenever anyone comes across a relevant word.

9 Consider an alphabet of vowel sounds and consonant sounds as a display or frieze around the walls.

10 If handwriting lessons are timetabled, add word patterns and sounds into those sessions.

11 Research free web resources to create your own crosswords and word searches linked to vocabulary in themes and spelling rules you are working on.

Grammar and punctuation: Whilst being mindful of reading for pleasure and text coherence, we focus on the grammar and punctuation arising from a text so that learners experience new learning in context. We have respected both teacher and learners' capacity for understanding and using correct metalanguage in the classroom and especially in writing activities.

Structure of texts: An exciting range of authentic texts is provided for discussion, performance, reflection and as models for learners' own writing. This is especially true in the final sessions of each unit when learners aim to write within the support of frameworks or scaffolds.

Interpretation of and creation of texts: Whilst the units provide a rich and broad selection of texts, it is also expected that learners are enjoying texts outside of the course, but aligned in some way to the topic or theme. Differentiation within each activity ensures that all learners can explore authentic texts and experiment with creative ideas and writing.

Appreciation and reflection of reading: We support the ethos of reading for pleasure and encourage learners to reflect and evaluate their wider reading from an early age. Links to Cambridge Reading Adventures (CRA) series are provided and offer a perfect bridge for learners between the texts in the Learner's Books, Book Band graded reading books in CRA and the wider world of authentic texts. We adopt 'assessment for learning' strategies to encourage learners to work independently and in pairs or groups to discuss their reading (and wider learning), to share experiences and to respond to others' ideas and experiences.

Presentation and reflection of writing: We encourage learners to adopt a write, reflect/evaluate and improve cycle of working from an early age. We encourage them to present their own work and listen for feedback as well as to talk about their own ideas and others'. Handwriting is an important part of writing and this series encourages best practice in handwriting but does not teach it explicitly. We recommend using the *Cambridge Penpals for Handwriting* series alongside *Cambridge Primary English* for teaching handwriting.

> Setting up for success

Our aim is to support better learning in the classroom with resources that allow for increased learner autonomy while supporting teachers to facilitate learner learning. Through an active learning approach of enquiry-led tasks, open-ended questions and opportunities to externalise thinking in a variety of ways, learners will develop analysis, evaluation and problem-solving skills.

Some ideas to consider, to encourage an active learning environment, are as follows:

- Set up seating to make group work easy.
- Create classroom routines to help learners to transition between different types of activity efficiently (e.g. move from pair work to listening to the teacher to independent work).
- Source mini-whiteboards, which allow you to get feedback from all learners rapidly.
- Start a portfolio for each learner, keeping key pieces of work to show progress at parent–teacher days.
- Have a display area with learners' work and vocab flashcards.

Planning for active learning

We recommend the following approach to planning:

1 **Plan learning intentions and success criteria:** these are the most important feature of the lesson. Teachers and learners need to know where they are going in order to plan a route to get there.

2 **Plan language support:** think about strategies to help learners overcome the language demands of the lesson so that language doesn't present a barrier to learning.

3 **Plan starter activities:** include a 'hook' or starter to engage learners using imaginative strategies. This should be an activity where all learners are active from the start of the lesson.

4 **Plan main activities:** during the lesson, try to: give clear instructions, with modelling and written support; coordinate logical and orderly transitions between activities; make sure that learning is active and all learners are engaged; create opportunities for discussion around key concepts.

5 **Plan assessment for learning and differentiation:** use a wide range of Assessment for Learning techniques and adapt activities to a wide range of abilities. Address misconceptions at appropriate points and give meaningful oral and written feedback which learners can act on.

6 **Plan reflection and plenary:** at the end of each activity and at the end of each lesson, try to: ask learners to reflect on what they have learned compared to the beginning of the lesson; build on and extend this learning.

7 **Plan homework:** if setting homework, it can be used to consolidate learning from the previous lesson or to prepare for the next lesson.

To help planning using this approach, a blank Lesson plan template is available to download from Cambridge GO (as part of this Teacher's Resource).

For more guidance on setting up for success and planning, please explore the Professional Development pages of our website **www.cambridge.org/education/PD**

> 1 Story writing with Roald Dahl

Unit plan

Session	Approximate number of learning hours	Outline of learning content	Resources
1.1 Setting the scene	1	Identify what a setting is, explore and talk about different settings, and write sentences to describe settings. Think about stories that could take place in a setting.	Learner's Book Session 1.1 Workbook Session 1.1
1.2 Looking at a setting	1	Read a description of a setting from *Matilda*. Use decoding skills and dictionaries to help with unfamiliar words, then answer questions about the extract. Find nouns and adjectives from the text.	Learner's Book Session 1.2 Workbook Session 1.2
1.3 Building a picture with words	1–1.5	Read a description from *Danny the Champion of the World* in an engaging way. Answer questions and draw a picture of a described setting. Explore the *ou* sound.	Learner's Book Session 1.3 Workbook Session 1.3
1.4 Writing a setting	1	Talk about familiar settings and list words that describe them. Compare the same setting in different weather conditions and meet new vocabulary for familiar adjectives. Write sentences to describe a known setting.	Learner's Book Session 1.4 Workbook Session 1.4 ⤓ Worksheet 1.1
1.5 Looking at characters	1	Read a description of Mr Wonka and explore ways of describing a character. Listen to a description of Charlie Bucket and then write a description of him.	Learner's Book Session 1.5 Workbook Session 1.5 ⤓ Worksheet 1.2

Session	Approximate number of learning hours	Outline of learning content	Resources
1.6 What happens next?	1	Read an extract from *The Enormous Crocodile* and answer questions about the setting and characters. Make predictions about how the story might end.	Learner's Book Session 1.6 Workbook Session 1.6
1.7 Looking at verbs	1	Review what a verb is and how essential verbs are to a sentence. Explore present and past tense verbs in sentences.	Learner's Book Session 1.7 Workbook Session 1.7 ⤓ Language worksheet 1A
1.8 Speech in texts	1–1.5	Explore speech in *The Enormous Crocodile* and the use of speech marks in texts. Explore alternative verbs for *said* and begin to use speech marks when writing dialogue.	Learner's Book Session 1.8 Workbook Session 1.8 ⤓ Worksheet 1.3 ⤓ Language worksheet 1B
1.9 Sequencing events	1–1.5	Sequence events in the story of *The Enormous Crocodile*. Explore story structure and how a story mountain can help to plan a story.	Learner's Book Session 1.9 Workbook Session 1.9 ⤓ Worksheet 1.4
1.10 Planning a story	1	Plan a story using ideas from Roald Dahl's characters. Draw a story mountain and write notes about setting and characters. Tell own story to a partner.	Learner's Book Session 1.10 Workbook Session 1.10 ⤓ Worksheet 1.5
1.11 Writing a story	1	Build a bank of adjectives for a story and use this, with a story plan, to write a story. Self-assess own story.	Learner's Book Session 1.11 Workbook Session 1.11 ⤓ Worksheet 1.6 ⤓ Differentiated worksheets 1A–C
1.12 Improving your story	0.5–1	Improve and proofread stories.	Learner's Book Session 1.12 Workbook Session 1.12 ⤓ Worksheet 1.6
Cross-unit resources			
Diagnostic check			
Learner's Book Check your progress			
Learner's Book Projects			
End-of-unit 1 test			

BACKGROUND KNOWLEDGE

It would be useful to have some familiarity with Roald Dahl's stories, in particular *Matilda, Charlie and the Chocolate Factory, Danny the Champion of the World* and *The Enormous Crocodile*. Try to use one of Roald Dahl's books as a class story. *The Magic Finger, George's Marvellous Medicine, Esio Trot* and *The Twits* are all short enough to read in full during this unit. Learners' reading and writing skills will benefit from listening to a book read aloud. These texts will also support learning on settings and character descriptions covered in this unit.

The early sessions in this unit focus on story components: setting and character descriptions. So that you can guide your learners in structuring their writing, it would help for you to be confident with basic story structure: introduction

– beginning – development – climax (the exciting part) – resolution (then what happens) – ending.

It will be helpful to be familiar with the following English subject knowledge:

* nouns and noun phrases
* adjectives
* synonyms
* compound words and words separated with a hyphen (dirt-path, wide-awake)
* word class order
* using dialogue
* punctuation: speech marks
* verb forms: past and present tense
* common irregular spellings for past tense verbs.

TEACHING SKILLS FOCUS

Metacognition – modelling your thinking

As with all skills, metacognition skills need to be taught. Ask yourself: *How often do I show learners I am thinking?*

Imagine that you are teaching a lesson on adding adjectives to a sentence. You could start by showing learners an object or picture and writing your own simple sentence on your board, e.g. *This is a flower*. Rather than ask learners what you could add to make the sentence more interesting, begin by showing your thinking out loud. For example, you could have this conversation with yourself:

Hmm. That's not a very interesting sentence (pause and pretend to think).
Ah. I know. I could add something about the flower (pause and do some more thinking).
I know. I could write, 'This is a red flower' (pause and read the sentence again).
Oh dear, that's still not very interesting. I'm sure there's a better word.

At that point you could continue thinking aloud or you could turn to your learners and ask them to suggest words you could use. You then continue the session on adding adjectives to sentences.

Modelling your thinking can provide valuable support to less confident learners by demonstrating that answers do not always come easily. It also allows thinking time so that when you turn to learners for help, all learners have had time to think of their ideas and will be keen to help you out.

At the end of the unit, reflect on how you felt the first time you modelled your own metacognitive thinking. Did this teaching style become easier the more you tried it? How did modelling your own thinking develop your learners' ability to give reasons? To what extent has it encouraged your learners' willingness and ability to edit and improve their work?

Cambridge Reading Adventures

There are several books in the series that would allow learners to explore character and setting descriptions.

- *Mei and the Pirate Queen* by Tony Brandman and Scoular Anderson
- *The Digger* by Jim Eldridge and Euan Cook
- *Hunters of the Sea* by Tony Bradman and Giorgio Bacchin
- *Skyscrapers* by Chris Oxlade

1.1 Setting the scene

LEARNING PLAN

Learning objectives	Learning intentions	Success criteria
3Rv.01, 3Rv.04, 3Rg.07, 3Rg.08, 3Ri.08, 3Wv.05, 3Wg.01, 3SLg.04	• Explore different settings for stories. • Talk about story settings. • Use and understand the words *noun* and *adjective*. • Write interesting sentences about settings.	• Learners can explore different settings for stories. • Learners can talk about story settings. • Learners can use and understand the words *noun* and *adjective*. • Learners can write interesting sentences about settings.

LANGUAGE SUPPORT

At this stage you can expect learners to identify specific adjectives (e.g. *cold*, *dirty*, *messy*, *green*, *massive*). The Learner's Book extracts also include words that intensify adjectives (e.g. <u>very</u> *pale*, <u>only</u> *one room*, <u>lots of</u> *teeth*). At this stage learners do not need to be concerned about the word class of these words. You should accept these words if learners include them as part of any lists of adjectives. The use of intensifiers is particularly apparent in Session 1.6 when learners meet the Notsobig One.

Worksheet 1.1 could be used with learners who need support in identifying adjectives.

Common misconceptions

Misconception	How to identify	How to overcome
Adjectives can be added after the noun without using a verb (e.g. *There are flowers colourful*).	When learners describe a setting (note the word class order).	Give learners several simple sentences containing an adjective. Cut each sentence into individual words. Ask learners to put the sentences in order. You could give each word to a different learner so that they have to physically put themselves in order.

Starter idea

Talk about a picture (10 minutes)

Resources: Learner's Book, Session 1.1: Getting started

Description: Ask learners to talk in groups about what they can see in the pictures in the Learner's Book. Ask each group to focus on one of the settings and note down words they could use to describe it. Ask each group to share their words and write them on the board.

Explain that all the things listed can be used to describe where a story takes place and that we call this the setting.

Ask specific questions about the picture to encourage learners to identify other features of the setting (*What time of day is it? What kind of weather is it? What would you hear?*).

Main teaching ideas

1 Talk about places (10 minutes)

Learning intention: To describe different settings shown in photographs.

Resources: Learner's Book, Session 1.1, Activity 1

Description: Ask learners to look again at the photographs in the Getting started activity. Elicit the names of the places (*a market, a beach, a wood/park/jungle, a fairground*). Ask learners to work in pairs to talk about the photos using the questions as prompts.

Ask individual learners to share what their partner said about somewhere they had visited.

Explain that all the places they have talked about could be used as a setting for a story.

> **Differentiation ideas:** Support learners with limited vocabulary by pairing them with more confident speakers. Challenge more confident speakers to ask their partner questions to elicit addtional information.

> **Assessment ideas:** Are learners able to choose appropriate adjectives when describing a photograph/setting?

Answers:
Learners' own answers.

2 Focus on nouns and adjectives (15–20 minutes)

Learning intention: To use and understand the terms *noun* and *adjective*.

Resources: Learner's Book, Session 1.1, Activity 2

Description: Ask learners what they already know about the words they have used to describe the photographs. Try to elicit the terms *nouns* and *adjectives*. Ask: *What is a noun* (words we use to name things)*? What is an adjective* (a word that describes the noun)*?*

Draw learners' attention to the Language focus box. Remind learners of the words they used when talking about the photographs. Discuss which words are nouns and which words are adjectives.

Ask learners to look at the four photographs again and to think of nouns and adjectives they could use for each one. Ask learners to write one sentence about each photograph using at least one noun and one adjective.

You could use this activity to consolidate basic sentence punctuation. Ask learners what each sentence needs at the start (a capital letter) and what it needs at the end (a full stop, a question mark, an exclamation mark).

> **Differentiation ideas:** Support learners by asking them to draw words you suggest (e.g. *boat, house, dog, blue, cloud, big*). Explain that if a word can be drawn, it is probably a noun.

Challenge learners to add more than one adjective before the noun (e.g. *You can see lots of colourful fruit; It is a cloudless blue sky*).

> **Assessment ideas:** Do learners know nouns are the names of things and that adjectives describe the nouns?

This is an opportunity to assess learners' understanding of simple sentence structures. Do they to use a capital letter at the start? Can they use a range of punctuation to end their sentences (full stop, question mark, exclamation mark). Can they use these features appropriately?

Answers:
Learners' own, but may include sentences such as: *It is a busy market; It is a beautiful beach; It is a quiet wood; It is a noisy fairground.*

3 Talk about a story setting (15 minutes)

Learning intention: To talk about story settings.

Resources: Learner's Book, Session 1.1, Activity 3

Description: Explain that a writer must include enough information in the description of their setting so the reader can imagine what it looks like.

Ask learners to choose one of the four photographs in the Getting started activity and to read their sentence from the previous activity to their partner.

Ask learners to work with their partners to think of other sentences to describe what they can see (e.g. *One of the stalls is selling yellow and green peppers; There are fluffy clouds in the blue sky; The ground is covered in green moss; The fair is busy and will be lots of fun*). Ask pairs to think of and discuss a story that could happen in that setting (e.g. losing and finding something; making friends; achieving something difficult; a holiday they have enjoyed; getting lost; having an adventure).

Invite several pairs of learners to share their ideas.

> **Assessment ideas:** Can learners use pairs of adjectives? (e.g. *the large blue ball*; *the red and white circus tent*).

Are they able to use quantifying or qualifying adjectives? (e.g. *lots of trees*; *many balloons*; *the tallest tree*).

Answers:
Learners' own answers.

Plenary idea

Classroom Twenty Questions (5–10 minutes)

Description: Explain that the classroom is another example of a setting. Ask one learner to choose an object in the classroom. Other learners must guess which object has been chosen by asking questions (e.g. *Is it large? Is it on the wall? Can I write with it?*). The learner choosing the object can only answer 'Yes' or 'No'. The learner who guesses correctly chooses the next object.

Homework ideas

Ask learners to:

- complete the Workbook activities for this session, if not completed in class
- bring in books or film versions of Roald Dahl stories for a class collection.

Answers for Workbook

1 Nouns: mountain, butterfly, book, office, rabbit, shirt, rain, computer.
 Adjectives: interesting, beautiful, young, happy, clever, sharp, blue.

2 Learners' own setting ideas with appropriate nouns and adjectives.

3 Learners' own pictures with appropriate nouns and adjectives labelling the picture.

1.2 Looking at a setting

LEARNING PLAN

Learning objectives	Learning intentions	Success criteria
3Rw.03, 3Rv.01, 3Rv.04, 3Rg.01, 3Rg.07, 3Rg.08, 3Ri.08, 3Ri.14, 3Ri.16, 3Ra.02, 3Wg.01, 3SLg.04, 3SLp.01, 3SLp.03	• Read a setting from *Matilda* to themselves. • Answer questions about a setting. • Find nouns and adjectives in a piece of writing.	• Learners can read a text about a setting to themselves. • Learners can answer questions about a setting. • Learners can find nouns and adjectives in a piece of writing.

LANGUAGE SUPPORT

Prepare learners for reading the extract by reminding them of strategies they can use to read unfamiliar words:

- Phonic knowledge: Remind them of the different *ow* sounds (*ow* as in *window* and *ow* as in *brown*).
- Segmenting: Discuss breaking words into syllables or looking out for compound words. Learners will have met compound words in Stage 2 (e.g. *playground, sandpit, classroom*).

However, the compound words in the extract may be less familiar to them (*newspaper, upstairs, overshadowing*).

- Explain that some compound words are separated with a line called a hyphen.
- Contextual information: Remind learners they can use the picture and their knowledge of houses to help them.

Common misconceptions

Misconception	How to identify	How to overcome
Numbers are not adjectives.	Show learners six red (toy) bricks. Ask learners to describe what they can see. Elicit the noun (*bricks*) and the adjectives *six red* (toy) bricks. Explain that to describe the group they have used two adjectives – one for number and one for the colour.	Repeat this activity using other groups of bricks that vary only by number.

Starter idea

Who has heard of Roald Dahl? (5 minutes)

Resources: Learner's Book, Session 1.2: Getting started; a selection of Roald Dahl titles (if available)

Description: Direct learners to the photograph of Roald Dahl in his shed. Ask: *Do you know who Roald Dahl is* (an author)*? Do you know the names of any books he has written?* (e.g. *The BFG, Matilda, Charlie and the Chocolate Factory*). Some learners may know these stories as film versions but not realise that Roald Dahl wrote them.

Encourage learners to look at any Roald Dahl books you have in school and to search for any pages with facts about the author. As a class, search for facts about Roald Dahl online.

Explain that in this unit you will be looking at some of the settings and characters in the books Roald Dahl wrote. Encourage learners to bring in any Roald Dahl books they have at home to create a class collection.

Main teaching ideas

1 Matilda visits Miss Honey (25–30 minutes)

Learning intention: To use a range of strategies to read unfamiliar words.

Resources: *Miss Honey's Home* (Learner's Book, Session 1.2, Activity 1); Track 01

Description: Explain that learners are going to read a description of a setting from *Matilda* by Roald Dahl, and that there will be some words they do not know. You could use the audio here and ask learners to follow the text as they listen.

Ask: *What could help you to read unfamiliar words* (e.g. sound them out, break them into small parts, use a picture, read the next part of the sentence to see if that helps)*?* Remind learners of any strategies they do not mention and point them to the Reading tip as necessary.

Before they begin reading, explore the glossary terms. Ask three learners to volunteer to read the words and the definitions.

Explore this vocabulary:

- Ask: *Which other words could Roald Dahl have used instead of 'human dwelling'?* (e.g. *house, cottage, building*).

- Can learners identify a wild area they know?

- Ask learners to use their arms to give themselves an embrace (cross arms and cuddle opposite arms).

Ask for volunteers to each read a sentence of the extract so that you can assess the range of strategies learners use to read unfamiliar words. When selecting learners to read individual sentences, consider the relative difficulty of each to ensure all learners can read the sentence.

Finally, ask all learners to read the text silently in their heads.

> **Differentiation ideas:** Support learners to use the contextual information in the picture to help them read unfamiliar words. Encourage them to miss out words they cannot decode and read on as this can help them guess the missed word.

Challenge learners to read the entire extract out loud.

> **Assessment ideas:** Note which learners confidently use a range of strategies to read unfamiliar words. Talk about the methods used. Ask: *How did you work out a word you were not sure about? How did you work out the meaning of a word you did not know?* Note which learners use punctuation when reading aloud.

2 Answering questions (10 minutes)

Learning intention: To answer questions about a setting.

Resources: Learner's Book, Session 1.2, Activity 2

Description: Explain that learners are going to work on their own to answer questions about the text.

Ask them to answer in full sentences using words from the text.

Allow time for learners to answer the questions and time to mark with peers.

> **Differentiation ideas:** Support learners by suggesting they give one- or two-word answers (e.g. Miss Honey; yes; no) instead of full answers.

> **Assessment ideas:** Did learners use capital letters at the start of each sentence and appropriate punctuation at the end? Did they use capital letters for proper nouns?

Answers:
Learners' own, but look for answers broadly similar to these:

a It is Miss Honey's house.

b It has one small chimney.

c There is no upstairs.

d Learners' own answers.

e Learners' own answers.

3 Think about nouns and adjectives (5–10 minutes)

Learning intention: To identify nouns and adjectives in a piece of writing.

Resources: Learner's Book, Session 1.2, Activity 3

Description: Remind learners of previous learning about nouns and adjectives.

Model how to set their work out in table form. Draw a line to form two columns. Write *Nouns* at the top of one and *Adjectives* at the top of the other column. Allow time for learners to draw the table and complete the activity by writing three nouns and three adjectives used in the setting text.

Ask learners to consider the Reflection text.

> **Differentiation ideas:** Challenge learners to identify adjectives describing size. Ask them to sort them into 'small' words and 'large' words.

Answers:

a Nouns include: cottage, bricks, roof, chimney, windows, nettles, grass

b Adjectives include: narrow, tiny, small, old, crumbly, little, enormous

Plenary idea

Picture frame game (10 minutes)

Resources: Something to form a screen (e.g. large book); paper; pen/pencil; coloured pencils

Description: Ask learners to work with partners and decide who is going to be 'A' and who is 'B'.

Explain that 'A' should think of a building (e.g. house, cottage, shed). 'A' must describe the building to 'B'. 'A' and 'B' both draw the building using 'A's description.

When 'A' has finished describing, both learners share their drawings. How accurately did 'A' describe their idea? How carefully did 'B' listen to the description?

If time is available, allow learners to swap roles.

Homework ideas

Ask learners to:

*   complete the Workbook activities for this session, if not completed in class
*   play the 'Picture Frame' game with a family member.

Answers for Workbook

1   Following words circled: bricks, roof, chimney, windows, window, sheet, newspaper, upstairs, place, path, wilderness, nettles, thorns, grass

2   Old, crumbly, pale, red, slate, one, small, two, little, front, larger, side, long, brown

3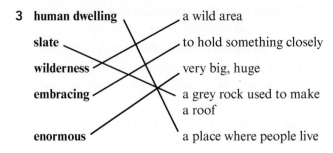

human dwelling — a place where people live

slate — a grey rock used to make a roof

wilderness — a wild area

embracing — to hold something closely

enormous — very big, huge

1.3 Building a picture with words

LEARNING PLAN

Learning objectives	Learning intentions	Success criteria
3Rw.01, 3Rw.03, 3Rv.01, 3Rv.02, 3Rv.04, 3Rg.01, 3Rg.07, 3Rg.08, 3Ri.08, 3Ri.14, 3Ri.16, 3Ra.01, 3Ra.02, 3Wg.01, 3Wp.02, 3SLm.05, 3SLg.04, 3SLp.01, 3SLp.03	• Read a setting from *Danny the Champion of the World*. • Answer questions about the setting. • Discuss different sounds the letters *ou* make in words. • Draw a picture showing the setting described.	• Learners can read a setting description to themselves and aloud. • Learners can answer questions about a setting. • Learners can recognise different *ou* sounds within words. • Learners can draw a picture of a setting they have read about.

LANGUAGE SUPPORT

This session focuses on learners reading aloud to peers in a way that holds their partner's interest. Learners can often add expression when reading dialogue but are unsure about how to do this in a narrative extract. Consider modelling reading a different extract to that used in the session by:

- reading more slowly
- using punctuation, such as pausing at commas and full stops
- stressing particular words to add emphasis
- varying your voice to add expression.

Learners may not understand these phrases: *fair-sized modern bathroom; wood-burning stove; home comforts.* Support learners using open questions to help them work out the meanings for themselves.

Learners may try to sound the *ou* in *through* as a digraph followed by a *gh* sound. Explain that when *ou* is followed by *gh* the four letters make a new sound together. Be prepared for learners to ask about other *ough* words and the different sounds made (e.g. *off* in *cough*; *ow* in *bough*; *oo* in *through*; *u* in *thorough*; *uff* in *rough*; *o* in *dough*).

Common misconceptions

Misconception	How to identify	How to overcome
s in *close* is always an *s* sound.	Sometimes the *s* in *close* has a *z* sound. Ask learners to read the sentences *He is standing close to the table* and *Please can you close the door.* Both words have a long *o_e* sound although *close* with a *z* sound is slightly longer.	Give learners six sentences using the two different *close* sounds. Ask them to underline the words with an *s* sound in red and the words with a *z* sound in blue.

Starter idea

Getting started (5 minutes)

Resources: Learner's Book, Session 1.3: Getting started; a copy of *Danny the Champion of the World*; internet access

Description: If possible, show learners the cover of *Danny the Champion of the World* (either from a book or online). Ask: *Does anyone know this Roald Dahl story?* Discuss learners' answers and elicit information about Danny from the front cover.

Make sure learners know that Danny's mother died when he was a baby and that he lives with his father in a caravan in the countryside. Check that learners understand the word *caravan*.

Allow learners time to talk to their partners about what Danny might have enjoyed and what he might have missed. Allow them to share their ideas.

You will need to be sensitive to learners who may have had an experience like Danny's.

Main teaching ideas

1 Read the description (20 minutes)

Learning intention: To read a setting description.

Resources: *The caravan* (Learner's Book, Session 1.3, Activity 1); Track 02; dictionaries

Description: Tell learners that they are going to read another setting description.

Explore the glossary terms and discuss any other unfamiliar words. Ask: *Can you tell me the strategies we used last time to read unfamiliar words?* Explain that this time you want them to read the extract in their heads, using their own reading strategies. You could ask learners to listen to Track 02 and follow the text as they listen.

When all learners have read the extract ask: *What have you learned about Danny's caravan? Are there any words you do not understand?* Use peer-support to ensure all learners understand the vocabulary. Encourage the use of dictionaries.

Explain that they are now going to take turns reading the text aloud to their partners. Direct learners to the Speaking tip and ask them to read each point to their partners. Ask: *What is different about reading aloud?* (e.g. slower than reading in your head, changing your voice, use some expression, say important words differently). Read the first paragraph of the extract aloud to show learners what you mean and then discuss the techniques you used.

Give learners time to read the extract out loud to one another.

> **Differentiation ideas:** Support learners by directing them to the *ou* sounds they will meet (see Language support).

Challenge learners to volunteer to read the first paragraph aloud to demonstrate adding expression and emphasis.

> **Assessment ideas:** Do learners use all the strategies discussed? Note any phonic patterns learners need to revisit.

The picture accompanying the extract in the Session 1.2 provided learners with a lot of contextual information. Note which learners are relying too heavily on pictorial information.

Which learners vary their voices to add expression? Do learners use punctuation well? Do learners identify appropriate words to emphasise? (e.g. *real old*; *at least a hundred and fifty years old*; *I really loved*; *I loved it especially*).

2 Answer the questions (10–15 minutes)

Learning intention: To answer questions about a setting.

Resources: Learner's Book, Session 1.3, Activity 2

Description: Explain that learners are going to work on their own to answer questions about the text. Remind learners to answer in sentences using words from the question and the extract.

Before learners begin, invite a learner to say what they will write as their answer to the first question to ensure learners know what you mean (e.g. *Danny's caravan was painted yellow, red and blue*; *Danny's caravan has yellow, red and blue patterns on it*).

> **Differentiation ideas:** Support learners with using words from the text in their answers.

Challenge learners by asking them to discuss what they think Danny means when he says of the home comforts: *They were all we needed.*

> **Assessment ideas:** Note which learners scan the text to find answers. Note which learners need support in answering inferential questions.

Answers:
Accept all answers that include the key information.

a   It was painted in yellow, red and blue. It had fine patterns all over it in yellow, red and blue.

b   No, it was at least 150 years old.

c   It has one room.

d   Danny and his father keep warm with a wood-burning stove.

e   Danny and his father have bunk beds, two chairs, a small table and a tiny chest of drawers.

f   Learners' own answers.

3 Focus on *ou* words (10–15 minutes)

Learning intention: To discuss the sounds made by the letters *ou*.

Resources: Learner's Book, Session 1.3, Activity 3; Workbook, Session 1.3; dictionaries

Description: Write *ou* on the board. Ask: *What sound do these letters make* (several different sounds)*? How do you know which sound to use?* Try to elicit that it depends on the rest of the word.

Ask learners to look at the words in the Learner's Book and identify the different *ou* sounds. Learners may find it difficult to distinguish between the *ou* sound in *our* and *house*. Explain that the sound is similar in these words, but there is more emphasis on the *ou* sound in words like *our* and *cow* than the *ou* sound in words like *mouse* and *house*. Be prepared to discuss the *ou* sound if learners suggest any words that have the *ough* pattern.

Allow time for learners to sort the four words into the three *ou* sounds. Ask them to find other words in the text with these *ou* sounds.

Use the Workbook Session 1.3 activities here to provide further practice.

> **Differentiation ideas:** Support learners by saying each word for them so they can hear the different sounds.

> **Assessment ideas:** Can learners identify the different *ou* sounds? Note those who need further support.

Answers:
b   Three
c   *ou* as in cow: our
    ou as in mouse: house
    ou as in stood: could, would

---

4   Draw a picture of a setting (10–15 minutes)

Learning intention: To draw a picture of a setting that learners have read about.

Resources: Learner's Book, Session 1.3, Activity 4; large pieces of paper; paints

Description: Tell learners to read the extract again. Ask: *Can you imagine the inside of Danny's caravan? What about the outside?* Explain that learners can draw either the outside or the inside of the caravan but that they must use Roald Dahl's description. Encourage learners to check the extract regularly for details.

Allow time for learners to compare their completed drawings with partners.

Ask: *Do you think Roald Dahl managed to make a clear picture of Danny's caravan using words? Was it easy or difficult to use Roald Dahl's words to create your picture? Does your drawing match Roald Dahl's words? Are there any details you think Roald Dahl could have included? Are there details he could have left out?*

> **Assessment ideas:** How accurately do learners use the extract? How much detail have they included? Which learners can express their opinions clearly? Which learners consider the opinions of other learners?

Plenary idea

Add a description (5 minutes)

Resources: *The caravan* (Learner's Book, Session 1.3); Track 02

Description: Remind learners that gypsy wagons are usually pulled by horses. Ask them to picture the horse in their mind. Ask: *What would it look like? Is it an old horse or a young horse?* Ask learners to write a short description of the horse they think pulled Danny's caravan.

Homework ideas

Ask learners to:

* find examples of *ou* words in their reading books

* draw a picture of another building that could be used as a setting; encourage learners to make it as detailed as possible.

Answers for Workbook

1   Learners' answers could include:
house: mouse, louse, douse
round: pound, sound, found
would: could, should
mouth: south
loud: proud, cloud

2

When *ou* sounds like the *oo* in *stood*	When *ou* sounds like the *ou* in *mouse*	When *ou* sounds like the *oo* in *too*	When *ou* sounds like the *ow* in *cow*
would	house	through	our
could	shout	you	hour
should	about		cloud
	out		count

3 Learners' answers could include:
I <u>should</u> tie my shoelaces before I trip up.
We <u>would</u> like to play football after school.
<u>Could</u> I borrow your ruler please?

Please can I go <u>out</u> with my friends?
<u>You</u> look very happy.
What is <u>your</u> name?

1.4 Writing a setting

LEARNING PLAN

Learning objectives	Learning intentions	Success criteria
3Rg.08, 3SLm.01, 3SLm.02, 3SLm.05, 3Wg.01, 3Ws.02, 3Wc.03, 3Wv.02, 3Wv.07, 3Wp.01, 3Ww.06	• Discuss different settings. • Write sentences describing two similar settings. • Write about a setting learners know well.	• Learners can discuss different settings. • Learners can write sentences describing two similar settings. • Learners can write about a setting they know.

LANGUAGE SUPPORT

There are number of opportunities in this session to develop vocabulary using synonyms. The plenary for this session is linked to building a class word wall. You may want to extend this activity to build other word wall categories in readiness for the independent writing learners will meet later in the unit.

Starter idea

Getting started (5–10 minutes)

Resources: Learner's Book, Session 1.4: Getting started

Description: Ask learners to name settings they visit most days. Encourage them to name individual rooms in the home, or areas outside, to develop the idea that a setting can be very specific. Direct learners to the speech bubbles in the Learner's Book.

Make a list on your board for each picture as learners name what they can see. Discuss the word types they have used (nouns, adjectives).

Main teaching ideas

1 Look at the settings (20–25 minutes)

Learning intention: To discuss different settings.

Resources: Learner's Book, Session 1.4, Activity 1; Worksheet 1.1; flashcards of adjectives to match the two pictures; thesauruses

Description: Talk about the two pictures together. Organise the learners into groups and ask each group to record the similarities and differences between the two pictures. For example:

Similarities	Differences
the place	the weather
both pictures have people in them	the mood of the people
	what the people are doing

Refer to the character's speech bubble and explain that a setting can also include information about the weather or the time of day (e.g. *It was a beautiful sunny day*; *It was early in the morning*).

Discuss the two lists and explain that the setting is the same, but the weather changes the atmosphere in each one, so we need different adjectives to describe it.

Give learners time to work in pairs to identify which adjectives should be applied to Picture 1 and which to Picture 2. Explain that learners are to write sentences about each of the pictures using some of these adjectives.

Explain that because each group of sentences describes one picture, learners do not need to number the sentences but can group them together into a paragraph and that they should write a paragraph for each picture. Encourage learners to peer assess as they share the paragraphs they write. Encourage them to think about: what they think is good; which sentences or words could be changed; whether there are any errors.

Use Worksheet 1.1 Ordering adjectives if learners are unsure about where to position adjectives.

> **Differentiation ideas:** Support learners by checking that they can read the adjectives. Provide flashcards of the adjectives for learners to match to the two pictures.

Challenge learners to use a thesaurus to find alternatives for some of the adjectives (e.g. *sad: miserable, unhappy*; *busy: bustling, hectic*; *dangerous: risky, threatening*).

> **Assessment ideas:** Note which learners understand that a description of a setting should include information about how a setting feels and the atmosphere it creates and which learners can organise their sentences into a paragraph.

Answers:

b

Picture 1	Picture 2
sunny lively light	dark rainy thundery
cheerful happy busy	empty stormy sad
warm colourful	dull gloomy cold
bright smiley	

c   Possible sentences:

Picture 1: It is a bright sunny day and people are playing in the park. You can see smiley happy children on the swings. Some people are sitting on the green grass eating a lovely picnic.

Picture 2: It is a cold wet day and everything looks gloomy and dull. The rain has made lots of puddles. The swings have no children playing on them but there is a duck on the lake.

2 Write a description of a setting you know (20 minutes)

Learning intention: To write about a setting learners know well.

Resources: Learner's Book, Session 1.4, Activity 2

Description: Ask learners to choose one of the settings they know very well and to think of adjectives to describe it. Allow time for learners to write a paragraph about their chosen setting.

Direct learners to work with their partner to share feedback, and then edit and improve their descriptions.

> **Differentiation ideas:** Support learners with organising their writing into sentences that form a paragraph.

> **Assessment ideas:** Note which learners:

- can identify ways to improve a piece of writing with the support of a partner
- find it difficult to change their original ideas
- can use a dictionary, word list or personal spelling log to check their spelling.

Answers:
Sentences will be different for every learner but should include several adjectives.

Plenary idea

Word wall (10 minutes)

Resources: Thesauruses; dictionaries

Description: Organise learners into groups, then allocate simple adjectives (e.g. big, small, bright, dull, happy). Ask each group to create a collection of more interesting adjectives that are synonyms of the adjective they have been allocated (e.g. big: large, huge, gigantic; bright: colourful, shiny, dazzling). Explain that their ideas will form part of a word wall that they can refer to when writing.

CROSS-CURRICULAR LINKS

Science: As an introduction to solids, liquids and gases, learners could classify and describe materials with adjectives based on their properties (e.g. dull, shiny, hard, soft, transparent, opaque).

Homework ideas

Ask learners to:

- complete the Workbook activities for this session, if not completed in class

- draw a picture of a setting they know well (e.g. a relative or friend's house, a park where they play, or somewhere they have visited on holiday).

Answers for Workbook

1 Possible answers:
Same: there is a shopping centre; both have cars; both have people.

Different: in one picture (A) it is sunny and in the other picture it is not (B); there are lots of people in Picture A but not in Picture B; one car has a window open in Picture A but not in Picture B; there is an umbrella in Picture B but not in Picture A.

2 Possible adjectives for Picture A: hot, sunny, busy, warm, happy
Possible adjectives for Picture B: cold, wet, gloomy, dull, cloudy.

3 Possible answers:
Picture A
It is a <u>sunny</u> day. The sky is <u>blue</u> so everyone feels <u>happy</u>. Some people are arriving. They are feeling <u>cheerful</u> as they walk towards the mall. Others have spent a <u>busy</u> time in the shops. They look <u>tired</u> as they walk back to their cars.
Picture B
It is a <u>gloomy</u> day. There is a <u>thunder</u> storm. The sky is <u>grey</u> so everyone feels <u>miserable</u>. The people who are arriving are feeling <u>cross</u> as they walk towards the mall. Other people are leaving. They look <u>unhappy</u> as they hurry back to their cars.

4 Possible answers:

1	beautiful	2	cheerful
3	sandy	4	joyful
5	warm	6	delicious
7	thrilled	8	wonderful

1.5 Looking at characters

LEARNING PLAN

Learning objectives	Learning intentions	Success criteria
3Rw.03, 3Rv.01, 3Rv.02, 3Rv.04, 3Rg.01, 3Rg.07, 3Rg.08, 3Ri.06, 3Ri.07, 3Ri.08, 3Ri.16, 3Ri.17, 3Ra.01, 3Ra.02, 3Wv.02, 3Wv.05, 3Wv.06, 3Wv.07, 3Wc.01, 3Wc.03, 3Wp.04, 3Ws.02, 3SLg.01, 3SLg.02, 3SLg.04, 3SLm.01, 3SLm.02, 3SLm.03	• Read and talk about a character description. • Write a character description.	• Learners can read and discuss a character description. • Learners can write a character description.

This session provides opportunities for learners to explore Roald Dahl's rich vocabulary.

The description of Mr Wonka includes several descriptions of colours (e.g. *plum-coloured, bottle green, pearly grey*). These words could be used as part of your word wall display.

In this session, learners will listen to a description of Charlie. No glossary is provided to support learners with words they may not know (e.g. *nervous, patiently, clutching, miracle, queue*). Be prepared to explain unfamiliar vocabulary, especially that which supports the description of Charlie's feelings.

Common misconceptions

Misconception	How to identify	How to overcome
Pairs and lists of adjectives are always separated by a comma (e.g. small, neat, pointed black beard).	Learners may ask why some lists of adjectives do not have commas separating them. The description of Mr Wonka includes many paired adjectives (e.g. *quick jerky little movements; bright twinkling eyes*).	Explain that a comma in a list separates the items because they are items that do not always belong together. Explain that when a writer uses more than one adjective, they sometimes want both adjectives to be linked to the noun, so a comma is not used. If you can put the word *and* or *or* between the adjectives, then a comma should be used. If you cannot, do not use a comma.

Starter idea

Think about a character (10 minutes)

Resources: Learner's Book, Session 1.5: Getting started; copy of *Charlie and the Chocolate Factory*; picture of a boy/girl from a book; internet access

Description: Show learners an image of *Charlie and the Chocolate Factory* (either from the book or online), then direct learners to the Getting started activity.

Ask: *How would you feel if you won a very special ticket to somewhere amazing? How do you think Charlie Bucket felt when he won a golden ticket?* Ask learners to discuss in pairs what a visit to a chocolate factory might be like.

Main teaching ideas

1 Meet Mr Wonka (20 minutes)

Learning intention: To read and talk about a character description.

Resources: *Mr Wonka* (Learner's Book, Session 1.5, Activity 1); Track 03

Description: Remind learners of the ways they have described characters so far (appearance, how they feel about something). Explain that when a writer describes a character, they include information about the character's appearance, how they feel, what they do and what the character thinks or says.

Direct learners to the description of Mr Wonka and discuss the glossary terms. Ask: *How will you work out the meaning of unfamiliar words* (phonic knowledge, segmenting unfamiliar words, contextual information)?

Listen to Track 03 and ask learners to follow the text. Then ask learners to re-read the description independently.

Now ask learners to discuss the description of Mr Wonka in a group. Ask group members to adopt specific roles (e.g. chairperson – to ensure everyone has a chance to speak; scribe – to write down ideas; reporter – to feedback the ideas). Allow time for discussion and then ask each group's 'reporter' to share their group's answers.

Can learners suggest why there is no information about how Mr Wonka might think or feel (e.g. when we meet a new person, we don't know what they think or feel about things)?

> **Differentiation ideas:** Support learners by directing them to take turns reading sentences. Explain any vocabulary they are unfamiliar with.

Challenge learners to read the glossary terms aloud for peers.

> **Assessment ideas:** Note which learners fulfil the role they have taken in the group.

Do you need to change group members for future group work?

Do learners listen to the opinions of others during the group task?

Which learners speak fluently and confidently using appropriate vocabulary?

Answers:

a	What Mr Wonka looks like:	b	What Mr Wonka does:
	little		stands on his own
	wears a black top hat		makes quick jerky little movements
	wears a plum-coloured velvet tail coat		cocks his head this way and that
	wears bottle-green trousers		takes everything in
	wears pearly grey gloves		
	carries a gold-topped cane		
	has a small, neat, pointed black beard		
	has a goatee		
	bright eyes that sparkle and twinkle		
	clever		
c	What Mr Wonka thinks or says:	d	What Mr Wonka feels:
	Learners' own answers.		full of fun and laughter

 2 Charlie waits to enter the chocolate factory (25–30 minutes)

Learning intention: To write a character description.

Resources: *Charlie* (Learner's Book, Session 1.5, Activity 2); Track 04; dictionaries; thesauruses

Description: Explain that learners will listen to a character description of Charlie and should make a note of adjectives that describe Charlie. Explain that learners do not need to write down every adjective they hear. They may need to listen to the description two or three times. Ask: *Do all the words describe Charlie's appearance? Do any words mention Charlie's feelings (nervous, excited, patient)?*

Explain vocabulary linked to Charlie's description (e.g. *nervous, patient*). Learners do not need to understand all the vocabulary (e.g. *miracle, queue*).

Ask learners to write their own descriptions of Charlie. Learners can use words from the description they have just listened to and add some ideas of their own. Remind them that adjectives come before the noun (e.g. *a quiet boy*) or after a noun and verb (e.g. *he was small and skinny*). Explain that Roald Dahl often emphasises an adjective by adding another word before it (e.g. *extraordinarily little, marvellously bright*). Encourage learners to share their descriptions.

> **Differentiation ideas:** Support learners with organising their ideas and with spelling as they write their descriptions.

Challenge learners to think about the adjectives Roald Dahl uses to describe colours (e.g. *plum-coloured, bottle green, pearly green*). Can they include interesting adjectives to describe colour? (e.g. *crimson, vermillion* or *scarlet* instead of *red*).

〉 **Assessment ideas:** Note which learners:

- identify appropriate vocabulary
- use the list of words they have recorded to write their own description
- attempt to write sentences in the style of Roald Dahl.

Audioscript: *Charlie*

At the factory gates crowds of people had gathered. Charlie was a quiet boy anyway but the crowds made him feel even more nervous than he thought he'd be. He stood, close to the gates, firmly holding the hand of Grandpa Joe. Charlie was small and skinny with messy hair and scruffy clothes. He stood clutching Grandpa Joe's hand but it wasn't clear which of the two was the most excited. Charlie had spent evening after evening talking to Grandpa Joe about exciting things but never did they believe they would be meeting Mr Wonka, the most amazing, fantastic, extraordinary chocolate maker in the whole world! Charlie was from a poor family who lived in a small home with all his grandparents who lay in bed all day, everyday. His family didn't have money to buy enough food to eat; what a miracle for little Charlie to be standing there in the queue, patiently waiting to meet Mr Wonka!

Answers:

a Adjectives: quiet, nervous, small, skinny, messy, scruffy, poor, patient

b Learners' descriptions of Charlie using some of the adjectives in **3 a.**

c Learners share their character description in groups.

Plenary idea

Building vocabulary (5–10 minutes)

Resources: Thesauruses; dictionaries; Worksheet 1.2

Description: Explain that Roald Dahl often emphasises an adjective by adding another word before it (e.g. *extraordinarily little, marvellously bright*). Ask learners to add extra words to other adjectives (e.g. old, tall, green) or use Worksheet 1.2 Changing adjectives.

Homework ideas

Ask learners to:

- complete the Workbook activities for this session, if not completed in class
- research words Roald Dahl has invented to share with other learners.

Answers for Workbook

1 Learners' own answers. Learners should use adjectives to describe the colour of the boy's clothes, adjectives to describe his hair, face and eyes beyond simple colour. Do they describe how he stands or what he might be thinking?

2 Learners' character descriptions should include some of their adjectives from Activity 1. Some learners may only include information about appearance. Other learners should include information about what their character does. A few learners may include how the character feels or what he says.

3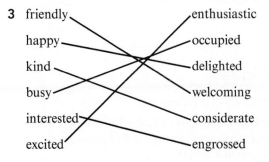

1.6 What happens next?

LEARNING PLAN

Learning objectives	Learning intentions	Success criteria
3Rw.03, 3Rv.01, 3Rv.02, 3Rv.04, 3Rv.05, 3Rv.07, 3Rs.02, 3Rg.01, 3Rg.04, 3Rg.07, 3Rg.08, 3Ri.06, 3Ri.07, 3Ri.08, 3Ri.11, 3Ri.12, 3Ri.16, 3Ri.17, 3Ra.01, 3Ri.12, 3Wv.03, 3SLg.01, 3SLg.02, 3SLg.04, 3SLp.01, 3SLg.03	• Read the beginning of *The Enormous Crocodile*. • Explore setting and character descriptions in the text. • Answer questions about the story. • Discuss what might happen next in the story.	• Learners can read the beginning of a story. • Learners can talk about the setting and characters in a story. • Learners can answer questions about a story. • Learners can discuss what might happen next in a story.

LANGUAGE SUPPORT

It would help to have background knowledge of crocodiles (e.g. they are reptiles; can be found throughout Africa, Asia, the Americas and Australia; they eat fish, birds and other animals).

There are many opportunities to explore comparative adjectives (e.g. big, bigger, biggest; muddy, muddier, muddiest). You may want to look at spelling rules for these words, such as rules for dropping *y* and changing to *–ier* / *–iest*.

The extract contains a lot of description about what both crocodiles think (*children are tough and chewy*; *children are nasty and bitter*; *you're the greediest crocodile*; *I'm the bravest crocodile*) and are opinions rather than facts. You could use this to explore fact and opinion in more detail.

At the end of the extract, Roald Dahl uses a simile to describe the Enormous Crocodile's terrible sharp teeth (*sparkled like knives in the sun*). Similes are not taught in this unit, but you may decide to make learners aware of the term.

Starter idea

Crocodiles (5–10 minutes)

Resources: Learner's Book, Session 1.6: Getting started; collection of books that include information about crocodiles; internet access

Description: Ask learners: *Have you ever seen a crocodile? What do they look like? What else can you tell me about them?*

Organise learners into pairs or groups and ask them to research crocodiles. Challenge them to find at least one interesting fact about them (e.g. closest relative to crocodiles are birds and dinosaurs; they can live for 50–60 years; they open their jaws to cool themselves).

Could learners answer all the Getting started questions? Ask learners to suggest questions for other learners to answer based on the information they have found.

Main teaching ideas

1 Read *The Enormous Crocodile* (15–20 minutes)

> **Learning intention:** To read the beginning of *The Enormous Crocodile*.
>
> **Resources:** *The Enormous Crocodile* (Learner's Book, Session 1.6, Activity 1); Track 05
>
> **Description:** Read the opening paragraph from the story, then ask: *What do you think the word*

enormous means? Can you tell me other words that mean the same as enormous (e.g. gigantic, massive, huge)? What do you think the Notsobig One means?

Before learners read the story, remind them that when they meet a word they do not understand they should read on to see whether the next part of the story makes the meaning clear.

When they have finished reading, check that learners have understood all the words. Ask: *Can you give me another word to replace 'tommy-rot'? What do you think 'gulp him up in one gollop' means?*

Ask learners to re-read the passage in pairs with one learner reading the Enormous Crocodile's words and the other learner reading the Notsobig One's words.

> **Differentiation ideas:** Support learners by reading the extract with them before they read it with their partners.

Challenge two learners to perform the dialogue for others.

> **Assessment ideas:** Note which learners can use expression when reading either the Enormous Crocodile's words or the Notsobig One's words. Do they vary their tone? Do they use italics and exclamation marks as clues to how to say the words?

2 Discuss answers to questions (10 minutes)

Learning intention: To explore setting and character descriptions.

Resources: Learner's Book, Session 1.6, Activity 2

Description: In previous sessions learners have read extracts that only describe the setting (Miss Honey's house, Danny's caravan) or only describe the character (Mr Wonka). When learners first read *The Enormous Crocodile* extract, they may overlook the setting and character descriptions and focus on the dialogue. Before learners discuss the questions, ask: *Does Roald Dahl describe the setting in this extract? Does he describe the characters?*

Make sure learners understand that some adjectives describe the children and that they should only find the adjectives describing the main characters. Explain that some of the adjectives are the crocodile's opinion of themselves or of the other crocodile (e.g. *greedy*, *brave*, *ugly*). Encourage

learners to decide whether they will include each crocodile's opinions.

Allow learners time to discuss answers to the questions.

You may choose to introduce the use of similes as a descriptive device. Ask: *Why do you think Roald Dahl chose the words 'his teeth sparkled like knives in the sun'? How does this description make you feel?* (e.g. scared, frightened, worried).

> **Differentiation ideas:** Support learners in understanding why the Notsobig One's name is clever. Ask: *Does 'Notsobig' mean the crocodile is small? Does the name tell you how big the Notsobig One is? Are any crocodiles small?*

Challenge learners to create a table of the differences between the two crocodiles.

> **Assessment ideas:** Which learners need support to identify adjectives that describe each crocodile?

Answers:

a   Africa or in a 'river in Africa'

b   biggest, brownest, muddiest

c   The Enormous Crocodile and the Notsobig One

d   The Enormous Crocodile: very big; huge; hungry; greedy; likes to eat children; boastful; thinks he's brave; thinks he's clever; he has lots of sharp white teeth; thinks children are juicy and yummy.

   The Notsobig One: thinks children are tough, chewy, nasty and bitter; doesn't like the Enormous Crocodile; is mean to the other crocodile.

e   All crocodiles are big and 'Notsobig' means this crocodile is just smaller than the Enormous Crocodile; 'Notsobig' means it is still a big crocodile.

---

3 Answer the questions (15-20 minutes)

Learning intention: To answer questions about a story.

Resources: Learner's Book, Session 1.6, Activity 3

Description: Direct learners to the questions in the Learner's Book. Remind them to use complete sentences to answer the questions in their notebooks.

Make sure learners understand that some of the answers require them to look for clues. For example, they should think about the words the Notsobig One uses when speaking to the Enormous Crocodile to work out what they think of each other (e.g. *you're so enormous and ugly*).

Once learners finish, discuss their answers to questions e and f. Can they explain how Roald Dahl revealed the feelings of the two crocodiles? (e.g. through the things the crocodiles said to each other; using speech).

Ask learners to describe the personalities of the two crocodiles. Encourage them to support their answers with reference to the extract (e.g. one is big-headed because he says he is the bravest crocodile in the river; one is mean because he tells the Enormous Crocodile that he's ugly).

> **Differentiation ideas:** Support learners through group discussion for questions e and f as this will help them participate in the question and answer time.

> **Assessment ideas:** Are learners able to infer the characters of the two crocodiles from what they say?

Answers:

a   *a nice juicy little child*

b   fish

c   thinks children are tough, chewy, nasty and bitter

d   Because he's the only crocodile who dares to leave the water and go through the jungle to the town.

e   Learners can answer yes or no to this question but should support their answer with an appropriate reason. For example:

   No – because the Enormous Crocodile keeps boasting and the Notsobig One says mean things.

   No – because the Enormous Crocodile thinks the Notsobig One talks *tommy-rot* and isn't very brave.

   No – because the Notsobig One calls the Enormous Crocodile greedy and ugly.

   Yes – because they are together in the river and they talk to each other.

f   Learners' own answers but they should be able to give reasons for them.

4 Secret plans and clever tricks (10 minutes)

Resources: Learner's Book, Session 1.6, Activity 4

Description: Explain that learners will work in a group to talk about what could happen next in the story. Discuss learners' answers to question f in the previous activity. Some learners may know the story and will be keen to share their ideas of what the Enormous Crocodile's plans are. Ask these learners to think of a secret plan that is not in the story. Challenge each group to choose one thing that could happen next, from all of their ideas.

Plenary idea

A good plan (5–10 minutes)

Description: Allow time for each group to share their suggestions for what happens next in the story. Were the ideas in the class similar, or very different? Take a class vote on which idea is the most interesting or exciting.

Homework ideas

Ask learners to:

* think of ten words that could describe the characters in the story and write their comparatives (e.g. big, bigger, biggest)

* complete the Workbook activities for this session, if not completed in class.

Answers for Workbook

1

Words that mean *enormous*	Words that mean the opposite of *enormous*
big	small
huge	tiny
gigantic	little

2 Possible answers:

Words that mean *brave*	Words that mean the opposite of *brave*
bold	cowardly
courageous	timid
fearless	cautious
heroic	fearful
daring	scared
adventurous	faint-hearted

3 Learners' own definitions, but examples might be:

crocodile:	a large, scaly reptile with short legs and large strong jaws
lunch:	a meal eaten in the middle of the day
sharp:	a very fine point, sometimes at the end of a knife, needle or pencil
gulp:	to swallow something quickly
bitter:	have an unpleasant taste; the opposite of sweet
greedy:	wanting to eat more and more food
jungle:	a tropical forest with lots of trees and leaves
secret:	something that no one else knows

1.7 Looking at verbs

LEARNING PLAN

Learning objectives	Learning intentions	Success criteria
3Rg.07, 3Rg.08, 3Rg.10, 3Rg.11, 3Ww.05, 3Wg.06	• Remember what a verb is. • Look at verbs in the past and present tense. • Understand that all sentences must have a verb.	• Learners know what a verb is. • Learners can recognise past and present verbs. • Learners understand all sentences needs a verb.

LANGUAGE SUPPORT

Most of the verbs in this session have regular spelling patterns. Be prepared for learners suggesting past tense verbs with irregular patterns that do not take the –ed ending (e.g. eats / ate; sits / sat; fly / flew; make / made). Language worksheet 1A gives opportunities for learners to note spelling rules for adding –ed and explore irregular past tense forms.

You should direct learners to the verbs ending in –s and –ed, while discussing tense, and focus on the different sounds of the verb inflections, e.g. the –s ending has an /s/ sound in *walks* but an /id/ sound in *started*.

Learners are likely to use other verb forms, such as the continuous (e.g. I was walking; I am trying) and perfect (e.g. I have had; he had had). They do not need to know the names of these verb forms at this stage.

Common misconceptions

Misconception	How to identify	How to overcome
The following words are not verbs: is, was, am, can, think.	When asking learners to 'act out' single words (e.g. eat, sleep, mouse, laugh, chair) learners can confuse the nouns and verbs. For example: in 'be a mouse' they might think the word 'mouse' can be demonstrated and therefore is the verb.	Ask learners: *Are you mousing or are you being a mouse?* Point out that the verb in that sentence is *being*. Suggest learners use the following test to identify verbs: if the words can follow *I* or *he* then it may be a verb (e.g. I know; I think; I can; I am; he is). If the word can follow *the* then it is not a verb (e.g. the child; the crocodile).

Starter idea

Simon Says (10–15 minutes)

Resources: Learner's Book, Session 1.7: Getting started; Language worksheet 1A

Description: Introduce the game Simon Says. Explain that you will call out various actions (e.g. clap your hands; jump up and down) but that learners should only carry out the action if Simon tells them to do it (e.g. Simon says jump up and down). Learners who carry out an action without Simon telling them are 'out' and should sit down. Continue until you only have a small group of learners still 'in'.

Ask learners to tell you what we call the words that you have been asking them to do (action words, doing words, verbs). Explain that when an action is in the past, it is called the past tense. Explain that most past tense verbs have an –ed ending. Ask learners to say what you and they are doing now (e.g. talking, sitting, listening) and explain that this is called the present tense.

Direct learners to the Language focus box then ask them to discuss the table in pairs.

Ask learners to suggest other past and present tense verbs. Language worksheet 1A could be used at this point.

Main teaching ideas

1 Are these sentences? (10–15 minutes)

Learning intention: To understand that every sentence must have a verb.

Resources: Learner's Book, Session 1.7, Activity 1

Description: Write a short sentence on the board (e.g. *The boy ran home*). Ask learners to identify the verb. Repeat this with other short sentences.

Then write another 'sentence' on your board (e.g. *The red apple*) and ask learners to identify the verb. When they are unable to do so, explain that that means it is not a sentence as every sentence must have a verb.

Direct learners to the Writing tip. Then ask them to work with their partner to identify which of a–f are sentences.

When learners have done this, ask them to write those that are sentences into their notebooks. Ask them to underline the verb in each sentence.

> **Differentiation ideas:** Challenge learners to add more information to the two non-sentences to turn them into sentences. Possible answers:

*   *The big crocodile* opens his mouth / eats lots of fish.
*   *Some dangerous crocodiles* live in Africa / are very old.

> **Assessment ideas:** Which learners need further support in identifying verbs, especially those that cannot be demonstrated (e.g. know, think, am, is)?

Answers:

a   Not a sentence.

b   He <u>swims</u> towards the river bank.

c   I <u>love</u> fish.

d   He <u>hears</u> some children.

e   Not a sentence.

f   They <u>eat</u> their lunch together.

2 Correct verb forms of *to be* (10–15 minutes)

Learning intention: To remember what a verb is.

Resources: Learner's Book, Session 1.7, Activity 2

Description: Write the following sentence on the board: *The queen was called Chang Ying.* Ask: *Is this a sentence? How do you know? Where is the verb?* Then write the sentence *Chang Ying is very pleasant.* Ask whether this is also sentence and ask learners to identify the verb.

Explain that both *was* and *is* are part of the verb *to be* and that they can be very hard to spot. Remind learners of the other *to be* words in the Language focus box.

Ask learners to work with a partner to choose the correct form of the verb for sentences a–d in the Learner's Book. Highlight that sometimes more than one form of the verb can be used. In this case, they should choose the one they think fits best.

> **Differentiation ideas:** Support learners using the suggestions in Common misconceptions before they complete the activity.

Challenge learners to identify more examples of *to be* verb forms in their reading book.

> **Assessment ideas:** Did learners identify an appropriate form of the verb *to be*?

Answers:

a   When he <u>was</u> two, the Enormous Crocodile liked eating fish.

b   Both *is* and *was* can be used in this sentence: He <u>is</u> very good at catching fish / He <u>was</u> very good at catching fish.

c   Now he <u>is</u> bigger he likes to eat children.

d   Both *am* and *was* can be used in this sentence: 'I <u>am</u> very hungry,' said the Enormous Crocodile / 'I <u>was</u> very hungry,' said the Enormous Crocodile.

3   Past and present tense change (10 minutes)

Learning intention: To look at verbs in the past and present tense.

Resources: Learner's Book, Session 1.7, Activity 3; Workbook, Session 1.7

Description: Remind learners of the Language focus box. Organise learners into pairs. Tell Learner A to ask Learner B to do something (e.g. *pick up your pen*). Learner B then repeats the sentence changing

it into past tense (*I picked up my pen / I have picked up my pen*). Learners can then swap roles.

Remind learners that the past tense tells you that the action has already happened, and the present tense means it is happening now. Ask learners to read the sentences a–e with their partner and write whether they are written in the past or present tense.

If there is time in class, you could use the Workbook activities to provide further practice with verbs.

> **Differentiation ideas:** Support learners with changing tense form. It may be more appropriate for them to complete the Workbook activities instead of the paired activity.

> **Assessment ideas:** Are learners able to change verbs from past tense to present tense? Which irregular past tense verbs do they recognise, and which can they spell?

Answers:

a   past tense

b   present tense

c   past tense

d   past tense

e   present tense

Plenary idea

Word group actions (5 minutes)

Description: Explain that you are going to set learners a challenge to see how well they know these word groups. Ask: *Who thinks they can identify nouns? What about adjectives? What about verbs?*

Learners first need to choose an action to represent each word group. For example:

- the action for nouns could be to touch a nearby object in the classroom (e.g. table or notebook)

- the action for adjectives could be to stretch arms up (to show tall / high) or out to the side (to show wide)

- the action for verbs could be to walk on the spot, or clap hands.

Explain that you will say a word and learners must perform the agreed action for that word group (e.g. you say 'crocodile' and learners point at the table, you say 'jumped' and learners walk on the spot / clap).

CROSS-CURRICULAR LINKS

Science and History: Learners will use the past tense in these subjects to write reports about investigations or recounts of an event.

Homework ideas

Ask learners to:

- complete the Workbook activities for this session, if not completed in class
- carry out a 'verb hunt' in their reading books and list the past tense and present tense verbs they find.

Answers for Workbook

1   a   A verb can be called a <u>doing, being or having</u> word.

b   A sentence must have a <u>verb</u> in it.

c   If something has already happened the verb is written in the <u>past</u> tense.

d   If something is happening now the verb is written in the <u>present</u> tense.

e   The most common verb in the English language is the verb <u>to be</u>.

1   a   He <u>had</u> a cup of chai after school.   past

b   The phone <u>rings</u> all day long.   present

c   We <u>are</u> all here today.   present

d   The baby owls <u>learned</u> to fly.   past

e   Hidaya <u>picked</u> her friends for her cricket team.   past

f   The tree outside my window <u>grows</u> very fast.   present

3   The words in bold should have been circled in each triangle.

am   ant   any

arm   **are**   at

be   bee   bed

where   **were**   warm

wash   **was**   want

was   win   with

in   **is**   it

art   all   **are**

went   want   **was**

1.8 Speech in texts

LEARNING PLAN

Learning objectives	Learning intentions	Success criteria
3Rv.05, 3Rg.04, 3Rg.07, 3Rg.08, 3Rg.10, 3Rg.11, 3Ri.16, 3Ra.01, 3Wv.03, 3Wg.01, 3Wg.03	• Explore text in speech. • Use speech marks to show dialogue. • Explore and use different verbs for speech in texts.	• Learners can recognise speech in a story. • Learners can add speech marks to show dialogue. • Learners can explore and use different verbs for speech in texts.

LANGUAGE SUPPORT

In this session learners explore writing dialogue. Learners will have seen dialogue in their reading books and know the term *speech marks*. They may also know this punctuation mark as *sixty-sixes* and *ninety-nines*. Encourage learners to avoid these terms as some texts will use only one mark at each end of the dialogue. The terms *speech marks* or *inverted commas* are more appropriate.

In this session learners should be introduced to the term *direct speech*. There is no need to introduce the term *indirect speech* at this stage.

In the extract, Roald Dahl uses the verb *said* for most of his dialogue. Although learners are asked to find

alternatives to *said* in one of the activities, it might be worth exploring why Dahl has used *said* as often as he has. Possible reasons are that he wants readers to focus on the adjectives describing the characters or he wants the dialogue to stand out, not the speaker.

Language worksheet 1B could be used as part of this session. Learners are asked to select alternative verbs for *said* using sentences from Cambridge Reading Adventures *Mei and the Pirate Queen*. The sentences use vocabulary that is suitable for all learners but they will need to check the meaning of the synonyms for *said* in a dictionary.

Common misconceptions

Misconception	How to identify	How to overcome
Speech marks go around the speech and who is speaking (e.g. *'I don't feel very well said the Enormous Crocodile. I think I have tummy ache.'*).	Note where learners place speech marks in their independent writing.	Show learners some speech in speech bubbles and the same speech written as dialogue. Ask them to spot the differences (no speech marks, bubbles do not have said, bubbles do not have the speaker's name). Ask learners to convert several examples of dialogue from their reading books into speech bubbles so that they are clear about which words require speech marks.

Starter idea

Speech bubbles (5–10 minutes)

Resources: Learner's Book, Session 1.8: Getting started

Description: Together, look at the cartoon in the Learner's Book. Ask learners to talk with their partner about what each character might be saying. Share ideas as a class.

Draw two stick people on the board with speech bubbles coming from each mouth. Write one of their suggestions in each bubble. Point out that only the words being spoken are written in the speech bubble.

Ask children how we know someone is speaking in a story (speech bubbles, speech marks, inverted commas). Encourage learners to find examples of speech in their reading books.

If there is time, you could ask learners to draw their own stick people and add speech to each of their bubbles. Note which learners add *he/she said* and correct this error.

Main teaching ideas

1   Looking at speech (15 minutes)

   Learning intention: To explore speech in a text.

   Resources: Learner's Book, Session 1.8, Activity 1

   Description: Ask learners to re-read the extract from *The Enormous Crocodile* from Session 1.6. Ask: *What are the two crocodiles doing in the text?* (talking together)

   Ask learners to tell their partners one thing the Enormous Crocodile says. How did they choose those words? (e.g. they are in the speech marks). Read the Language focus text about speech marks together. Discuss questions a–d together.

Answers:
a   The words are in speech marks.

b   two

c   the Enormous Crocodile and the Notsobig One

d   It tells you – it says 'the Enormous Crocodile asked' or 'cried the Enormous Crocodile'.

2   Add missing speech marks (10–15 minutes)

Learning intention: To use speech marks to show dialogue.

Resources: Learner's Book, Session 1.8, Activity 2; Worksheet 1.3

Description: Write an example of dialogue, including who is speaking, on the board (e.g. *I am feeling hungry, said the Enormous Crocodile*). Ask: *Where should I put the speech marks?* Add the speech marks to your sentence (e.g. *'I am feeling hungry,' said the Enormous Crocodile*).

Ask learners to talk to their partners about parts a–e. When they have agreed where the speech marks go, ask them to write the sentences in their notebooks. If necessary, remind learners to put the exclamation marks and question marks inside the speech marks.

Do learners notice anything else about the way dialogue is set out (different line for a new speaker)? Explain that it is set out like this so that the reader is not confused about who is speaking.

> **Differentiation ideas:** Use Worksheet 1.3 Dialogue in stories to support learners who need additional practice identifying direct speech.

> **Assessment ideas:** Note which learners: put speech marks around the speaker too

put punctuation inside the speech marks

omit the punctuation linked to the dialogue.

Answers:
a   'Shall we walk to the river?' asked Anja.

b   'Yes, good idea!' said Juan.

c   'We will have to be careful,' explained Anja.

d   'Why?' asked Juan.

e   'There may be crocodiles,' laughed Anja.

3   Alternatives for *said* (10 minutes)

Learning intention: To explore and use different verbs for speech in texts.

Resources: Learner's Book, Session 1.8, Activity 3; Language worksheet 1B; a selection of reading books; thesauruses

Description: Ask learners which word group *said* belongs to (verbs). Direct learners to the Key word box and the Language focus box about writing dialogue.

Ask learners to re-read *The Enormous Crocodile* extract with their partner and list all the verbs used instead of *said* (*asked, cried, snorted*). Ask: *Is the speaking verb always in the same place* (no, sometimes in front of the speaker, sometimes after the speaker)?

Ask learners to work with a partner and think of as many words that could be used in place of *said*. Encourage the use of a thesaurus. You could use Language worksheet 1B here.

Share ideas, then look at the extract together and discuss words Dahl could have used in place of *said*. Direct learners to part c and ask them to complete the task with a partner.

Discuss the effect of using different dialogue verbs. Ask learners to think about how that could affect a story.

> **Differentiation ideas:** Support learners with finding other dialogue verbs in fiction texts.

Challenge learners to find other ways a character says something (e.g. *said a loud voice*; *said nervously*). Ask them to think of five other ways to describe how a character said something.

> **Assessment ideas:** Note the range of dialogue words learners use. Do the words give the reader an idea of the speaker's feelings or attitude?

Answers:
a   asked, cried, snorted

b   Learners will have their own ideas for each alternative. Possible answers are: replied, exclaimed, declared, grumbled, announced, muttered, boasted, responded, snapped, whispered.

4 Copy the sentences (15 minutes)

Learning intention: To explore and use different verbs for speech in texts.

Resources: Learner's Book, Session 1.8, Activity 4

Description: Direct learners to sentences a–e in the Learner's Book. Explain that the five sentences are a dialogue between Anja and Juan. Encourage learners to read all five sentences before they begin to add speech marks and dialogue verbs.

Explain that learners could use the verb *said* one or two times but should not use it for every sentence. Remind them to check that they have followed the rules for speech using the Language focus boxes in this session.

Share some examples by asking three learners to take the roles of Anya, Juan and a narrator. Peer assess whether learners have chosen appropriate verbs.

Direct learners to the reflection prompt at the end of Activity 4.

> **Differentiation ideas:** Support learners by asking them to work with a partner. One of them should take the role of Anya and the other should take the role of Juan. Remind learners that they only say the words that each character speaks and to think about how they have said it to give them ideas about dialogue verbs they could use.

> **Assessment ideas:** Did learners choose appropriate dialogue verbs? Did they match the speaker's character?

Answers:
Possible answers include:

a 'Is that a crocodile over there?' asked Anja.

b Juan replied, 'Where?'

c 'Over there, near the tree in the water,' whispered Anja.

d 'Oh yes! I can see it,' gasped Juan.

e Anja exclaimed, 'Quick, let's run!'

Plenary idea

Character speech bubbles (10 minutes)

Description: Ask learners to choose an animal that they can draw easily (e.g. cat, rabbit, fish). Learners decide what type of personality their character has.

Ask them to write a speech bubble for their character to show their character's personality (e.g. *I have the fluffiest tail in the whole burrow; I wish my whiskers were as long as yours; I wish I was as brave as you*).

Homework ideas

Ask learners to:

- complete the Workbook activities for this session, if not completed in class

- search for alternative verbs for *said* in their reading books.

> ### CROSS-CURRICULAR LINKS
>
> IT: Write simple code to animate characters and make them talk. Learners could animate some of the dialogue between the two crocodiles or use the dialogue they wrote with their partner to create a short animation. There are several free downloadable programmes that could support this activity (e.g. Scratch).

Answers for Workbook

1 a Words that Miho said: Where are you going?; Where have you been?; I have been so worried; Nothing is that important; Boys should do what their mother tells them to do; You are a good boy!

   d Words that Yuu said: I'll be back later, mother; I'm sorry; I had forgotten to do something important, but then I remembered it; But this was very important!; I had forgotten to get your present. But then I remembered. Look!

2 shrieked, shouted, demanded, mumbled, complained, declared, stated

3 Learners' own answers.

1.9 Sequencing events

LEARNING PLAN

Learning objectives	Learning intentions	Success criteria
3Rs.01, 3Rs.02, 3Ri.07, 3Ri.17, 3Ws.01, 3Ws.02, 3Wp.02, 3SLm.01, 3SLm.05, 3SLg.01, 3SLg.04, 3SLp.03, 3SLp.04	• Order the main events in *The Enormous Crocodile*. • Discuss the structure of stories using *The Enormous Crocodile* as an example. • Act out the story by following the story mountain.	• Learners can order events in a story. • Learners can understand how a story relates to a story mountain. • Learners can act out a story.

LANGUAGE SUPPORT

The more opportunities learners are given to retell a story the better they will be at writing their own. Encourage learners to think about events in their lives that they could tell others, such as celebrating a birthday, buying something new, visiting a zoo or a new baby being born. Alternatively, encourage them to retell stories they have read or a story they know well.

Starter idea

What makes a story? (5 minutes)

Resources: Learner's Book, Session 1.9: Getting started; extracts from *Matilda* (Session 1.2), *Danny the Champion of the World* (Session 1.3) and *Charlie and the Chocolate Factory* (Session 1.5)

Description: Remind learners of the extracts you read from *Matilda*, *Danny the Champion of the World* and *Charlie and the Chocolate Factory*. Ask learners: *Are these extracts stories?* Learners are likely to say: they are part of the story; just about the people in the story; they do not tell you what the story is. Ask: *What makes a story a story?* Elicit that a story needs a beginning, a middle and an end and that something happens in the story.

Ask whether learners can remember their ideas about the Enormous Crocodile's secret plans and their predictions for how the story ended. Ask: *How did The Enormous Crocodile begin? How do you think it will end?* Allow time for learners to talk about this together.

Main teaching ideas

1   Sequence events in a story (15 minutes)

Learning intention: To order the main events in *The Enormous Crocodile*.

Resources: Learner's Book, Session 1.9, Activity 1

Description: Explain that all stories have a beginning, middle and ending. Read the description of the Learner's Book activity together, then ask for volunteers to read each of the events listed in part b.

Explain that when sequencing a story, it helps to identify the beginning and the end of the story first, then decide what happens in the middle.

When learners have completed the task, discuss the answers together to ensure all learners have the correct order.

Direct learners to the reflection prompt at the end of Activity 1.

> **Differentiation ideas:** Support learners by pairing less confident readers with more confident ones.

> **Assessment ideas:** Do learners understand the components of a story (e.g. beginning, end, something happens, characters). Can learners identify the key elements of a story?

Answers:
b   iv–i–vi–ii–v–iii

2   Sequence events in a story (15–20 minutes)

Learning intention: To discuss the structure of stories using *The Enormous Crocodile* as an example.

Resources: Learner's Book, Session 1.9, Activity 2; Workbook, Session 1.9, Activity 1; Worksheet 1.4

Description: Direct learners to the story mountain in the Learner's Book and explain that this story shape is the shape of most stories.

1   The **introduction** sets the scene and introduces the main character(s)/setting.

2   The **beginning** introduces a problem or difficulty that the main character will have to overcome.

3   The **development** explains the problem a bit more or adds more problems/difficulties.

4   In **the exciting part**, the main character has to prove himself/herself and show whether he/she can overcome the problem.

5   **Then what happens** explains the outcome of the exciting part.

6   **The ending** wraps up the events and ends the story.

Organise learners into pairs and ask them to draw a simple story mountain in their books (e.g. an inverted V) or use the Focus activity in the Workbook, then write each event from Learner's Book Activity 1 in the appropriate part of the mountain.

When learners have completed their story mountains, discuss the position of each event.

> **Differentiation ideas:** Support learners who find it difficult to hold different ideas in their head, by providing a template of the story mountain and printed events to stick in the appropriate place. You could use provide Worksheet 1.4 Sequencing events from *The Enormous Crocodile* for this purpose.

> **Assessment ideas:** Do learners understand the components of a story? (e.g. beginning, end, something happens, characters). Can learners identify the key elements of a story?

Answers:
1 Introduction: iv; 2 Beginning/Problem: i;
3 Development: vi; 4 Exciting part: ii; 5 Then what happens: v; 6 Ending: iii.

3   Act out the story (25–30 minutes)

Learning intention: To act out a story.

Resources: Learner's Book, Session 1.9, Activity 3; completed story mountain showing the events of *The Enormous Crocodile* in the correct order

Description: Read the sequence of events in the correct order so that learners become familiar with it as a story. Ask learners to identify the characters in the story (the Enormous Crocodile, the Notsobig One, jungle animals, children).

Ask learners to organise themselves into groups of six to eight. Explain that each group should decide:

•   who will be the 'director'

•   who will play the crocodiles

•   which jungle animals they will include

•   how many children will be in their play.

Explain that the director's role is to make sure their group follows the story mountain plan and to make sure each group member is involved. Allow time for learners to rehearse their plays and then time to perform each one.

Before groups perform, introduce the idea of 'freeze frame': first the director organises actors into a series of still poses at each point of the story mountain. The director takes a photo (or mimes taking a photo) of each pose. After each photo (real or imaginary) actors explain how their character felt at that particular point in the story.

Encourage learners to peer assess, explaining what they think each group did well and how they could improve it.

Plenary idea

Question and answer (5 minutes)

Description: Ask learners to talk about what they have learned about story writing in this session. Discuss ways they could use story mountains in other curriculum areas. Can learners explain how it could help them organise their ideas in other subjects?

Learners could apply the story mountain format in:

- **History:** to identify the key events in a topic they are currently studying. They could use their story mountain to write a recount of the event.

- **Science:** to explain the sequence of events in an animal's life cycle or the moon's orbit.

Homework ideas

Ask learners to:

- complete the Practice and Challenge activities in the Workbook

- think about the characters they have met during this unit and to choose a favourite, then draw a picture of that character and annotate the picture with reasons why they prefer that character.

Answers for Workbook

Encourage learners to select a story they have read recently or know very well.

1 Learners' own answers. Remind learners that they are not to write the whole story; they should only write a one or two sentences for each of the six points on the story mountain.

2 Learners' own answers.

3 Learners' own answers.

1.10 Planning a story

LEARNING PLAN

Learning objectives	Learning intentions	Success criteria
3Rs.02, 3Ri.07, 3Ri.17, 3Wv.03, 3Wv.05, 3Wv.07, 3Wg.01, 3Wg.03, 3Wg.06, 3Wg.07, 3Ws.01, 3Ws.02, 3Wc.01, 3Wc.02, 3Wc.03, 3Wc.05, 3Wp.02, 3Wp.04, 3SLm.03, 3SLm.05, 3SLg.02	• Think of a new idea for a story. • Draw a story mountain based on the main events in the story. • Plan a story including information on setting and characters. • Include dialogue in a new story.	• Learners can think of a new idea for a story. • Learners can draw a story mountain based on the main events in the story. • Learners can plan a story that includes information on setting and characters. • Learners can include dialogue in a new story.

LANGUAGE SUPPORT

Throughout this session you should encourage learners to talk to a partner about their ideas as this will help them identify weaknesses in their plan.

When learners have completed their plan, encourage them to say their plan quietly to themselves. Saying the words rather than just thinking them is important because it helps learners to remember what they plan to write and allows them to rehearse their thinking. This should help to prevent learners moving away from their plan once they begin writing.

Throughout this session be prepared to model a story of your own and *think aloud* as you select words or choose one idea over another. As you think aloud mention ideas from a Roald Dahl story to model where your ideas are coming from (e.g. *I know the Enormous Crocodile liked juicy children, I think my Scary Bear will like to frighten children; I think Danny wakes up one morning and finds a pony outside his caravan*).

Note which learners can plan and tell a coherent story.

Starter idea

Talk about Roald Dahl character's (5–10 minutes)

Resources: Learner's Book, Session 1.10: Getting started; Roald Dahl books from this unit; internet access

Description: Show learners the covers of the Roald Dahl books, or share online versions. Ask learners to name the characters they have met in this unit.

Ask learners to talk to their partner about the character they like best and explain why they like that character. If learners were given this activity as homework for the previous session, learners can talk to their partners about their homework. Invite some learners to share their reasons.

Ask learners to write the name of the character in their notebooks and to think of three adjectives they could use to describe that character.

Main teaching ideas

1 Ideas for a story (30–35 minutes)

Learning intentions: To think of a new idea for a story; to draw a story mountain based on the main events in the story.

Resources: Learner's Book, Session 1.10, Activity 1; Worksheet 1.5

Description: Explain that learners are going to write their own story. Tell them that sometimes thinking about stories they already know (e.g. a reading book such as *The Enormous Crocodile*) can help them come up with ideas for their own stories.

Ask learners to look at the story suggestions in the Learner's Book. Learners can use one of these ideas but more confident learners could write a story using an idea of their own. Ask: *Who will be the main character in your story?* Allow learners time to discuss their ideas with a partner.

Explain that learners will plot their story ideas on a story mountain. Draw a simple mountain on the board and talk through the six points. Ask learners to draw a large story mountain in their notebooks and plot their story ideas on to it.

If any learners have chosen the same story idea, they could work together.

> **Differentiation ideas:** Support learners who find it difficult to think of their own ideas and find writing difficult by suggesting they write a new version of

The Enormous Crocodile. Ask them to think of a new animal (e.g. snake, monkey). *Where will it live? What kind of character will it have* (e.g. grumpy, mean, mischievous, boastful)*? What will it be called* (e.g. Mean Snake, Notsomean Snake, Mischievous Monkey, Notsomischievous Monkey)*?* Learners could note their ideas in Worksheet 1.5 Thinking of ideas for a story before they add them to the story mountain as this worksheet follows *The Enormous Crocodile* structure.

> **Assessment ideas:** Note which learners were able to think of their own ideas. Could learners identify six key points for their story? Did they follow the story mountain structure?

2 Think about the setting and characters (5 minutes)

Learning intention: To include information about setting and characters.

Resources: Learner's Book, Session 1.10, Activity 2

Description: Explain that now learners should think about the setting and characters for their story.

Suggest ways learners could introduce their story (e.g. 'It was lunchtime and Matilda was trying to read the new football poster on the school noticeboard'; 'Mr Wonka's Chocolate Factory was incredibly huge'; 'Danny's tiny, old pony wandered slowly along the country lanes').

Explain that learners should make notes about words they could use in their story mountain. Remind them that they should only write key words (e.g. lunchtime – Matilda reading notice; factory incredibly huge; pony wandering – countryside) or draw pictures.

Allow learners time to share their ideas with a partner, then add their ideas to their story mountain.

> **Differentiation ideas:** Provide support with choosing vocabulary by directing learners to adjectives / noun phrases from the word wall collections or personal word lists.

Challenge learners to think of interesting adjectives or noun phrases.

> **Assessment ideas:** Did learners choose interesting adjectives? Did any learners include Roald Dahl-style descriptions? Note which learners included noun phrases.

3 Thinking about dialogue (15 minutes)

Learning intentions: To include dialogue in a new story; to plan a story including information on setting and characters.

Resources: Learner's Book, Session 1.10, Activity 3

Description: Ask: *Can you think of anything else we could add to the story?* Elicit the answer *speech/dialogue*.

Remind learners of the conversation between the two crocodiles. Encourage them to think of one thing their main character will say. Who are they talking to? How will that character respond? Encourage learners to share their ideas. Allow them time to think about this and to add possible dialogue to the side of their plan.

Explain that now learners have their story plan they should try telling their story quietly to themselves. Then learners should tell their stories to a partner and work together to check that the story makes sense. Ask: *Are your ideas in the right order? Could your partner follow the story?*

Tell learners to add any new ideas to their story mountain plan.

> **Differentiation ideas:** Support learners by asking questions about any parts that do not make sense and helping to identify what they need to change/add.

> **Assessment ideas:** Note the dialogue verbs learners choose. Note which learners are willing to make changes to their plans.

Plenary idea

Tell a story (5 minutes)

Resources: Learners' story plans

Description: Invite learners to share their story plans with the class.

CROSS-CURRICULAR LINKS

The planning skills from this session can be used across the curriculum whenever learners are organising their ideas for either a written or oral presentation.

Homework ideas

Ask learners to:

- draw a cartoon strip for the story they have planned. Each cartoon strip should have at least six boxes. Ask learners to add speech bubbles to at least four of the boxes.

- complete the Workbook activities for this session, if not completed in class.

Answers for Workbook

Learners' own answers.

1.11 Writing a story

LEARNING PLAN		
Learning objectives	**Learning intentions**	**Success criteria**
3Ww.02, 3Wv.02, 3Wv.03, 3Wv.05, 3Wv.07, 3Wg.01, 3Wg.03, 3Wg.06, 3Wg.07, 3Ws.01, 3Ws.02, 3Wc.01, 3Wc.03, 3Wc.05, 3Wp.01, 3Wp.04, 3SLm.05	• Remember how important adjectives are when writing a description. • Remember that different dialogue words make writing more interesting. • Write a story using a plan.	• Learners can write adjectives linked to setting and characters. • Learners can write verbs linked to dialogue. • Learners can write a story using a plan.

LANGUAGE SUPPORT

In preparation for editing and improving stories, it may be valuable to introduce the Differentiated worksheets on adjectives at this point. These worksheets are designed to introduce your learners to adjectives they are unfamiliar with. They will also help to consolidate their understanding of how adjectives are used within sentences.

Starter idea

Share your story (5 minutes)

Resources: Learner's Book, Session 1.11: Getting started

Description: Allow learners time to look at their plans and retell their story to a new partner to remind themselves of the flow of ideas and any dialogue they used. Explain that when learners tell the story, they should try to use words that they think a writer would use and not the ones they use when they speak. Explain that they should try to add dialogue when they tell their stories. Tell learners that they could try to use a different voice for their character.

Main teaching ideas

1 Think about adjectives (5 minutes)

Learning intentions: To remember how important adjectives are when writing a description; to remember that dialogue words make writing more interesting.

Resources: Learner's Book, Session 1.11, Activity 1

Description: Explain that before learners start writing, you would like them to think about the adjectives and verbs that they will use. Direct learners to the a, b and c prompts in the Learner's Book and ask them to add their ideas to their plans.

Ask learners to look at the words they have chosen for their setting. Ask: *Can you put your words into an interesting sentence? Do your words paint a picture for the reader?* (e.g. All around were enormous flowering plants and towering trees that seemed to touch the sky; It was hard to believe that someone so tiny could be so amazingly strong).

Ask learners to share their ideas for verbs to use instead of *said*. Ask: *Do the verbs make the character sound the way they behave? Do the verbs match the voice you used when you told your story to a partner?*

> **Differentiation ideas:** Support learners with spelling interesting words and using their adjectives in sentences.

Answers:
Learners' own answers.

2 Write a story (30–40 minutes)

Learning intention: To write a story using a plan.

Resources: Learner's Book 1.11, Activity 2; learners' plans from Session 1.10; dictionaries

Description: Tell learners that they can check spellings in dictionaries, personal word lists and use the word wall as they write their stories but that they will also be given time to check these when they have finished writing.

Give learners time to write their stories. When they have finished, encourage them to self-assess their stories against the points in the Learner's Book or by using Worksheet 1.6.

> **Differentiation ideas:** Support learners by reminding them of their plans and the vocabulary they have noted.

Challenge learners to organise their writing into paragraphs and to set out dialogue using speech marks and a new line for each speaker.

Answers:
Learners' own answers.

Plenary idea

Review your work (5–10 minutes)

Resources: Worksheet 1.6

Description: Ask learners to read through their story, saying it quietly to themselves. Ask them to check their story using the points in Worksheet 1.6 Checklist for writing a story and in the Learner's Book.

Homework ideas

Ask learners to:

*   complete the Workbook activities for this session, if not completed in class

*   complete Differentiated worksheets A–C.

Answers for Workbook

1 Marco loved riding his bike but he was getting too big for it. He needed a new bike but he knew his papa didn't have enough money. One day he saw a notice for a bike race. The prize was a new bike. Marco wanted that new bike but first he would have to win the race on his little bike.

2

Word	Difficult bit	Word	Similar word	Similar word
was	wa	was	want	wand, watch
said	ai	said	again	rain, afraid, stain
there	ere	there	where	were

3 Learners' own answers.

1.12 Improving your story

LEARNING PLAN

Learning objectives	Learning intentions	Success criteria
3Ww.02, 3Ww.05, 3Wv.02, 3Wv.03, 3Wv.05, 3Wv.07, 3Wg.01, 3Wg.03, 3Wg.06, 3Wg.07, 3Ws.01, 3Ws.02, 3Wc.01, 3Wc.03, 3Wc.05, 3Wp.01, 3Wp.04, 3Wp.05	• Improve the story learners have written. • Check own stories for errors.	• Learners can improve their story. • Learners can proofread their writing for errors.

LANGUAGE SUPPORT

Learners will improve and proofread their stories in this session. Both of these tasks can be difficult concepts for young learners. You could introduce the idea of improving a story by telling learners that when Roald Dahl was writing *Matilda*, he got halfway through and decided it was not right and so started the story again. It may also help learners to know that Roald Dahl said 'any writers who think their writing is marvellous is in for a shock', so they should expect to make changes to what they write.

Proofreading is best explained to learners as checking for mistakes. Learners may find this easier if they work with a partner.

Starter idea

Sharing ideas (5 minutes)

Resources: Learner's Book, Session 1.12: Getting started; learners' draft stories from Session 1.11

Description: Invite a few learners to read the opening of their story or piece of description they are proud of. If you have noted any good examples of description or dialogue, ask these learners to read these aloud. Elicit comments from other learners.

Ask all learners to read through their stories silently and to think about the questions in the Learner's Book.

Main teaching ideas

1 Improving stories (15–20 minutes)

Learning intention: To improve a story learners have written.

Resources: Learner's Book, Session 1.12, Activity 1; learners' stories from Session 1.11; thesauruses

Description: Explain that learners are going to find ways of improving their stories. You could show learners something you have written (e.g. *Two monkeys were sitting in a tree. One of the monkeys was cheeky. The other was not so cheeky*).

Model how you would improve your story. Say: *Hmm, I have not used many adjectives or interesting noun phrases.* Say: *I know, I could start with 'One beautiful morning.'* Add this, then say: *And I could describe the tree.* Then insert: *at the very top of a huge green* before *tree*. Re-read your improved story and ask: *Does my story sound more interesting with these improvements?*

Ask learners to re-read their stories and look for things to improve. Tell them that they should also check that their stories make sense and try to include interesting synonyms for adjectives and verbs (e.g. *said*). Suggest that learners make changes with a different-coloured pen.

Direct learners to the question prompts in the Learner's Book and allow time for them to improve their stories. Ask them to re-read their plans. Ask: *Did the story follow your plan? Have they included dialogue?*

> **Differentiation ideas:** Support learners whose stories are different to their plans. Try to establish the reason why. Do their stories still make sense?

Challenge learners to find alternative word choices using a thesaurus.

> **Assessment ideas:** To assist your learners and you, ask them to use a different-coloured ink when they add improvements to their writing (a 'polishing' pen). This small change can make the task more appealing as well as make it easier for you to see learners' improvements.

Answers:
Learners' own answers.

2 Proofreading a story (10–15 minutes)

Learning intention: To check a story for errors.

Resources: Learner's Book, Session 1.12, Activity 2; Worksheet 1.6; dictionaries

Description: Explain that learners are now going to proofread their stories. Explain that proofreading means checking for mistakes. Ask: *What type of mistakes could you have made?* (e.g. spelling mistakes; missed-out words; missing punctuation, such as full stops, capital letters or speech marks).

Ask learners to look at the Learner's Book. Who can explain what *checking grammar* means? Explain that checking grammar means checking:

- tenses and *–ed* verb endings to make sure they have used the past tense
- that they have chosen appropriate pronouns
- that they have used complete sentences.

Remind learners what they already know about spelling. Ask: *Have you used spelling strategies and patterns you know? Have you checked your spelling of high-frequency words?* You could suggest that learners put a line under any words they think they have misspelled and cannot correct.

Encourage learners to read their stories aloud to a partner or themselves. This should help them identify any final mistakes. Encourage partners to check that:

- sentences begin with capital letters and end with the appropriate punctuation
- speech marks are around the words spoken.

Finally, ask learners to revisit the success criteria you had agreed with them or use Worksheet 1.6 Checklist for writing a story to self-assess their finished story.

> **Differentiation ideas:** Encourage less confident and more confident learners to work in pairs as they proofread their writing. This will provide support for some learners and challenge other learners to express their ideas clearly.

Plenary idea

Sharing stories (5 minutes)

Resources: Learners' stories

Description: Learners will be eager to share their stories now they are finished. Invite several learners to read their finished stories aloud. Remind them that they should project their voices and add expression as they read to sustain the attention of their listeners.

Homework ideas

Ask learners to:

- complete the Workbook activities for this session, if not completed in class
- design a front cover for their finished story.

Answers for Workbook

1 Learners' own answers.

2 Learners' own answers but possible dialogue might be:

Girl: I wonder what it could be?
Boy: I hope it's something we can play with together.

3 'Where are we going?' asked Anja.
'Shall we ~~going~~ back to my house to make some sweets?' Jonah replied.
Jonah had just remember<u>ed</u> it <u>was</u> his grandmother's birthday the next day. <u>H</u>e wanted to make som<u>e</u>thing for her.
'W<u>h</u>at a great idea,' laughed Anja. 'I could make some sweets for my br<u>o</u>ther too<u>. It</u> was his birthday ~~next~~ last week.'

CHECK YOUR PROGRESS

1 Learners' own sentences describing the setting.

2 Learners' own sentences describing a character from the setting.

3
Nouns	Verbs	Adjectives
school	screamed	black
child	asked	silly
ball	laughed	quick

4 **b** Dialogue is what characters in a story say.

   d We put speech marks around words which characters actually say.

PROJECT GUIDANCE

Group project: Learners will need access to some of Roald Dahl's books that include a profile of the writer, or access to the internet.

Learners work in a group to research and prepare questions for an interview with Roald Dahl. They then use role play to conduct the interview. Encourage learners to switch roles so that they all have the opportunity to act as Roald Dahl and an interviewer. Learners will not have done any formal work on note taking at this point so may need some guidance to avoid them copying all the information they find.

This project requires learners to use critical thinking as they select useful and interesting facts to support the interview.

Observe learners as they work together. Did they keep other learners interested during the interview?

Assess learners by asking:

- *How did you allocate tasks?*
- *Did everyone contribute?*
- *Could you find relevant facts about Roald Dahl?*
- *Did you ask appropriate questions?*

CONTINUED

Pair project: The first learner creates a character, writes adjectives to describe them and then role plays (or draws a picture of) that character. Their partner then writes down adjectives that describe this character. Learners should compare the two sets of adjectives they wrote and then swap roles. Observe learners as they work together.

- Were they able to transfer the written description into a believable character?
- How confident were they in role play?

Solo project: Ask learners to choose a photograph of a happy memory and write about it. If learners do not have a photo, ask them to imagine a memory, creating a picture in their mind. Remind learners to explain what, when, where and who the memory is about and how they feel.

If this project is being completed at home, ensure that each learner understands that while parents may help them in choosing an appropriate photograph, the work should be their own.

Setting up and assessing the projects

Start by deciding which of these projects you will use. Some projects are better managed in class (e.g. the group project) but other projects could be used as alternative homework tasks. Consider whether you will allocate a project or whether you will offer your learners a choice of project.

Resources will depend on the project(s) used. Try to anticipate the resource or organisational needs of each project (e.g. access to the internet for research, dressing up clothes to support role play). When projects are completed, learners should peer and self-assess – both giving and receiving feedback. As you assess each learner's contributions ask yourself these questions:

- Did the learner(s) engage with the project independently, or did they need support? If so, what kind of support did they need? How much support did they need?
- Did the learner(s) demonstrate the skills they had covered in this unit, particularly in the paired and solo projects? Did they:
  - use the success criteria checklist features effectively
  - work co-operatively as part of a group to plan and prepare the project
  - work well alone (if working on the individual project)
  - act respectfully towards peers in group discussions and when giving feedback?

> 2 Let's have a party

Unit plan

Session	Approximate number of learning hours	Outline of learning content	Resources
2.1 Looking at celebrations	1	Explore, talk about and research celebrations. Use dictionaries and alphabetical order to find definitions.	Learner's Book Session 2.1 Workbook Session 2.1 Worksheet 2.1
2.2 Writing lists	1	Start to plan a class party. Explore how to make lists and recap knowledge of verbs.	Learner's Book Session 2.2 Workbook Session 2.2
2.3 Fiction or non-fiction?	1	Explore key features of fiction and non-fiction texts. Use these features to classify narrative text, instructions and an invitation.	Learner's Book Session 2.3 Workbook Session 2.3 Language worksheet 2A
2.4 Following instructions	1	Read and follow a set of instructions. Identify and use command (imperative) verbs and sequencing words.	Learner's Book Session 2.4 Workbook Session 2.4 Language worksheet 2B
2.5 Writing an invitation	1–1.5	Identify the features of an invitation and then write one. Explore rules for adding –ing and –ed to verbs.	Learner's Book Session 2.5 Workbook Session 2.5
2.6 Following and writing instructions	1	Explore the features of written instructions. Write some instructions. Develop reading and spelling skills through exploring compound words.	Learner's Book Session 2.6 Workbook Session 2.6 Worksheet 2.2
2.7 Contents pages and indexes	1	Explore the features of recipes as another style of instruction. Explore contents and index pages.	Learner's Book Session 2.7 Workbook Session 2.7
2.8 Making lists	1	Develop skills in writing lists and ordering items alphabetically. Write a simple recipe.	Learner's Book Session 2.8 Workbook Session 2.8 Worksheet 2.3 Differentiated worksheets 2A–C

Session	Approximate number of learning hours	Outline of learning content	Resources
2.9 Giving instructions	1–1.5	Explore differences between written and oral instructions. Practise giving oral instructions for simple games.	Learner's Book Session 2.9 Workbook Session 2.9
2.10 Planning a game	1	Review a set of instructions and consider how to improve them. Invent a party game and give instructions for it to others.	Learner's Book Session 2.10 Workbook Session 2.10
2.11 Writing instructions	1	Write instructions for a party game using command and sequencing verbs.	Learner's Book Session 2.11 Workbook Session 2.11 ⬇ Worksheet 2.3
2.12 Improving your instructions	1–1.5	Edit and proofread written instructions.	Learner's Book Session 2.12 Workbook Session 2.12 ⬇ Worksheet 2.4
Cross-unit resources			
Learner's Book Check your progress			
Learner's Book Projects			
End-of-unit 2 test			

BACKGROUND KNOWLEDGE

It will be helpful to be familiar with the following English subject knowledge:

- alphabetical order
- how dictionaries are organised, especially those available to your learners
- numbered and bullet-pointed lists
- fiction genres (e.g. traditional tales, fantasy, real-life stories, animal stories, poetry, myths, legends)
- non-fiction genres (e.g. information texts, recipes, instructions, newspapers, invitations)
- adding –ing and –ed to words
- command verbs
- sequencing words

- the present continuous form
- features of non-fiction texts (e.g. glossary, index, headings, contents page, photographs)
- prepositional adverbs and the language of direction: right, left, forwards, backwards
- compound words
- colons.

Command (imperative) and sequencing verbs are a key focus in this unit.

Instructions also use modal verbs (e.g. you will need, you could use, you can). Your learners will be familiar with modal words but do not need to formally identify or refer to them at this stage. Learners will meet modal verbs in greater detail at Stage 5.

CONTINUED

In this unit, your learners explore a range of instruction texts, including some they may be unfamiliar with. If possible, provide a variety of recipe books for your learners to look at. Learners will develop their understanding of:

- verb forms (present, imperative)
- how non-fiction books are organised
- alphabetical order
- how to write lists
- compound words.

TEACHING SKILLS FOCUS

Active learning: Think–Pair–Share

Active learning is a style of teaching that directly involves the learner. There are many ways of developing an active learning approach but Think–Pair–Share is a simple first step.

Introduce the Think–Pair–Share strategy with your learners. Explain that learners first *Think* about a question on their own. When you signal it is time to *Pair*, learners share their ideas or the answer in pairs. Both learners contribute to this quietly. You then give the signal to *Share*, at which point pairs share their ideas or answer with a group or the whole class. Often learners who are reluctant to share their ideas in case they are incorrect gain confidence once they have checked, having talked to others, that their answer is correct.

Think–Pair–Share can be used with very simple questions. For example, you could ask which word group does the word *jump* belong to. You then ask learners to Think–Pair–Share, and within a very short time you have class agreement that *jump* is a verb. Nevertheless, all learners have been involved in the question/answer process. Alternatively, you could ask for the definition of *verb*. The Think–Pair–Share process will take a little longer, but again all learners will have been involved. As a result, learners are more likely to remember what verbs are in the future.

The more you use this approach, consider whether your learners are more engaged in lessons. What effect has it had on your less confident learners and less confident speakers? Are they more willing to speak or give answers in class? Do you feel more engaged with your learners? Has this approach provided more assessment for learning opportunities?

Cambridge Reading Adventures

There are several books in the series that could be used to provide additional opportunities for instruction writing.

- *What's for Lunch?* by Catherine Chambers
- *Connections* by Scoular Anderson
- *The Changing Climate* by Jon Hughes
- *Journey to Callisto* by Mauritz DeRidder and John Stuart

2.1 Looking at celebrations

LEARNING PLAN

Learning objectives	Learning intentions	Success criteria
3Rv.01, 3Rs.03, 3Ri.04, 3Ri.15, 3SLm.01, 3SLm.02, 3SLm.03, 3SLm.05, 3SLs.01, 3SLs.02, 3SLg.02, 3SLg.04	• Discuss different celebrations. • Research what a celebration is. • Use a dictionary.	• Learners can discuss different celebrations. • Learners can research what a celebration is. • Learners can use a dictionary.

LANGUAGE SUPPORT

When exploring dictionaries, make sure your learners understand what the abbreviations mean (e.g. n., v., adj., pl.) and the phonetic spelling of the word in brackets. Some words have more than one definition and you may need to help your learners work out which definition is appropriate to the context.

Make sure your learners know that dictionaries do not list plural forms; these are included in an entry for the root word.

Common misconceptions

Misconception	How to identify	How to overcome
Alphabet letters are incorrectly ordered (e.g. l, m, n, p, o) or omit letters (e.g. i, j, k, m, n).	Ask learners to recite the alphabet and note those learners who have difficulty with specific parts.	Encourage learners to recall the alphabet in short sections. Ask three or four learners to recite the alphabet as a group, with one learner saying the first three letters, then another learner to follow on with the next three, etc.

Starter idea

Let's celebrate (5 minutes)

Resources: Learner's Book, Session 2.1: Getting started

Description: Ask learners to tell you what they understand by the word *celebrate* (e.g. doing something special; having a party; when it is your birthday). Direct learners to the photographs of different celebrations and ask them to talk to their partners about each one. Invite a few learners to share their ideas.

Answers:
Photographs show: a wedding, a birthday party, a street carnival, Chinese New Year

Main teaching ideas

1 **Talk about a celebration (15 minutes)**

   Learning intention: To discuss different celebrations.

   Resources: Learner's Book, Session 2.1, Activity 1

Description: Your learners will be familiar with a variety of celebrations. Many of these celebrations have recognised traditions, but families may also have developed traditions that have a special meaning to that learner. During this session, learners are encouraged to share personal celebrations and you will need to remind them that it is important to listen respectfully to each other.

Explain that learners are going to think about some of the events they have celebrated themselves. Draw learners' attention to the Listening tip. Explain that you will be looking for good listening skills in this activity, from those who are joining in, by asking questions.

Ask learners to tell their partner one celebration they have enjoyed. Then ask learners to share their partner's answers. Write the different events on the board.

Direct learners to the prompts in the Learner's Book. Invite one learner to tell the class about their own chosen celebration, making sure they cover all five points. Remind others to ask thoughtful questions.

> **Differentiation ideas:** Support learners who lack confidence in sharing their ideas verbally by organising them into small groups to share their ideas with the class together.

Challenge learners who are confident at speaking to be the spokesperson for each group.

2 Use a dictionary (20–25 minutes)

Learning intention: To use a dictionary.

Resources: Learner's Book, Session 2.1, Activity 2; Worksheet 2.1; dictionaries; alphabet letters

Description: Ask: *Why do we use dictionaries* (to check how we spell a word, to find out what a word means)? Explain that the correct term for the meaning of a word is *definition*, and that they are going to use a dictionary to find the definition of *celebration*.

Ask learners to explain how a dictionary is organised (e.g. it is in alphabetical order). Ask learners to say or sing the alphabet. If your learners need more practice recalling alphabetical order, you could distribute individual alphabet letters among a group of learners, then invite learners to put the letters (or themselves) in the correct order. To provide more challenge, jumble letters from random points in the alphabet.

Organise your learners into pairs or small groups depending upon the number of dictionaries you have available. Ask learners to find the definition of *celebration* (e.g. a special social event, such as a party, when you celebrate something). Ask: *Who found the word first? How did you find the word quickly?* Use learners' answers to draw attention to the alphabetical order within each letter section.

Allow time for learners to look more closely at the *c* words in the dictionary and to talk to their partners about how words beginning with *c* are organised. Draw their attention to what happens with all the words that begin *ce* (e.g. cease, cedar, cedilla, ceilidh, ceiling, celebrate). Try to elicit that you look at the first letter, then the second letter, then the third letter, etc., and that these are also in alphabetical order. You could use Worksheet 2.1 Alphabet mix-up here if there is time in class.

> **Differentiation ideas:** Support learners to become more familiar with alphabetical order by providing a list of words that all begin with the same letter (e.g. pedal, post, party, puppy). Explain that they must look at the second letter of each word to order the words. When they have done this give them another group of words where the first two letters are the same (e.g. tap, take, tar, taste, talk) and encourage learners to look at the third letter.

Challenge learners by providing them with words that have the first three or four letters the same. Ask them to order them alphabetically and find the definitions of each word (e.g. festive, festivity, festoon, fester, festival; lights, lightweight, ligature, lightning, ligament, lighthouse).

> **Assessment ideas:** Note which learners are confident using a dictionary. Which learners understand the way a dictionary is organised?

3 Research celebrations (15–20 minutes)

Learning intention: To research celebrations.

Resources: Learner's Book, Session 2.1, Activity 3; Workbook, Session 2.1; internet access; reference books

Description: You could use the Workbook activities here to encourage learners to think about words associated with celebrations.

Look at the list of celebrations your learners suggested in Activity 1. Explain that each group of learners must find out more about one of these celebrations. Assign a celebration to each group.

Ask: *What could you use to find information about the celebration (e.g. internet, books)? What kind of information will you look for (e.g. when the event is celebrated; who celebrates it; some of the food eaten during the celebration; traditions of that celebration)?*

Give learners time to research their celebration and feed back to the class.

> **Differentiation ideas:** Support your learners by suggesting they find the information using these headings: *name of celebration; when it is celebrated; who celebrates it; food eaten; special traditions.*

Challenge learners to create fact files for each celebration.

> **Assessment ideas:** Note which learners were confident carrying out research. Did they make appropriate notes? Were they able to feedback to the class?

Answers:
Celebrations could include: Diwali, Holi, Eid, Ramadan, Yom Kippur, Hannukah, Christmas, Easter, Bonfire Night, Halloween, Mardi Gras, Chinese New Year, Guru Nanak Jayanti, marriage/weddings, birthdays

Plenary idea

Making words from a word (5 minutes)

Description: Write *CELEBRATE* on the board and ask learners to find as many new words as possible from the letters, using each letter only once.

Allow learners time to find as many words as they can without using any resources.

Homework ideas

Ask learners to:

- find at least 50 words from a new word (see Plenary idea)
- complete the Workbook activities for this session, if not completed in class
- complete Worksheet 2.1 Alphabet mix-up if not completed in class.

Answers for Workbook

1 Possible answers: party, food, special clothes, lights, fun, families, friends, presents, decorations, games.

2 Possible definitions include:

   a ceremony: (a set of) formal acts, often fixed and traditional, performed on important social or religious occasions

   b festival: a special day or period, usually in memory of a religious event, with its own social activities, food, or ceremonies

   c anniversary: the day on which an important event happened in a previous year

   d fiesta: a public celebration in Spain or Latin America, especially one on a religious holiday, with different types of entertainment and activities

   e carnival: (a special occasion or period of) public enjoyment and entertainment involving wearing unusual clothes, dancing, and eating and drinking, usually held in the streets of a city.

3

2.2 Writing lists

LEARNING PLAN

Learning objectives	Learning intentions	Success criteria
3Rw.03, 3Rv.03, 3Rg.08, 3Rs.02, 3Ri.04, 3Ri.09, 3Ri.15, 3Ws.04, 3Wc.05, 3Wc.06, 3SLm.03, 3SLm.05, 3SLg.01, 3SLg.03, 3SLg.04	• Plan a party. • Write lists. • Identify verbs.	• Learners can plan a party. • Learners can write lists. • Learners can identify verbs.

LANGUAGE SUPPORT

Encourage learners to write lists that are brief but are meaningful to them. It is important that learners understand that lists should not include sentences or long phrases. Some learners will be happy to use single items (e.g. date, when, where, invitations, party food, games) whereas other learners may prefer to include a little more detail (e.g. agree a date, send invitations, buy food).

Starter idea

Words within a word (5 minutes)

Resources: Learner's Book, Session 2.2: Getting started

Description: Write *party* on the board and challenge learners to find as many words as possible from the letters in two minutes (e.g. art, apt, pat, pay, rat, ray, tap, tar, try, pry, rap, part, pray, trap, tray). Note that using *parties* would result in a huge number of words.

Ask: *Who has been to a party?* Direct learners to the Getting started activity and allow them time to talk to their partners about a party using the prompt in the Learner's Book.

Main teaching ideas

1 Talk about parties (15–20 minutes)

Learning intention: To plan a party and write a list.

Resources: Learner's Book, Session 2.2, Activity 1

Description: Explain that during this unit learners will plan a class party. Be clear about whether this is a real event or an imaginary event. Explain that learners should first make a list of all the things that they need to do to make the party a success.

Organise your learners into groups of five or six and explain that each group needs to allocate the following roles:

- Chairperson: makes sure every group member has an opportunity to speak

- Scribe: makes a note of everyone's ideas

- Spokesperson: explains their group's ideas to the rest of the class

Direct learners to the prompts in Activity 1 and check that all learners understand how to produce a list. Direct them to an example of a list in the classroom. Explain that numbering each item in the list is useful when things need to be done in order. Allow learners time to discuss their ideas and to write their lists, then share each group's ideas. Make a note of key ideas if you plan to have a real party.

> **Differentiation ideas:** Support learners who are reluctant to offer ideas by encouraging them to be the chairperson.

Challenge learners who readily share their ideas to play more of a listening role in this activity.

> **Assessment ideas:** How well do learners fulfil their assigned role? Note which learners carry out each role so that other learners are given this opportunity in future groups.

Answers:
Learners' own ideas.

2 Verb forms (15 minutes)

Learning intention: To identify verbs.

Resources: Learner's Book, Session 2.2, Activity 2

Description: Explain that the lists they have made are often called 'to do lists' because they are lists of all the actions that need to be done.

Ask: *Who can remember what action words are called* (verbs)*? Who can give me some examples* (e.g. jump, dance, make, laugh)*?* Direct learners to Activity 2a in the Learner's Book and ask them to answer the questions about verbs in their notebooks. Then ask learners to complete Activity 2b, perhaps using a coloured pen or crayon to underline the verb in each sentence.

Once learners have completed the activity, ask them to swap their books with a partner and peer mark as a class so that you can correct any misunderstandings.

> **Differentiation ideas:** Support learners who are slow at writing by providing a copy of the four sentences in Activity 2b so that they can focus on the task of identifying verbs.

Challenge learners to write two more sentences and ask their partner to identify the verb in each one.

> **Assessment ideas:** Note which learners need support in identifying verbs, particularly versions of *to be*. Do learners overuse some verbs? Ask: *Which words could you use instead of 'get'?*

Answers:
a   A verb is a doing or action word.

To describe how to do something or to describe what we are doing.

No – all sentences must have a verb.

b   Write ideas for a class party.

Send invitations to the party.

Parties are fun!

Some people dance at parties.

Plenary idea

Organising lists (5 minutes)

Resources: selection of fiction and non-fiction books or leaflets

Description: Ask learners where they might find a list (e.g. rules for a game; a phone book; a shopping list; sets of instructions; chapters in a book; the register). Challenge learners to think of as many ways of organising a list as they can (e.g. numbers, alphabetically, bullet points). Some learners may find it helpful to look through books or leaflets for ideas. Discuss why each way of organising a list might be useful (e.g. numbers help you know the order you need to do something; bullet points keep things separated).

Homework ideas

Ask learners to:

*   write a list of things they do during a short period at home (e.g. before they have their evening meal; the hour before going to bed; before coming to school); encourage learners to identify the verb in each item on their list

*   complete the Workbook activities for this session, if not completed in class.

Answers for Workbook

1   Learners' own answers but are likely to include: write invitations, prepare games, put up decorations, buy popcorn, buy juice, choose a date, decide where to hold the party, decide who should come, make cakes, buy food, organise some music, put up balloons, make party hats.

2   Lists should include: the date of the party, where it is, time it will start, time it will finish, the reason for the party, whose party it is, who is sending the invitation. Lists may also include: what to bring, when to reply, what to wear.

3   Learners' own answers but could include: dance, talk, eat, drink, have (fun), celebrate, play (games), laugh, give (presents), open (presents), receive (presents).

2.3 Fiction or non-fiction?

LEARNING PLAN

Learning objectives	Learning intentions	Success criteria
3Rw.03, 3Rg.07, 3Rg.08, 3Rs.02, 3Rs.03, 3Ri.01, 3Ri.04, 3Ri.05, 3Ri.06, 3Ri.07, 3Ri.14, 3Ri.16, 3SLm.01, 3SLm.02	• Discuss the difference between fiction and non-fiction. • Recognise fiction and non-fiction texts. • Answer questions about specific texts.	• Learners can discuss the difference between fiction and non-fiction. • Learners can recognise fiction and non-fiction texts. • Learners can answer questions about specific texts.

LANGUAGE SUPPORT

At this stage, many of your learners will use the terms *story* or *fact* to distinguish between fiction and non-fiction texts. Learners may be less familiar with the range of texts classed as non-fiction and may not have considered recipes and invitations as part of the non-fiction text group.

It is worth explaining that 'RSVP' at the end of Amelia's invitation stands for the French words **r**é*pondez* **s**'*il* **vou**s *plait*, meaning *please reply*. A long time ago educated people and the royal courts in Europe preferred to speak French and RSVP is an example of one of the French phrases that is still used today in formal invitations.

Common misconceptions

Misconception	How to identify	How to overcome
Fiction books only have text and pictures. The text is not factual.	Learners sort books into fiction/non-fiction incorrectly.	Use the four points in the Reading tip to decide whether a book is fiction or non-fiction. Show learners examples of fiction books that have many features of a non-fiction text (e.g. boxed text, headings). Remind learners that they should check against several aspects of a genre. Encourage learners to look for other fiction books that use features of a non-fiction text (e.g. contain letters, include recipes, include diagrams and maps).

Starter idea

Book review (5 minutes)

Resources: Learner's Book, Session 2.3: Getting started

Description: Show learners one of your favourite books and explain why you like it. Ask learners to talk to their partner about the kind of books they like reading. Invite some learners to share their partner's examples.

Direct learners to the Getting started activity. Discuss the meaning of *fiction* and *non-fiction*, and direct learners to the Key words box if necessary. Encourage learners to give examples of both fiction and non-fiction texts, citing those that they have read or looked at.

Main teaching ideas

1 Fiction or non-fiction sort (10–15 minutes)

Learning intention: To discuss the difference between fiction and non-fiction.

Resources: Learner's Book, Session 2.3, Activity 1; selection of fiction and non-fiction books

Description: Direct learners to the Reading tip in the Learner's Book and allow time for learners to read through the four points with a partner. Hold up a book and tell learners that you need them to help you decide which category it belongs to. Read each Reading tip, referring back to your example text each time. Check that your learners understand where to find 'the blurb' and what the term *blurb* means. Check that your learners know where they would find a contents page and index in a book.

Introduce the book-sorting activity. If you have enough books, your learners could complete the sorting task in pairs. Otherwise, organise your learners into groups of four or five so that each group has a selection of books to sort. When each pair or each group has sorted their piles, ask them to write a label for each pile to show whether it is fiction or non-fiction.

Ask each pair or group to peer assess how well another pair or group have sorted their books, using 'thumbs up' and 'thumbs down' to indicate correctly or incorrectly sorted books. If any pairs or groups give a 'thumbs down' to a sorted book discuss as a class why this book is incorrectly sorted.

> **Differentiation ideas:** Support learners by pairing or grouping them with more confident learners.

This will also challenge more confident learners to explain their reasoning clearly, using the points in the Reading tip.

> **Assessment ideas:** Learners will use 'thumbs up' and/or 'thumbs down' to express preferences in this activity. Introduce your learners to other non-verbal responses: hands on heads; fold arms; fingers on the tips or noses; hands on knees. Varying the action encourages learners to think more carefully about their response.

Answers:
Learners' own answers.

2 Fiction or non-fiction texts (10–15 minutes)

Learning intention: To recognise fiction and non-fiction texts.

Resources: *A surprise, How to make a sponge cake, Vovó's surprise party invitation* (Learner's Book, Session 2.3, Activity 2); Tracks 06, 07 and 08; Language worksheet 2A

Description: Invite three learners to read each of the texts in Activity 2 aloud. Remind them to segment unfamiliar words in the text (e.g. *ex–cite–d, won–der–ed, dec–or–ate, in–vite–d*). After each text is read, discuss the meaning of any words that are unfamiliar to your learners (e.g. *softened, sift, dressed to impress, RSVP*). Explain that as well as looking for clues to sort books into fiction and non-fiction, we can also look for clues to help sort short pieces of text into fiction and non-fiction. Ask learners to re-read and discuss the texts with a partner.

Ask learners to read and answer the first question in part b individually (check that they can read *invitation* and *instruction*.) You could use the Language worksheet 2A here to explore other *–tion* words. Ask: *What does 'features of each text type' mean* (e.g. how a text is set out, whether there are headings)? Ask learners to discuss the following two questions of part b with a partner. Refer them to the Key word box if they need a reminder of features of text types.

Choose three learners to act as scribes as other learners feed back the features they identified in each of the texts (e.g. Text 1 is telling you a story; Text 2 has different headings; Text 2 tells you what you have to do; Text 3 is set out on different lines; Text 3 has information in it about times and places; Text 3 is about something that is real). You could use the Workbook activities to reinforce understanding of text types.

> **Differentiation ideas:** Support learners during the discussion by working with them and encouraging them to think about the layout and the style of each text.

Challenge learners to act as scribes during the feedback about text features.

> **Assessment ideas:** Can learners identify differences between texts? Can they use layout features of information texts and fiction texts to explain their reasoning?

Answers:

a   'A surprise' – fiction; 'How to make a sponge cake' – non-fiction; Invitation – non-fiction

b   Invitation – Text 3; Story – Text 1; instructions – Text 2

Differences between the texts: Learners' responses but possible answers should include:

- Text 1: is telling you a story; it isn't about real people.

- Text 2: has different headings; tells you what you must do.

- Text 3: is set out on different lines; has information in it about times and places; is about something that is real.

Story features: the people and events are not real; it has descriptions of characters and settings; it tells you how the characters feel or what they think; sometimes there is dialogue; there may be pictures showing something that is happening in the story; it has a beginning, a middle and an end.

Instructions: headings; list of what you need; list of what to do; information to help you; steps are in order; tells you how long it will take.

Invitation: Tells you what is happening; tells you when it is happening; tells you where it is happening; tells you what you should do; is set out on different lines; it has colons after some of the words.

3 Answer questions about texts (10–15 minutes)

Learning intention: To answer questions about specific texts.

Resources: Learner's Book, Session 2.3, Activity 3

Description: Explain that learners should now read the three texts again answer questions a–f in the Learner's Book.

> **Differentiation ideas:** Support learners by prompting them to refer to the texts for answers to the questions.

Challenge learners to answer in complete sentences and use correct punctuation.

> **Assessment ideas:** Note which learners met the learning intention.

Answers:

a   João's grandmother

b   He will make a cake for her birthday.

c   Possible answers: No, because the old people will only want to talk; No, because the old people will not want to play games; Yes, because he is going to make a cake as a surprise.

d   They don't play games; they just eat and talk.

e   Mix the baking powder with the flour.

f   Rio de Janeiro

Plenary idea

Spelling pattern spotting (5 minutes)

Resources: Dictionaries

Description: Write *invitation* and *instruction* on the board. Ask: *What do you notice about the two words* (e.g. both begin with *in*; both end *–tion*)? Challenge learners to think of other words beginning with *in–* or ending *–tion* (e.g. instruct, inspect, interest, injure, injury, inside, inspection, infection, fiction, function, friction, mention, fraction).

Homework ideas

Ask learners to:

- complete the Workbook activities for this session, if not completed in class

- design their own invitation card for Vovó's surprise party.

Answers for Workbook

1 a Fiction: a book or story about imaginary characters and events; a book that is not about real people and not about facts.

   b Non-fiction: writing about real events and facts.

2 Learners' own answers.

3 a non-fiction

   b it is set out on different lines; it has facts about when and where the event is; it tells you to RSVP

   c to invite someone to a party

   d the person being invited to the party

   e invitation text

4 a non-fiction

   b it has a heading numerical list, linking/ sequencing words: 'First, Then, Finally' and instructions, it has facts about how long to cook the cake for and how much of the ingredients you need

   c to tell you how to make a cake

   d someone who wants to bake a cake and doesn't know what they need or what they have to do

   e instruction text

2.4 Following instructions

LEARNING PLAN

Learning objectives	Learning intentions	Success criteria
3Rw.03, 3Rv.06, 3Rg.05, 3Rg.07, 3Rg.08, 3Rs.01, 3Rs.02, 3Rs.03, 3Rs.04, 3Ri.04, 3Ri.05, 3Ri.09, 3Ri.17, 3Ra.02, 3SLm.01, 3SLm.02, 3SLm.03, 3SLm.05, 3SLs.01, 3SLs.02, 3SLg.01, 3SLg.02, 3SLg.03, 3SLg.04	• Read instructions. • Follow instructions to make an invitation. • Recognise command verbs and sequencing words.	• Learners can read instructions. • Learners can follow instructions. • Learners can recognise command verbs and sequencing words.

LANGUAGE SUPPORT

Instruction texts often include modal verbs, such as *will* in 'You will need'. Note that modal verbs have not been included in the Learner's Book or Workbook activities in order to keep the focus on command/imperative verbs.

When exploring sequencing words in instruction texts, the words used are usually: first; second; next; finally; then; meanwhile; later; afterwards; last; before; when. However, it is worth noting that the word *and* is used as a sequencing word in the party invitation instructions.

For example, *Draw a party picture on Card 3 <u>and</u> cut it out.*

You may wish to direct learners to the use of colons in the text examples. Explain that colons are used to introduce an item or series of items. Explain that capital letters should not be used after a colon unless the word begins with a proper noun. Learners could be encouraged to use colons when they write lists and instructions. At this stage it is suggested that you do not make any reference to colon use in other text types.

Starter idea

Talk about the class party (5–10 minutes)

Resources: Learner's Book, Session 2.4: Getting started

Description: Ask learners to reform the groups they were in when they first discussed the class party. Explain that this time different learners should take on the chairperson, scribe or spokesperson role in each group. Direct learners to the Getting started prompts. Explain that each group must agree a party theme and begin to think about who to invite. Allow time for group discussion and then ask each spokesperson to share the group's ideas for a party theme.

If planning is for a real party, agree a theme as a class, either by choosing the idea that most groups suggest or by having a class vote. If planning is for an imaginary party, each group can plan parties with different themes.

> **Assessment ideas:** How well do learners fulfil the roles of chairperson, scribe and spokesperson? Do learners adapt their vocabulary to match the topic? Do learners listen to others and build on their contributions?

Main teaching ideas

1 Reading instructions (10 minutes)

Learning intention: To read instructions.

Resources: *How to make a pop-up card* (Learner's Book, Session 2.4, Activity 1); Track 09; Workbook, Session 2.4

Description: Direct learners to the Learner's Book and check that they understand the abbreviations for centimetres. Read the instructions as a class then ask learners to answer the questions in their notebooks.

You could use the Workbook activities now, to provide further practise with instructions.

> **Differentiation ideas:** Support learners by working with them in a group. Allow them to give verbal answers to each question and provide prompts if needed.

Challenge learners to suggest additional instructions or resources that could be included (e.g. thickness of card; draw a line on the short side of Card 2; suggestions about what the party picture might look like).

Answers:

a instruction text

b Possible answers: so that you have everything ready before you start; so that you don't forget anything.

c Possible answers: so that you can check that your pop-up card looks the same; in case you are not sure about some of the instructions; they give you extra help so that you don't make a mistake.

d Possible answers: so that you can do everything in the right order; so that you don't mix things up; so that you know what to do first.

2 Follow instructions (15–20 minutes)

Learning intention: To follow instructions to make an invitation.

Resources: Learner's Book, Session 2.4, Activity 2; three pieces of card for each learner; scissors; rulers; glue; colouring pens and pencils

Description: Explain that learners will now follow the instructions to make a pop-up card of their own that can be used to invite people to their party. Ask them to design a picture that matches their theme and explain that the party details will be added in another lesson. Make sure learners know which pieces of card are Card 1, Card 2 and Card 3. Allow time for learners to make their cards.

Encourage learners to self-assess their work and think about how they could have improved their cards. Direct learners to the reflection questions. Ask: *Did you find the instructions easy to follow? Which features did you find the most helpful?*

> **Differentiation ideas:** Support learners who have fine motor difficulties with cutting and folding.

Challenge learners by asking them to support learners in following each instruction step.

> **Assessment ideas:** Note which learners follow the written instructions accurately. Which learners needed support?

Answers:
Learners' finished pop-up card will provide evidence of how well they have followed the instructions.

3 Good instructions (15 minutes)

Learning intention: To recognise command and sequencing verbs.

Resources: Learner's Book, Session 2.4, Activity 3; Language worksheet 2B

Description: Ask learners to read the instructions for making a card again. Ask: *What do you notice about the way each instruction is written* (they are short sentences; they do not say 'you'; some start with verbs; some start with time words)? Ask: *Why have the instructions been written this way* (e.g. easier to follow; only gives you the important information; makes the order clear)? Explain that instructions use a special form of the verb known as a *command* or *imperative* verb, and also use special words called *sequencing words*.

Direct learners to the Language focus box and read this together. You could use Language worksheet 2B to provide further practice. Ask learners to complete Activity 3 and write their answers in their notebooks, and then check their answers with a partner. Ask: *Did you find all the verbs? Where were they? Which sequencing words did you find?*

> **Differentiation ideas:** Support learners by organising them into pairs with a more confident learner for the activity.

Challenge learners to write one alphabetical list of both command verbs and sequencing words.

> **Assessment ideas:** As you explore the vocabulary used in instruction writing, note which learners identify the command verbs. Do your learners understand the purpose of sequencing words? Can they suggest other sequencing words (e.g. before, later, last of all, after, afterwards)? Can they suggest alternatives to the word *then* (e.g. afterwards, secondly, following that)?

Answers:

a The verbs are at the start of each instruction or follow the sequencing word: make, fold, draw, fold, fold, open, glue, stick, draw, cut, glue.

b sequencing words: first, then, next, finally

Plenary idea

Simon Says (5 minutes)

Description: Explain that the game Simon Says uses a lot of command verbs. Remind learners how to play Simon Says: they should only carry out an action when Simon tells them to do it (e.g 'Simon says, clap your hands'). If Simon has not told them to do something (e.g. 'Clap your hands') but they still do it, then they are out of the game.

Choose a learner to call out the commands for others to follow. Play the game until there are only a few learners that are not out.

CROSS-CURRICULAR LINKS

Maths: The pop-up card activity provides a starting point for exploring standard and imperial measurements of length. Learners could:

- measure various classroom objects using one or both units of measurement
- draw lines of different lengths
- prepare card of different sizes for their pop-up card activity.

Homework ideas

Ask learners to:

- design a poster showing examples of command verbs or sequencing words
- design a wordsearch using sequencing words
- complete the Workbook activities for this session, if not completed in class.

Answers for Workbook

1 a verbs: make, need, measuring, do, mix, stir, mix, use, push, knead, put, keep

 b sequencing words: then, finally

2 a First fold the card in half.

 b Next fold the small card.

 c Stick the small card into the big card.

 d Then draw a picture.

 e Finally stick the picture on the small card.

3 Possible answers include: headings, bullet points, numbered points, command verbs, sequencing words, list of what you need, instructions in order.

2.5 Writing an invitation

LEARNING PLAN

Learning objectives	Learning intentions	Success criteria
3Rg.05, 3Rg.07, 3Rg.08, 3Rg.10, 3Rs.02, 3Rs.03, 3Ri.04, 3Ri.15, 3Ri.16, 3Ww.02, 3Wg.06, 3Ws.01, 3Ws.04, 3Wc.02, 3Wc.05, 3Wc.06, 3Wp.01, 3Wp.03, 3Wp.04, 3Wp.05, 3SLm.05, 3SLs.01	• Discuss the information needed in an invitation. • Write and present an invitation for a particular purpose and audience. • Listen and respond appropriately. • Add _–ing_ and _–ed_ to words.	• Learners can discuss the information needed in an invitation. • Learners can write and present an invitation for a particular purpose and audience. • Learners can listen and respond appropriately. • Learners can add _–ing_ and _–ed_ to words.

LANGUAGE SUPPORT

How you organise your learners for Activity 2 will depend upon whether you are planning a real class party or planning an imaginary party.

Ask each planning group to decide who will be invited to the party. If the party is real, you will need to agree as a class who to invite and who each learner is writing their invitation to. Is each learner inviting another learner in the school? Are learners inviting parents?

In this session, learners explore rules for adding _–ing_ and _–ed_ to verbs with short and long vowels. Learners will be familiar with the term _past tense_ from Unit 1. Although the present continuous tense

is used in this unit (e.g. I am inviting; I am sending) there is no need discuss it at this point.

Prior to adding _–ing_ and _–ed_ endings to verbs, your learners need to know which letters of the alphabet are vowels (a, e, i, o, u) and which are consonants (all other letters). Your learners also need to be aware that there is one consonant exception – the letter _y_ – which behaves like a vowel when it occurs at the end of a verb (e.g. enjoy, enjoying, enjoyed; stay, staying, stayed; cry, crying, cried) and has its own set of rules (e.g. add _–ing_ to the root verb when the verb ends in _y_; change _y_ to _i_ when adding _–ed_ for all regular verbs).

Common misconceptions

Misconception	How to identify	How to overcome
You only need to add _d_ to form the past tense of some verbs (e.g. invite – invited; change – changed)	Note how learners explain rules for adding _–ed_. Note which learners think 'you just add d' when giving explanations about how some past tenses are formed.	Play a verb-addition game where learners add either _–ing_ or _–ed_ to a root word to form a new word. Learner A writes a root word on their whiteboard or card. Learner B writes + _ing_ or + _ed_ on their whiteboard or card. Learner C writes the correct new verb. Ensure that learners always remove necessary letters from the root word before adding _–ing_ or _–ed_.

Starter idea

Amelia's invitation (3–5 minutes)

Resources: Learner's Book, Session 2.5: Getting started

Description: Ask learners to talk to their partner about the invitation João sent to Amelia in Session 2.3. Direct them to the discussion prompts in the Learner's Book and ask learners to make notes in their books. Discuss answers as a class, checking that all learners have noted the correct information.

Answers:
Vovó's party; Santa Teresa Colombo Café in Rio de Janeiro; 4.30 pm; it says *will be at*.

Main teaching ideas

1 Exploring invitations (10–15 minutes)

Learning intention: To discuss the information needed in an invitation.

Resources: Learner's Book, Session 2.5, Activity 1

Description: Direct learners to Activity 1 and discuss parts a–c as a class. Ask: *Why do we need to include RSVP* (e.g. so that we know who is coming)*? Why is RSVP useful?* (e.g. it is very short) *Are there any other phrases that we could use that are less formal?* (e.g. Please reply; Please let us know if you can come; Please say whether you can come) *Do we need to give a date that we want people to reply by?* (learners' answers will vary).

Direct learners to answer part d in their notebooks.

> **Differentiation ideas:** Support and challenge learners by dividing your class into groups comprising some learners who would like to be challenged and some learners who would benefit from additional support.

> **Assessment ideas:** Did learners identify the features of invitation texts?

Answers:
a writing is in the centre of the page; it's on different lines so that the information is clear

b what, where, when, extra information

c please reply

d Learners' answers should include: what the party is for; when it will be; where it will be; what people should wear; who the invitation is to.

2 Writing an invitation (20–25 minutes)

Learning intention: To write and present an invitation for a particular purpose and audience.

Resources: Learner's Book, Session 2.5, Activity 2; dictionaries

Description: Check that all your learners know what the details are for your party (e.g. what the party is for, where the party will be, when the party will take place, any additional information such as the theme or how to be dressed).

If groups are planning an imaginary party, you may need to allow more time for each group to agree the details. Remind learners to use the notes they have made as a group or as a class. Allow time for them to write their rough invitations in their books.

Remind learners of what it means to proofread their writing (e.g. check spelling accuracy, check party details are correct, check layout). Once they have proofread their work, ask learners to type or write their final invitation. Remind them that their invitations must be beautifully presented as they are to be sent to other people, and, if handwriting the invitations, writing must be neat and legible.

Once learners have cut and stuck their written invitation onto their pop-up card, direct them to peer assess their finished invitations with their partners.

> **Differentiation ideas:** Support learners with the layout for their invitations, especially if using a computer.

Challenge learners to use a variety of writing styles (e.g. illuminated letters for some of the words, bubble writing for the name of the invitee, colons to introduce items).

> **Assessment ideas:** Note which learners can identify and correct misspelled words. Note which learners used set their invitation out correctly. Learners' own class party invitations

3 Listening activity (10–15 minutes)

Learning intention: To listen and respond appropriately.

Resources: *Party invitation* (Learner's Book, Session 2.5, Activity 3); Track 10

Description: Explain that learners are going to listen to a conversation between Tuhil and Anya and that the conversation includes all the information they need about a party. Ask learners to talk to their partner about the kind of information they expect to hear and share ideas (e.g. what kind of party it will be, when it will be, where it will be).

Show learners how to prepare for listening by writing headings such as *What? When? Where? Other information?* on the board. Play the audio. Once learners have listened to the audio, ask each pair to compare notes. Ask: *Do you have all the information you need to write an invitation for the party?*

Allow learners time to write an invitation from Tuhil to Anya in their books, then ask them to peer assess each other's invitations.

> **Differentiation ideas:** Support learners by providing prompts for the listening task (e.g. What? When? Where?). Position each prompt on a new line to support learners with layout.

Challenge learners to use the correct punctuation in the invitation.

> **Assessment ideas:** Note which learners need support in identifying the relevant information. You should note which learners set out the invitation correctly (e.g. new line for each piece of information, appropriate punctuation) and which learners needed scaffolding for this in the form of a template or guidance on which details to listen out for.

Audioscript: *Party invitation*

Tuhil: Hey Anya! Would you like to come to my birthday party? It is in three weeks time.

Anya: That would be great, when exactly is it?

Tuhil: It is on the 18th February. I'm inviting all the class so it should be fun. I thought I might have a fancy dress party. Come dressed as your favourite character from a film. The best fancy dressed person will win a prize.

Anya: That sounds brilliant. I already know who I will come as.

Tuhil: Who?

Anya: That can be a surprise!

Tuhil: Ok [laughing]. It will be at Grantham Hall, down Silver Street.

Anya: Great, I know where that is, we can walk there from our house. What time is it so I can tell Mum?

Tuhil: It will start at 3pm and finish at 6pm. There will be lots of food, Mum has already started buying food for it!

Anya: Hope I remember everything to tell Mum.

Tuhil: No problem if you don't, I'm sending invitations out after this weekend. The invitation will have everything you need to know on it.

Anya: Brilliant, I have to go as I'm meeting my sister but thanks for the invite!

Answers:

Learners' invitations should include the following information:

Anya

Is invited to: Tuhil's birthday party

It will be at: Grantham Hall, Silver Street

On: 18th February, 3 pm–6 pm

Come dressed as your favourite film character

RSVP

---

4 Adding –*ing* and –*ed* to verbs (15–20 minutes)

Learning intention: To add –*ing* and –*ed* to words.

Resources: Learner's Book, Session 2.5, Activity 4; Workbook, Session 2.5

Description: Ask learners to look again at the invitation to Voló's surprise party in Session 2.3.

Write the two sentences from Activity 4 on the board and ask learners which verb is used in both sentences (to invite). Explain that in the first sentence the verb is about something that is going to happen, and the second sentence is about something that has happened.

Write *invite* on the board and ask: *How has the spelling changed in the word 'inviting'?* (e.g. it has –*ing* on the end, the e has gone) Direct learners to the word *invited* and explain that the e has been removed and –*ed* has been added to form the past tense. Direct learners to the Language focus box and read to the end of the rule for words with consonants.

Write *jump, talk, pretend* and *behave* on the board and show learners how to check the letter before the last letter and apply the rule for adding –*ing* and –*ed* to each word.

Ask learners to read the Language focus box rule about words with single vowels. Write *grin, dip, snow* and *snap* on the board and ask learners to apply the rule by adding *–ing* and *–ed* to each word in their notebooks.

Direct learners to the final Language focus box rule, then allow time for them to complete the activity in their books. You could then use the Workbook activities to provide further practice.

> **Differentiation ideas:** Support learners by providing a copy of the alphabet with vowels highlighted in a different colour.

Challenge learners to think of two more verbs and apply the rules for *–ing* and *–ed*.

> **Assessment ideas:** This activity offers an opportunity for you to assess your learners' spelling and understanding of verb tenses. Note which rules learners have most difficulty with. A classroom display of the rules, with numerous examples, would be a useful prompt for most of your learners.

Answers:
a   helped; pushed; zipped; waved; hopped
b   sitting; sweeping; waiting; baking; boxing

Plenary idea

Wordhound (5 minutes)

Description: Say that you are all going to play a game called Wordhound. Explain that you will think of a word (e.g. *working*) and will draw a dash on the board for each letter (e.g. _ _ _ _ _ _ _). You could provide the initial letter of the word. Explain that they need to use their knowledge of spelling patterns to suggest the next letter. (e.g. only a, e, h, i, o, and r can follow w). As consecutive letters are guessed, learners will find it easier to predict letters. Each time they get a letter wrong, you will draw

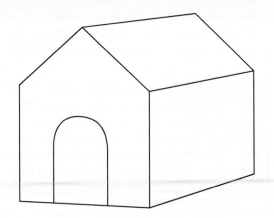

a line to create a picture of a dog kennel. The aim is to guess the letter before the dog kennel is completed. Supply the letter for learners if they fail to guess a letter before the kennel is completed. You then move on to the second letter and start drawing a new kennel.

Unlike the game Hangman, Wordhound encourages learners to think of spelling patterns and sequences of letters that are often found together. Once they have guessed the first three letters (*wor*), learners should quickly guess the remainder of the word.

Homework ideas

Ask learners to:

• decorate the invitation to Anya

• carry out a word hunt of *–ed* and *–ing* verbs using their reading books

• complete the Workbook activities for this session, if not completed in class.

Answers for Workbook

1   a   landing
    b   stooped
    c   bumping
    d   reading
    e   helped
    f   meeting

2   Possible answers to complete the sentence: you just add the *–ed* or the *–ing*; you don't need to change the end of the word.

3   a   tuning
    b   burying
    c   flapping
    d   tipping
    e   saving
    f   skating
    g   towing
    h   rubbing
    i   behaving

4   a   Taila <u>plans</u> a party.
        Taila planned a party.
    b   She <u>invites</u> all her friends.
        She <u>invited</u> all her friends.

c   She <u>wants</u> to play lots of games.
She <u>wanted</u> to play lots of games.

d   She <u>cooks</u> some lovely food.
She <u>cooked</u> some lovely food.

e   Her friends <u>arrive</u>.
Her friends <u>arrived</u>.

f   She <u>dances</u> with her friends.
She <u>danced</u> with her friends.

2.6 Following and writing instructions

LEARNING PLAN

Learning objectives	Learning intentions	Success criteria
3Rw.03, 3Rv.02, 3Rv.06, 3Rg.05, 3Rg.08, 3Ri.02, 3Ri.04, 3Ri.05, 3Ww.05, 3Wg.04, 3Wg.06, 3Ws.04, 3Wc.05, 3Wc.06	• Recognise different activities where instructions are followed. • Write instructions. • Recognise compound words to help spell and read words correctly.	• Learners can recognise different activities where instructions are followed. • Learners can write instructions. • Learners can recognise compound words to help spell and read words correctly.

LANGUAGE SUPPORT

Your learners may benefit from a maths lesson exploring language for direction and location prior to this session (e.g. right, left, forwards, backwards, quarter turn, right-angled turn to the left).

When forming compound words in Activity 3, your learners may omit less familiar vocabulary (e.g. *bedbath, anyhow, anybody*). Whilst learners do not need to know the less well used *bedbath, anyhow* and *anyway* should be mentioned, if omitted. *Anyhow* is a more informal version of its synonym *anyway*. *Anybody* is also a more informal version of its synonym *anyone*. Both informal versions are more likely to occur in spoken English as opposed to written English.

Common misconceptions

Misconception	How to identify	How to overcome
All words with two or more syllables are compound words without understanding that a compound word contains two words that make sense in their own right.	Note learners' answers during Learner's Book Activity 3 and the Practice activity in the Workbook. Which learners identified any of the following as compound words: *battery, cucumber, different, remember*?	Remind learners that compound words contain two words that make sense on their own. Ask learners to look closely at examples of compound words used in the session, particularly the clusters of consonants in the middle of the words. Note the combinations (e.g. cla<u>ss</u>room, hai<u>rb</u>rush, ba<u>tht</u>ime, too<u>thp</u>aste, some<u>th</u>ing, any<u>wh</u>ere). Explain that compound words usually have several consonants together that do not form a trigraph.

Starter idea

Getting started (5 minutes)

Resources: Learner's Book, Session 2.6: Getting started

Description: Ask learners to make a list in their notebooks of all the things we use instructions for. Allow learners time to write their ideas (e.g. recipes, playing games, making objects, doing what someone asks, listening to the satnav/GPS when we're in the car).

Ask learners to compare their list with a partner or other members of their group. Were their lists the same?

Main teaching ideas

1 Following directions (15 minutes)

Learning intention: To recognise different activities where we follow instructions.

Resources: *How to get from school to the playground* (Learner's Book, Session 2.6, Activity 1); Track 11

Description: Explain that some instructions tell us how to get from one place to another and that instructions of this kind are called *directions*. Ask learners to suggest why this might be (e.g. they use words such as turn right, turn left, head north).

Direct learners to Activity 1 and select six learners to take turns reading an instruction aloud to the class. Ask: *Can you give me an example of a command verb* (leave, turn, walk, cross, go)*? Can you find any sequencing words* (next, and)*?* Read and discuss the Writing tip.

Invite a learner to give directions to another learner to direct them from their seat to another part of the classroom. Ask the rest of the class to indicate whether the instructions were clear using 'thumbs up/thumbs down'. Ask: *Were the instructions short? Were the instructions simple? Which command verbs and sequencing words did you hear?*

> **Differentiation ideas:** Support learners by providing more opportunities to give instructions within the classroom. If learners confuse right and left, encourage them to put up both hands with the knuckles facing them with thumbs turned out. Explain that the thumb makes an L shape on their left hand. Encourage learners to do this whenever they confuse left and right.

> **Assessment ideas:** As learners give verbal directions to others, note their use of command verbs and sequencing words. Do learners keep their directions short and simple?

2 Writing instructions (20–25 minutes)

Learning intention: To write instructions.

Resources: Learner's Book, Session 2.6, Activity 2; Worksheet 2.2; map of your school

Description: Explain that learners are going to write directions for the people coming to the class party. Explain that it is important that no instructions are left out and that the instructions are in the right order. If your learners need more practice at reading and following instructions prior to writing their own, use Worksheet 2.2 Muddled routes.

Elicit where the directions should start (e.g. the school car park, the main entrance to the school) and where the directions should end (e.g. the room that will be used for the party). Ask learners to talk to their partner about the route and allow learners time to write their directions.

Before learners finalise their directions, allow each pair time to follow the directions for themselves or provide each pair with a plan of the school so that they can plot the directions if they cannot follow the route themselves. Explain that as learners follow the route, they should consider whether there are directions they have omitted or whether some directions are unclear. Remind learners of your behaviour expectations before they leave the classroom. Once learners return to the classroom, allow time for them to amend their directions and change, or add, command verbs and sequencing words.

> **Differentiation ideas:** Support learners by dividing your class into groups comprising some learners who would like to be challenged and some learners who would benefit from additional support.

Challenge learners by encouraging them to swap directions with another pair to peer assess the directions.

> **Assessment ideas:** It is important that you assess your learners' ability to write short, simple directions using command verbs and sequencing words, and not the accuracy of their directions. Do your learners consider the needs of the reader when they write directions?

Answers:
Learners' own answers.

3 Compound words (10–15 minutes)

Learning intention: To recognise compound words to help spell and read words correctly.

Resources: Learner's Book, Session 2.6, Activity 3; Workbook, Session 2.6

Description: Write *playground* on the board and ask learners what they notice about this word (e.g. it can be split into two small words: play/ground). Ask learners to work with their partner and make a list of words of objects in the classroom that are made up of two smaller words (e.g. classroom, whiteboard, windowsill, cupboard, bookcase). Explain that these words are called *compound words* and direct learners to the Reading tip.

Ask learners to work in pairs to complete part b. Ask learners to share ideas and then to complete part c independently.

You could use the Workbook activities to provide further practice if there is time in class.

> **Differentiation ideas:** Support learners by encouraging them to begin with *hair* and try placing the other words after it to identify possible compound words. Once they have tried all possibilities and identified hair + brush and hair + band, encourage them to try pairs beginning with *bed*.

Challenge learners to think of other compound words (e.g. aircraft, afternoon, background, birthday, cardboard, doorbell, downstairs, farewell, football, hotdog, grandmother, laptop, lunchtime, outside, passport, pillowcase, rainbow, shipwreck, whenever, zigzag).

> **Assessment ideas:** Note which learners can combine two smaller words to form a compound word. Do any learners suggest non-words? Do learners need to check that their compound word exists?

Answers:

a *Playground* can be split into two smaller words.

b hairbrush, hairband, bedroom, bedtime, bedbath, bathroom, bathtime, playroom, playtime, toothpaste, toothbrush

c everything, everyone, everybody, everywhere, anything, anyone, anywhere, anyhow, anybody, someone, something, somewhere, somebody, nothing, nowhere, nobody

Plenary idea

Compound word sentence (5–10 minutes)

Description: Ask learners to use a compound word from Activity 3b in an instruction sentence (e.g. Put the toothpaste on your toothbrush; Tidy your bedroom; Put your coats on for playtime).

Homework ideas

Ask learners to:

- complete the Workbook activities for this session, if not completed in class

- write directions for a route at home (e.g. the kitchen to their bedroom, their house to a neighbour's, their house to a nearby shop, their house to the bus stop).

Answers for Workbook

1 Learners should tick: **a** Then walk to the traffic lights; **c** Be kind to each other; **d** Turn left after the letterbox; **f** Add the milk and stir.

2 classroom, fingernail, letterbox, midnight, outside, teapot, understand, upstairs

3 Learners' own sentences. All sentences should be instructions and include a compound word.

2.7 Contents pages and indexes

LEARNING PLAN

Learning objectives	Learning intentions	Success criteria
3Rv.03, 3Rs.02, 3Rs.03, 3Ri.01, 3Ri.04, 3Ri.05, 3Ri.07, 3Ri.14, 3Ri.15, 3Ri.16, 3Ri.17, 3Ra.01, 3Wc.02, 3Wp.02, 3SLm.03, 3SLm.05, 3SLg.01, 3SLg.02, 3SLg.04	• Recognise that instructions are found in recipe books. • Understand the use of a contents page and index. • Use a contents page and an index.	• Learners can recognise that recipes are a form of instructions. • Learners can understand why we use a contents page and an index. • Learners can use a contents page and an index.

LANGUAGE SUPPORT

This session builds on previous work on features of non-fiction books and learners' knowledge of the alphabet. Your learners will be familiar with contents and index pages but may lack confidence in using them to locate information. Make sure you explore these features carefully and allow learners time to look at a range of non-fiction books.

Starter idea

Thinking about parties (5–10 minutes)

Resources: Learner's Book, Session 2.7: Getting started

Description: Say: *I am thinking of two words. You will try to guess these words in a game of Wordhound.* Draw five dashes followed by four dashes (for *party food*) on the board. Remind learners of the rules for Wordhound (see Session 2.5, Plenary idea), then invite them to guess each letter in turn. The first three letters of the first word will need several guesses but then learners should be confident with guessing the remaining letters and word. Once *party food* has been guessed, direct your learners to the Getting started prompts and ask them to talk in pairs or threes. Allow time for learners to discuss each prompt.

Main activity ideas

1 Party food (10 minutes)

Learning intention: To recognise that instructions are found in recipe books.

Resources: Learner's Book, Session 2.7, Activity 1; selection of recipe books

Description: Organise your learners into their party-planning groups and ask them to appoint a new chairperson, scribe and spokesperson. Direct learners to part a.

Explain that each group must choose one item of party food for the class party. If possible, provide a selection of recipe books for learners to explore for ideas. If learners are planning an imaginary party, each group can decide all the party food items. Allow time for groups to discuss.

Ask the spokesperson from each group to share their party food choice(s). Make a note of all the items shared. Ask: *What kind of book would tell you how to make your party food? Where would you find a recipe book? Why would I find recipe books in the non-fiction section of a library?* If possible, visit the school or local library to look at how non-fiction books are organised.

> **Differentiation ideas:** Support learners who have never looked at or used a recipe book by providing copies for them to explore.

> **Assessment ideas:** All your learners should have held at least one of the group roles by now. Ask learners to peer assess each other using these prompts:

- *Are the scribe's notes too long? Do they include unnecessary words (e.g. X said that ... ; Y said ...)?*

- *Does the chairperson give every member of the group a chance to speak? Does the chairperson talk too much?*

- *Does the spokesperson report group ideas accurately? Did they report back clearly?*

Answers:
a   Learners' own answers.

b   a recipe book; libraries, kitchens, bookshops

2   Fruit rockets (10–15 minutes)

Learning intention: To recognise that instructions are found in recipe books.

Resources: *Fruit rockets* (Learner's Book, Session 2.7, Activity 2); Track 12

Description: Direct learners to the activity. Allow time for them to read the text, then ask: *What type of text is this?* Try to elicit the answer *instruction text.* Ask learners to work with their partner to identify the instruction text features and then to note these features in their notebooks. Allow a few minutes for learners to make their notes. Then ask: *What sort of book does the page come from?*

Discuss the features your learners have noted and point out any omitted features.

> **Differentiation ideas:** Support learners by reading unfamiliar words with them and ask direct questions (e.g. *Does the text tell you what to do? Are there numbers to help you with the order? Does it have short lines and simple sentences?*).

Challenge learners to identify the maths terms used in the text (e.g. *centimetre, half, triangles, base, top, above, middle, long, two, digits 1, 2* and *3*).

> **Assessment ideas:** Learners should now be confident in recognising features of instruction

texts. Note which learners still need support in identifying these features. Encourage these learners to focus on the layout of the text first, noting the short lines and simple sentences.

Answers:
a   Instruction text; layout, bullet points, numbered points, command verbs, sequencing words, list of what you need, headings.

b   A recipe book.

3   Contents pages and index (15 minutes)

Learning intentions: To understand the use of a contents page and index; to use a contents page and index.

Resources: Learner's Book 2.7, Activity 3; Workbook, Session 2.7; selection of recipe books and non-fiction books

Description: Direct learners to the example contents and index pages in the Learner's Book. Ask them to find the fruit rockets recipe on the contents page. Allow time for learners to talk to their partners about the contents page and index using the question prompts in part a.

Ask learners to write the title *Contents page and index* in their notebooks and then draw a table underneath with two columns: one column headed *Same* and the other column headed *Different.* Allow time for learners to complete the table to record the similarities and differences and then to share their results.

Ask: *When would you use a contents page?* (e.g. to find out where some information is; to find a list of what is in the book) Ask: *When would you use an index?* (e.g. to find a small item that would not need a whole section; if I was looking for a recipe using a particular fruit) Elicit that, in this example, the contents page lists all the recipes in the book; the index only lists the ingredients used in the recipes but not the equipment. Explain that contents pages guide you to large topics, whereas index pages help you find smaller pieces of information.

Provide learners with a variety of non-fiction books and allow them time to explore the two types of page. Learners can complete the Workbook activities now to provide further practice if there is time in class.

> **Differentiation ideas:** Support learners by giving them easier non-fiction texts to explore. You can also support learners by providing them with a pre-prepared blank table.

Challenge learners to explore glossaries. Ask them to identify:

- how glossaries are the same and different to contents and index pages

- how a glossary is the same and different to a dictionary.

> **Assessment ideas:** Which of your learners continue to confuse alphabetical order? Are there particular sections that learners muddle? Could you provide more opportunities for playing alphabet games?

Answers:

Same	Different
Each item has page numbers with it	Index is in alphabetical order
	Index lists more than one page number for some items
Every item or chapter has a new line	Contents page has sub-headings
	Contents page numbers are aligned in a vertical row
	Index page numbers are next to each item

a   Possible reasons for when you would use each page:

- contents: to look where to find information about a topic; to see which topics are included in the book

- index: to find specific information.

Contents and index pages would be found in information texts (e.g. recipe books, books on particular topics).

4   Finding recipes (5–10 minutes)

Learning intention: To use a contents page and index.

Resources: Learner's Book, Session 2.7, Activity 4; selection of or internet access to recipe books

Description: Remind learners of the food items they chose at the beginning of the session. Organise learners into their party-planning groups and provide each group with a selection of recipe books or access to the internet. Allow time for each group to add additional party food items to their lists.

> **Differentiation ideas:** Support learners using computers by providing links for accessible party food recipes online.

> **Assessment ideas:** Note which learners achieved the Learning intention.

Answers:
Learners' own answers.

Plenary idea

Finding items quickly (5 minutes)

Resources: Contents page and index in Learner's Book Activity 3

Description: Direct learners to the example contents page and index in Activity 3 in the Learner's Book. Explain that you will call out an item or topic and that they should put up their hands as soon as they have located the page number. You could introduce a competitive element by inviting two learners to compete against each other. The fastest learner each time goes on to play against a new learner.

Homework ideas

Ask learners to:

- complete the Workbook activities for this session, if not completed in class

- speak to a family member about their favourite party food and write it out neatly as a recipe or draw a picture of it.

Answers for Workbook

1 a Text A

   b index

   c at the beginning of a book

   d at the end of a book

   e recipe book

2 a Nutty banana whirl, Orange refresher

   b page 31

   c 24, 28, 31

   d 31

   e carrot, butter, sugar

3 a no

   b Possible reasons: it starts at page 28; it stops at page 33; some of the items in the index start before page 28 (start at page 6); some of the items in the index are on pages after page 33 (pages 34, 35, 37)

2.8 Making lists

LEARNING PLAN

Learning objectives	Learning intentions	Success criteria
3Rv.03, 3Rs.02, 3Rs.03, 3Ri.05, 3Ri.14, 3Ri.15, 3Ri.17, 3Wg.01, 3Wg.04, 3Wg.06, 3Ws.02, 3Ws.04, 3Wc.05	• Write useful lists. • Write words in alphabetical order. • Write a recipe.	• Learners can write useful lists. • Learners can write words in alphabetical order. • Learners can write a recipe.

LANGUAGE SUPPORT

Make sure learners understand when it is appropriate to use alphabetical order (e.g. dictionaries, class lists, indexes) and that they know that alphabetical order is not always appropriate.

Starter idea

Party planning (5–10 minutes)

Resources: Learner's Book, Session 2.8: Getting started

Description: Ask learners to remind you of all the things they have already done for their party. Write each one on the board (e.g. chosen a theme, set the date, written invitations, chosen the food). Ask: *How is this list helpful* (e.g. it helps us remember things, it reminds us of things we haven't done)? Direct learners to the Getting started activity. Ask them to write their lists in their notebooks.

Main teaching ideas

1 Fruit Rocket lists (15–20 minutes)

Learning intentions: To write useful lists; to write words in alphabetical order.

Resources: Learner's Book, Session 2.8, Activity 1; Differentiated worksheet pack

Description: You could use Differentiated worksheets 2A–C here to provide practice with sorting by alphabetical order. Ask learners to read the fruit rockets recipe in Session 2.7 again.

Ask: *What kind of list would you write using this recipe?* Elicit the answer 'a shopping list'. Ask: *Will your list look the same as the list in the recipe? How will your list be different?*

Allow learners time to write their shopping lists. Remind them to include all the items they need, not just the fruit.

Write your own shopping list for fruit rockets on the board and allow time for learners to assess their own lists for layout and items. Explain that learners now need to re-write their lists in alphabetical order. Allow time for learners to re-write their lists then peer assess with their partners.

〉 **Differentiation ideas:** Support learners by providing a copy of the alphabet and reminding them to look at the second letter when two words begin with the same letter.

Challenge learners by asking them to sort a list of items that involves using third and fourth letters (e.g. peach, pomegranate, pineapple, pear, persimmon, papaya, plum, prune, passion fruit).

〉 **Assessment ideas:** Note which learners are confident with sorting alphabetically using two and three letters in a word.

Answers:
a   banana, pineapple, skewers (three wooden), strawberries, watermelon.

2   Party food ideas (10 minutes)

Learning intention: To write useful lists.

Resources: Learner's Book, Session 2.8, Activity 2; Workbook, Session 2.8; recipe books; computers

Description: Ask learners to think about the lists they have just written. Ask: *Is alphabetical order a helpful way of organising the list?* Discuss ways of organising a shopping list that could be helpful (e.g. fruit items together, dairy items together). If there is time in class, use the Workbook activities here to provide further practice with using contents and index pages.

Remind learners of the party food ideas agreed in a previous session. Allow time for learners to locate one of the recipes and to write a shopping list for it with their partner. Talk about how learners chose to organise their lists.

〉 **Differentiation ideas:** Challenge learners to collate a single shopping list for the class.

Answers:
Learners' own shopping lists.

3   Write a recipe (30 minutes)

Learning intention: To write a recipe.

Resources: Learner's Book, Session 2.8, Activity 3; Worksheet 2.3

Description: Ask learners to think about something they like to eat. Explain they are going to write a recipe for it. Steer learners towards snacks that are simple to make. Your learners may not have prepared items of food and may not be able to think of a recipe they can use for the writing task. You could prepare a very simple item in class and learners could use this idea to write the recipe (e.g. a sandwich, a boiled egg, an ice-cream cone with sprinkles on top, a pancake, filling a taco shell with a ready-made filling).

Discuss some of their ideas and check that everyone has thought of one item they could write a recipe for. Tell learners that it does not matter if their recipe is not exactly right. What you want to see is how well learners write a recipe using recipe features. Ask learners to read the prompts in the Learner's Book and allow time for them to write their recipe. When they have finished, ask learners to peer assess their writing with a partner.

〉 **Differentiation ideas:** Support learners by suggesting a food item and helping them to identify the equipment and instruction steps. You may wish to provide Worksheet 2.3 Instruction-writing template to help them.

〉 **Assessment ideas:** Note which learners wrote their recipes using recipe features.

Answers:
Learners' own recipes.

Plenary idea

Alphabetical order (5–10 minutes)

Resources: A soft ball

Description: Ask learners to form a large circle – include yourself in the circle. Explain that Learner A will say a letter of the alphabet, then throw a ball to Learner B who will then say the next letter of the alphabet. The game continues in this manner. When learners are confident with the game you can add more challenge, e.g. Learner A says a letter and throws the ball to Learner B who says the next letter. Learner B then says a new letter and throws the ball to Learner C who says the next letter. The game continues in this way.

Homework ideas

Ask learners to:

- complete the Workbook activities for this session, if not completed in class

- visit a shop/supermarket to find the cost of each item on their list

- make a list of all their family members in alphabetical order.

Answers for Workbook

1 Learners' own answers.

2 Answers from Activity 1 arranged in alphabetical order.

3 Learners' own answers.

2.9 Giving instructions

LEARNING PLAN

Learning objectives	Learning intentions	Success criteria
3Wc.05, 3SLm.01, 3SLm.02, 3SLm.03, 3SLm.04, 3SLm.05, 3SLs.01, 3SLg.01, 3SLg.02, 3SLg.03, 3SLg.04, 3SLr.01, 3SLr.02	• Discuss different party games. • Select which information to include when giving spoken instructions. • Speak fluently and confidently when giving instructions.	• Learners can discuss different party games. • Learners can select which information to include when giving spoken instructions. • Learners can speak fluently and confidently when giving instructions.

LANGUAGE SUPPORT

Although learners will hear you giving instructions throughout their school day, they will need time to practise doing so themselves. Demonstrate how you explain a simple game and ask learners to think about what you are doing and saying. Do learners spot the non-verbal cues you use (e.g. eye contact, smiles of encouragement) and the verbal cues (e.g. praise, step-by-step to allow listeners time, an encouraging voice, making sure listeners can hear you)?

Starter idea

Children's games (5–10 minutes)

Resources: Learner's Book, Session 2.9: Getting started

Description: Ask: *Which games do you know?* Ask learners to look at the photographs in the Getting started activity, then discuss the games as a class, using the question prompts provided.

Main teaching ideas

1 Party games (15–20 minutes)

Learning intention: To discuss different party games.

Resources: Learner's Book, Session 2.9, Activity 1

Description: Ask learners to think about the roles involved in planning a party and explain that in this session, learners will spend a lot of time talking in their groups. Discuss the value of learners taking specific roles in a group and whether it has helped the group. Ask: *What is important when you talk in a group? Would group rules help your group work better? Are some learners better suited to particular roles?* Allow time for learners to discuss these points and draw up a list together using what they have learned about list making.

Remind learners about the party games in the photographs, then ask them to discuss the party games they enjoy playing. Remind learners of the rules they have agreed for group working and to think about how they will decide the three games to play at their party.

> **Differentiation ideas:** Support learners who lack confidence in speaking to keep a list of learners who have had an opportunity to speak as a prompt for the chairperson.

Challenge learners who write quickly, neatly and accurately to act as scribe.

> **Assessment ideas:** At this point, all group members should have experienced the role of either scribe, chairperson or spokesperson when working in a group. Use this activity for learners to self-assess and peer assess how well they work in groups. Encourage your learners to speak freely about the effectiveness of their group but remind them of the importance of being sensitive to the feelings of others. Ask: *Does it help to have specific roles in a group? Who showed skills as a scribe? As a chairperson? As a spokesperson? Was everyone in the group given an opportunity to share their ideas? Did other group members listen politely?* Assess each group's ability to follow their rules for group work. How did they organise their lists? Were learners able to take turns?

Answers:
Learners' own answers.

2 Write instructions (15–20 minutes)

Learning intention: To select which information to include when giving spoken instructions.

Resources: Learner's Book, Session 2.9, Activity 2; a picture cut into nine large jigsaw-type pieces; coloured pens

Description: Ask learners what they need to remember when writing instructions (e.g. keep them

simple, use command verbs, write them in order). Ask: *When I give instructions to you in class, do I give them in the same way as written instructions? How do I provide the instructions?* (e.g. you give them bit by bit; you don't tell us it all at once; you say our names or say 'Group 1' etc.).

Place the jigsaw pieces randomly on the board. Invite a volunteer to make the jigsaw (however, they can only make the puzzle by following instructions from other learners). Ask: *When you are telling someone how to make something, do you use the same words as written instructions?*

Direct learners to the Learner's Book and ask them to complete the activity with a partner.

> **Differentiation ideas:** Support learners in identifying the differences between written and oral instructions by reading a set of instructions, then giving the same instructions orally. Ask them to spot the differences.

Challenge learners to work with a partner and role play giving instructions orally.

> **Assessment ideas:** Note which learners achieved the learning intention.

Answers:
Learners' own answers.

3 Instructions for a game (20–25 minutes)

Learning intention: To speak fluently and confidently when giving instructions.

Resources: Learner's Book, Session 2.9, Activity 3; Workbook, Session 2.9; space to play games; equipment for the games

Description: Ask for two volunteers and explain that you are going to give them instructions for playing a simple game (e.g. noughts and crosses). Explain that you will tell them exactly what to do.

After you have delivered the instructions, ask learners to discuss all the things you did as you gave the instructions (e.g. looking at each volunteer, praising them, speaking slowly and clearly). Show learners the Workbook activities for this session and ask them to complete these in their groups.

Allow time for groups to complete the Focus and Practice sessions and collect the equipment needed for their game. Ask each group to choose one person to explain how to play their game to another group member. Other group members should peer assess how well the speaker gave the instructions. Allow learners to switch roles if there is time.

> **Differentiation ideas:** Support learners by encouraging them to choose games that are simple to explain.

Challenge each group instructor to explain the game to a member of a different group.

> **Assessment ideas:** Note which learners spoke clearly. Which learners used non-verbal cues well? Were learners able to adapt their language?

Plenary idea

Play a game (5–10 minutes)

Resources: equipment for the game

Description: Choose a learner to teach their game to the whole class.

Homework ideas

Ask learners to:

- write instructions for a game they enjoy playing at home.

Answers for Workbook

1 Learners' own answers.

2 Learners' own answers.

3 No written answers needed.

2.10 Planning a game

LEARNING PLAN

Learning objectives	Learning intentions	Success criteria
3Rg.01, 3Rg.05, 3Rs.02, 3Ri.06, 3Ri.07, 3Ri.09, 3Ri.10, 3Ri.17, 3Wg.04, 3Ws.01, 3Ws.04, 3Wc.02, 3Wc.05, 3Wc.06, 3SLm.01, 3SLm.02, 3SLm.03, 3SLm.04, 3SLm.05, 3SLs.01, 3SLs.02	• Discuss instructions for party games. • Plan a new party game. • Discuss our party game plans with others.	• Learners can discuss instructions for party games. • Learners can plan a new party game. • Learners can discuss their party game plans with others and listen to feedback.

LANGUAGE SUPPORT

Avoid explaining instructions that learners do not understand. Instead, use questioning to help learners solve the misunderstanding themselves.

Starter idea

 ### Party games (5 minutes)

Resources: *How to play Fruit Basket* (Learner's Book, Session 2.10: Getting started); Track 13

Description: Ask learners to talk to their partners about the games discussed and played in the previous session. Ask: *Which games did you like best? Which games did you find difficult to understand?* Direct learners to the Getting started activity. Invite learners to take turns to read one point of the Fruit Basket instructions aloud.

Main teaching ideas

1 Fruit Basket instructions (15–20 minutes)

Learning intention: To discuss instructions for party games.

Resources: Learner's Book, Session 2.10, Activity 1; Workbook, Session 2.10; open space large enough to play Fruit Basket

Description: Ask learners to re-read the instructions for the game with a partner and make notes on anything that does not make sense. For example, have they understood that each group of nine or more players should be divided into smaller groups with each of these groups named a different fruit? Discuss learners' notes and then explain that they will play the game and should make sure that none of the instructions need changing.

As soon as learners begin playing the game, points that have not been understood will be obvious by learners' confusion. Be prepared to stop the game and spend time discussing misunderstood points. For example, learners may be unsure about what the player in the middle does once they have called out a fruit. Does the player find a new place in the circle or do they stay in the middle? To help learners reason this for themselves, ask: *What happens when one player leaves the circle and stands in the middle?* (they leave a space in the circle) *Why do we need a space in the circle?* (so that there is an empty space for players to run to) *Would that make it easy to find a new space?* From this, learners should understand that if the player in the middle *stayed* in the middle, all the other players would be able to find a new place, no-one would ever be out and the player in the middle would never change.

Allow additional time for learners to play the game. Encourage them to consider how they could change the instructions for the game to make them clearer. Ask learners to talk to their partners about what they have learned about writing instructions for games. Ask: *Which instructions did you find hardest to follow?* (e.g. the long ones, number 5, number 6) You could use the Workbook activities here to provide practice with ordering instructions.

> **Differentiation ideas:** Support learners by inviting them to read aloud one of the easier instruction steps (e.g. 2, 4 or 7).

Challenge learners by inviting them to read aloud a more complex instruction step (e.g. 5 or 6).

> **Assessment ideas:** Understanding written instructions will be challenging for many learners and they may expect you to explain the game rules to them. It is important that you allow them to play the game without your intervention initially. Once learners have played the game, you can explore points with them. For example, what does *roughly equal groups* mean? Would it help to write this instruction in a different way (e.g. groups of three or four)?

Answers:
Learners' own answers.

2 Invent a party game! (20–25 minutes)

Learning intention: To plan a new party game.

Resources: Learner's Book, Session 2.10, Activity 2

Description: Ask learners to work in pairs or small groups to think about a party game they know well and to make rough notes of instructions for this game. Allow time for learners to do this.

Then explain that new games are often invented just by changing one or two simple things about an existing game. Ask learners to suggest how Fruit Basket could be changed (e.g. change the name and have different categories, such as vegetables, animals, TV programmes; have more players and more fruits).

Direct learners to the advice in the speech bubble on the page and allow time for pairs or groups to talk about possible changes to their games. Encourage learners to use the prompts in the Learner's Book to help them make their notes for how to play the game.

> **Differentiation ideas:** Support learners by working with them as a group.

Challenge learners to work in pairs and to use headings for each section of the instructions.

Answers:
Learners' own answers.

3 Practise your instructions (10 minutes)

Learning intention: To discuss the new party game plans with others.

Resources: Learner's Book, Session 2.10, Activity 3

Description: Remind learners of the differences between writing instructions and saying instructions. Explain that before learners teach others how to play their game, they need to practise saying their instructions aloud to themselves or with a partner. Allow time for learners to practise. Then ask learners to explain their game to a learner from another pair or group. Encourage constructive feedback about how the game could be improved.

> **Differentiation ideas:** Support learners by pairing with a partner of a similar level and supporting pairs as they practise explaining their games.

> **Assessment ideas:** Assess how well your learners change their written instructions when they explain them to others. Do they use non-verbal cues (e.g. hand gestures, eye contact, smiles)?

Answers:
Learners' own answers.

Plenary idea

Play a new game (5 minutes)

Resources: Fruit Basket instructions from the Getting started activity

Description: Ask learners to suggest a change to Fruit Basket and play the new version of the game.

Homework ideas

Ask learners to:

- complete the Workbook activities for this session, if not completed in class
- change one or two things about a game they play at home then play it with friends or family.

Answers for Workbook

1   Possible order of instructions: 2/7/4/1/6/3/5

2   Learners' tips could include: list of equipment, numbered points, headings, short sentences, command verbs.

3   Possible improvements could be:

   a   if the player in the middle calls out 'Fruit Basket', everyone must find a new position

   b   the player in the middle calls one of the group names and everyone must find a new place quickly. The last player to find a place must stand in the middle.

2.11 Writing instructions

LEARNING PLAN

Learning objectives	Learning intentions	Success criteria
3Ww.05, 3Wv.02, 3Wv.04, 3Wg.01, 3Wg.04, 3Ws.02, 3Ws.03, 3Ws.04, 3Wc.05, 3Wc.06, 3SLm.04, 3SLm.05, 3SLr.01	• Write instructions. • Use sequencing words and command words appropriately.	• Learners can write instructions. • Learners can use sequencing words and command words appropriately.

When you recap command verbs at the start of this session, encourage learners to suggest synonyms for common verbs (e.g. get – find, take, pick; put – place, add; mix – stir, combine).

Starter idea

Instruction writing (5–10 minutes)

Resources: Learner's Book, Session 2.11: Getting started

Description: Ask learners to talk in pairs about what they have learned about writing instructions, then share their ideas. Ask learners to suggest command verbs that could be used and write these on the board. Then ask learners to suggest sequencing words and make another list of these on the board.

Direct learners to the Getting started prompts and ask them to write their checklist. Share learners' ideas and write each item on the board. Allow learners time to add or change any items in their individual checklists.

Main teaching ideas

1 and 2   Write instructions for a party game (40–45 minutes)

Learning intentions: To write instructions; to use sequencing words and command words appropriately.

Resources: Learner's Book, Session 2.11, Activities 1 and 2; Workbook, Session 2.11; Worksheet 2.3; learners' notes from Session 2.10

Description: If there is time in class, use the Workbook activities to provide practice with reviewing instructions before learners look at their own. Ask learners to use the notes they wrote in the previous session to write their game instructions. Remind them to use the command verb and sequencing word lists on the board. Allow time for learners to write their instructions. Check that learners use their notes, your lists of words and their checklists.

⟩ **Differentiation ideas:** Support learners by providing Worksheet 2.3 Instruction-writing template as a template to support the layout of the instructions, and text prompts.

Challenge learners to add a picture or diagram to illustrate their game.

⟩ **Assessment ideas:** Have learners used their notes and checklist to write instructions? Which learners remembered to start each instruction with a command verb or sequencing word?

Answers:
Checklists could include: a title, command verbs, sequencing words, bullet points, numbered points, section headings, short, simple sentences, list of equipment, number of players.

Plenary idea

Party game rules (5–10 minutes)

Resources: Learners' instructions from previous activity

Description: Invite learners to read the instructions for their game. Explain that other learners will peer assess their instructions using the checklist on your board. Ask learners to make their assessments using a 'thumbs up' and/or 'thumbs down' method. When each learner has explained their game, ask: *Does this sound like a fun game? Would you enjoy playing this game?*

⟩ **Assessment ideas:** Invite learners who have used the checklist well to explain their games. During the peer assessment, go through each item on the checklist step-by-step to help reinforce each point and to support learners.

Science:

- Living Things: Write instructions for an investigation about plants and water.

- Forces: Write instructions for an investigation about friction.

Homework ideas

Ask learners to:

- use their instructions to play their party game at home

- complete the Workbook activities for this session, if not completed in class.

Answers for Workbook

1 a Things the writer has done well: learners' answers could include: used short, simple sentences; set every point on a new line; used some command verbs.

b Things the writer could improve: learners' answers could include: number each instruction; start each instruction with a command verb or sequencing word.

c Learners' own answers.

2 Possible answers:

First, sit in a circle.

Everyone be quiet. / Listen carefully.

Get your paper mouse.

Hold onto your mouse's tail.

Someone has the cone. / Next, one player has a cone.

The player with the cone must bang the cone down on the mice.

Try to pull your mouse out. / Now everyone must try to pull their mouse out.

3 Learners' own answers.

2.12 Improving your instructions

LEARNING PLAN

Learning objectives	Learning intentions	Success criteria
3Ww.05, 3Ww.06, 3Wv.02, 3Wv.07, 3Wg.01, 3Wg.04, 3Ws.03, 3Ws.04, 3Wc.05, 3Wc.06, 3Wp.01, 3Wp.04, 3Wp.05, 3SLm.04, 3SLm.05, 3SLs.01, 3SLg.02, 3SLg.04, 3SLp.01, 3SLr.01	• Improve the instructions that have been written. • Check instructions for errors. • Listen and respond appropriately to others' instructions.	• Learners can improve the instructions they have written. • Learners can proofread their writing. • Learners can listen and respond appropriately to others' instructions.

LANGUAGE SUPPORT

You may want to spend some time discussing speaking skills when giving a presentation. Encourage learners to think about their audience and what will help to engage them and keep them interested. It might be worth discussing the language used to describe different speaking styles (e.g. mumbling, monotone, muttering, shouting). You could even introduce words such as *varying pitch* (your voice going up and down).

Starter idea

Checklists (5–10 minutes)

Resources: Learner's Book, Session 2.12: Getting started; learners' checklists from Session 2.11; agreed class checklist from previous session

Description: Ask learners to look at the checklist from the previous session. Remind them of the lists of command verbs and sequencing words. Ask: *Are there any words we could add to the lists?*

Ask learners to read their instructions from Session 2.11 aloud and consider if they make sense. (Remind learners to read quietly when they read aloud.)

Main teaching ideas

1 Proofread your instructions (10 minutes)

Learning intentions: To improve instructions that have been written; to check instructions for errors.

Resources: Learner's Book, Session 2.12, Activity 1; Workbook, Session 2.12, Activity 2; learners' instructions and checklists; dictionaries; coloured pens or pencils

Description: Explain that learners should work with a partner to proofread both sets of instructions. Remind learners of what to check when proofreading, using the prompts in the Learner's Book. You could use the Practice activity in the Workbook to provide proofreading practice. Explain that learners should use a coloured pen or pencil to make their changes so that their edits can be clearly seen.

> **Differentiation ideas:** Support learners by working with a group and looking at each proofreading prompt together.

> **Assessment ideas:** It is helpful to group learners in pairs when they are proofreading their writing, as a partner is more likely to spot errors. Consider pairing learners who are working at a similar writing level at the start of the task. Such pairings ensure each learner is equally involved in the task and avoids a scenario where a more confident writer identifies many errors in a less confident writer's work. Note which learners used dictionaries confidently.

2 Final copy (15–20 minutes)

Learning intention: To use neat handwriting.

Resources: Learner's Book, Session 2.12, Activity 2; Worksheet 2.4; paper and pens for presenting work

Description: Tell learners that you want them to use neat, joined handwriting. Show learners how you want them to write the title for their instructions by writing an example on the board (e.g. *How to play Fruit Basket*). Talk about which letters need capital letters. If you expect learners to use joined handwriting, remind them that capital letters should not be joined to the next letter. Allow learners time to write their instructions neatly.

When learners have completed their final copy, you could show them Worksheet 2.4 Checklist for writing instructions. Ask learners to use the checklist to assess whether they have included all the features of instructions in their writing.

> **Differentiation ideas:** Support learners by showing them how to form the letters if you have an agreed handwriting style in school. If possible, give them a piece of lined paper to put underneath their work to form guidelines.

> **Assessment ideas:** When learners are creating a final version of their instructions, provide a sheet with thick ruled lines to place beneath their work. Learners should see the thick lines through their paper. This will help them to space their lines and keep each line straight. Assess which learners are not forming some letter shapes correctly. Which learners can join their handwriting?

3 Follow instructions (25–30 minutes)

Learning intention: To listen and respond appropriately to others' instructions.

Resources: Learner's Book, Session 2.12, Activity 3; equipment for the games; space to play the games

Description: Direct learners to the Speaking tip and allow time for them to rehearse giving instructions orally. Explain that it will be difficult to try everyone's game; invite volunteers to teach their game to a group. However, you could have several games played at the same time if you have the space. This would allow all learners a chance to explain their games to others.

Encourage learners who are observing to peer assess the speaker and the players. Ask: *Did the speaker use a clear voice to explain to rules? Were the rules easy to follow? Did the players listen carefully? Did the players follow the rules accurately?* Allow as many learners as possible to read out their game instructions.

> **Assessment ideas:** As groups play their games, observe which speakers explain well and which games work well. Invite those learners to explain their games to everyone and then carry out the peer assessment.

Plenary idea

New games (5 minutes)

Description: Ask learners to talk in their party-planning groups about the new party games they have played. Ask them to think about which games worked well. Would they include any of the new games in their list of party games in place of existing ones?

Homework ideas

Ask learners to:

- choose another game and suggest how the game could be changed or improved

- complete the Workbook activities for this session, if not completed in class.

Answers for Workbook

1 Possible answers:

   a   need to be simple; need to be in order; need to include any equipment; need to start with command verbs or sequencing words

   b   Learners' own answers.

2 Possible instructions:

Dear <u>Mbeke</u>

You are invited to <u>Lisha's birthday party</u>.

It will be at the <u>New Club, Ikwere Road</u>

on <u>18th November</u>

at <u>3 pm until 5 pm</u>.

(possibly included: Come dressed as an animal)

3 Possible answer: From my house I will turn left into New Road, and walk past the houses and shops on my right. When I reach Ikwere Road I will walk over the crossing and then turn right and walk past the park and the School. I will follow the road round to the right and New Club will be in front of me.

CHECK YOUR PROGRESS

1 possible answers: all use command verbs and sequencing words; ordered points; list of equipment; numbered steps; headings

2 contents pages, index pages, invitations, dictionaries, lists

3 Learners' own answers.

4 possible answers:

   a   Foot<u>ball</u>, foot<u>path</u>

   b   any<u>where</u>, any<u>body</u>, any<u>one</u>

5   a   walking

   b   smiled

   c   sitting

PROJECT GUIDANCE

These projects develop learners' skills in writing instructions and lists. You will find it helpful to refer to the guidance about *Setting up and assessing the projects* in the Project guidance for Unit 1.

Group project: This project involves both individual and group elements. As a group, learners should decide which recipe ideas they will use and how they will present them. Encourage learners to talk to family members about favourite recipes. Learners could choose a theme for their recipes (e.g. recipes from around the world, favourite meals).

Pair project: This project asks learners to make a list of all the tasks involved in preparing for a party. Encourage them to use party food and party game ideas that have been suggested during the unit.

Learners' lists should include:

- preparing the party food, including how they will organise who prepares each item
- which decorations need making

- collecting materials for the decorations then making the decorations
- decorating the room
- which games to play, including the order they will be played in
- gathering (or making) equipment for the games.

Solo project: Learners are asked to write instructions about caring for an animal. Talk about the kind of animal it could be (e.g. dog, cat, fish) or suggest an animal they know well and would like to look after.

Did learners' instructions include:

- headings
- numbered steps
- a list of what is needed
- sequencing words
- command or imperative verbs?

> 3 Poems from around the world

Unit plan

Session	Approximate number of learning hours	Outline of learning content	Resources
3.1 Words that make pictures	1	Explore a world map and read the poem *Dancing Poinciana*. Explore how the language in a poem helps us to to visualise the content.	Learner's Book Session 3.1 Workbook Session 3.1
3.2 Reading with expression	1	Read a poem from Trinidad about a hurricane. Explore how to add expression when performing a poem. Revise *–ing* verb endings.	Learner's Book Session 3.2 Workbook Session 3.2
3.3 Performing a poem	1.5	Explore a traditional poem from Mongolia. Prepare a short drama based on the poem. Write own poems using noun phrases.	Learner's Book Session 3.3 Workbook Session 3.3 ⬇ Worksheet 3.1 ⬇ Language worksheet 3A
3.4 Onomatopoeia	1	Explore onomatopoeic words in an African poem. Write an extra verse for the poem. Explore the effect of pronouns on verb endings.	Learner's Book Session 3.4 Workbook Session 3.4 ⬇ Differentiated worksheets 3A–C
3.5 Writing a haiku	1	Read a haiku about a cat and listen to an audio description about a tiger. Explore syllables and adjectives before writing an animal haiku.	Learner's Book Session 3.5 Workbook Session 3.5 ⬇ Language worksheet 3B ⬇ Worksheet 3.2
3.6 Reviewing poems	1–1.5	Compare three poems from the unit and write a review of one of them. Perform a favourite poem from the unit.	Learner's Book Session 3.6 Workbook Session 3.6

Cross-unit resources
Learner's Book Check your progress
Learner's Book Projects
End-of-unit 3 test

BACKGROUND KNOWLEDGE

It will help to have some geographical knowledge of the location and features of the countries associated with the poems in this unit. You should also be able to locate other major countries on a world map.

It will be helpful to be familiar with the following English subject knowledge:

- rhyme
- syllables
- figurative language (including personification, simile, metaphor, onomatopoeia)

- present continuous (progressive) tense
- rules for adding –ing to verb tenses
- the effect of pronouns on verb endings
- noun phrases
- pronouns
- performance poetry.

In this unit, all learners are expected to draw tables. Learners need to understand how to prepare a table. Some learners will need careful instruction on how to do this.

TEACHING SKILLS FOCUS

Cross-curricular learning

This unit offers the opportunity to develop cross-curricular teaching. As you read each poem, you could explore the geography, art and music of that country. Learners could:

- draw maps showing cities, rivers, mountain ranges and seas or oceans
- compare the temperature and climate with their own country
- research the country's art and music.

Alternatively, you could choose one poem from the collection and research that country or continent in detail. For example, you could choose:

- *Song of the Animal World*: study rainforests, create a rainforest in your classroom, make animal masks, listen to African music and make African musical instruments.

- *Dancing Poinciana*: explore island life, research hurricanes, create a sound scape of wind, study painters from the Bahamas (e.g. Brent Malone or Maxwell Taylor).

Whichever approach you use, think about the learning intentions and success criteria you will cover. Did a cross-curricular approach engage your learners more? Did it deepen their understanding of the poems?

3.1 Words that make pictures

LEARNING PLAN

Learning objectives	Learning intentions	Success criteria
3Rw.03, 3Rv.01, 3Rv.04, 3Rv.07, 3Rs.02, 3Ri.02, 3Ri.06, 3Ri.07, 3Ri.10, 3Ri.14, 3Ri.17, 3Ra.01, 3Ra.02, 3Ra.03, 3SLg.03, 3SLg.04	• Locate and discuss some countries around the world. • Read a poem from The Bahamas. • Answer questions about a poem.	• Learners can locate and discuss diifferent countries. • Learners can read a poem. • Learners can answer questions about a poem.

LANGUAGE SUPPORT

In *Dancing Poinciana*, the poet describes a tree without ever mentioning that a poinciana is a tree. When an object is described without actually being mentioned it is known as figurative language.

To support learners in understanding the poem, show photographs of the poinciana tree and its blossoms, or allow learners time to research the poinciana tree. *Is it a tall or short tree? How big are the blossoms?* Learners could also research The Bahamas. *What do The Bahamas look like from the air?*

Common misconceptions

Misconception	How to identify	How to overcome
Misunderstanding figurative language in poems.	Learners use the pronoun *she* when they talk about the poem, *Dancing Poinciana*, e.g. 'She is dancing'. Some learners may even say, 'She is dancing under a tree.'	Use *Dancing Poinciana* as an example. Ask learners to explain what trees look like when the wind blows. Encourage learners to talk about the tree moving back and forth and explain that this is known as swaying. Encourage learners to talk about other ways to describe what a tree does (e.g. when the leaves rustle it can sound like whispering). Tell learners that writers like to describe things as if they were people.

Starter idea

Countries of the world (10 minutes)

Resources: Learner's Book, Session 3.1: Getting started; a large world map and atlas if possible

Description: Explain that in this unit learners will be looking at poems from all over the world. Ask learners to look at the world map in the Learner's Book, then invite a learner to locate the country they live in on a large map.

Organise learners into pairs and allow time for them to locate countries they know and discuss what they know about those countries. Using a large world map, invite two learners to the front of the class to compete against each other at finding a country. Say: *Can you find China?* The learner who finds the country first then competes against another learner to find another country you name. Try to include all the countries and the continent mentioned in this unit (The Bahamas, Trinidad and Tobago, Mongolia, Africa, Japan).

Main teaching ideas

1 Dancing Poinciana (15 minutes)

Learning intentions: To locate and discuss some countries around the world; to read a poem from The Bahamas.

Resources: *Dancing Poinciana* (Learner's Book, Session 3.1, Activity 1); Track 14; dictionaries; world map or atlas

Description: Ask: *Have you ever read a poem from our country? What type of things would a poet want to include in a poem about our country?* (e.g. weather, food, birds, scenery) Encourage learners to name features about their country that are important and that they think a visitor would notice. Explain that poets like to choose words that give the reader clues about what a poem is about.

Explain that you are going to read a poem from another country and that learners should listen for clues about what the poet is describing. You could listen to the audio and ask learners to follow the text.

Write the title *Dancing Poinciana* on the board and show learners how to break the second word into small segments to help them read it (e.g. poin-ci-an-a). Explain that the *c* is a soft *c* sound.

Read *Dancing Poinciana* aloud so that learners can hear the rhythm of the poem and picture what is happening. Ask: *Did you work out what the poem is about?* (e.g. a large plant / a tree) *Which word clues helped?* (e.g. blossoms, petals, treetops) Ask learners to read the poem with their partner and to note any words they do not know (e.g. *regal, sway, stained, crimson*). Direct them to the Reading tip.

Invite a learner to add a label to the world map to mark The Bahamas and direct learners to the map showing The Bahamas in the Learner's Book.

⟩ **Differentiation ideas:**

- Support learners with finding the appropriate definition of unknown words.

- Challenge learners to explain the meaning of unfamiliar words to others.

⟩ **Assessment ideas:** Learners with a limited general knowledge about the country they live in will find the initial task challenging. Can learners name the animals, birds or plants that are associated with the country?

Do your learners understand what the poet is referring to with each description? Assess which learners understand the implicit meaning of the poem and which learners do not look beyond the explicit meaning.

Answers:

a   Learners' own answers.

b   A tree.

c   Learners locate The Bahamas on the world map.

2 The Bahamas (15–20 minutes)

Learning intention: To answer questions about a poem.

Resources: Learner's Book, Session 3.1, Activity 2; Workbook, Session 3.1

Description: Ask: *Can you imagine the poinciana tree that the poet is describing? What is the tree doing?* Invite a learner to demonstrate the tree moving from side to side.

Explain that when writers choose words that paint a picture of their meaning it is known as using *figurative language*. Explain that writers use figurative language to make their writing more interesting. Ask learners to read the poem again, and this time to look for clues (or figurative language) the poet has used about the country.

Allow learners time to discuss the poem and ask: *Which words gave you clues about the country?* (e.g. *sea of green* makes you think of the sea; it could be an island; *Fire in the sky* makes you think of a hot sun; it is where poinciana trees grow) *Could the poem have come from any other country?* (e.g. yes, if the poinciana tree grows there) You could use the Workbook activities here if there is time in class. Ask learners to the questions in part c in their notebooks.

⟩ **Differentiation ideas:** Support learners by dividing your class into groups comprising some learners who would like to be challenged and some learners who would benefit from additional support.

Challenge learners to find other countries where the poinciana tree grows.

⟩ **Assessment ideas:** To assess whether learners have understood the unfamiliar vocabulary (e.g. *sway*, *regal*), ask them to perform the words, (e.g. regal: standing tall and straight like a king or queen; sway: moving gently from side to side). Ask direct questions: *How does the tree dance? How does the tree look regal? How can blossoms be 'dazzling'?*

Answers:

a Possible answers: sea of green; poinciana trees grow there; the sun sounds hot because it is like a fire in the sky.

b Possible answers: the tree sways; the tree moves gently; 'regal' makes it sound tall and straight; the tree is bright red with crimson petals and red blossoms.

c Learners' own answers.

Plenary idea

Picture clues (5 minutes)

Resources: A selection of pictures or photographs of familiar objects (e.g. an umbrella, a bird, a wild animal)

Description: Invite a learner to look at one of the pictures. Explain that they must not say what the picture is. The learner should provide clues for what the picture shows, one at a time (e.g. a striped umbrella: it has a long handle; it is green, yellow and white; it has a canopy; it protects you from the rain). The rest of the class try to guess what the picture is after each clue. The learner who guesses correctly can then provide clues for a different picture.

> **CROSS-CURRICULAR LINKS**
>
> Science (Living Things): Use the poinciana tree to identify parts of a plant and look at leaf patterns in different types of tree.
>
> Maths (Symmetry): Look at different leaf types to find which ones have the most lines of symmetry and which have none. Use the poinciana flower to explore more intricate symmetrical designs.

Homework ideas

Ask learners to:

- complete the Workbook activities for this session, if not completed in class

- write another verse of *Dancing Poinciana* (e.g. about the leaves), writing in the same style as the existing poem.

Answers for Workbook

1 red; *red as sunset*

2 Possible answers: No, because fires do not have blossoms or petals.

3 sky

4 d: noble

5 the sea, the ocean

6 b: a gentle breeze

7 Possible answers: the tree is dancing and swaying which means it is not a very strong wind; the tree is moving gently so the wind is only gentle; the sun is in the sky so it does not sound like a storm or a hurricane.

8 dance, sway

9 Learners' own answers.

3.2 Reading with expression

LEARNING PLAN

Learning objectives	Learning intentions	Success criteria
3Rw.03, 3Rv.01, 3Rv.04, 3Rv.07, 3Rg.01, 3Rg.07, 3Rg.08, 3Rs.02, 3Ri.02, 3Ri.06, 3Ri.07, 3Ri.10, 3Ri.12, 3Ri.16, 3Ri.17, 3Ra.01, 3Ra.02, 3Ra.03, 3Ww.02, 3Ww.05, 3SLm.01, 3SLm.05, 3SLg.03, 3SLg.04, 3SLp.01, 3SLp.02, 3SLp.03, 3SLr.01	• Read a poem silently. • Answer questions about the detail in a poem. • Recognise verbs with –*ing* endings. • Read aloud with expression.	• Learners can read a poem silently. • Learners can answer questions about the detail in a poem. • Learners can recognise verbs with –*ing* endings. • Learners can read aloud with expression.

LANGUAGE SUPPORT

Hurricanes are also known as typhoons. Explain to your learners that hurricanes and typhoons are the same weather condition, and the word used depends upon the area of the ocean where the storm occurs. Hurricanes occur in the North Atlantic, and central and eastern parts of the North Pacific, whereas typhoons occur in the Northwest Pacific.

Common misconceptions

Misconception	How to identify	How to overcome
Verbs with –*ing* endings do not need –*ing* to be added for the present continuous tense.	Learners do not add –*ing* to verbs such as *sing, bring* when they write the present continuous form.	First, remind learners that verbs are doing or action words. If the word cannot be performed it is not a verb. Remind learners of the two tenses used in the poem from this session (the present tense and the present continuous tense). Explain that some present tense verbs are spelled with –*ing* (e.g. ring, sing, fling, bring) so we need to add another –*ing* for the present continuous (e.g. ringing, bringing). Suggest that learners ask themselves: *Is the action happening once or is it continuing?*

Starter idea

What is a hurricane? (5 minutes)

Resources: Learner's Book, Session 3.2: Getting started

Description: To avoid any learner becoming distressed during this lesson, be sensitive to those who may have experienced any kind of extreme weather event. Consider talking to individual learners about the topic beforehand.

Ask learners to name different weather conditions they know. Explain that some of these conditions are known as 'extreme weather' because they are severe and can cause damage.

Write *hurricane* on the board and show learners how to break up the word (e.g. hurr-i-cane) to make it easier to read. Explain that in some parts of the world hurricanes are known as typhoons. Direct learners to the questions and photographs in the Learner's Book.

Remind learners of the importance of treating each other's feelings with respect as learners discuss the questions and photographs with their partners.

Main teaching ideas

1 Read *Hurricane* (15–20 minutes)

Learning intentions: To read a poem silently; to answer questions about the detail in a poem.

Resources: *Hurricane* (Learner's Book, Session 2.3, Activity 1); Track 15; map showing Trinidad and Tobago

Description: Explain that learners are going to read a poem from Trinidad, then ask learners to find Trinidad on a map. Before reading the poem, or playing the audio, ask learners to list the strategies they use to read unfamiliar words. Write *clothesline*, *neighbours* and *mountain* on the board and ask for volunteers to read each word. Ask: *What is a clothesline? What are neighbours?*

Allow learners time to read the poem silently then ask: *What is happening in the poem* (e.g. people are getting ready for the hurricane)? Ask one learner to volunteer to read the poem aloud to make sure learners are familiar with all the words. Ask: *How do people know the hurricane is coming? What signs can they see? What can they feel? What do the people do to prepare for the hurricane?*

Direct learners to the questions in the Learner's Book, then ask them to use these ideas to answer the first two questions and to write their own response to part c in their notebooks.

When learners have completed the first three questions, ask: *Why do you think the poet repeated some of the lines of the poem?* (to tell you the hurricane was getting nearer each time) *What is different about the first three verses and the last verse?* (the first three are about people and the last verse is about the hurricane) *Why do you think the last verse is different?* (the first verses are about people getting ready but in the last verse the hurricane has arrived).

Explain that writers choose words, repeat words and organise verses in particular ways to interest (engage) the reader. Ask learners to talk with their partner about what they thought about the poem. Did it interest them? Did it engage them?

⟩ **Differentiation ideas:** Support learners by working with them in small groups to answer the questions.

⟩ **Assessment ideas:** As you question learners about the poem, note which learners can understand the implicit meaning of the poem. Encourage learners who limit their answers to the facts (e.g. people are shutting their windows and bolting the doors; people are whispering together) to think more deeply about why people are doing these things. Can learners explain what the people in the poem might be thinking? Can learners infer what the people might be feeling?

Answers:

a   Any three answers from: rain coming, dark clouds (gathering), wind (rising), raindrops, branches falling, treetops swaying, big wind rising.

b   Any three answers from: shut windows, bolt doors, bring in the clothesline, pull down the blinds.

c   Possible answers: hurricanes are dangerous, so they need to get inside; it is raining and they do not want to get wet; they do not want to get hit by falling branches; they need to find somewhere safe to shelter.

d   Learners' own answers.

2 Revise –*ing* verb endings (15 minutes)

Learning intention: To recognise verbs with –*ing*.

Resources: Learner's Book, Session 2.3, Activity 2

Description: Explain that there are several verbs in the poem and ask: *Who can tell me what a verb is?* (a *doing* word; an *action* word)*? Can you tell me some of the verbs in the poem?* (e.g. *shut, bolt, falling, coming, gather*) Write five or six of the verbs suggested on the board using two columns, one for verbs without *–ing* and the other for verbs with *–ing*. Explain that the verbs without *–ing* are present tense verbs, which means the action happens at that time, and that verbs with *–ing* mean the action is continuing to happen, known as the present continuous tense.

Ask learners to make a list in their notebooks of all the verbs in the poem ending with *–ing*. Tell learners to only write each verb once. Then ask: *How would you spell the present tense form of 'falling'? How would you spell the present tense form of 'coming'?* Ask learners to note the changes to the spelling with a partner, then direct learners to the Language focus box.

Allow time for learners to complete the task by writing each verb in its two forms in their notebooks. Encourage them to peer mark their answers.

> **Differentiation ideas:** Support learners by helping them to identify when *–ing* has just been added to the verb (climb, fly, sway). Then help them identify where a letter has been doubled before the *–ing* (running) and finally where an *e* may have been removed (coming).

Challenge learners to identify the verbs in the poem that do not end in *–ing* and to re-write these verbs with *–ing* (shut = shutting; bolt = bolting; gather = gathering; pull = pulling; whisper = whispering).

> **Assessment ideas:** Note which learners copied the spelling of each verb correctly from the poem. Did learners double the last letter or drop the *e* when necessary? Which learners can identify how the spelling of the verb changed when *–ing* was added? Can learners say which of the spelling rules in the Language focus box have been used? Note which learners can spell both forms of each verb accurately.

Answers:

a   coming, climbing, rising, falling, flying, swaying, running, blowing

b   coming = come; climbing = climb; rising = rise; falling = fall; flying = fly; swaying = sway; running = run; blowing = blow.

3   Performing *Hurricane* (15–20 minutes)

Learning intention: To read aloud with expression.

Resources: Learner's Book, Session 2.3, Activity 3

Description: Explain that learners are to listen to you reading *Hurricane* aloud. Do not add any expression as you read it. When you have read the poem, ask: *Do you think I read the poem the way the poet would have read it? Did I keep you interested in the poem?*

Ask learners to discuss in pairs how the poem could be read. Before they begin, ask:

*   *What do you think the people in the poem are feeling as they prepare for the hurricane?*

*   *How will you show what they are feeling with your voice?*

*   *How can you use your voice to show that the hurricane is coming nearer?*

*   *Could you say some parts of the poem softer or louder than other parts?*

*   *Could you say parts of the poem more quickly or more slowly?*

*   *Could you change how you say some of the words?*

Allow pairs to practise reading the poem together, then ask for pairs to volunteer to perform the poem to the class.

Explain that learners are now going to work as a group to read the poem. Remind them to use the prompts in the Speaking tip as they plan a group performance of *Hurricane*. Allow time for each group to discuss how to perform the poem and to practise reading it together.

> **Differentiation ideas:** Support learners who find it difficult to add expression by grouping them with more confident performers.

Challenge learners who are confident with using expression to be the first volunteers to perform the poem.

> **Assessment ideas:** As learners read the poem, note which learners show their understanding of the poem through the expression used.

Which learners:

- say parts of the poem more slowly or more quietly
- manage to show how worried or frightened the people would be as they prepare for the hurricane
- use a faster and/or louder voice in the last verse to show that the hurricane has arrived
- can follow the pace of others during the group performance; do any learners find it difficult to match the rhythm of the poem?

Plenary idea

Group performance (5–10 minutes)

Description: Invite each group to perform *Hurricane* to the class. Remind learners to add expression and to use clear voices. Ask learners to peer assess each group's performance using the prompts in the Speaking tip.

CROSS-CURRICULAR LINKS

Geography: The poem *Hurricane* could be the starting point for a study of extreme natural events around the world (e.g. volcanic eruptions, tornadoes, earthquakes, floods, droughts). Identify on a map where this weather condition is known as a hurricane and where it is known as a typhoon.

Homework ideas

Ask learners to:

- complete the Workbook activities for this session, if not completed in class
- make a list of different extreme natural events that occur around the world (e.g. drought, flood, volcanic eruption, earthquake, tornado, hurricane, typhoon, whirlwind, monsoon, heatwave).

Answers for Workbook

1   counting, running, skipping, laughing, standing, looking, looking, staring, believing, standing, talking, spending, giving, carrying, running, telling, weeping, flowing, smiling

2

smile	smiling		come	coming
say	saying		dance	dancing
go	going		howl	howling
run	running		stare	staring
drop	dropping		fly	flying
walk	walking		pull	pulling
like	liking		flash	flashing
stand	standing		hurry	hurrying
rush	rushing		roar	roaring
clap	clapping		become	becoming

3   Learners' own sentences.

3.3 Performing a poem

LEARNING PLAN

Learning objectives	Learning intentions	Success criteria
3Rw.03, 3Rv.01, 3Rv.02, 3Rv.04, 3Rv.07, 3Rg.01, 3Rs.02, 3Ri.02, 3Ri.03, 3Ri.06, 3Ri.07, 3Ri.10, 3Ri.17, 3Ra.01, 3Ra.03, 3Wv.03, 3Wv.05, 3Wv.06, 3Wv.07, 3Wc.01, 3Wc.02, 3Wp.01, 3Wp.03, 3SLm.01, 3SLm.04, 3SLm.05, 3SLg.02, 3SLg.03, 3SLp.01, 3SLp.02, 3SLp.03, 3SLp.04	• Read and discuss a traditional poem. • Plan and present a short performance based on a poem. • Include noun phrases in a poem. • Present a poem for display.	• Learners can read and discuss a traditional poem. • Learners can plan and present a short performance based on a poem. • Learners can include noun phrases in a poem. • Learners can present a poem for display.

LANGUAGE SUPPORT

The style of the poem used in this session is very different to *Dancing Poinciana* and *Hurricane*: it does not rhyme, it is not organised into verses and there are no repetitive lines. Encourage learners to identify the imagery and figurative language used in the poem. You may need to read the poem aloud to help learners identify that most lines are in two parts: one part is about the dragon and the second part about what happens.

One of the learning intentions for this session is to write a poem using noun phrases that include powerful vocabulary. However, as the purpose of this session is to use descriptive vocabulary, this session only discusses adjective + noun as noun phrases. Draw learners' attention to noun phrases in the text (e.g. *a great dragon; his huge, leathery wings*). Encourage learners to think carefully about the adjectives they choose and to use pairs of adjectives.

Common misconceptions

Misconception	How to identify	How to overcome
All poems should rhyme.	Learners ask for help to find *the words that rhyme in The Thunder is a Great Dragon*.	Show learners a picture of an animal (e.g. a lion). Ask each learner to write a sentence describing the animal. Choose four or five sentences and write them on the board under each other. If learners have started their sentence with the name of the animal (e.g. *The lion*) change it to a pronoun (*His*). Ask: *Have we written a story* (no)? *Have we written a poem* (yes)? *Do any of the words rhyme* (no)? *Does that matter* (no)?

Starter idea

What do we know about Mongolia? (10 minutes)

Resources: Learner's Book, Session 3.3: Getting started; atlas; world map; access to reference books or the internet

Description: Explain that in this session learners will be reading a poem from Mongolia. Ask for a volunteer to find Mongolia on a world map and to add a label to mark it. Ask: *What kind of weather would you expect in Mongolia? Will it be hot like The Bahamas?* Direct learners to the question and prompts in the Learner's Book and allow time for learners to find information about Mongolia in books or on the internet. Encourage learners to share some of the facts they have found.

Main teaching ideas

1 *The Thunder is a Great Dragon* (15 minutes)

Learning intention: To read and discuss a traditional poem.

Resources: *The Thunder is a Great Dragon* (Learner's Book, Session 3.3, Activity 1); Track 16

Description: Explain that *The Thunder is a Great Dragon* is an example of a traditional poem from Mongolia. Listen to Track 16 and then ask learners to read the poem together with a partner. Remind learners to use the strategies they know to work out unfamiliar words (e.g. segmenting, phonic knowledge, contextual clues).

Allow time for learners to read the poem then ask: *How is this poem the same as Dancing Poinciana and Hurricane?* (it is about weather) *How is it different to the other two poems?* (it does not have verses, it does not rhyme; the other poems were about something real (a tree and a hurricane) but this poem is more about a dragon).

Ask learners to discuss with their partner how they know *The Thunder is a Great Dragon* is a poem. If necessary, suggest that learners look closely at the words and layout, and think about how the poem is different to a story. Explain that a poem can be any piece of writing that paints a picture using words and that poems do not need to rhyme or have verses. Ask learners to re-read the poem with their partner and to practise reading it, adding expression.

Allow time for learners to practise the poem then organise learners into groups and direct them to parts b–d. Allow time for groups to discuss each question and invite one learner to feedback the answers from each group.

> **Differentiation ideas:** Support learners with understanding the imagery in the poem by asking them what they know about thunder. How could learners describe thunder? Then ask them what they know about dragons.

Challenge learners to make a list of other mythical creatures they know (e.g. unicorns, centaurs, mermaids, yetis, fairies, leprechauns, the Loch Ness Monster).

> **Assessment ideas:** On this initial exploration of the poem, consider: Could learners explain the meaning of the poem? Could learners say why a dragon was a suitable creature for explaining thunder? Did learners identify the rhythm of the poem?

Answers:

a   Learners' own readings.

b   Dragons are mythical creatures in Mongolia.

c   The dragon chases away and kills all the evil things; learners' own choices.

d   Learners' own answers.

2   Time for drama (20 minutes)

Learning intention: To plan a short performance based on a poem.

Resources: Learner's Book, Session 3.3, Activity 2; a space large enough for a performance

Description: Ask: *Did you use any actions when you were reading the poem* (e.g. striking the stones together)? *Which parts of the poem could you add actions to?* Keep learners in the same groups and

tell them that each group is going to prepare a short performance about the poem. Explain that each group should decide which roles they need and how they can use actions as well as voices. Ask groups to think about any props they could use, and any sound effects they could add. Allow 5–10 minutes for groups to rehearse then ask each group to present their performance to the class.

> **Assessment ideas:** Did learners listen carefully to the ideas of other learners? Did all groups show the meaning of the poem in their performances? Which learners took a lead in organising the group and which learners contributed most to the discussion? Which learners used clear, expressive voices?

3   Write a poem (25–30 minutes)

Learning intentions: To include noun phrases in a poem; to present a poem for display.

Resources: Learner's Book, Session 3.3, Activity 3; Workbook, Session 3.3; Worksheet 3.1; Language worksheet 3A; thesauruses

Description: Revise pronouns by asking learners to look at the poem again and ask: *Who is **he** in the poem (the dragon)? Who are **them** (the evil spirits)? How does the dragon make thunder in the poem* (he strikes two stones together)? Explain that adding adjectives to describe a noun makes the noun more interesting to the reader. It engages the reader. Remind learners that when adjectives are added to a noun, this is called a noun phrase.

Direct learners to the Language focus box and ask them to give examples of noun phrases in the poem. Encourage learners to check whether it is a noun phrase by asking them to swap the noun phrase with a pronoun. You could use the Workbook activities here if there is time in class.

Ask learners to talk to a partner about ways a dragon could make thunder instead of striking two stones and how the dragon could behave. Remind learners to use noun phrases with powerful adjectives to describe the dragon. Explain that this helps the reader to create a picture in their minds.

Remind learners that the dragon pursues and slays evil spirits in the poem. Suggest learners use a thesaurus to find alternatives (synonyms) for these words. You could use Language worksheet 3A at this point.

Ask learners to use some of these ideas to write their own poem about a dragon that makes thunder.

Encourage learners to produce a final version of their poem for presentation.

> **Differentiation ideas:** Support learners by encouraging them to think of noun phrases that describe a dragon flying in the sky and making a noise. You could use Worksheet 3.1 Describe the picture here to support learners with ideas for their descriptions.

Challenge learners to share some of their descriptions and synonyms to provide ideas for others.

> **Assessment ideas:** Do learners understand what is meant by a noun phrase? Can they identify examples in the poem? Before learners write their own poems, consider using the Workbook activities as these provide more examples of noun phrases and will give learners more ideas for their own poems.

In poetry writing, consider the following:

- Which learners chose powerful words and followed the style of the poem?
- Did any learners continue to write poems with rhyme?
- Which learners used a thesaurus to find appropriate synonyms?

Answers:

Learners' own poems.

Plenary idea

My dragon poem (5–10 minutes)

Description: Ask learners to share their dragon poems with a partner to gain peer feedback.

Which noun phrases did your partner like? Can partners suggest better adjectives?

Homework ideas

Ask learners to:

- complete the Workbook activities for this session, if not completed in class
- think of another creature that could sound and behave like thunder and write a new poem in the style of *The Thunder is a Great Dragon*.

Answers for Workbook

1 a The huge, scaly dragon
   b the bright swords of light
   c two large, shiny stones
   d a dark, smelly cave
   e the tall mountain range

2 a It flew high above the mountain.
   b People stood and watched as they shot through the clouds.
   c A dragon crashed them together.
   d The people shelter from the thunder and lightning in it.
   e At last the dragon flies over it to another area.

3 Learners' own answers.

3.4 Onomatopoeia

LEARNING PLAN

Learning objectives	Learning intentions	Success criteria
3Rw.03, 3Rv.02, 3Rv.04, 3Rv.07, 3Rg.08, 3Rs.02, 3Ri.02, 3Ri.06, 3Ri.07, 3Ri.14, 3Ri.16, 3Ri.17, 3Ra.01, 3Wv.02, 3Wv.05, 3Wv.06, 3Wv.07, 3Wc.01, 3Wc.02, 3Wp.02, 3Wp.04, 3SLm.05, 3SLp.01, 3SLp.02	• Discuss different words found in a poem. • Recognise onomatopoeic words. • Write a verse for a poem.	• Learners can discuss different words found in a poem. • Learners can recognise onomatopoeic words. • Learners can write a verse for a poem.

LANGUAGE SUPPORT

Some onomatopoeic words are real words and learners should spell these accurately (e.g. crash, buzz, swoops, bangs, giggles). Onomatopoeic words used in poetry to describe the sound an animal or object makes or how it moves are often invented words (e.g. Weeee, Grrrrr, Rrragh, Hisssss). Words associated with an animal can also vary from country to country (e.g. the noise a cat makes might be meow, miaow or nyan).

To help learners with onomatopoeic sounds, consider teaching the traditional song *Old Macdonald had a Farm*. Play an online version of the song. Encourage learners to add the noises associated with each farm animal in English and their own language (e.g. cow: moo; pig: oink; hen: cluck; donkey: hee-haw; dog: bow-wow; turkey: gobble).

Starter idea

The River Congo (5 minutes)

Resources: Learner's Book, Session 3.4: Getting started; world map; atlases

Description: Ask learners to recall which countries the poems in previous sessions have come from. Challenge learners to guess where the poem in this session is from. Give learners clues (e.g. the country is in the second-largest continent, the name of the country is also the name of a famous river). Direct learners to the map in Session 3.1 and invite a learner to locate Africa. Then direct learners to the map in the Learner's Book for this session and ask them to locate the River Congo on this map and the world map. Allow time for learners to share any other information they know about the River Congo.

Main teaching ideas

1 Exploring words in a poem (10–15 minutes)

Learning intention: To discuss different words found in a poem.

Resources: *Song of the Animal World* (Learner's Book, Session 3.4, Activity 1); Track 17

Description: Ask learners to look at *Song of the Animal World* and ask: *What do you notice about the layout of the poem?* Listen to the audio. Try to elicit from learners that the poem is like a play because there are parts for different speakers. Explain that the words in bold do not need to be read.

Remind learners to add expression as they read the poem. Invite learners to read the parts of narrator, bird, fish and monkey. Explain that other learners will read the words for the chorus.

After reading the poem, ask: *Which word group do most of the words in the poem belong to?* (verbs) *Do all the verbs describe how the animal moves?* Ask learners to make a list in their notebooks of the verbs in the poem.

> **Differentiation ideas:** Support learners by recapping that a verb is an action or doing word. Suggest that learners work in pairs with one learner finding the verb and the other learner writing the list of verbs.

Challenge learners to organise their lists into three columns: movement verbs, being verbs (e.g. am, is), other verbs (e.g. goes, start, stuffed, sings).

> **Assessment ideas:** The poem introduces verbs that learners may not know. Consider which learners could explain the meaning of less familiar verbs and which verbs did you need to explain?

Answers:

Fifteen verbs describing movement: start, twist, slips, slides, twists, leaps, flies, passes, climbs, floats, swoops, runs, hops, jumps, dances (three times)

2 Looking at the sounds in the poem (15–20 minutes)

Learning intention: To recognise onomatopoeic words.

Resources: Learner's Book, Session 3.4, Activity 2; Workbook, Session 3.4; Differentiated worksheet pack

Description: Ask: *Does this poem give you any clues about which country it is from?* (a country where monkeys live; near a river; a lively place because everything dances and sings) Ask learners to re-read the poem with their partner and to think about the chorus words for each animal. Ask: *How will you say each word? What do the words sound like when you say them?*

Direct learners to the Language focus box and write *on-o-mat-o-poe-ia* on the board to show how the word can be segmented. Make sure that learners understand what this term means. You could use the Workbook activities to provide further practice with onomatopoeia if there is time in class.

Ask learners to look at their list of verbs from the previous activity and to say what most of the verbs describe (e.g. movement). Ask them to say each movement verb aloud with a partner to see which verbs could also be onomatopoeic words (e.g. slides, swoops, hops). Encourage learners to explain their choices.

Focus on the use of pronouns:

*   Discuss the verse about the fish. Ask: *Why is the verb twist at the beginning and twists later in the verse?*

*   Direct learners to the writing tip and ask them to give examples of pronouns. Make a list of each pronoun on the board.

*   Ask learners to choose three verbs from the poem with their partner and write each verb with four different pronouns, changing the verb spelling to match the pronoun (e.g. I leap, she leaps, it leaps).

You could use Differentiated worksheets 3A–C to provide additional practice with pronouns.

Ask learners to respond to use a 'thumbs up/down' response as you ask: *Is this a happy poem? Is it a sad poem?*

> **Differentiation ideas:** Support learners in recognising an onomatopoeic word by exaggerating how the word is said (e.g. say *hops* and *jumps* quickly and say the *p* very clearly; say *swoops* slowly to emphasise the *oo* sound).

Challenge learners to think of other onomatopoeic verbs (e.g. buzz, splash, snap).

> **Assessment ideas:** When exploring onomatopoeia, consider: Could learners identify the onomatopoeic words in the poem? Could learners exaggerate sounds in onomatopoeic words to increase the effect? Note which learners invented their own onomatopoeic words. Note which learners need

additional support with pronouns. Are there certain pronouns learners confuse, such as *he, she, it*?

Answers:

a   Learners' own answers; Plop! Cheep! Screech!

b   twist, slips, slides, twists, leaps, dances, flies, climbs, floats, swoops, runs, hops, jumps, start, passes, dances

c   Learners' own answers but could include: glug, tweet or whoop.

d   happy

3   Write another verse (20–25 minutes)

Learning intention: To write a verse for a poem.

Resources: Learner's Book, Session 3.4, Activity 3; thesauruses

Description: Explain that learners are going to write a new verse for *Song of the Animal World* with their partners, and that the verse must have the same style as the other verses. Organise learners into pairs and direct them to the prompts and table in the Learner's Book. Explain that they should use the information in the poem to fill in the boxes about the bird and the monkey. Suggest that learners use their own knowledge of birds and monkeys to add some information to the last column. Before learners complete the blank row, explain to them that when they have chosen their animal, they will need to think of a word for how their animal sounds. Ask: *Will the word for your animal be a real word or an invented word? How will you spell the word? What will the word sound like? Will your word be onomatopoeic?* Remind learners to use interesting verbs to describe the movement of their chosen animal.

Allow time for learners to complete the table and then use their ideas to write a new verse. When they have written their verse, organise learners into groups of four to peer assess whether each pair used onomatopoeic words and interesting verbs for their verses.

> **Differentiation ideas:** Support learners by providing a copy of the table to fill in, and help them think of verbs to describe the way their animal moves.

Challenge learners to use thesauruses to find alternative words for the verbs they choose for their animal.

> **Assessment ideas:** From the word choices learners use in their own poetry verses, assess learners'

vocabulary knowledge. Do learners use simple verbs? Which learners have the confidence to explore new verbs? Can learners change the verb spelling to match the pronoun?

Answers:

Animal	How it sounds	Where it lives	How it moves	Other information
fish	Plop!	the water	twists, slips, slides, leaps	swims through the water
bird	Cheep!	Learners' own ideas (**trees/ nests**)	flies, climbs, floats, swoops	sings eats seeds and worms has colourful feathers
monkey	Screech!	branches / in trees	runs, hops, jumps,	lives with his wife and baby / lives in families eats a lot (mouth stuffed full) jumps with tail in the air makes lots of noise

Learners' own answers for **b** and **d**.

Plenary idea

A new *Song of the Animal World* (10 minutes)

Description: Organise learners into groups of three or four pairs. Make sure each pair has chosen a different animal for their own verses. Explain that they are going to use their verses to perform a new version of *Song of the Animal World*. Remind learners to begin their new poem with the chorus and to repeat the chorus after each verse.

Ask each group to assess whether their new poem sounded like a poem from Africa. Ask: *Was it lively? Did the onomatopoeic sounds suggest the rainforest?*

CROSS-CURRICULAR LINKS

Geography (Rainforests): Learners could create a rainforest display to show the different layers and the animals that live at each layer.

Homework ideas

Ask learners to:

* complete the Workbook activities for this session, if not used in class
* draw a picture to accompany the verse they wrote.

Answers for Workbook

1 snake – hiss
  donkey – hee-haw
  cat – meow
  bear – growl
  chicken – cluck
2 Learners' own sentences.
3 the bird
4 c: the sound the animal makes when it sings
5 It moves to the left.
6 slides
7 screech
8 dives

3.5 Writing a haiku

LEARNING PLAN

Learning objectives	Learning intentions	Success criteria
3Rw.03, 3Rv.01, 3Rv.02, 3Rv.07, 3Rg.08, 3Rs.02, 3Ri.02, 3Ri.03, 3Ri.17, 3Ra.01, 3Ra.02, 3Wv.02, 3Wv.05, 3Wv.06, 3Wv.07, 3Wc.01, 3Wc.02, 3Wp.04, 3SLm.05, 3SLp.01	• Explore what a haiku is. • Write a haiku. • Structure a poem using syllables.	• Learners can say what a haiku is. • Learners can write a haiku. • Learners can structure a poem using syllables.

LANGUAGE SUPPORT

Identifying the number of syllables in a word requires learners to hear each sound in a spoken word, in the same way that segmenting words requires the learner to split a word into its separate sounds. The ability to hear each sound in a word (syllable) can be very beneficial to learners who are unsure about how to segment a word.

The better learners become at hearing syllables in words, the better they will become at segmenting words and therefore at reading new vocabulary. For this reason, it is worthwhile spending time making sure learners understand what syllables are and that they can identify them.

Starter idea

Focus on Japan (5 minutes)

Resources: Learner's Book, Session 3.5: Getting started; world map; atlases

Description: Tell learners that this session is about a special kind of poem called a haiku. Ask: *Can anyone tell me which country haiku comes from?* Try to elicit that haikus are Japanese poems. Invite a learner to find Japan on the world map.

Ask learners to share any other information they know about Japan, then allow time for learners to discuss what else they would like to know.

Main teaching ideas

 1 **What is a haiku? (15 minutes)**

Learning intention: To explore what a haiku is.

Resources: *Cat haiku* (Learner's Book, Session 3.5, Activity 1); Track 18; Language worksheet 1B

Description: Invite a learner to read the definition of a haiku aloud. Ask: *What is a syllable?* Try to elicit that a syllable is a way of counting the number of beats or

parts that give the word its rhythm. Invite a learner to read the Language focus information aloud.

Ask learners to say their own name and to clap their hands for each syllable in their name. If there is time, encourage learners to stand in different parts of the room depending upon the number of syllables in their name. So, for example, all learners with names of one syllable stand together, learners with two syllable names stand together, etc. You could use Language worksheet 3B to provide more practice with syllables.

Ask learners to look at the verbs in the cat haiku and invite learners to read a verb aloud and mime the action. Ask learners to read the haiku quietly while their partner claps their hands silently for each syllable. Ask learners to re-read the haiku but this time one partner reads the haiku and claps the syllables and the other partner counts the syllables (number of claps) in each line. Ask: *Do the syllables match the haiku pattern?*

Ask learners to discuss part c in the Learner's Book with a partner, and to write ideas in their notebooks.

Invite learners to read the haiku aloud using expression.

> **Differentiation ideas:** Support learners with counting syllables by clapping each syllable with them.

Challenge learners to research what other things are special in Japan (e.g. willow trees; almond and cherry blossom; birds, such as the crane, owl and rooster).

> **Assessment ideas:** When exploring syllables, consider: Which learners can identify syllables easily and which learners need more practice in identifying syllables? Do these learners also find reading unfamiliar words difficult?

Did learners notice the connection between the number of syllables in a word and how the word could be segmented?

Encourage learners to make this link. Ask: *How did I segment this word* (e.g. 'onomatopoeia') *to read it? How many syllables are there?*

Answers:

b   5, 7, 5

c   Learners' own answers but could include: Japanese people like cats; cats are special in Japan; some words are onomatopoeic.

d   Learners' own readings.

---

2   *Tiger news report* (20–25 minutes)

Learning intention: To write a haiku.

Resources: *Tiger news report* (Learner's Book, Session 3.5, Activity 2); Track 19

Description: Explain that learners are going to listen to some information about tigers. Tell learners that tigers no longer live in Japan but are important animals in Japanese art and culture. Ask them to make notes about what the tiger looks like and what is happening to the tiger. Remind learners to only write important words, such as adjectives, and not write in sentences. (You may wish to check that learners know what adjectives are.) Play the audio.

When learners have listened to the audio, ask them to compare notes with their partner and to use their notes to answer parts a and b in the Learner's Book.

Explain that learners should work with their writing partner to use some of the words in their notes to help them write a haiku about the tiger (part c). Allow learners time to write their haiku and to use the character prompt to check the haiku has the correct number of syllables in each line.

> **Differentiation ideas:** Support learners by writing the haiku as a group. Ask learners how many syllables there are in *tiger*. Did learners write down an adjective with three syllables to describe the tiger (e.g. beautiful, powerful)? Which of their sentence ideas could they use (e.g. with large heads and long whiskers)? Remind learners to count the number of syllables in each word.

Challenge learners to write a haiku on their own. Suggest that learners choose a theme for their haiku. Will the haiku describe the tiger, or will the haiku explain that tigers are endangered?

During the listening activity consider which learners demonstrated good listening skills? Which learners used the note taking skills taught in Unit 2? Did learners make appropriate notes by writing only key words?

Audioscript: *Tiger news report*

Tigers. They are beautiful. They are strong, they are powerful.

They are one of the biggest of the wild cats. Their large heads and long whiskers are striking. Did you know that a white spot surrounded by black can be found on the back of their ears?

The black stripes on their light brown fur camouflage tigers in their environment but they are still endangered. Their habitats, the places where they live, have been destroyed and many tigers have been killed for their skins.

Tigers are often found roaming on their own, not as part of a group. They help to keep a balance in the environment in which they live. They eat plant-eating animals like deer, who, if left to overgraze would damage the land and disrupt the balance of the local environment.

The number of tigers in this world have dropped significantly but finally their numbers are beginning to increase due to the continued efforts by conservation groups to protect them. In 12 years it is hoped the number of tigers in the world will have doubled to 8000 tigers worldwide. What can you do to help support the survival of tigers in our world?

Answers:

a   Possible answers: large heads, long whiskers, black stripes on light brown fur.

b   Possible sentences: Tigers are powerful. Their black stripes with light brown fur is striking. Tigers are strong and beautiful.

c   Learners' own haikus (individual, paired or group).

3 My animal haiku (20–25 minutes)

Learning intention: To structure a poem using syllables.

Resources: Learner's Book, Session 3.5, Activity 3; Worksheet 3.2; dictionaries; thesauruses

Description: Ask: *Who has a favourite animal?* Say: *Tell your writing partner why you like that animal and what you think is special about that animal.* Explain that learners are going to write a haiku about their favourite animal. Ask learners to write a list of adjectives that describes their animal, and then to write the number of syllabus each adjective has. Remind learners to use a dictionary and thesaurus.

When learners have made an adjective list, ask them to make a list of verbs to describe how the animal moves and to write the number of syllables in each verb.

Finally, encourage learners to think of noun phrases to describe the animal and to write the number of syllables next to these. Allow time for learners to use some of these ideas to write their haiku.

When learners have finished writing their haiku, ask them to work through the peer assessment prompts in the Learner's Book with their partner. You could ask learners to peer assess their writing using Worksheet 3.2 Checklist for writing a haiku.

> **Differentiation ideas:** Support learners by organising pairs or groups of learners who have chosen the same animal to write a haiku together. Provide additional support by working with one of the groups.

Challenge learners to write a haiku without including the name of their chosen animal. Explain that learners must describe the animal very well so that it is easy for other learners to guess what their animal is.

> **Assessment ideas:** During the haiku-writing activity, did learners follow the haiku syllable pattern in their poems? Did learners help to create a picture in the mind of the reader with their word choices?

Answers:

Learners' own answers.

Plenary idea

Building vocabulary (10 minutes)

Description: Write a simple adjective or verb on the board (e.g. big, brave, walk, run). Ask learners to suggest synonyms for the word. To add additional challenge, ask learners to suggest synonyms that have a certain number of syllables.

Homework ideas

Ask learners to:

•   complete the Workbook activities for this session, if not used in class

•   make a list of names in their family and sort the list according to the number of syllables in each name.

Answers for Workbook

1   Sud/den/ly /a/wake. 5
    Stre/tching/, yaw/ning/, ar/ching/ back. 7
    Stalk/ing/, poun/cing/: cat. 5

2   Learners' own answers.

3   Learners' own answers.

4   Learners' own answers.

5   Learners' own answers.

3.6 Reviewing poems

LEARNING PLAN

Learning objectives	Learning intentions	Success criteria
3Rv.02, 3Rv.04, 3Rv.07, 3Rs.02, 3Ri.03, 3Ri.06, 3Ri.07, 3Ri.10, 3Ri.14, 3Ri.15, 3Ri.16, 3Ri.17, 3Ra.02, 3Ra.03, 3Ra.04, 3Ww.02, 3Ww.05, 3Ww.06, 3Wv.02, 3Wv.05, 3Wv.06, 3Wv.07, 3Wg.01, 3Ws.02, 3Wc.02, 3Wc.05, 3Wp.02, 3Wp.04, 3Wp.05, 3SLm.01, 3SLm.04, 3SLm.05, 3SLg.02, 3SLp.01, 3SLp.02, 3SLp.04, 3SLr.01	• Compare poems. • Write a review about a poem. • Perform a poem.	• Learners can compare poems. • Learners can write a review about a poem. • Learners can perform a poem.

LANGUAGE SUPPORT

Introduce learners to the terms *gesture* and *expression* before they plan their performance as this will make it easier to discuss ways of performing and improving their performance.

Starter idea

Looking back at poems (10 minutes)

Resources: Learner's Book, Session 3.6: Getting started

Description: Ask: *Can you remember the poems we have read in this unit? Can you remember where they are from?* Ask learners to re-read each of the poems with a partner. Allow time for learners to read the poems and then share their opinions of each poem as a class.

Main teaching ideas

1 Compare poems (20–25 minutes)

Learning intention: To compare poems.

Resources: Learner's Book, Session 3.6, Activity 1

Description: Explain that learners are going to compare three poems from the unit. Ask: *What does compare mean?* Before learners choose their poems, ask them to copy the table from the Learner's Book into their notebooks.

Explain that in the *Language* column, learners should write about words that rhyme, are onomatopoeic, powerful verbs, powerful adjectives or syllables. Write this list on the board as a prompt for learners.

Explain that in the *Interesting things* column, learners can include words they liked in the poem and any part of the poem they found interesting (e.g. *Dancing Poinciana* did not say it was tree; *The Thunder is a Dragon* only had one verse).

Allow learners time to complete the table in their notebooks.

› **Differentiation ideas:** Support learners to draw the table. Show them how you would draw the table and ask learners to copy each of your steps as you do it. Challenge learners to add extra rows to the table and to compare all five poems in the unit.

> **Assessment ideas:** Did learners identify the language used in each poem? What type of information did learners add to the *Language* and *Interesting things* columns? Which learners left some boxes in the final two columns blank? What does this tell you about learners' ability to identify explicit and implicit meanings?

Answers:

Learners' own answers. Possible answers could be:

Title	Country	Topic	Language	Interesting things
Dancing Poinciana	The Bahamas	A tree	Some of the words rhyme.	The poet does not say it is a tree.
Hurricane	Trinidad	A hurricane	The verses have a repetition pattern to them.	Every verse ends with the rain coming and the hurricane coming up the mountain.
The Thunder is a Dragon	Mongolia	Thunder / a dragon	It has lots of adjectives.	The poem is a bit like a story. It is about dragons and evil spirits.
Song of the Animal World	Congo	Animals / fish, bird and monkey	A lot of the words are onomatopoeic.	The poet makes up some of the words (e.g. *Viss!*, *Gnan!*).
Haiku about a cat	Japan	A cat	The syllables are important. It has 17 syllables. The syllables are in a 5,7,5 pattern.	Cats are very special animals in Japan. The poem is exactly like a cat.

Learners' own answers for **b** and **c**.

2 Review a favourite poem (15 minutes)

Learning intention: To write a review about a poem.

Resources: Learner's Book, Session 3.6, Activity 2; Workbook, Session 3.6

Description: Explain that learners are to choose their favourite poem from the unit and write a review about it. Ask: *What is a review?* Try to elicit from learners that a review tells other people:

- what something is about
- what is good or bad about it
- what you (the 'reviewer') enjoyed about it.

Direct learners to the self-assessment prompt ('How am I doing?') in the Learner's Book and explain that learners should refer to this list as they write their review. Remind learners to write their review using complete sentences and to use capital letters and full stops to begin and end their sentences.

Allow time for learners to write their reviews. Then ask learners to work with a partner as they self-assess their reviews. Encourage partners to question each other using the points in the self-assessment prompt.

> **Differentiation ideas:** Support learners using a template based on the prompts from the Learner's Book (you could also use the Workbook activities if there is time in class).

Challenge learners to say how many stars they would give their favourite poem out of a possible five stars.

> **Assessment ideas:** Assess learners' ability to organise their comments. Did learners use capital letters and full stops for sentences? Did they remember to use capital letters for proper nouns? Did they spell the most common words accurately? Did they use the rules taught for different verb endings?

Answers:

Learners' own answers.

3 Performance! (10–15 minutes)

Learning intention: To perform a poem.

Resources: Learner's Book, Session 3.6, Activity 3

Description: Explain that learners are going to re-read their favourite poem. Tell them to think about how they will perform the poem and direct them to the Speaking tip. Ask: *Will you add any actions when you perform your poem? Could you add any sound effects?*

Allow time for learners to practise their performance. Then, tell them to work with their partners to find ways to improve the performance. Explain that partners should say what is good about the performance and think of one thing their partner could do to improve the performance (e.g. use musical instruments to add sound effects; ways to add more expression).

Differentiation ideas: Support learners who are less confident with speaking by rehearsing the poem with them and suggesting how to add expression.

> **Assessment ideas:** During and after performances note which learners used appropriate expression in their performances and which learners used clear voices. Note how well learners used the self-assessment tips. Did learners reflect on their performance? Were they willing to amend and improve their performance?

Plenary idea

Decision alley (10–15 minutes)

Resources: Poem titles written in large lettering on card or paper

Description: Explain that you want to know which poem was the favourite for most learners. Tell all learners to stand at the back of the room and create a short pathway (alley) for learners to walk through. Then, place the titles of the five poems in different parts of the room on the other side of the pathway. Explain that learners are at one end of a *decision alley* and that when they reach the other end of the alley they should walk towards the title of their favourite poem. Explain that there are no right or wrong answers. Allow learners to make their decisions. Ask: *Which poem is the class favourite? Why? Which poem didn't you like? Why did you not like this poem?*

Homework ideas

Ask learners to:

*   complete the Workbook activities for this session, if not used in class

*   draw a picture to accompany their favourite poem.

Answers for Workbook

Learners' own answers.

CHECK YOUR PROGRESS

2 Learners' answers should refer to the language (e.g. underwater garden, starry anemones, fish hiding).

3 No, but it links to any country that has coral reefs.

4 Learners' own answers.

5 Learners could include:

*   nouns: city, fishes, (underwater) garden, forest, trees, anemones, predators

*   adjectives: teeming, underwater, lost, skeleton, starry, frightened, prowling, alien, unseen, luminous

*   noun phrases: a teeming city, an underwater garden, luminous eyes, a skulking place, frightened fishes.

6 Learners' own onomatopoeic words. Possible answers: gloop, blubbing, gliding, bluh.

7 **a** Ba/ham/as (3)

    b Car/ib/be/an (4)

    c Mon/gol/i/a (4)

    d Af/ric/a (3)

PROJECT GUIDANCE

These projects develop learners' skills in writing, performing and researching of poems from around the world. You will find it helpful to refer to the guidance about *Setting up and assessing the projects* in the Project guidance in Unit 1.

Group project: The group project focuses on learners' animal haikus from Session 3.5. Organise learners into groups based on:

- the habitat of their animal (e.g. domestic, farm, desert, jungle, savannah, ocean)
- the species their animal belongs to (e.g. fish, birds, mammals, insects, reptiles)
- the continent where their animal is usually found.

Learners should present their haiku using neat joined handwriting and illustrate it to match the words in the haiku. Provide materials for learners to illustrate and create the book.

Pair project: Provide a selection of poetry books or internet access to allow pairs to research other poems from around the world. Learners will need time to rehearse their poem. Assess learner's ability to:

- read aloud with expression
- use expression that is appropriate to the meaning and sound of the words
- use speech, gesture and movement to add interest to their performance
- use non-verbal communication techniques for different purposes
- show awareness of an audience (e.g. by adapting language and tone to engage them)
- respond politely to another point of view with a personal point of view.

Solo project: Learners are asked to write a short poem about the country they live in. Encourage learners to re-read the poems in the unit and to use the pattern of one of these poems to write their own. Remind learners that their poem does not need lots of verses.

Learners could present a final copy using neat joined handwriting then illustrate their poem. Learners could decide how they would perform their poem and present it to a small group or the class.

> 4 Myths and legends

Unit plan

Session	Approximate number of learning hours	Outline of learning content	Resources
4.1 Looking at a traditional story	1	Read the traditional story *Bear and Fire* and answer questions about it. Express opinions about the story.	Learner's Book Session 4.1 Workbook Session 4.1
4.2 What is a myth?	1.5	Explore characters in the story then perform it in groups. Explore the features of a myth and identify myth features in *Bear and Fire*.	Learner's Book Session 4.2 Workbook Session 4.2
4.3 Looking at pronouns	1	Identify pronouns in sentences. Use pronouns to write sentences.	Learner's Book Session 4.3 Workbook Session 4.3
4.4 What is a legend?	1	Explore the features of legends and read the legend of *Mulan*. Answer questions about the story. Identify and spell words with common suffixes.	Learner's Book Session 4.4 Workbook Session 4.4 ⬇ Language worksheet 4A
4.5 Looking at paragraphs	1.5	Explore and identify examples of paragraphs. Explore and identify adverbs and sentence openers that are used as paragraph openings.	Learner's Book Session 4.5 Workbook Session 4.5 ⬇ Worksheet 4.1
4.6 Joining sentences	1	Recap word-class groups and explore simple and multi-clause sentences. Identify clauses within simple sentences. Write multi-clause sentences using connectives.	Learner's Book Session 4.6 Workbook Session 4.6
4.7 Making links	1	Explore the similarities and differences in myths and legends.	Learner's Book Session 4.7 Workbook Session 4.7 ⬇ Worksheet 4.2

Session	Approximate number of learning hours	Outline of learning content	Resources
4.8 Rewriting a myth	1.5	Explore different story settings and listen to a different version of the *Bear and Fire* myth. Role play retellings of the myth and plan a retelling of the myth using a storyboard.	Learner's Book Session 4.8 Workbook Session 4.8 Worksheet 4.1
4.9 Exploring a legend	1	Read an extract from *Sinbad and the Roc* and discuss features of legends. Identify and expand words with apostrophes for omission.	Learner's Book Session 4.9 Workbook Session 4.9 Language worksheet 4B
4.10 Planning a legend	1	Use a storyboard to plan the next steps in *Sinbad and the Roc*. Select adverbs and sentence openers to use as paragraph openings in stories.	Learner's Book Session 4.10 Workbook Session 4.10 Worksheet 4.3 Differentiated worksheets 4A–C
4.11 Writing a legend	1	Rehearse telling a legend about Sinbad using a storyboard. Write the legend. Use dialogue and alternative words for *said* in stories.	Learner's Book Session 4.11 Workbook Session 4.11 Worksheet 4.4
4.12 Improving your legend	1	Proofread legends. Self-assess a finished story.	Learner's Book Session 4.12 Workbook Session 4.12 Worksheet 4.5
Cross-unit resources			
Learner's Book Check your progress			
Learner's Book Projects			
End-of-unit 4 test			

BACKGROUND KNOWLEDGE

It will be helpful to be familiar with the following English subject knowledge:

- features of myths and legends
- nouns and proper nouns
- pronouns – especially personal, possessive and intensive pronouns
- noun phrases
- apostrophes for omission
- use of speech marks
- rules for setting out speech
- structuring writing using paragraphs
- using adverbs and sentence openers as paragraph openings
- identifying adverbs and sentence openers by time, place and cause.

CONTINUED

It will be helpful for learners to be familiar with the following English subject knowledge:

- some awareness of different story genre
- some knowledge of myths and legends
- full stops, question marks and exclamation marks for different sentence types
- commas for lists.

TEACHING SKILLS FOCUS

Differentiation: Paired work

Learners are often organised into pairs to complete a task. When you do this, do you consider how individuals are paired? Do you consider learners' reading, writing and speaking abilities when you pair them? All these factors can make a huge difference to what learners achieve when paired.

When pairing learners for a speaking activity, consider pairing learners who lack confidence with speaking with a learner who has a little more confidence in this area. A less confident speaker may feel overwhelmed if their partner is too confident and this will result in neither learner benefitting.

The same considerations apply to reading and writing pairings. Try to organise your learners so that one learner is only a little more able than the other learner. As well as supporting the less confident reader or writer, it will challenge the stronger learner in the pair to feel good about sharing what they know.

Once you have considered your pairings, tell learners who their partners will be. Once learners know who their partner is in each situation they will be able to get into their pairings quickly.

Cambridge Reading Adventures

There are several books in the series that are based on myths and legends, and would allow learners to explore examples of this genre.

- *Yu and the Great Flood* by Tony Brandman and Nicola Hitoride
- *A Tale of Two Sinbads* by Ian Whybrow and Shahab Shamshirsaz
- *Tamerlane and the Boy* by Tom and Tony Bradman, and Arpad Olbey

4.1 Looking at a traditional story

LEARNING PLAN

Learning objectives	Learning intentions	Success criteria
3Rv.01, 3Rv.04, 3Rg.01, 3Rg.04, 3Ri.02, 3Ri.12, 3Ri.14, 3Ri.15, 3Ri.16, 3Ra.01, 3Ra.02, 3Ra.03, 3SLm.01, 3SLg.02, 3SLg.03, 3SLg.04, 3SLp.01, 3SLp.03	<ul><li>Read a traditional story.</li><li>Answer questions about a traditional story.</li><li>Listen to the viewpoint of others and share a personal viewpoint.</li></ul>	<ul><li>Learners can read a traditional story.</li><li>Learners can answer questions about a traditional story.</li><li>Learners can listen to the viewpoint of others and share opinions of their own.</li></ul>

The story *Bear and Fire* uses many words to describe fire. As well as checking that learners understand all the words in the text, you may need to check what experience learners have of fire. Remind them that fire can be dangerous.

As learners answer questions about the story, note which learners:

- use the text to support their answers
- make reasonable inferences about why Fire was angry with Bear and chased him away
- give explanations without reference to the text
- give reasons based on personal knowledge (e.g. bears are dangerous).

Starter idea

Different types of story (5 minutes)

Resources: Learner's Book, Session 4.1: Getting started

Description: Ask: *What types of story do you know?* Write learners, suggestions on the board. Direct learners to the book covers in the Learner's Book. Allow time for learners to talk with a partner about the different covers and decide what type of stories they are for.

Main teaching ideas

1 Bear and Fire (15–20 minutes)

Learning intention: To read a traditional story.

Resources: *Bear and Fire* (Learner's Book, Session 4.1, Activity 1); Track 21; map of North America

Description: Explain that during this unit learners will find out about stories known as myths or legends. Say: *Myths and legends are very old stories that have been told many times. We are going to start by reading a traditional story of the Alabama tribe of North America.* Direct learners to the information in the Learner's Book and invite a learner to read it aloud. Use the following prompts to elicit learners' understanding of fire:

- Does anyone have a real fire in their home?
- Who knows how a fire is made?
- Has anyone made a fire using a flint, moss and sticks?
- Has anyone sat around a campfire?

Show learners a map of North America and locate Alabama. Direct learners to the Reading tip and then invite a learner to read the definition for 'dwindle' aloud.

When learners have read *Bear and Fire*, ask: *What did Fire mean when he called 'Feed me. Feed me.'?* (Fire needs more logs and sticks to keep it burning)

What does 'Fire ate the wood' mean? (Fire burned all the wood so needed more) *What does 'Fire leapt and danced in delight' mean?* (it is describing how the flames move).

Discuss learners' answers then check that learners understand the vocabulary in the story (e.g. blazed, wandering, flickering).

⟩ **Differentiation ideas:** Support learners by pairing them with confident readers.

Challenge groups of learners by inviting them to read the story aloud, adopting the different roles of narrator, Fire and Man.

⟩ **Assessment ideas:** As learners read the text, note which learners use punctuation. Which learners overlook full stops? Which learners notice the speech marks? Which learners use expression for the dialogue?

Note which learners notice the capital letters for Bear, Fire and Man. Are learners able to explain why these words have capital letters (e.g. because they are the characters' names)?

2 Answering questions (15 minutes)

Learning intention: To answer questions about a traditional story.

Resources: Learner's Book, Session 4.1, Activity 2; Workbook, Session 4.1

Description: Ask learners to re-read the story and then to write the answers to the questions in their notebooks. Remind learners to keep looking back at the text to find the information for their answers. You could use the Workbook activities here to provide further practice if there is time in class.

⟩ **Differentiation ideas:** Support learners by rehearsing their answers verbally in a small group before writing answers in their notebooks.

Answers:

a   Fire warmed Bear and his people and gave them light.

b   Bear probably knew that Fire would burn the forest down if he took it into the forest.

c   Fire told Man what it needed.

d   Man liked the colours of the flames and the hissing sound Fire made when it ate the wood.

e   Fire was happy with Man because Man fed him, and Bear had left him alone and hungry.

3   Talk about the story (5–10 minutes)

Learning intention: To listen to the viewpoint of others and share a personal viewpoint.

Resources: Learner's Book, Session 4.1, Activity 3

Description: Talk about how different people enjoy different types of stories. Explain that, sometimes, different people also have different opinions about a story. Remind learners that it is important to listen politely to each other's opinions.

Ask learners to put their hands up if they liked the story. Invite learners to say what they liked about the story. Ask: *Is there anything you do not like about the story?* Allow time for learners to share their opinions.

⟩ **Differentiation ideas:** Support learners who are reluctant to speak in a large group by organising them into a small group.

Challenge learners to record the opinions of other learners on the board.

Answers:

Learners' own answers.

Plenary idea

All about the fire (5 minutes)

Description: Ask learners to re-read the story *Bear and Fire* and find descriptions of what a fire is like (e.g. it warms you, gives light, blazes, burns, smokes, flickers, dwindles, goes out, leaps, dances, hisses). Ask learners to think of other words they could use to describe a fire (e.g. glows, roars, crackles, sparks, spits).

Homework ideas

Ask learners to:

*   complete the Workbook activities for this session, if not completed in class

*   research and write a set of instructions about how to make a fire, including a list of safety rules and risks of things that could go wrong. (Note: learners should never start a fire without an adult.)

Answers for Workbook

1   warmth, light

2   At the edge of the forest.

3   Bear was deep in the forest so he could not hear Fire.

4   a   Man
   b   Man gave him sticks and logs.
   c   Fire told him that was what he ate.

5   Fire felt angry because Bear had left him and not fed him.

6   happy

7   Fire felt worried because he had nearly gone out.

8   Possible answers: scared, frightened, nervous.

9   happy – possible reasons: he felt warm; he enjoyed watching the colours of the flames; he liked the hissing sound Fire made.

10   Learners' own answers.

11   Learners' own answers.

4.2 What is a myth?

LEARNING PLAN

Learning objectives	Learning intentions	Success criteria
3Rg.08 3Rs.02, 3Ri.02, 3Ri.03, 3Ri.06, 3Ri.07, 3Ri.10, 3Ri.12, 3Ri.15, 3Ri.17, 3Ra.01, 3Wv.05, 3Wg.01, 3SLm.01, 3SLm.04, 3SLm.05, 3SLp.04	• Recognise and discuss the features of a myth. • Answer questions about characters in a story. • Create a character in drama.	• Learners can recognise and discuss the features of a myth. • Learners can answer questions about characters in a story. • Learners can create a character in drama.

LANGUAGE SUPPORT

Many of the questions featured in this session require implicit understanding of the text (e.g. suggesting words to describe Man and Bear). Learners also need knowledge of how a word changes in context (e.g. warmed – warmth; happily – happy).

Support learners to understand the text more fully using targeted questioning:

- *What makes Fire happy? Does he say 'Thank you' to Bear or Man for finding him food? Is Fire grateful?*
- *Man had never seen a fire before. How do you think he felt when Fire shouted 'Feed me'?*
- *At the end of story, Fire was angry with Bear. How do you think this made Bear feel? Why?*

Common misconceptions

Misconception	How to identify	How to overcome
Bear, Man and Fire are individual characters.	When answering the questions in Session 4.2, learners continue to think Bear, Man and Fire are the names of individual characters because learners know proper nouns start with capital letters.	Explain that in a myth characters do not usually have actual names because the story is not about a single animal or person. Characters in myths represent all things in that category. Explain that Bear, Man and Fire mean *all* bears, *all* people, *all* fires.

Starter idea

What is a myth? (10 minutes)

Resources: Learner's Book, Session 4.2: Getting started

Description: Ask learners to think about what was said about traditional stories in the previous session. Explain that some traditional stories are known as *myths*.

In small groups, ask learners to talk about what they think a myth is. Allow time for discussion and feedback. Write learners' ideas on the board.

Direct learners to the Getting started activity and ask them to read the information in the box. Ask learners to compare the information about myths with their own ideas. Ask: *Can you think of any stories you know that may be a myth?* If learners suggest *Bear and Fire* as a possible myth, suggest that you all read the story again to find out.

> **Assessment ideas:** This session provides an opportunity for Assessment for Learning (AfL). Note learners' pre-knowledge of myths and how well their knowledge compares with the information in the Getting started section. Which learners have a good understanding of myths? Which learners will need careful support?

Main teaching ideas

1 *Bear and Fire* (15 minutes)

Learning intention: To recognise and discuss the features of a myth.

Resources: Learner's Book, Session 4.2, Activity 1; *Bear and Fire* (Learner's Book, Session 4.1); Track 21

Description: Ask learners to read *Bear and Fire* again. Allow time for learners to re-read the text.

Read the first question out loud. Ask learners to discuss the question with their partner and then discuss the answer as a class. Elicit the correct answer and correct any misconceptions.

Discuss the other questions using paired and class discussion. Ask: *Which features of a myth did you find? Can you give me an example from the text of feature of a myth?*

> **Differentiation ideas:** Support learners by reading the story to them so that they can focus on the content of the story and not on decoding the words. Then, discuss the questions as a group. Record answers on the board.

Challenge learners to read the story silently and then write answers in their notebooks. Remind learners to use full sentences and accurate punctuation.

> **Assessment ideas:** Note which learners need support with uncovering the implicit meaning. Note which learners give answers that are based on their reactions without evidence in the text.

Answers:

a Bear, Man and Fire are names that mean it is really about *all* bears, *all* men and *all* fires.

b *In the beginning* means a very long time ago when the world was just beginning.

c No, because bears and fires cannot speak. What happens in the story could not really happen. Bears cannot carry fire and fires cannot speak.

d Yes: characters and things have names like Bear, Man and Fire; bears cannot speak in real life; Fire is not really a person; the text explains how something happened and how man was able to make fire; the text explains why animals, like the bear, are afraid of fire.

2 Exploring characters (20 minutes)

Learning intention: To answer questions about characters in a story.

Resources: Learner's Book, Session 4.2, Activity 2; Workbook, Session 4.2, Activities 1–3; dictionaries; thesauruses

Description: Explain that learners are going to answer questions about the characters in the story. Tell them that sometimes a story tells us what a character is like but sometimes we must find clues in the story. Explain that when answering the questions learners should choose words they think describe the character best.

Before learners answer the questions, check that they understand the words in part b. Invite volunteers to find each word in a dictionary and share the definitions with the class. Direct learners to the Writing tip. Check that learners can recall what a pronoun is. Ask learners to suggest examples of noun phrases (e.g. the hungry fire, a flickering flame, a hissing sound). Ask learners to answer the questions. Encourage them to discuss their ideas with a partner and to use a dictionary or thesaurus as necessary. When learners have completed the questions, ask: *Did you find the clues in the text about all of the characters?* Use the Focus and Practice activities of the Workbook to provide further practice.

> **Differentiation ideas:** Support learners by discussing the questions as a group. Record learners' responses to parts a–d on the board and ask learners to complete part e in their notebooks.

Challenge learners to write answers in their notebooks. Remind learners to use full sentences and accurate punctuation.

> **Assessment ideas:** Note which learners were able to suggest noun phrases. Which learners could recall examples of pronouns?

Answers:

a He helped Bear and his people and then they abandoned him.

b   Possible answers: proud, friendly, excitable, happy, angry.

c   Learners' own answers. Possible answers: helpful, kind, happy, friendly.

d   Learners' own answers. Possible answers: thoughtless, sad, frightened.

e   Learners' own noun phrases.

3 Performance time (20–25 minutes)

Learning intention: To create a character in a story.

Resources: Learner's Book, Session 4.2, Activity 3; a space large enough for groups to perform in

Description: Direct learners to the Learner's Book and organise them into groups of three to five. Ask learners to name the characters in the story (e.g. Bear, Man, Fire, Bear's friends). Ask learners to suggest ways to make characters interesting to watch (e.g. loud and clear voices, adding expression to what is said, facial expressions, actions that can be easily seen).

Encourage learners to use their own words for the dialogue and not to read from the text. Allow time for learners to rehearse.

If there is time, ask learners to peer assess each group's performance. Did they use some facial expression or gestures? Did they speak clearly and add expression? What could they do to improve the performance?

> **Differentiation ideas:** Support and challenge learners by organising groups that allow all learners to take on roles that match their confidence in performing.

Plenary idea

The Whisper game (10 minutes)

Resources: Space in which to play the game

Description: Ask learners to sit in a large circle. Remind them that myths are stories that have been passed from person to person by word of mouth. Explain that you are going to whisper a phrase into the ear of the learner on your right. That learner will then whisper it on to the learner on their right and so on until all learners have heard the whisper. Ask the learner on your left to say what they heard. Ask the learner on your right to say the phrase you gave them. The phrase is always something very different to the original phrase!

Explain that myths change over time too and that there can be many versions of the same myth.

Homework ideas

Ask learners to:

*   complete the Challenge section of the Workbook
*   draw a picture to illustrate their favourite part of the story *Bear and Fire*.

Answers for Workbook

1   Learners should circle four statements:

*   The characters are named after something from the natural world.
*   It is not a story that would happen in the real world.
*   It is an old story from Native Americans.
*   It explains why people have fire.

2   Nouns: blaze, flame, sparkle
Verbs: glowing, blaze, shining, flickering, sparkle, dwindle
Adjectives: glowing, fiery, shining; brilliant, flickering

3   Learners' own sentences.

4   Learners' own myths.

4.3 Looking at pronouns

LEARNING PLAN		
Learning objectives	**Learning intentions**	**Success criteria**
3Rg.01, 3Rg.08, 3Rs.01, 3Ri.14, 3Ri.15, 3Ri.16, 3Ra.02, 3Wg.04, 3Wp.02	• Identify pronouns. • Use pronouns in a sentence.	• Learners can identify pronouns. • Learners can use pronouns in a sentence of their own.

LANGUAGE SUPPORT

There are many types of pronoun. At Stage 3, learners should learn to identify personal pronouns (e.g. I, he, she, it, they), possessive pronouns (e.g. my, mine, his, theirs) and intensive pronouns (e.g. myself, himself, themselves). Learners will learn to identify other types of pronoun in later stages. For this reason, *this* has not been included in the answers to the exercises in this session. Learners do not need to know the names for types of pronoun.

Some words belong to multiple word classes depending upon the role the word plays in the sentence. In this session, learners may inaccurately identify words as pronouns when the word in the text is being used as a possessive adjective. This is dealt with in Common misconceptions. Learners do not need to know the word class of such non-pronouns as this could lead to learners becoming confused about adjectives.

Common misconceptions

Misconception	How to identify	How to overcome
His and *its* are always pronouns.	Ask learners to identify the pronouns in a piece of text. Learners identify *his* and *its* as pronouns in 'his people', 'its wood', 'its flames'.	Explain that *his* and *its* can both be a pronoun and used to show something belongs to something else (i.e. a possessive adjective). Encourage learners to check whether a word is a pronoun by re-inserting the noun or noun phrase in its place. If learners need to re-insert the word with a *noun + apostrophe* (e.g. Bear's, Fire's), then the word is not a pronoun.

Starter idea

Noun categories (5–10 minutes)

Resources: Learner's Book, Session 4.3: Getting started

Description: Explain that learners are going to play the Category Game with a partner. Explain that you will say a category name (e.g. fruits, birds, animals, things eaten for breakfast) and, as quickly as possible, each pair must think of five items that belong to that category. When pairs have thought of five items they should call out 'Category!'. Ask the first pair to call out to say their items. If learners' items belong to that category the pair gets a point. Repeat the game with a new category.

After playing the game for a short time ask: *Which word class do all the words belong to?* (nouns) Direct learners to the Getting started activity and ask them to identify the nouns with a partner.

Tell learners that some nouns are called proper nouns because they are the special name for that person, place or organisation. Give learners examples of proper nouns. Ask: *How can we recognise a proper noun?*

(it has a capital letter) Ask learners to suggest examples of proper nouns.

Answers:
2 night, food, forest, bear, flame

Main teaching ideas

1 Identify pronouns (15–20 minutes)

Learning intention: To identify pronouns.

Resources: Learner's Book, Session 4.3, Activity 1; Workbook, Session 4.3, Activity 1

Description: On the board, write the sentence *Bear was looking.* Ask learners to identify the noun in the sentence. Explain that sometimes the noun is replaced by a word from another word class. In this sentence, *Bear* can be replaced by the word *He*. Write this sentence on the board: *He is looking.* Ask: *Can you remember which word class he belongs to?* Ask learners to suggest other pronouns. Write the pronouns on the board.

Direct learners to the Language focus box and allow time for them to read the information. Use the Focus activity in the Workbook here to provide practice with identifying pronouns.

Write this sentence on the board: *Fire warmed Bear and his people and it also gave them light.* Ask learners to identify the pronouns in the sentence (it, them). If learners identify *his* as a pronoun explain that in this sentence *his* means 'Bear's people' and is part of the noun phrase *Bear and his people,* so is not being used as a pronoun (see Common misconceptions). Ask learners to suggest a pronoun that could replace the noun phrase *Bear and his people* in the sentence (e.g. them).

Ask learners to discuss in pairs which nouns *it* and *them* have replaced (Fire, Bear). Tell learners to look out for another non-pronoun in sentences a–d in the Learner's Book (its).

Allow time for learners to complete the sentence activity in the Learner's Book. Ask learners to peer mark as you provide the answers.

> **Differentiation ideas:** Support learners by providing a list of pronouns (e.g. it, he, she, I, you, them, they, we, himself).

Challenge learners to identify the noun or noun phrase in each sentence that the pronoun has replaced.

> **Assessment ideas:** Note which learners understand that pronouns can replace single nouns and noun phrases. Did learners choose appropriate pronouns to replace nouns and noun phrases?

Answers:
a   Fire warmed Bear and his people and <u>it</u> also gave <u>them</u> light.
b   Bear put Fire down and left <u>it</u> behind while <u>he</u> went to look for food.
c   When <u>it</u> had burned up all of its wood, Fire started to call for help.
d   Man heard <u>it</u>. <u>He</u> came to help and <u>he</u> fed <u>it</u> sticks.

2   Using pronouns (15 minutes)

Learning intention: To identify pronouns.

Resources: Learner's Book, Session 4.3, Activity 2; Workbook, Session 4.3, Activities 2 and 3

Description: Ask learners how they recognised which words were pronouns in the sentences (e.g. knowing examples of pronouns; knowing when a word was meaning one of the nouns in the story). Explain that learners are going to re-read *Bear and Fire* and find more pronouns. Ask learners to make a list of the pronouns they find.

When learners have completed the task, ask them to peer mark their answers. You could use the Practice and Challenge activities of the Workbook to provide further practice.

> **Differentiation ideas:** Support learners by asking them to organise the list of pronouns under three headings: *Bear (and his people)*, *Fire* and *Man*.

Challenge learners by asking them to decide how to organise their list of pronouns (e.g. noun groups (bear, fire, man); male/female/neither male or female/plural; first/second/third person) and to think of additional pronouns to include.

> **Assessment ideas:** Note which learners can identify pronouns in a text.

Answers:
it, them, him, me, they, I, you, he, himself

3   Writing pronoun sentences (10–15 minutes)

Learning intention: To use pronouns in sentences.

Resources: Learner's Book, Session 4.3, Activity 3

Description: Write the following sentence on the board: *Fire warmed Bear and his people and it also gave them light.* Ask: *Does the sentence make sense* (yes)? Write on the board: *It warmed him and his people and it also gave them light.* Ask: *Is this sentence easy to understand* (no)? Explain that when we replace nouns and noun phrases with pronouns we need to make sure that it is easy for a reader to understand which noun the pronoun has replaced.

Direct learners to the activity in the Learner's Book. Explain that the sentences can include ideas from the story and the pictures. Allow time for learners to write the sentences.

> **Differentiation ideas:** Support learners by suggesting the sentences contain only one pronoun. Remind learners to use a capital letter at the start of the sentence and for proper nouns.

Challenge learners to use pronouns in different types of sentences.

> **Assessment ideas:** Can learners write sentences using pronouns? Are the sentences easy to understand?

Answers:
Learners' own sentences.

Plenary idea

Storytelling (5–10 minutes)

Resources: Space for learners to sit in a large circle

Description: Tell learners that they are going to retell the story in order. Ask learners to sit in a circle. Explain that each learner must only say one sentence of the story. The next learner continues and so on until the story has been told. Remind learners to use pronouns in their retelling.

Homework ideas

Ask learners to:

*   write about an activity or hobby they enjoy; ask learners to underline all the pronouns in the writing.

Answers for Workbook

1   Nouns: twigs, bear, food, flames
    Verbs: leapt, ate, chased, danced
    Pronouns: they, it, him, them

2   Fire was worried. <u>It</u> had almost gone out. But Man heard <u>its</u> calls for help and <u>he</u> came. Fire told Man what <u>it</u> liked to eat and Man went to look for twigs and sticks. <u>He</u> placed <u>them</u> down beside Fire. While Fire devoured <u>them</u>, Man warmed <u>himself</u>.

Nouns or noun phrases	Pronouns
Fire	it
Man	he / him
twigs and sticks	they / them

3

Male	*he*	*him*	*himself*
Female	she	<u>*her*</u>	<u>*herself*</u>
Plural	<u>*they*</u>	*them*	<u>*themselves*</u>
Neither male nor female	<u>*it*</u>	<u>*it*</u>	*itself*

4.4 What is a legend?

LEARNING PLAN		
Learning objectives	**Learning intentions**	**Success criteria**
3Rw.01, 3Rw.03, 3Rv.01, 3Rg.01, 3Rs.02, 3Ri.03, 3Ri.06, 3Ri.07, 3Ri.10, 3Ri.12, 3Ri.14, 3Ri.15, 3Ri.16, 3Ra.01, 3Ra.02, 3Ww.03, 3Wg.01, 3Wp.04	• Recognise and discuss the features of a legend. • Identify the main points and hidden meanings in a text. • Identify and spell words with a range of suffixes.	• Learners can recognise and discuss the features of a legend. • Learners can identify the main points and hidden meanings in a text. • Learners can identify and spell words with a range of suffixes.

Mulan is the most famous heroine in China, dating back to the 1st century. When you discuss the legend of Mulan, be sensitive to learners who may have experienced a member of their family being called to fight an invader or threat from others. Make sure discussions focus on Mulan's bravery and willingness to help her family.

You may want to explain unfamiliar vocabulary in the text (e.g. (weaving) *loom, nervous, confuse, troops*). Alternatively, you could take the opportunity to develop learners' dictionary skills and ask them to build a spelling log of new vocabulary.

Common misconceptions

Misconception	How to identify	How to overcome
Word endings (e.g. *–ed, –ly, –er*) are always suffixes.	Ask learners how many suffixes there are in *suddenly*. Note which learners identify one (*–ly*) and which learners identify two (e.g. *–en, –ly*).	Explain that if you remove *–ly, sudden* is a word but if you remove *–en, sudd* is not a word. Explain that when you remove a suffix the remaining letters must be a word. Remind learners that this is the root word. If the part of the word remaining is not a word on its own then the ending is not a suffix.

Starter idea

What is a legend? (10 minutes)

Resources: Learner's Book, Session 4.4: Getting started

Description: Ask learners to recall the features of a myth and note them on your board. Explain that in this session learners will read a legend. Then ask learners to read the Language focus box with a partner. Ask: *What is the same about a myth and a legend* (e.g. both myths and legends are passed on by word of mouth)*? What is the main difference between a myth and a legend* (e.g. myths are about things that are always unreal but legends include some things that are real)*?*

Read the first bullet point about legends aloud and check that learners understand the terms *hero* and *heroine*. Ask learners to suggest people who are heroes or heroines in history or their culture. Read the remaining two bullet points aloud.

Main teaching ideas

1. **Read the legend of *Mulan* (15–20 minutes)**

   Learning intention: To recognise and discuss the features of a legend.

Resources: *Mulan* (Learner's Book, Session 4.4, Activity 1); Track 22; dictionaries

Description: Explain that you are going to read a legend about a famous Chinese heroine called Mulan. Then, listen to the audio.

Direct learners to the Glossary terms in the Learner's Book. Then, ask learners to read the text to themselves quietly. Remind them to break unfamiliar words into small parts and to use the clues in the text to help them work out what the word means. When learners have finished reading, discuss any unfamiliar vocabulary they identified. Encourage other learners to offer explanations.

Ask learners which features of legends they noticed in the story. Remind them to refer to the Getting started section and the character and speech bubble.

> **Differentiation ideas:** Support learners who find it difficult to read large quantities of text by re-reading the text to them.

Challenge learners who are confident at reading to read sections of the text aloud.

> **Assessment ideas:** Note which learners could explain the meaning of unfamiliar vocabulary.

Answers:

There is a heroine as the main character – Mulan; the heroine completed a dangerous task; pretending she was a boy so that she could join the army; Mulan is a well-known Chinese heroine.

2 Answer the questions (15–20 minutes)

Learning intention: To identify the main points and hidden meanings in a text.

Resources: Learner's Book, Session 4.4, Activity 2

Description: Ask learners to re-read the text with a partner and then write their answers to the questions in their notebooks. Remind learners to refer to the text and to use capital letters for the start of each sentence and proper nouns.

Allow time for learners to answer the questions and then peer mark their answers. Ask: *Which questions had answers that were easy to find in the text* (a and b are explicit)*? Which questions expected you to use the clues in the text* (c, d and e are implicit or require learners to infer Mulan's feelings and character)*? Were you able to use the clues?*

> **Differentiation ideas:** Support learners by directing them to appropriate sections of the text for each question.

Challenge learners to think of two more questions that they could ask their partners about the text.

> **Assessment ideas:** Learners are encouraged to answer questions about the text using sentences. Note which learners:

- show implicit and explicit understanding of the text
- use complex sentence structures
- spell high-frequency words accurately
- spell more complex words accurately.

Answers:

a   Because every family needed to send a man to join the army and there was no one in her family who could go.

b   She tied her hair up and used her deepest voice.

c   Possible answers: scared, brave, pleased, proud.

d   Learners' own answers.

e   Learners' own answers.

3 Exploring suffixes (15–20 minutes)

Learning intention: To identify and spell words with a range of suffixes.

Resources: Learner's Book, Session 4.4, Activity 3; Workbook, Session 4.4; dictionaries

Description: Write *quietly* on the board. Ask: *What would the word be if I removed '–ly' from the end of the word?* Explain that a group of letters (e.g. *–ly*, *–ment* and *–ed*) that can be added to or removed from the end of a word is called a *suffix*. Explain that a word with the suffix removed is known as the *root word*. Write the word *suffix* on the board. Direct learners to the word *fix* within the word *suffix* and say: *We fix the letters to the root word.*

Direct learners to the Language focus box. Read the *bright* words with each suffix. Then read each suffix so that learners know how to say each of them. Read the second part of the Language focus box. Ask: *Can you think of any other words with more than one suffix* (e.g. nervously, protectiveness, exhaustively)*?*

Explain that learners should look for the root word when deciding whether a word ending is a suffix or not. Encourage learners to use a dictionary to check the meaning of words if necessary. Allow time for learners to complete the activity in the Learner's Book. Ask: *Which words did you find? Which suffixes did you notice?* You could use the Workbook activities to provide further practice with suffixes now if there is time in class.

> **Differentiation ideas:** Support learners by asking them to find words with the suffixes *–ed*, *–ing*, *–our*, *–ive* and *–ion* from *'I'm just the right age...'* to the end of paragraph 1.

Challenge learners to record the words they find in a table with three columns: *Word, Root word, Suffix.*

> **Assessment ideas:** As learners explore suffixes, assess their vocabulary knowledge. Learners with limited vocabulary are likely to find it more difficult to identify suffixes. Some learners may benefit from being given the root word prior to identifying the word with its suffix.

Answers:

Words with suffixes in paragraph 1: morning, working, quietly, weaving, cooking, happily, playing, sighed, sighing, asked, poster, being, threatened, looked, looked, suddenly, practised, fighting, tried, speedy, protective, armour.

4 Exploring suffixes (10 minutes)

Learning intention: To identify and spell words with a range of suffixes.

Resources: Learner's Book, Session 4.4, Activity 4; Language worksheet 4A

Description: Ask learners to re-read the last two paragraphs of the story and to use these paragraphs to complete the task in the Learner's Book. Use Language worksheet 4A to provide further practice with suffixes.

› **Differentiation ideas:** Challenge learners to use the whole text and to find up to ten words with suffixes to add to the table they created in the previous exercise.

Answers:
Possible answers: arrived = –ed; deepest = –est; exhausting = –ing; officer = –er; beautiful = –ful.

Plenary idea

Twenty Questions game (5 minutes)

Description: Tell learners that they are going to play a version of Twenty Questions in teams of four or five. Explain that you are thinking of a story. The story could be a myth, a legend or an ordinary story. Tell learners that they should ask questions to find out which story type you are thinking of. Explain that you can only answer 'yes' or 'no'.

› **Assessment ideas:** This activity will help you assess which learners have a good understanding of the features of both myths and legends.

Homework ideas

Ask learners to:

* complete the Workbook activities for this session, if not completed in class
* draw a picture of a section of the story *Mulan* and write two or three sentences about that part of the story.

Answers for Workbook

1 Learners should underline: tied, looked, arrived, nervous, notice, used, deepest, exhausting, missed, worked.

2   a   quietly = quiet
    b   looked = look
    c   suddenly = sudden
    d   deepest = deep
    e   exhausting = exhaust
    f   impressed = impress

3   Possible answers:
    a   dangerous: something could hurt or harm you
    b   nervous: feeling worried or anxious about something
    c   beautiful: very pretty
    d   deepest: the lowest you can go
    e   quietly: to make as little noise as possible
    f   impressed: to think that someone has done something well

4.5 Looking at paragraphs

LEARNING PLAN		
Learning objectives	**Learning intentions**	**Success criteria**
3Rv.02, 3Rv.04, 3Rv.06, 3Rs.01, 3Rs.02, 3Rs.03, 3Rs.04, 3Ri.07, 3Ri.12, 3Ri.17, 3Wv.04, 3Wv.05, 3Ws.02, 3Ws.03, 3Wc.02, 3Wp.02	• Recognise paragraphs. • Identify adverbs and sentence openers that act as adverbs. • Identify the most important events of a story. • Understand how paragraph openings establish links in a story.	• Learners can recognise paragraphs. • Learners can identify adverbs and adverbial phrases. • Learners can identify the most important events of a story. • Learners can understand how paragraph openings establish links in a story.

Learners will explore a variety of adverbs and sentence openers that contain adverbs (e.g. *Later that day, In the morning, Soon*) in this session. In order to support learners' independent writing later in this unit, it would be helpful to establish a word bank of adverbs and sentence openers that learners can use. The plenary task in this session invites learners to create individual posters of adverbs and sentence openers. If time is short, reduce the task to asking learners to suggest adverbs and sentence openers for a class word bank.

Common misconceptions

Misconception	How to identify	How to overcome
Learners think that new lines for each speaker are the same as new paragraphs.	Ask learners to record words at the start of paragraphs. Learners may include words at the start of speech (e.g. when reading or counting paragraphs in *Bear and Fire*).	Remind learners that new paragraphs are started when there is a new idea. Ask learners to read the dialogue between Man and Fire in the story *Bear and Fire*. Ask learners what the main idea is in the section where Fire says *Feed me! Feed me* (e.g. Fire needs feeding). Now ask what the main idea is when Man says *What should I feed you?* (e.g. Fire still needs feeding). Continue to where Fire dances in delight. Elicit from learners that the conversation between Man and Fire has all been about the same idea (e.g. Fire needs feeding) so it is all part of the same paragraph.

Starter idea

What is a paragraph? (5 minutes)

Resources: Learner's Book, Session 4.5: Getting started; a selection of fiction and non-fiction books

Description: Organise learners into groups of four or five. Give each group a selection of books. Ask learners to look at a page in a book and talk to each other about how the writing is set out. Try to elicit that the writing is broken into sections. Ask learners to recall what these sections are called. Try to elicit the term *paragraph*. Direct learners to the Learner's Book and allow a few minutes for them to discuss how paragraphs make the story easier to understand.

Main teaching ideas

1 Looking for paragraphs (15 minutes)

Learning intention: To recognise paragraphs.

Resources: Learner's Book, Session 4.5, Activity 1

Description: Direct learners to the Language focus box. Ask for a volunteer to read the first explanation about a paragraph. Ask learners to read the two paragraphs from *Bear and Fire*.

Organise learners into pairs and ask them to agree what the first paragraph is about (e.g. Bear and Fire being together). Then ask learners to agree what the second paragraph is about (e.g. Bear leaves Fire and goes to look for food). Confirm with learners that the two paragraphs are about two different things.

Ask for a second volunteer to read the second explanation about a paragraph. Ask: *What does 'indented' mean?* (e.g. set a little further in than the main text) Remind learners that dialogue (or speech) is also set out on a new line for each speaker. Explain that the way dialogue is laid out is not the same as using a paragraph.

Direct learners to the text *Bear and Fire* and ask partners to count the number of paragraphs in the story. Remind learners that you can often identify paragraphs because they are often indented.

> **Differentiation ideas:** Support learners by pairing with confident readers.

Challenge learners to identify the main point in each paragraph (e.g. paragraph 3: *Man came along and fed Fire*; paragraph 4: *Fire belonged to Man*).

> **Assessment ideas:** Learners who can identify the main point of a given paragraph will find it easier to understand that paragraphs are used to contain single ideas. Note which learners find this task challenging.

Answers:
five paragraphs

2 Paragraph beginnings (10–15 minutes)

Learning intention: To understand how paragraph openings establish links in a story.

Resources: Learner's Book, Session 4.5, Activity 2; Workbook, Session 4.5, Activities 1 and 2; *Bear and Fire* (Learner's Book, Session 4.1); Track 21

Description: Ask learners to recall what a phrase is. Direct them to the character text if necessary. Ask learners to look at *Bear and Fire* again with a partner and identify the phrase at the beginning of each paragraph. Remind learners not to include phrases at the start of speech. Allow time for learners to copy the phrases into their notebooks.

Ask a volunteer to read the information in part b. Discuss each of the phrases, then direct learners to the Writing tip and read the tip aloud. Ask learners to suggest other phrases that could be used to begin a paragraph (e.g. All at once; Suddenly; Once upon a time; Long, long ago; Later; The next day). Use the Focus and Practice activities in the Workbook for further practice.

> **Differentiation ideas:** Support learners by pairing them with more confident readers.

> **Assessment ideas:** Which learners were able to suggest phrases for paragraph openings? Do learners understand the purpose of these phrases?

Answers:
a   In the beginning; One day; At that moment; A long time later.
b   Possible answers: they put the story in order; they tell you when something happened.

3 Paragraph details (20 minutes)

Learning intention: To identify the most important events of a story.

Resources: Learner's Book, Session 4.5, Activity 3; Worksheet 4.1; A3 sheets of paper; pencils and crayons

Description: Direct learners to part a. Show learners how to fold the paper to create the boxes, or provide learners with an A3 copy of Worksheet 4.1 Story boxes. Encourage learners to use the illustration in the Learner's Book to draw the additional sections in each box.

Direct learners to part b and ask: *What would help you identify the most important events of the story?* If necessary, ask learners to count the number of paragraphs in the story to elicit from learners that each paragraph will have a new idea about each part of the story.

Ask learners to discuss each paragraph with a partner and agree the main point. Allow time for learners to draw pictures and add the words and phrases to describe the event.

> **Differentiation ideas:** Support learners by reading the text one paragraph at a time. Ask learners what kind of picture they think of when they hear the paragraph (e.g. paragraph 1: Mulan telling the family the news; paragraph 2: Mulan dressing up as boy). Support learners to recognise that what they picture in their mind is the clue to the main point of that part of the story.

Challenge learners to write a short sentence for each picture and to underline the key words or phrase within each sentence.

> **Assessment ideas:** Can learners identify the main points in each paragraph?

Answers:

b   Possible answers for five most important events (possible phrases underlined):

Mulan's family have to send one man from every family to join the army to help their country.

Mulan disguised herself as a boy and began life in the army.

Mulan took part in her first battle.

Mulan led her troops into many winning battles but still missed her family.

Mulan returned to her family.

4   Finding adverbs (10 minutes)

Learning intention: To identify adverbs and sentence openers that act as adverbs.

Resources: Learner's Book, Session 4.5, Activity 4

Description: Direct learners to the activity. Explain that if the adverbs are part of a sentence opener (e.g. *Soon it was time*) learners should underline the phrase. Allow time for learners to complete the task and then peer mark as a class.

> **Differentiation ideas:** Support learners by identifying the adverbs in a group.

Challenge learners to identify other adverbs and sentence openers in the books used in the Getting started activity.

> **Assessment ideas:** Learners who can identify adverbs and sentence openers will find it easier to understand how these paragraph openings signal a change. Note which learners are unable to identify sentence openers.

Answers:
Early one morning; At dawn; Soon it was time; Time passed; When she arrived; Her story travelled

Plenary idea

Adverb posters (10 minutes)

Resources: A4 or A3 paper for each learner; coloured pens and crayons

Description: Ask learners to recall the sentence openers discussed earlier in the session. Explain that they are going to design posters to show the adverbs and sentence openers that they have identified during this session. Encourage learners to use handwriting that is large, neat and colourful.

Homework ideas

Ask learners to:

*   complete the Challenge activity in the Workbook
*   finish adverb posters, if not completed in class
*   write a list of what they did at home using adverbs or sentence openers to organise the list (e.g. First; To begin with; First of all; After that; Next; Before; The last thing).

Answers for Workbook

1   Answers arranged in Venn diagram:
When: Yesterday; Eventually; In the year 2050; During the night; Later; In the morning; At six o'clock
When and where: When she reached the castle
Where: Outside; Under my bed; Near the lake; In the garden

2   Learners' own answers. Possible answers:
a   Yesterday the chief called a meeting and explained that the dragon was eating too many people.

b   Eventually they decided to ask if anyone would fight the dragon.

c   When she reached the castle the girl said that she would like to try. Everyone laughed.

d   During the night the girl set off to find the dragon.

e   Near the lake she saw the dragon's cave.
f   Outside there was an enormous dragon.

3   Learners' own answers.

4.6 Joining sentences

LEARNING PLAN

Learning objectives	Learning intentions	Success criteria
3Rg.05, 3Rg.06, 3Rg.07, 3Rg.08, 3Rs.01, 3Wv.05, 3Wg.04, 3Wg.05, 3Wp.01	• Identify the subject and verb/verb phrase in a sentence. • Identify multi-clause sentences using simple connectives of time, place and cause. • Write multi-clause sentences using simple connectives of time, place and cause.	• Learners can identify the subject and verb/verb phrase in a sentence. • Learners can identify multi-clause sentences using simple connectives of time, place and cause. • Learners can write multi-clause sentences using simple connectives of time, place and cause.

LANGUAGE SUPPORT

During this session, encourage learners to recognise and use technical terms for different parts of a sentence (e.g. subject, verb phrase, clause, multi-clause). Encourage learners to begin to build a word bank for different types of connective so that they have this to draw on for future writing.

Common misconceptions

Misconception	How to identify	How to overcome
That *and* always indicates a multi-clause sentence.	Ask learners to identify multi-clause sentences. Some learners may include examples such as *Man and Fire were very happy together; ... her family and home.*	Explain to learners that *and* can be used to pair names or items (e.g. *Man and Fire; family and home*). Ask learners to think of words that are usually paired together (e.g. bread and butter, fish and chips, rice and noodles). Here, *and* is a connective connecting two words, but it is not connecting two clauses.

Starter idea

Word class recap (15 minutes)

Resources: Learner's Book, Session 4.6: Getting started; individual whiteboards if available; whiteboard pens

Description: Recap different word classes learners know (e.g. nouns, adjectives, pronouns, sentence openers, verbs). Tell learners that you will name a word class and they should write an example on their whiteboards. Tell learners to keep the word hidden until you say *Show me.* If no small whiteboards are available, you can ask for several examples from learners before moving on to a new word class.

For each word class ask: *Can you give me an example of a... ?* After a minute, say: *Show me.* Check that learners have written a word from that word class. Direct learners to the Getting started activity.

Main teaching ideas

1 Joining simple sentences (10 minutes)

Learning intention: To identify the subject and verb/verb phrase in a sentence.

Resources: Learner's Book, Session 4.6, Activity 1

Description: On the board, write: *Her little brother was playing with his toys.* Ask: *What is the subject of this sentence?* Try to elicit from learners that the subject of the sentence is *Mulan's little brother.* Explain that the verb or verb phrase is always linked to the subject of the sentence and that together they make a clause. Ask: *What is the main clause in* She tied her hair up so she looked like a boy? (*She tied her hair up*) Explain that a clause has a complete meaning on its own but that sometimes extra information is added to create interest (*so she looked like a boy*).

Direct learners to the Language focus box and read the information about simple sentences. Allow time for learners to complete the activity in the Learner's Book.

> **Differentiation ideas:** Support learners through small group work.

Challenge learners to identify and underline the clause in each sentence, as well as the subject and verb/verb phrase.

> **Assessment ideas:** Note those who cannot identify the subject of the sentence.

Answers:
Learners may include the verb phrase in some sentences. If learners identify a verb phrase, learners should also underline the verb phrase as part of the clause.

a   Mulan; made up
b   Mulan; found
c   battles; were dangerous
d   Mulan; walked out

2 Writing multi-clause sentences (15 minutes)

Learning intention: To write multi-clause sentences using simple connectives of time, place and cause.

Resources: Learner's Book, Session 4.5, Activity 2; Workbook, Session 4.5

Description: Direct learners to the Language focus box and read the information about multi-clause sentences. On the board, write: *The Emperor*

offered Mulan a reward. Mulan asked to go home to her family.

Ask: *Are these both simple sentences? How do you know* (they both have one verb)? Invite learners to suggest connectives to join the two sentences together (e.g. and, so). Explain that finding the link between the two sentences will give learners a clue about which connective to use.

Organise learners into pairs and ask them to discuss possible clauses to add to each sentence in the Learner's Book. Direct learners to the Writing tip. Allow time for learners to complete the task, then share some examples of learners' answers. Ask: *Are your new sentences single clause or multi-clause sentences* (multi-clause)? *How do you know?* (because they have two verbs; because the clauses are joined with a connective) Use the Workbook activities to provide further practice.

> **Differentiation ideas:** Support learners by encouraging them to try each connective at the end of each simple sentence to see which sounds right, before they add an additional clause.

Challenge learners to write additional sentences using other connectives (e.g. or, because, if).

> **Assessment ideas:** Note which learners miss out some pronouns when joining two simple sentences with a connective. Do any learners find it difficult to choose appropriate connectives?

Answers:
Learners' own answers. Possible suggestions for completing each sentence:
a   Mulan's family didn't want her to join the army but Mulan would not be stopped.
b   Mulan left home early one morning and joined the other soldiers.
c   Her family were very grateful because Mulan was helping them.
d   Mulan arrived home then changed into a dress.

3 Finding multi-clause sentences (15–20 minutes)

Learning intention: To identify multi-clause sentences using simple connectives of time, place and cause.

Resources: Learner's Book, Session 4.5, Activity 3

Description: Remind learners that a clause has a subject plus a verb or verb phrase. Ask: *What type* of *word connects two clauses* (a connective)? Direct learners to the activity in the Learner's Book.

Tell learners to write each sentence in neat and clear handwriting and use correct punctuation.

> **Differentiation ideas:** Support learners by asking them to read each paragraph in pairs. Ask them to look for connectives as they read the text.

Challenge learners to identify other sentences in the text that could be joined with a connective. Ask them to write these in their notebooks and to underline the connective in each one.

> **Assessment ideas:** Note learners who need further handwriting practice. Did learners use correct sentence punctuation?

Answers:
Possible sentences:
Her mother was cooking and her little brother was happily playing.
She tied her hair up so she looked like a boy.
She missed her family, but she didn't give up.
I have practised fighting with Father and I should be the one to join the army.
She went inside the house so she could let down her hair and put on a dress.

Plenary idea

Connectives Flower (5 minutes)

Description: This game is played using the rules of Hangman but involves drawing a flower in a pot instead of the hangman's scaffold. For each incorrect answer draw the following parts:

*   the two sides and bottom of the pot
*   an oval rim to the pot
*   a stalk
*   two leaves
*   five petals.

Learners must guess the connective before the drawing is complete. Explain that you are thinking of a connective (e.g. because, although, nevertheless, therefore). Draw a dash on the board for each letter of the word you have chosen. Tell learners that they must suggest letters for the word. If the letter is in the word, you will write the letter on the appropriate dash (or dashes). Explain that each time learners suggest a letter that is wrong, you will add another part of a flower.

Homework ideas

Ask learners to:

*   complete the Workbook activities for this session, if not completed in class
*   find ten examples of multi-clause sentences using books, newspapers and magazines.

Answers for Workbook

1   a   Jamilla had to find her watch so she could find out if she was late.

    b   The cricket captain was nervous but he was sure they were going to win.

    c   The snow covered everything overnight.

    d   Kyle was hungry but he had no time to eat his lunch.

2   Learners' own sentences.

3   Learners' own sentences.

4.7 Making links

LEARNING PLAN

Learning objectives	Learning intentions	Success criteria
3Ri.03, 3Ri.06, 3Ri.07, 3Ri.10, 3Ri.12, 3Ri.13, 3Ri.15, 3Ri.16, 3Ri.17, 3Ra.02, 3Ra.03, 3Wp.02, 3SLg.01, 3SLg.02, 3SLg.03, 3SLg.04	• Identify features of myths and legends. • Compare and contrast myths and legends. • Explore myths and legends in learners' own cultures.	• Learners can identify the features of myths and legends. • Learners can compare and contrast myths and legends. • Learners can explore myths and legends in their own cultures.

LANGUAGE SUPPORT

Some learners may benefit from you recapping some of the vocabulary used in *Bear and Fire*, and *Mulan*.

Starter idea

Choose your favourite (5 minutes)

Resources: Learner's Book, Session 4.7: Getting started

Description: Organise learners into small groups and ask each group to assign specific roles to group members (scribe, chairperson, reporter). Direct learners to the Getting started activity and draw their attention to the Listening tip.

Allow time for discussion and then ask the reporter from each group to feed back a summary of the group's views.

Main teaching ideas

1 Features of myths and legends (15 minutes)

Learning intention: To identify the features of myths and legends.

Resources: Learner's Book, Session 4.7, Activity 1

Description: Explain that learners will continue to work in their groups and that group members should swap roles. Direct learners to the Learner's Book and allow them time to re-read the features of myths in Session 4.1 and the features of legends in Session 4.4.

Ask the following questions to aid discussions: *Do you have information about when myths or legends take place? Do both types of story involve real characters? What else have you noticed?*

> **Differentiation ideas:** Support learners by displaying features of both text types.

> **Assessment ideas:** Note which learners understand the features of myths and legends.

Answers:
Possible answers: both myths and legends take place long ago; legends often give some idea of when they happened; characters are not real people in myths; events unlikely to happen in myths but might happen in legends.

2 Comparing stories (20–25 minutes)

Learning intention: To compare and contrast myths and legends.

Resources: Learner's Book, Session 4.7, Activity 2; Worksheet 4.2; *Bear and Fire* (Learner's Book, Session 4.1); Track 21; *Mulan* (Learner's Book, Session 4.4); Track 22

Description: Direct learners to the task in the Learner's Book. Allow learners time to re-read *Bear and Fire* and *Mulan*. Ask learners to suggest what they might write in the *When?* box for *Bear and Fire*. Explain that answers do not need to be long.

The last paragraph of the legend of Mulan refers to the events having *travelled far and wide* and *still being told to this day*. This is the only information that places the legend in the past so learners may need support in completing the *When?* box of the table.

Allow time for learners to complete the rest of the table, then ask: *What is the same about the two stories* (e.g. they both happened a long time ago)? *What is different about the stories* (e.g. the characters do not really exist in *Bear and Fire* but are real in *Mulan*)?

> **Differentiation ideas:** Support learners as they complete the first column. Consider providing Worksheet 4.2 Comparison chart as a template for the activity.

Challenge learners by asking them to add a fourth column to the table and to compare a third story (e.g. another myth or legend they know).

> **Assessment ideas:** Note which learners were able to complete each box in the table. Which learners needed additional support?

Answers:
Possible answers:

	Myth *Bear and Fire*	Legend *Mulan*
When?	It happened a very long time ago because the text says *In the beginning*.	It happened a long time ago. The text says *it's still being told to this day*.
Where?	Near a forest.	In Mulan's home country and in an army camp.
Characters	Bear, Man and Fire. Characters come from the natural world and could not really exist.	Mulan, her family, the soldiers, the Emperor.
Main event	Fire gets hungry and Man feeds him sticks. Man learned how to use fire to keep him warm.	Mulan joined the army and became a well-known officer because she helped her troops win many battles.

Theme/ lesson	It explains how people found fire.	We can all be brave when it is important.

3 Other myths and legends (5–10 minutes)

Learning intention: To explore myths and legends in learners' own cultures.

Resources: Learner's Book, Session 4.7, Activity 2; Workbook, Session 4.7

Description: With a partner, learners should suggest sentences to explain what a myth is and what a legend is (e.g. a myth is about something that could never happen but explains something difficult; a legend is about a famous person and makes that person seem more powerful or braver than they were). Ask learners to share their sentences.

Ask: *Have you heard any other myths about fire* (e.g. *Rabbit Steals the Fire*)? *Have you read or heard any myths about animals or the weather* (e.g. Thunder – Thor riding his chariot across the sky)? *Do you know any legends about other famous people? Are there any legends about a country you know? Do you know any local legends?*

Allow time for learners to discuss myths and legends they know with their talk partners. You could use the Workbook activities to provide a story to discuss if there is time in class.

Answers:
Learners' own answers.

Plenary idea

Myth or legend? (5–10 minutes)

Description: Invite a learner to share a myth or legend they know. Tell the volunteer that they must not say whether the story is a myth or legend. Explain that as they listen to the story, learners must decide whether the story is a myth or a legend.

CROSS-CURRICULAR LINKS

History: Research legends about a character from a particular period of history within learners' own culture.

Homework ideas

Ask learners to:

- complete the Workbook activities for this session, if not completed in class

- talk to family members about myths and legends they know, then write a short paragraph about each one.

Answers for Workbook

1 **a** a myth
   b Possible learners' answers: there are characters from the natural world; it explains how something is; it happened in the long ago past; these are events that do not happen in the real world, such as sticks becoming bored.

2 Possible answers:

	A Visit from Strangers from Another Place
When?	In the long ago past.
Where?	Far, far away and a land where Aboriginal people lived.

	A Visit from Strangers from Another Place
Characters	Kanbi and Jitabidi Fire sticks Aboriginal people
Main event	Aboriginal people saw fire for the first time and enjoyed the heat and the light fire gave.
Theme/ lesson	Fire can be dangerous if left alone but can also be a wonderful gift, giving heat and light.

3 **a** They lived far, far away; **c** They had fire.

4 Kanbi and Jitabidi went to explore the world and hunt for possum.

5 Kanbi and Jitabidi knew there was a fire because they heard the flames and smelled the smoke.

6 The Aboriginal people thought the fire was a loud, orange monster.

7 The Aboriginal people liked the heat and light the fire gave.

8 Kanbi and Jitabidi

9 *agreed*

4.8 Rewriting a myth

LEARNING PLAN

Learning objectives	Learning intentions	Success criteria
3Rs.01, 3Rs.02, 3Ri.02, 3Ri.03, 3Ri.16, 3Ri.17, 3Ra.05, 3Ws.01, 3Wc.01, 3Wc.02, 3Wp.02, 3Wp.04, 3SLm.01, 3SLm.05, 3SLs.01, 3SLg.02, 3SLp.04	• Role play a retelling of a myth. • Compare two versions of a myth. • Write a retelling of a myth using a storyboard.	• Learners can role play a retelling of a myth. • Learners can compare two versions of a myth. • Learners can write a retelling of a myth using a storyboard.

Starter idea

Different settings (5 minutes)

Resources: Learner's Book, Session 4.8: Getting started

Description: If appropriate, remind learners of their work on settings from Unit 1. Ask: *What do we mean by the 'setting' of a story? What is the setting for* Bear and Fire? Direct learners to the Learner's Book and ask them to write their lists with a partner.

Main teaching ideas

1 Listen to a myth (15 minutes)

Learning intention: To compare two versions of a myth.

Resources: *Bear and Fire, the myth* (Learner's Book, Session 4.8, Activity 1); Track 23

Description: Ask: *What was the theme of* Bear and Fire? (how Man found fire) If you have used the Workbook activity for Session 4.7, ask: *What was the theme of the Aboriginal story in Session 4.7 of the Workbook?* (how the Aboriginal tribe found fire) Explain that because myths are passed on from person to person the same myth can be told in different ways and in different settings.

Explain that learners are to listen to another version of *Bear and Fire.* Encourage learners to make notes about the characters and setting as they listen.

Allow time for learners to complete the first two questions in their notebooks. Discuss the features of a myth that learners noticed in the story.

> **Differentiation ideas:** Support learners by pairing them with more confident learners.

Challenge learners to create a two-column table to record the events in both stories and colour code what is the same and what is different.

Audioscript: *Bear and Fire, the myth*

Fire and Bear began as really good friends. Bear carried Fire with him everywhere; he realised how important Fire was. It kept him warm and provided light. Fire was happy with their friendship until Bear did something silly.

One day, Bear and Fire were out walking along a beautiful beach. The sun was out and there was only a very gentle breeze. Unusually Bear decided to put Fire down while he went off looking for food. Fire didn't mind, it was burning well and felt happy looking out at the sea.

As time passed, Fire began to worry. It continued to burn well, Bear had left him with plenty of wood, but the sea was getting closer. Occasionally a splash of water would hit Fire and it would hear a sizzle and the flames would drop. Fire realised water wasn't good. He started shouting…loudly!

Bear was too far away and couldn't hear but in the distance Man was walking along the beach. He heard the calls of 'Help! Help!'. Looking around

Man spotted Fire in the distance. He ran towards Fire as quickly as he could.

Fire cried, "Please help me, move me away from the water, once I get wet I am nothing."

Quickly, Man carefully picked up Fire and moved him away from the sea. He then placed Fire well out of reach of the incoming waves. He fed Fire with more sticks until his blaze was strong again.

Eventually Bear returned and was surprised to see that Fire had moved. Fire was angry. Bear's actions could have put Fire out forever! Fire told Bear to leave, and that they wouldn't ever be friends again. So from that day to this, Fire has belonged to Man.

Answers:

a   Same: Fire and Bear were good friends; Bear went to look for food and left Fire alone; Fire almost went out; Man came along and gave Fire food; Fire and Man became friends; Bear returned; Fire was angry with Bear; Fire belonged to Man.

b   Different: the setting is a beach not a forest; the sea was beginning to put Fire out; Man moved Fire to a safer place; Fire explained why he was angry with Bear.

c   Yes. Possible reasons: it explains events that could not happen in the real world, such as Fire's talking; it explains a natural event, such as what happens to Fire when it gets wet.

2 Role play (20 minutes)

Learning intention: To role play a retelling of a myth.

Resources: Learner's Book, Session 4.8, Activity 2; Workbook, Session 4.8, Activity 1

Description: Organise learners into pairs and ask them to discuss what is the same and what is different about the two versions of the fire myth. Establish that although the two versions of the myth were slightly different, they were both still about how man found fire. Use the Focus activity in the Workbook to support this.

Direct learners to the activity in the Learner's Book. Organise learners into groups of three and ask groups to decide what the setting for their role play of the story will be. Encourage learners to use settings from the lists written at the start of the session. Allow time for learners to try different settings for their role play. Then ask each group to share the setting they thought worked best.

> **Differentiation ideas:** Support learners as they choose a setting. Guide learners to develop their role play using questioning. Ask: *What kind of character has Fire to begin with? Why does that character put Fire down? What happens to Fire? What kind of character comes along and notices what has happened to Fire? How do the characters feel at the end of the story?*

Challenge learners to think of something a character might say, then use expression in their role play to show the character's personality.

> **Assessment ideas:** Note which learners listened well to the ideas of others. Were learners able to identify a suitable setting for their new myth?

3 Make a storyboard (20–25 minutes)

Learning intention: To write a retelling of a myth using a storyboard.

Resources: Learner's Book, Session 4.8, Activity 3; Workbook, Session 4.8, Activity 1; Worksheet 4.1

Description: Explain that learners are to draw their own version of the fire myth using a storyboard. Direct learners to the definition of a storyboard if appropriate. Remind learners of the story box grids used in Session 4.5 of the Learner's Book. Explain that the storyboard will look similar, and that learners can use one of the ideas they used in their roleplay for their myth, or a completely new idea.

Before learners start, encourage them to plan which part of the myth will be in each box. You could refer learners back to the Focus activity in the Workbook to use as a planning prompt. Allow time for learners to complete their storyboards.

Direct learners to the How are we doing? questions and allow time for learners to share their stories with their partners.

> **Differentiation ideas:** Support learners by choosing one of the versions suggested in the role play and plan the storyboard with a partner or as a group. Provide a copy of Worksheet 4.1 Story boxes for learners to complete.

Challenge learners to support a less confident learner.

> **Assessment ideas:** Were learners able to give constructive feedback about the new stories to their

partners? Was feedback given sensitively? Could learners adapt the story to today's world?

Answers:
Learners' own ideas.

Plenary idea

Check your myth (5 minutes)

Resources: Learners' storyboards from Activity 3

Description: Ask learners to check that their storyboard myth covers all the features of myths. Encourage learners to use the information about myths in Session 4.2.

Homework ideas

Ask learners to:

*   complete the Practice and Challenge activities in the Workbook

*   make as many words as they can out of 'Bear and Fire' (e.g. in, if, be, ran, rain, red, bee, ear, bed, bad, bead, bread, bend, bird, idea, read, dear, band, beard, friend, afraid). You could set a target of 20 words.

Answers for Workbook

1

Bear and Fire	Pattern
Bear owned Fire.	introducing characters 1 and 2
Bear left fire by the edge of the wood and wandered off. Fire got hungry	character 1 leaves character 2 character 2 needs character 1
Man came and fed Fire	<u>character 3 helps character 2</u>
Man and Fire became friends	characters 2 and 3 become friends
Bear came back	character 1 returns
<u>Fire chased Bear away</u>	character 2 chases character 1 away
Fire now belonged to Man	<u>characters 2 and 3 stay friends</u>

2   Learners' own answers for their own myths.

3   Learners' own answers based on their own myths.

4.9 Exploring a legend

LEARNING PLAN

Learning objectives	Learning intentions	Success criteria
3Rw.02, 3Rw.03, 3Rg.01, 3Rg.03, 3Rs.02, 3Ri.02, 3Ri.03, 3Ri.06, 3Ri.07, 3Ri.10, 3Ri.12, 3Ri.14, 3Ri.15, 3Ri.16, 3Ri.17, 3Ra.01, 3Ra.02, 3Wg.02	• Read and answer questions about a legend. • Identify the features of a legend. • Understand how the apostrophe takes the place of missing letters in words.	• Learners can read and answer questions about a legend. • Learners can identify the features of a legend. • Learners can understand how the apostrophe takes the place of missing letters in words.

LANGUAGE SUPPORT

The stories of Sinbad the Sailor form part of the Persian sagas recorded in *The Thousand and One Nights*.

Learners will be used to seeing apostrophes in texts and hearing their use in spoken English. At Stage 3, learners are introduced to apostrophes for omission and do not need to use apostrophes for possession until Stage 4.

Common misconceptions

Misconception	How to identify	How to overcome
An apostrophe always indicates that a letter has been missed out.	Ask learners to find all the contractions in *Sinbad and the Roc*. Learners may include *Roc's* (egg) where the apostrophe is used for possession.	Encourage learners to expand words with apostrophes to check for omission, then check that it makes sense when put with the next word (e.g. it's time = it is time; let's go = let us go; wasn't an island = was not an island; Roc's egg = Roc is egg). Tell learners that if the expanded version makes sense then the apostrophe has been used for contraction. If the expansion does not make sense then the apostrophe is not being used for contraction.

Starter idea

Who is Sinbad? (5 minutes)

Resources: Learner's Book, Session 4.9; stories about Sinbad the sailor

Description: Explain that in this session learners will explore legends about a sailor called Sinbad. Direct learners to the Getting started activity. If available, provide any stories about Sinbad the sailor for learners to explore.

Main teaching ideas

1 Read *Sinbad and the Roc* (20 minutes)

Learning intention: To read and answer questions about a legend.

Resources: *Sinbad and the Roc* (Learner's Book, Session 4.9, Activity 1); Track 24

Description: Before reading the story, ask learners to tell you what they know about the sea. Ask: *What does the phrase 'the sea was calm' mean? What does 'tossed about on the waves' mean?*

Ask for three volunteers to narrate each paragraph and for another volunteer to read what Sinbad says. When volunteers have read the story extract, explain that they should read the extract before answering the questions.

Allow time for learners to answer the questions in their notebooks, then direct learners to the Reflection question. Encourage learners to think about the strategies they used to find the answers to the questions. Ask: *When you checked the text did you always read the text carefully from the beginning?* Explain that reading sections of a text quickly to find an answer is known as *scanning* the text.

⟩ **Differentiation ideas:** Support learners by allowing them to give short answers to questions a to f and to answer questions g and h verbally in a group.

Challenge learners to give a reason for their answer to part g and use evidence from the text for their word choices to describe Sinbad's character.

⟩ **Assessment ideas:** Note which learners can scan a text to find answers to specific questions. Learners need to understand implicit meaning in order to answer questions about the Roc and Sinbad's characters. Note which learners can do this.

Answers:
a   Sinbad the sailor
b   He had no money left.
c   To faraway lands
d   A great storm blew up and the food and water were washed overboard.
e   Sinbad thought he would find food and water there.
f   It was a giant bird; the Roc's egg was huge.

g   Learners' own answers.
h   Possible answers: kind and generous (because he gave his money to the poor); brave (because he was not scared in the storm; he did not run away from the giant bird); calm (because he did not panic when the storm washed the food and water into the sea); adventurous (because he loved adventures).

2 Is *Sinbad and the Roc* a legend? (5–10 minutes)

Learning intention: To identify the features of a legend.

Resources: Learner's Book, Session 4.9, Activity 2

Description: Ask learners to re-read the features of a legend in Session 4.4. Then direct learners to Activity 2 in the Learner's Book. Ask learners to discuss the three questions with a partner. When learners have had time to discuss the questions, ask: *Do your answers match the features of a legend?*

⟩ **Differentiation ideas:** Challenge learners to support less confident readers.

⟩ **Assessment ideas:** Can learners recognise the features of a legend in *Sinbad and the Roc*?

Answers:
a   Yes – Sinbad the sailor.
b   Sinbad is in a storm at sea and then meets a giant bird.
c   It is probably about events linked to a culture.

3 Contractions (10 minutes)

Learning intention: To understand how the apostrophe takes the place of missing letters in words.

Resources: Learner's Book, Session 4.9, Activity 3; Workbook, Session 4.9; Language worksheet 4B

Description: Write *It's time for another adventure* on the board, then ask: *What is the name of the punctuation mark in the first word?* (apostrophe) Direct learners to the Language focus box. Ask: *Which letter has been missed out in 'It's'?*

In pairs, learners should re-read *Sinbad and the Roc* and list any words with an apostrophe to show a letter has been missed out (e.g. *It's*, *Let's*, *didn't*, *wasn't*, *That's*, *isn't*). You could use Language worksheet 4B at this point. Use the guidance in Common misconceptions if learners identify *Roc's* as a contraction.

Direct learners to the activity in the Learner's Book. Allow time for learners to complete the activity then peer mark answers. You could ask learners to complete the Workbook activities now.

> **Differentiation ideas:** Support learners who think every word with an apostrophe is a contraction using the guidance in Common misconceptions.

Challenge learners to collect other examples of contractions in other texts in a two-column list showing the contracted form and the expanded form (e.g. shan't = shall not; wouldn't = would not; haven't = have not; won't = will not).

> **Assessment ideas:** Are learners able to expand the contractions? Note which learners included *Roc's* as a contracted word. If further assessment is needed, provide learners with pairs of words and ask learners to write the contracted form.

Answers:
a   It's = It is
b   Let's = Let us
c   That's = That is
d   isn't = is not

Plenary idea

More contractions (5 minutes)

Resources: A variety of fiction texts

Description: Ask learners to find other examples of contracted words in their reading book or the fiction books available. If learners began a collection of contractions in the Workbook 4.9 Challenge activity, invite them to share the examples.

CROSS-CURRICULAR LINKS

Geography: Learners could explore the trade routes around the Indian Ocean at the time of Sinbad the sailor. What kind of things did they carry? Which countries were involved?

Homework ideas

Ask learners to:

- complete the Workbook activities for this session, if not completed in class

- research the elephant bird egg with a family member. The elephant bird may well have been the Roc mentioned in the stories of Sinbad. The elephant bird's egg is about 160 times greater in volume than a hen's egg and the elephant bird is thought to have been more than three metres tall!

Answers for Workbook

1   hasn't = has not; aren't = are not; could've = could have; you're = you are; it's = it is; she'll = she will

2   a   he'll = he will
    b   should've = should have
    c   isn't = is not
    d   that's = that is
    e   I'm = I am

3   Learners' own sentences.

4.10 Planning a legend

LEARNING PLAN

Learning objectives	Learning intentions	Success criteria
3Rv.06, 3Rs.02, 3Rs.04, 3Ri.11, 3Wv.04, 3Wv.05, 3Ws.01, 3Ws.02, 3Ws.03, 3Wc.01, 3Wc.02, 3Wc.03, 3Wp.02, 3Wp.04	• Predict what happens next in a story. • Plan a legend. • Use a variety of adverbs or sentence openers to begin paragraphs.	• Learners can predict what happens next in a story. • Learners can plan a legend. • Learners can use a variety of adverbs or sentence openers to begin paragraphs.

Starter idea

Who are the characters? (5 minutes)

Resources: Learner's Book, Session 4.10: Getting started

Description: Ask learners to re-read the extract from *Sinbad and the Roc*, then direct them to the Getting started activity.

Ask learners to discuss the characters in the story with their partners. If there is time, allow learners to research the giant Roc.

Draw three columns on the board and add the headings *Sinbad*, *The Roc* and *The sailors*. Record what learners know about each character in the appropriate column: *Sinbad* (e.g. kind, brave, generous, helpful), *The Roc* (e.g. gigantic bird, likes to eat snakes, has a nest of sticks, the Roc's egg is as big as a hill) and *The sailors* (e.g. afraid, worried, listen to Sinbad).

Main teaching ideas

1 What happens next? (10–15 minutes)

Learning intention: To predict what happens next in a story.

Resources: Learner's Book, Session 4.10, Activity 1; Worksheet 4.3; *Sinbad and the Roc* (Learner's Book, Session 4.3); Track 24

Description: Ask learners to re-read *Sinbad and the Roc* from Session 4.9. Explain that this is an extract and is only part of the story. Direct learners to the prompts in the Learner's Book and the picture of

Sinbad at the harbour's edge. Ask: *What do you think happened next?*

Ask learners to work with their partners as they discuss each prompt. Tell learners that there are no right or wrong answers but remind them to use what they know about Sinbad's character when making their predictions. Remind learners that Sinbad often finds treasure during his adventures and likes to use it to help other people. Ask: *Does this give you any ideas about what might happen next?*

Allow learners time for discussion, then invite learners to share their ideas.

❭ **Differentiation ideas:** Support learners in a group by agreeing simple answers to each prompt (e.g. a giant turtle; Sinbad hides from the Roc; Sinbad rides on a turtle's back; he gives the treasure to some poor people). Then use additional questions: *How did he meet the turtle? Where did Sinbad hide? Where did he find the treasure?* Ask learners to use the questions in Worksheet 4.3 Planning a legend decision tree and to colour the boxes they select.

Challenge learners to include at least one new character in the story.

❭ **Assessment ideas:** Can learners suggest ways to develop the story?

Answers:
Learners' own answers.

2 Create a storyboard (25 minutes)

Learning intention: To plan a legend.

Resources: Learner's Book, Session 4.10, Activity 2; Workbook, Session 4.10, Activity 1

Description: Explain that learners are now going to write their own story about Sinbad the sailor, based on what they know of the story so far. Direct learners to the activity for instructions for making a storyboard, or use the storyboard in the Focus section of the Workbook.

Ask: *How does the story begin?* (Sinbad goes to sea to find treasure but there is a big storm) *What does Sinbad do?* (he rows to an island) *What happens when he gets to the island?* (Sinbad realises that it is not an island, it is the Roc's nest) Write the answers to the questions on the board as prompts for your learners. Explain that learners should use these prompts to draw the pictures for the first three boxes on their storyboard. Explain that learners should fill in the other storyboard boxes using their own ideas for the ending. Tell them that they can add more boxes to the storyboard if they need to.

When learners have completed their storyboards, explain that each storyboard box will be a new paragraph in their story.

> **Differentiation ideas:** Support learners by reminding them to use each of the boxes they selected in Worksheet 4.3 to complete their storyboard. Explain that each coloured box will be a new paragraph.

Challenge learners to add notes of any new characters' names and to write a short description of each character and their role in the story.

> **Assessment ideas:** Note which learners made predictions that showed an understanding of how legends develop.

3 Paragraph beginnings (10 minutes)

Learning intention: To use a variety of adverbs or sentence openers to begin paragraphs.

Resources: Learner's Book, Session 4.10, Activity 3; Workbook, Session 4.10; Differentiated worksheet pack

Description: Ask learners to look at the beginning of the first two paragraphs in the Sinbad extract in Session 4.9 (*Once upon a time*; *At first*). Ask: *Can you remember what we call these words?* (adverbs, sentence openers) Ask learners to suggest other adverbs or sentence openers to use as paragraph beginnings. You could use Differentiated worksheets 4A–C.

Tell learners to choose an adverb or adverbial phrase to use in each paragraph of their own story and to write the adverb in the appropriate box on their storyboard. Learners could use the workbook activities for their planning.

> **Differentiation ideas:**

- Support learners with more limited vocabulary by providing a bank of adverbs to choose from (e.g. next, then, after that, finally). Encourage learners to use these words to sequence their story.

- Challenge learners to use interesting adverbs or sentence openers (e.g. suddenly, all at once, before, finally, at long last, in the distance, slowly and carefully).

> **Assessment ideas:** Note which learners can select appropriate sentence openers to sequence their stories.

Plenary idea

What did they say? (5–10 minutes)

Description: Ask learners to discuss the following questions with their partner: *What do you think Sinbad might have said when he realised he was in the Roc's nest? What do you think Sinbad's sailors might have said when they saw the Roc? What do you think people would have said when Sinbad returned home and gave them treasure?*

Homework ideas

Ask learners to:

- complete the Workbook activities for this session, if not used in class, or use the templates to plan a completely new adventure about Sinbad

- draw a picture of the Roc and add descriptive information about the bird (e.g. claws as sharp as knives, eyes that can see something two kilometres away). Note that some legends say that the Roc's wings were so enormous that they could block out the sun.

- use Differentiated worksheets 4A–C to provide further practice with adverbs and sentence openers if not used in class.

Answers for Workbook

1 Learners' own answers.

2 Possible characters and answers include:

Character	Description	Role in story
Sinbad	A sailor who has lots of adventures Likes giving money to poor people Very brave	Main character – is trying to rescue another sailor who is trapped on an island Manages to escape
Enormous serpent	Eats sailors Lives in a cave on a desert island	Is keeping Jack a prisoner Has lots of treasure at the back of its cave
Polly the parrot	Has a loud squawk Always says 'Go away' when the serpent is near	Helps Sinbad

Character	Description	Role in story
Jack	A sailor who is trapped on an island	Needs rescuing

3 Possible answers could include:

Paragraph 1	Many years ago; One day, when Sinbad ... ; In a far-away land
Paragraph 2	The following day; All at once; Later that night
Paragraph 3	Suddenly; Slowly; Quietly
Paragraph 4	Without a noise; As quick as lightning; Creeping silently
Paragraph 5	Before long; After a while; Swiftly
Paragraph 6	Finally; The next day; Happily

4.11 Writing a legend

LEARNING PLAN

Learning objectives	Learning intentions	Success criteria
3Ww.02, 3Ww.05, 3Ww.06, 3Wv.02, 3Wv.03, 3Wv.04, 3Wv.07, 3Wg.01, 3Wg.02, 3Wg.03, 3Wg.05, 3Ws.01, 3Ws.02, 3Ws.03, 3Wc.01, 3Wc.03, 3Wc.05, 3Wp.03, 3Wp.04, 3Wp.05, 3SLs.02, 3SLg.02	• Write a legend. • Use dialogue in a story. • Evaluate own and others' writing, suggesting improvements for sense, accuracy and content.	• Learners can write a legend. • Learners can use dialogue in a story. • Learners can evaluate own and others' writing, suggesting improvements for sense, accuracy and content.

Common misconceptions

Misconception	How to identify	How to overcome
When using dialogue, a comma always goes after what has been said, even when asking a question or exclaiming, OR question marks and exclamation marks go after the speaker (e.g. 'What are you doing', asked the sailor?).	Ask learners to include dialogue when writing their legends. Note where learners place punctuation for speech.	Ask learners to draw a stick person with a speech bubble. Then ask learners to write what the character says inside the speech bubble. Learners will see that a full stop, question mark or exclamation mark goes at the end of what has been said within the speech bubble. Explain that all the spoken words in a speech bubble must go inside the speech marks. You will need to explain that the full stop is replaced by a comma to show it is not the end of the sentence.

Starter idea

Recipe for a legend (5 minutes)

Resources: *How to write a legend* (Learner's Book, Session 4.11: Getting started); Track 25

Description: Explain that learners will be using their storyboard plans to write a legend of about Sinbad. Direct learners to the recipe for a legend in the Learner's Book. Ask learners to check that their storyboard plans include all the things from the recipe.

Main teaching ideas

1 Evaluate your storyboard (10 minutes)

Learning intention: To evaluate own and others' writing, suggesting improvements for sense, accuracy and content.

Resources: Learner's Book, Session 4.11, Activity 1

Description: Direct learners to part a. Encourage them to consider any changes they could make to their storyboard.

Direct learners to part b. Explain that as learners tell the story, partners should be thinking:

- Does the story make sense?
- Are there gaps in the story?
- Would another adverb be better?
- Does any dialogue match the character?

Allow time for learners to share storyboard ideas and make improvements.

> **Differentiation ideas:** Support and challenge learners by pairing less confident writers with more confident writers.

> **Assessment ideas:** Did learners identify changes when they proofread their stories? Were they able to give and accept constructive feedback?

2 Write your legend (25–30 minutes)

Learning intentions: To use dialogue in a story; to write a legend.

Resources: Learner's Book, Session 4.11, Activity 2; Workbook, Session 4.11; Worksheet 4.4; thesauruses

Description: Before learners begin to write, direct them to the Language focus box and remind them of the ideas they had about what Sinbad might say (Session 4.10, Plenary idea).

Ask learners to think about the speech verbs they could use instead of *said* and encourage them to add these words to their storyboard. If learners need further practice with setting out dialogue, use the Workbook activities or Worksheet 4.4 Adding speech marks at this point. Remind learners that they should use the ideas on the storyboard as they write their stories.

If appropriate, invite or select learners to write their stories using an IT programme. At this point in the writing process learners should not have access to onscreen tools such as spelling or grammar checkers.

Allow time for learners to write their stories.

> **Differentiation ideas:** Support learners by providing word banks for high-frequency words, adverbs and sentence openers, and words that can be used instead of *said*.

Challenge learners to use a thesaurus to find synonyms of words, such as *big*, *little* and *afraid*.

> **Assessment ideas:** Note the resources learners used to support their vocabulary choices and spelling.

Answers:
Learners write their legends.

3 Check your legend (5–10 minutes)

Learning intention: To evaluate own and others' writing, suggesting improvements for sense, accuracy and content.

Resources: Learner's Book, Session 4.11, Activity 3

Description: Once learners have finished writing their legends, ask: *Do you think your story is ready for someone else to read? What could you check before you share you story – missing words, missing punctuation?* Allow time for learners to read through their story and add any missing words or punctuation.

> **Differentiation ideas:** Support and challenge learners by pairing less confident writers with more confident writers.

Answers:
Learners read out their legends.

Plenary idea

Time to be proud (5 minutes)

Resources: Learners' legends from Activity 2

Description: Ask learners to find an opening sentence for a paragraph, or dialogue that they are very pleased with. Invite them to read the example they are proud of to other learners.

Homework ideas

Ask learners to:

* complete the Workbook activities for this session, if not used in class

* complete Worksheet 4.4 if not completed in class.

Answers for Workbook

1

How the words are said	Verbs
quietly	murmured, muttered, whispered
in a questioning way	*asked*, demanded, enquired, questioned
loudly	shouted, exclaimed
very loudly	screamed, shrieked
sadly	wailed, sobbed, cried

2
a shout → shouted
b query → queried
c smile → smiled
d reply → replied
e enquire → enquired
f cry → cried
g laugh → laughed
h ask → asked
i notice → noticed
j add → added

3 Possible dialogue verbs included but accept any appropriate dialogue verb.
a 'It is time we left,' <u>called</u> Hussain.
b 'We better hurry or we will be late,' <u>replied</u> Jacob.
c Tom <u>asked</u>, 'Has the film started?'
d 'That was a brilliant story,' <u>said</u> Leah.
e Meena <u>exclaimed</u>, 'I want to go and watch it again!'

4.12 Improving your legend

LEARNING PLAN

Learning objectives	Learning intentions	Success criteria
3Ww.03, 3Ww.05, 3Ww.06, 3Wv.02, 3Wv.03, 3Wv.04, 3Wv.05, 3Wg.01, 3Wg.02, 3Wg.03, 3Wg.05, 3Ws.01, 3Ws.02, 3Ws.03, 3Wc.01, 3Wc.03, 3Wp.01, 3Wp.04, 3Wp.05, 3SLm.05, 3SLs.02, 3SLg.02, 3SLp.01, 3SLp.03	• Proofread the completed story.	• Learners can proofread their stories.

Starter idea

Re-read your legend (5 minutes)

Resources: Learner's Book, Session 4.12: Getting started; learners' legends from Session 4.11

Description: Direct learners to the Getting started activity and allow time for learners to re-read their legends.

Main teaching ideas

1 Improve your legend (15–20 minutes)

Learning intention: To proofread the completed story.

Resources: Learner's Book, Session 4.12, Activity 1; Workbook, Session 4.12; Worksheet 4.5

Description: Say: *In the last session you checked your legend for small errors.* Ask: *What else should you do before your legend is finished?* Try to elicit that learners should proofread their writing and look for ways to improve their legend.

Direct learners to Activity 1 and read through each of the bullet points. Ask: *Can you tell me some good joining words? Who can suggest a better word for big? Who can suggest some synonyms for frightened?*

Direct learners to the Reflection prompt and discuss their ideas as a class (e.g. use phonic knowledge; break the word into syllables; consider whether the word looks right; use the first two letters to check in a dictionary; ask a partner). If appropriate, direct learners to the Workbook activities for this session and ask them to read the information about punctuation.

Ask: *What kind of punctuation would you put at the end of a sentence when something terrible happens?*

What kind of punctuation shows that a question has been asked? Where should you put the speech marks if you have used dialogue?

Write this sentence on your board: *Sinbad grabbed some sticks leaves rocks and a net.* Invite learners to add the missing punctuation (e.g. Sinbad grabbed some sticks, leaves, rocks and a net). Remind learners that there is no need to add a comma before the word *and*.

Ask: *Have you used any shortened words in your writing? Have you used an apostrophe to show which letters you have missed out?*

Allow time for learners to proofread their legends and identify what they could improve. Once learners have completed proofreading their legends, direct them to the How am I doing? prompts. Allow learners time to respond to the two bullet points. You could ask learners to peer assess their legends using Worksheet 4.5 Checklist for writing a legend.

> **Differentiation ideas:** Support learners by allowing access to onscreen proofreading tools or provide word lists of high-frequency words or any word banks that have been created during this unit of adverbs or sentence openers.

Challenge learners to set out dialogue correctly, using speech marks and a new line for each speaker.

> **Assessment ideas:** Once learners have completed their legends, assess their writing against the five key learning intentions that have been taught in this unit.

Answers:

Learners proofread their legends.

Note which learners can:

- identify and use pronouns appropriately
- recognise and discuss the features of myths and legends
- write paragraphs and understand how their openings establish links in a story
- write multi-clause sentences using simple connectives of time, place and cause
- plan, write and proofread a legend.

If you wish, you can also assess which learners can:

- spell words with a range of common suffixes, including –ed, –ment, –ness, –less
- use full stops, question marks and exclamation marks correctly
- use apostrophes to mark omission of letters in shortened form
- use speech marks to punctuate speech
- use neat and clear handwriting
- present text using an IT programme.

Plenary idea

Share your legend (10–15 minutes)

Resources: Learners' own legends

Description: Organise learners into groups of five or six. Ensure that groups include learners who are less confident in reading and learners who are more confident in reading. Ask learners to take it in turns to read their legends aloud in the group. Other group members say what they liked about the legend.

Homework ideas

Ask learners to:

- complete the Workbook activities for this session, if not used in class
- present a final copy of their legend either using neat, careful handwriting or in printed form.

Answers for Workbook

1. a 'I have been listening to the traders,' said the queen.

   b 'What have you found out?' asked her advisers.

   c 'They say that this new king is very wise,' replied the queen.

   d 'Have you heard the stories? The man is already a legend.'

   e I want to find out how wise he really is.

2. Learners' own sentences.

3. Learners' own paragraphs.

CHECK YOUR PROGRESS

1.

	Myths	Legends
The stories were told before they were written down.	✓	✓
The stories are set in the past.	✓	✓
The stories explain how or why something happens.	✓	
The stories are about heroes or gods.	✓	✓

2. a The elephant lived in the jungle but the trees made the elephant unwell.

   b The cow was feeling hungry so it/she ate all the flowers in the park.

   c Does Stefan like cats or does he prefer dogs?

   d The teacher looked at the children and they stopped talking.

   e The giant looked down at the people and he laughed.

PROJECT GUIDANCE

Group project: The plenary task in Session 4.12 could provide a starting point for the group project. Once learners have shared their legends, learners in the group could choose the legend most of them prefer.

Before learners plan their performance, decide whether groups will perform to the class, whether parents or other visitors will be invited and where performances will take place.

Allow learners time to agree roles and make or collect any props they think will be useful. Discuss the key features of performance:

- reading and speaking with expression appropriate to the meaning of the words
- using speech, gesture and movement to create their character.

Allow learners time to practice their performance and perform their story.

Groups should evaluate what went well in their performance and what could be improved.

Pair project: You may wish learners to complete the paired project before beginning the solo project. Rehearsing opinions about stories learners know well will provide support for many learners when they write their own reviews about a new legend.

This paired task provides learners with an opportunity to talk about their likes and dislikes of particular myths or legends. Learners should support their opinions with examples from the stories. Working with a partner will give learners an opportunity to consider how to explain their opinions to another learner and how to organise their thinking.

Solo project: Learners will need access to the internet or a selection of books for this solo project. If learners are using the internet, it would help to know a myth or legend from history, or from their own culture, before beginning their search.

Before learners write their reviews, discuss what should be included. Explain that their review should be like a book 'blurb' but also include a star rating and say which age range the story would be most suitable for.

> 5 Writing to each other

Unit plan

Session	Approximate number of learning hours	Outline of learning content	Resources
5.1 What do we write?	1	Read an email, formal letter and postcard. Answer questions about these text types.	Learner's Book Session 5.1 Workbook Session 5.1
5.2 Scanning or reading carefully?	1	Discuss the differences between scanning and reading a text to answer questions. Explore prepositions.	Learner's Book Session 5.2 Workbook Session 5.2 ⬇ Language worksheet 5A
5.3 Looking at synonyms	1	Scan/read a letter to answer questions. Explore synonyms in a text and record them in a table.	Learner's Book Session 5.3 Workbook Session 5.3 ⬇ Worksheet 5.1
5.4 What does a letter look like?	1	Explore the layout of letters. Plan and write a letter.	Learner's Book Session 5.4 Workbook Session 5.4 ⬇ Worksheet 5.2
5.5 Looking at homophones	1	Use scanning/reading carefully to answer questions about a letter and party invitation. Explore regular and irregular nouns. Explore homophones.	Learner's Book Session 5.5 Workbook Session 5.5
5.6 A letter of complaint	1	Discuss letters of complaint and formal and informal letter writing. Recall multi-clause sentences and simple connectives.	Learner's Book Session 5.6 Workbook Session 5.6
5.7 Beginning and ending letters	0.5	Explore greetings and endings of formal and informal letters.	Learner's Book Session 5.7 Workbook Session 5.7
5.8 Looking at sentences in a letter	1	Identify statement, exclamation and question sentences in a letter. Explore verb tense and agreement.	Learner's Book Session 5.8 Workbook Session 5.8

Session	Approximate number of learning hours	Outline of learning content	Resources
5.9 Other written communication	1.5	Explore the features of emails and SMS messages, including identifying verbs, pronouns and sentence structure. Write an email.	Learner's Book Session 5.9 Workbook Session 5.9 ⬇ Worksheet 5.3 ⬇ Differentiated worksheets 5A–C
5.10 Talking about mail	1	Create a mind map of types of mail. Develop speaking and listening skills through retelling events.	Learner's Book Session 5.10 Workbook Session 5.10
5.11 Writing a letter	1	Plan ideas and make notes. Write a letter.	Learner's Book Session 5.11 Workbook Session 5.11 ⬇ Worksheet 5.4 ⬇ Worksheet 5.5
5.12 Improving your letter	1.5	Proofread a letter for grammar, spelling and punctuation errors, and make some improvements. Rewrite a letter using neat, joined handwriting.	Learner's Book Session 5.12 Workbook Session 5.12 ⬇ Worksheet 5.6 ⬇ Language worksheet 5B

Cross-unit resources

Learner's Book Check your progress

Learner's Book Projects

Mid-point test

End-of-unit 5 test

BACKGROUND KNOWLEDGE

For the teacher

With increasing use of emails and SMS messaging, it is likely that learners have limited experience of receiving or sending letters. If possible, you could share with your learners one of the fiction books that include letters. Some books are written as letters (e.g. *Love from your Friend, Hannah* by Mindy Warshaw Skolsky, *Dear Greenpeace* by Simon James). Some books include letters and postcards that can be taken out of the book and read (e.g. *The Jolly Postman, or Other People's Letters* by Janet Ahlberg, *Meerkat Mail* by Emily Gravet).

It will be helpful to be familiar with the following English subject knowledge:

- formal and informal language
- nouns and proper nouns
- adverbs
- prepositions
- synonyms
- differences between scanning a text and reading carefully
- letter-writing structure
- apostrophes for contractions
- regular and irregular past tense verbs.

For the learner

It will be helpful for learners to be familiar with different types of mail, including formal and informal letters, postcards, email and messaging. It will also be helpful for learners to be familiar with the following English subject knowledge:

- vocabulary for different family relationships, particularly *aunty*, *nephew* and *grandmother*.

TEACHING SKILLS FOCUS

Skills for Life: Cross-curricular learning

- This unit is an opportunity to develop your learners' skills for life. Learners are more likely to use email and messaging than formal letter writing so it is important that they understand the protocols when writing formal letters. It is also important that learners understand the difference between formal and informal language and when to use each form.

- If you have links with teachers in other schools, you could explore the possibility of cross-school communication links. Communication could be through postal or electronic exchanges. Could you arrange an internet call with learners in another school? Why not arrange pen-pal communication between learners in each school? You should seek permission from leaders of the school and parents before setting up any such links. Arranging a class-to-class link may be more acceptable to leaders, parents and learners. One-to-one links may feel too personal and intrusive.

- Such cross-school links will provide an authentic reason for writing, which will benefit your learners.

5.1 What do we write?

LEARNING PLAN

Learning objectives	Learning intentions	Success criteria
3Rw.02, 3Rw.03, 3Rv.01, 3Rg.01, 3Ri.04, 3Ri.05, 3Ri.06, 3Ri.10, 3Ri.15, Ri.16, Ri.17, 3Ra.01, 3Ra.02, 3Wg.01, 3Wp.01, 3SLm.01, 3SLg.02, 3SLg.04	• Read and explore a range of written communication. • Answer questions about a text.	• Learners can read and explore a range of written communication. • Learners can answer questions about a text.

LANGUAGE SUPPORT

When you introduce the characters Mrs Sabella and Arturo, check that your learners understand the family terms *aunty* and *nephew*. Introduce the term *relation* as meaning a member of the same family. Explain that each relation has a different *relationship* within the family (e.g. mother, father, son, daughter, brother, sister).

If learners are unfamiliar with the *Horrid Henry* books by Francesca Simon, you may need to explain who Horrid Henry and Perfect Peter are. Horrid Henry is the main character and is always being blamed for things. Perfect Peter is Henry's annoying younger brother who usually gets Henry into trouble.

Common misconceptions

Misconception	How to identify	How to overcome
Mail means email.	Ask learners what type of mail they receive. Learners may say they do not receive any mail because they do not have an email address.	Explain that mail is any communication that is written and sent to another person. Mail can mean all letters and packages delivered by a postal service. Explain that mail can also mean email and SMS messages.

Starter idea

All kinds of mail (5 minutes)

Resources: Learner's Book, Session 5.1: Getting started; examples of different types of mail (if possible)

Description: Ask: *What kind of mail can you get* (e.g. letters, postcards, email, SMS messages, bills, advertising)? Direct learners to the images in the Getting started activity, or show them examples of real mail. Ask: *Were there any types of mail you missed?* Ask learners to discuss the remaining questions in pairs or small groups.

Main teaching ideas

1 Meet Mrs Sabella and Arturo (25–30 minutes)

Learning intention: To read and explore a range of written communication.

Resources: *Email to Aunty Sonia, Letter of complaint, Letter to Class 3 (1)* (Learner's Book, Session 5.1, Activity 1); Tracks 26, 27 and 28; Workbook, Session 5.1; dictionaries

Description: Read the introduction to Activity 1 to your learners, then discuss the relationship between the characters. Look at a map showing Argentina and the United Kingdom and locate where Aunty Sonia and Arturo live. Ask: *How do you think Aunty Sonia would travel from Buenos Aires to England?*

Direct learners to the word *complain* in the formal letter. Ask learners to explain the meaning of the word or invite a learner to read the definition from a dictionary. Ask them to recall the methods that will help them understand unfamiliar words (e.g. breaking words into small parts, using context and picture clues, reading further on in the sentence, phonic patterns).

You could listen to the audios of each piece of correspondence and ask learners to follow the texts. When learners have read the texts, ask them to discuss the questions with a partner. Then talk about learners' answers and their reasons as a class. You could use the Workbook activities to reinforce understanding of each type of mail.

> **Differentiation ideas:** Support learners by pairing less confident readers with a more confident partner.

Challenge learners by inviting volunteers to read the texts to the class.

> **Assessment ideas:** Use this activity to assess whether learners are familiar with postal mail. Do learners identify the different mail types correctly? Do learners comment about the different writing styles in the three texts? Your learners will explore formal and informal language in a later session, but it would be helpful to direct them towards the different styles in this session if time allows. Note which learners share their opinions with confidence.

Answers:
a   Arturo's 'thank you' letter: it has email addresses at the top; it tells you what the email subject is.

b   The message to Class 3: it has a picture on one side and the message on the other; there is no date. (Do not accept answers about it being short as this could apply to other types of mail.)

c   The letter addressed to 'Dear Sir': it has the address; a formal greeting, the date and a signing off.

2 Questions about mail (10–15 minutes)

Learning intention: To answer questions about a text.

Resources: Learner's Book, Session 5.1, Activity 2

Description: Say: *Have another look at the three items of mail. Were there any words you did not understand* (e.g. promptly, faithfully, grateful)? Explain the meaning of any unknown words or invite learners to find the definitions in a dictionary. Direct learners to the questions in the Learner's Book. Ask them to write answers to questions a to d in their notebooks.

Encourage learners to use complete sentences with capital letters and full stops. Ask: *Which words in your sentence need capital letters* (e.g. initial words and proper nouns)? If necessary, remind learners that proper nouns are names of people or places.

When learners have completed questions a to d, discuss the answers. Then discuss questions e and f. You could encourage learners to bring in postcards they have received for a postcard display.

> **Differentiation ideas:** Support learners by directing them to the appropriate texts as they answer questions b to d.

Challenge learners to identify all the words with the suffix –ly in the texts (e.g. kindly, really, nearly, particularly, promptly, faithfully, luckily) and write a definition for each word to share with the class.

> **Assessment ideas:** Note learners who punctuate sentences correctly, including those who use capital letters for proper nouns.

Answers:
a   Text 2
b   Mail taking over five weeks to arrive
c   Aunty Sonia
d   For the two books: the book by Francesca Simon and the book about cars.
e   Learners' own answers.

f   Learners' own answers. Possible reasons might be: enjoy seeing pictures from other places; tells you what friends or family are doing on holiday; lets you know they are thinking about you.

Plenary idea

Family portrait (10 minutes)

Resources: Pencils and crayons

Description: Ask learners to list all of Mrs Sabella's relations (sister, mother, Arturo). Ask them to draw a family portrait of each family member and then label each person showing their family relationship (e.g. sister, daughter, aunty, son, nephew, mother, grandmother). Ask: *Who can tell me what Arturo's family name is* (*Garcia*)? *How do you know* (from his email address)?

CROSS-CURRICULAR LINKS

History: Learners could use Arturo's family to explain what a family tree is and how it is laid out. Use this example to look at the family tree of someone they are currently studying in history.

Homework ideas

Ask learners to:

- complete the Workbook activities for this session, if not completed in class
- draw a family portrait of their own family, labelling the different relationships.

Answers for Workbook

Learners' own answers.

5.2 Scanning or reading carefully?

LEARNING PLAN

Learning objectives	Learning intentions	Success criteria
3Rw.03, 3Rw.04, 3Rv.01, 3Rg.01, 3Rg.09, 3Ri.04, 3Ri.06, 3Ri.10, 3Ri.14, 3Ri.15, 3Ri.16, 3Ra.01, 3Ra.02, 3Wg.01, 3Wg.04, 3Wg.08, 3Wp.01, 3SLm.01, 3SLs.02, 3SLg.02, 3SLg.04	• Scan or read texts to locate relevant information to answer questions. • Take turns in a discussion. • Explore the different purposes of prepositions.	• Learners can scan or read texts to locate relevant information to answer questions. • Learners can take turns in a discussion. • Learners can explore the different purposes of prepositions.

LANGUAGE SUPPORT

Just as learners are taught to *read* a text, they need to be taught how to *scan* a text. Encouraging learners to talk about how they found an answer to a question is a good step in teaching scanning skills. Praise methods such as looking for particular words in a text or remembering that the information was at the beginning, middle or end of a text.

Common misconceptions

Misconception	How to identify	How to overcome
Scanning a text means reading every word in a text very quickly.	Observe learners carefully as they scan a text. Learners who move their heads rapidly are often simply moving over a text without reading anything.	Explain that scanning a text involves thinking about the text before reading it so that learners can make a sensible decision about where particular information may be in a text. Ask: *Where in a letter will you find information about where someone lives (e.g. in the address)? Where will you find the address (e.g. at the top of the letter)? Where you find the name of the letter writer (e.g. at the end of a letter)?* Explain that thinking like this helps you move to the correct place in a text quickly to find an answer.

Starter idea

Scanning or reading (5–10 minutes)

Resources: Learner's Book, Session 5.2: Getting started

Description: Ask: *What do you do when you first see a new text* (e.g. look at the title or for proper names within a text; look at a picture; look at the layout)*?* Explain that how we read a text changes depending on what we are trying to do. Invite a learner to read the Reading tip to the class.

In pairs, ask learners to discuss texts that can be scanned and texts that need to be read carefully. Share their ideas and make a list on the board (e.g. we scan timetables, non-fiction books and dictionaries; we carefully read a story and a poem).

If learners need help with how to scan a text, ask them whether they read:

- every word on the page when they look for a word in a dictionary
- every day in a timetable if they want to know what is happening on a Tuesday
- every word in a story book or poem
- the whole letter if they want to know who wrote it.

Main teaching ideas

1 Scan a text (10 minutes)

Learning intention: To scan texts to locate relevant information to answer questions.

Resources: Learner's Book, Session 5.2, Activity 1

Description: Explain that learners are going to scan a note to find the answers to some questions. Direct learners to the Reading tip for this activity. Explain that as soon as learners have written the answers to the question neatly in their notebooks, they should put up their hands.

When half the class have answered each question, ask: *Did you need to read the whole letter? Where did you look to find the answer to the first question?*

Answers:
a   Mrs Sabella
b   England
c   Her mother is very ill.

2 Read carefully (15 minutes)

Learning intention: To read texts to locate relevant information to answer questions.

Resources: *Letter to Class 3 (2)* (Learner's Book, Session 5.2, Activity 2); Track 29

Description: Ask learners to follow the text as they listen to the audio. Explain that we need to read carefully to find some answers, such as when we have to find information from different parts of the letter to answer a question. Ask learners to re-read the note to Class 3 very carefully, then direct them to the questions. Remind learners to keep referring to the text to find the answers. Ask them to write answers in their notebooks using neat joined handwriting and complete sentences.

> **Differentiation ideas:** Support and challenge learners by dividing your class into groups comprising some learners who would like to be challenged and some learners who would benefit from additional support.

> **Assessment ideas:** Did learners refer to the text? Note which learners have difficulty answering questions about details implicit to the text.

Answers:
a   Mrs Sabella will be staying with her sister and her family.
b   Arturo is Mrs Sabella's nephew.
c   Class 3 are to: work hard for Mrs Diaz; show Mrs Diaz how wonderful they are; show Mrs Diaz how much they have learned so far this year.
d   Yes, because she says she will miss them and they are wonderful children.

3   Sharing answers (10 minutes)

Learning intention: To take turns in a discussion.

Resources: Learner's Book, Session 5.2, Activity 3

Description: Ask learners to work in pairs to discuss their answers from Activities 1 and 2. Remind them of the importance of respecting each other's opinions and ask: *What will you do if you have an answer that is different to your partners? Will your answers always be the same? Could there be more than one way of answering some questions?*

Invite learners to share what they know about the differences between scanning and reading carefully. Try to elicit from learners that when you scan a text you only read parts of the text and scanning can help you find information quickly.

> **Assessment ideas:** Note which learners understand the difference between scanning a text and reading a text carefully.

4   Where are the prepositions? (15 minutes)

Learning intention: To explore the different purposes of prepositions.

Resources: Learner's Book, Session 5.2, Activity 4; Workbook, Session 5.2; Language worksheet 5A

Description: Write *preposition* on the board and ask learners to read the word using segmenting (*pre/pos/ ition*). Direct learners to the word *position* within the word. Ask: *What does preposition mean? Can you give me an example of a preposition*? Direct learners to the Language focus box and read the explanation together. Ask: *What is a noun? Can you give me some examples of pronouns?*

Tell learners to now write their own sentences using prepositions. Ask: *What will all the sentences need* (e.g. capital letter for the first word; a full stop, exclamation mark or question mark to end; a verb; capital letters for proper nouns; a preposition)? Ask learners to underline the preposition in their sentences. Use Language worksheet 5A or the Workbook activities to provide further practice with prepositions.

> **Differentiation ideas:** Support learners by suggesting that they use ideas from Mrs Sabella's note.

Challenge learners to write two more sentences using different prepositions.

> **Assessment ideas:** Did learners use appropriate prepositions in their sentences?

Answers:
Learners' own sentences.

Plenary idea

Asking questions (5–10 minutes)

Resources: *Letter to Class 3 (2)* (Learner's Book, Session 5.2); Track 29

Description: Ask learners to re-read the note Mrs Sabella left for her class with their partner. Explain that they should take turns thinking of a question about the note to ask their partner. Allow learners to ask two or three questions each. Then ask: *Who was able to scan the text to find an answer? Who asked questions that required partners to read the text carefully?*

Homework ideas

Ask learners to:

- complete the Workbook activities for this session, if not completed in class

- draw pictures showing the position of one object in relation to another (e.g. a bowl on the table, a cat under a table, a child hiding behind a tree) and write a sentence to match the picture.

Answers for Workbook

1 **a** The cat ran <u>through</u> the bush.

    b A bus stopped <u>at</u> the traffic lights.

    c The children ran <u>down</u> the hill.

    d We enjoy going <u>to</u> the shop.

    e I slipped <u>in</u> the mud.

    f Samra hid <u>behind</u> the curtain

2 **a** under

    b out

    c far

    d above

3 Learners' own prepositions could include: to – from, high – low; on – off; in front of – behind.

4 Learners' own answers.

5 Learners' own sentences.

6 Learners' own answers.

5.3 Looking at synonyms

LEARNING PLAN

Learning objectives	Learning intentions	Success criteria
3Rw.01, 3Rw.02, 3Rw.03, 3Rw.04, 3Rv.01, 3Rv.02, 3Rg.01, 3Ri.04, 3Ri.06, 3Ri.07, 3Ri.10, 3Ri.14, 3Ri.15, 3Ri.16, 3Ra.02, 3Wv.02, 3Wp.02, 3SLm.02, 3SLg.02	• Scan or read texts to locate relevant information to answer questions. • Explore and use synonyms.	• Learners can scan or read texts to locate relevant information to answer questions. • Learners can explore and use synonyms.

LANGUAGE SUPPORT

The letter from Mrs Sabella contains some words with silent letters (e.g. parliament, favourite, government). Discuss these words and encourage learners to explore other words with silent letters (e.g. interesting, foreign, school, reign, Wednesday, fascinate).

Identifying synonyms is a valuable way of developing vocabulary knowledge. Learners with limited vocabulary may need to check the meaning of words before completing a matching task.

Common misconceptions

Misconception	How to identify	How to overcome
The digraph *th* is always pronounced *th* as in *the*.	Note how learners pronounce *Thames*. Do learners use a *th* sound or a *t*?	Explain that in English, *th* usually makes a *th* sound but there are a few exceptions (e.g. Thames, Thomas, Beethoven, Thailand, Lesotho, Kathmandu, thyme). There are also a few exceptions in compound words (e.g. lighthouse, foothold, knighthood, sweetheart).

Starter idea

Synonyms (5 minutes)

Resources: Learner's Book, Session 5.3: Getting started

Description: Read the statement in the Getting started activity and allow learners time to write their lists.

Invite learners to share their words for *happy* with the class. Write their ideas on the board. Then repeat this as learners share their words for *sad*. Remind them that groups of words with the same or a similar meaning are called synonyms.

Main teaching ideas

1 Talk about Mrs Sabella's letter (15–20 minutes)

Learning intention: To scan or read texts to locate relevant information to answer questions.

Resources: *Letter to Class 3 (3)* (Learner's Book, Session 5.3, Activity 1); Track 30

Description: Explain that Mrs Sabella has written a letter to her class. Direct learners to the glossary terms. Talk about the silent *n* in *government*. If learners are unfamiliar with regnal numbers, explain that *II* after *Queen Elizabeth* stands for 'two' and is read as *the second*. Explain that the current Queen Elizabeth is the second British queen called Elizabeth.

Invite volunteers to read a paragraph of the letter to the class. As volunteers read each paragraph, discuss vocabulary learners find difficult to read (e.g. *Thames, Parliament, bridge, Eye*). Discuss any vocabulary learners do not understand (e.g. *strolled*).

Organise learners into small groups to talk about the questions.

> **Differentiation ideas:** Support learners by dividing your class into groups comprising some learners who would like to be challenged and some learners who would benefit from additional support.

Challenge learners to act as the scribe for their group.

Answers:
Possible answers might include:
- Mrs Sabella and Arturo had a day out.
- Mrs Sabella and her nephew, Arturo.
- Friday 16th May; do not accept references to 'yesterday'.
- central London
- Mrs Sabella's sister looked after her mother.

2 Answer some questions (20 minutes)

Learning intention: To scan or read texts to locate relevant information to answer questions.

Resources: Learner's Book, Session 5.3, Activity 2

Description: Remind learners of their previous learning about scanning and reading texts carefully. Direct them to the Reflection point. Allow a short time for learners to think about the skill they used to answer the group questions. Ask them to answer the questions.

Direct learners to the Reflection point again. Ask: *Did you use the same skill to answer these questions as when you answered the previous questions? Did all the questions require you to read the text carefully? Were there any questions where you could scan to find the answer? Which ones?*

Discuss the answers to each question and ask learners to peer mark answers.

> **Differentiation ideas:** Support learners with reading the more difficult words.

Challenge learners to write an extra question for a partner to answer.

> **Assessment ideas:** Can learners scan the text for answers? Can they find implicit information (e.g. why or when it happened)? Do learners refer to the date below the address when explaining when Mrs Sabella and Arturo had their day out? Can they select appropriate answers to each question? Do learners include things that were listed in the letter but not seen by Mrs Sabella (e.g. things on the river, fireworks)?

Answers:

a   Possible answers: Buckingham Palace, the Houses of Parliament, the River Thames, Westminster Bridge, the London Eye. (Note: do not accept things that are listed as using the river.)

b   The number of windows. She *counted 68 windows!*

c   It is where the UK government makes laws.

d   When there are fireworks; when there are special celebrations like New Year's Eve.

e   It says we went for a ride. It says, you *can see some excellent views of London from the top.*

3   Interesting synonyms (10–15 minutes)

Learning intention: To explore and use synonyms.

Resources: Learner's Book, Session 5.3, Activity 3; Workbook, Session 5.3; Worksheet 5.1; thesauruses

Description: Ask: *What do we mean when we talk about interesting words* (e.g. words that are not ordinary, better words for the same thing)? Explain that when we use an interesting word in place of an ordinary word, the two words must have a similar meaning. You could use Worksheet 5.1 A nice day out or the Workbook activities here to provide more practice with synonyms.

Read the introduction to the activity, then direct learners to the Language focus box. With a partner, learners should make a list of interesting words in the letter (e.g. *enjoyable, huge, imagine, strolled, massive*). Why do learners think Mrs Sabella used these words?

Direct learners to Activity 3 and together read the words in the boxes above the table. Then ask learners to copy and complete the table. Ask learners to compare answers in small groups.

Then ask learners to add one more synonym to each row. Encourage learners to use a thesaurus.

> **Differentiation ideas:** Support learners by grouping them with other learners working at a similar level.

Challenge learners to choose two more ordinary words to add to the table and find synonyms for.

Answers:

Ordinary words	Synonym
big	huge, massive, wide
nice	amazing, beautiful, fun
walked	strolled
building	house, palace
boat	speedboat, water taxi
think	imagine

Learners add one more synonym for each ordinary word.

Plenary idea

Interesting sentences (10 minutes)

Description: Write a short sentence on the board (e.g. *They liked their day out*). Ask learners to write two sentences using more interesting words for *liked*. Then ask learners to compare their sentences with a partner. How many different words for liked did they use? Which sentence did they think sounded the most interesting?

CROSS-CURRICULAR LINKS

Maths (Time): Give learners a set of times linked to Mrs Sabella's day out (e.g. time she arrived at an attraction, queuing time, time on the London Eye). Ask learners to calculate time intervals in minutes.

Homework ideas

Ask learners to:

- complete the Workbook activities for this session, if not completed in class

- create a word search using synonyms for a frequently used word (e.g. big, little, kind, good).

Answers for Workbook

1. big — massive
   little — tiny
   good — brilliant
   sad — miserable
   nasty — horrid
   odd — strange

2. Learners' own sentences.

3. Learners' own synonyms.

5.4 What does a letter look like?

LEARNING PLAN

Learning objectives	Learning intentions	Success criteria
3Rw.02, 3Rs.02, 3Rs.03, 3Rg.05, 3Ri.04, 3Ri.05, 3Ri.14, 3Ri.15, 3Ww.05, 3Ww.06, 3Wv.05, 3Wv.07, 3Wg.01, 3Wg.02, 3Wg.04, 3Ws.01, 3Ws.02, 3Ws.04, 3Wc.02, 3Wc.05, 3Wc.06, 3Wp.01, 3Wp.03, 3Wp.04, 3SLm.01	• Explore and recognise the layout of a letter. • Plan a letter. • Write a letter.	• Learners can explore and recognise the layout of a letter. • Learners can plan a letter. • Learners can write a letter.

LANGUAGE SUPPORT

Although the layouts of the two letters in this session have many common features, the language of each one is very different. Point out the difference in formality (the difference between formal and informal language is covered in Session 5.6).

Learners often have difficulty choosing the correct starting point for writing an address – they often start too far to the right and run out of space. Encourage learners to start the first line of the address in the middle of the page.

Starter idea

Compare letters (10 minutes)

Resources: Learner's Book, Session 5.4: Getting started

Description: Organise learners into groups and ask each group to choose a scribe. Allow learners to discuss the letters for a few minutes. Invite scribes to share the points identified by each group. Elicit that the letters have the following features in common: an address and date, who the letter is written to, who the letter is from,

both say *Dear*. Try to elicit the following differences: the style of greeting (*Dear Sir* / *Dear Class 3*), the ending (*Yours faithfully* / *From*), the signature (*Sonia Sabella* / *Mrs Sabella*).

Ask: *Did both letters sound friendly? What did you notice about the words used in the two letters?*

Share learners' ideas about how a letter from England gets to Argentina (e.g. aeroplane).

Main teaching ideas

1 Explore the layout (10 minutes)

Learning intention: To explore and recognise the layout of a letter.

Resources: Learner's Book, Session 5.4, Activity 1; Workbook, Session 5.4, Activity 1

Description: Direct learners to the Language focus box and read the list of features. Ask: *Why is it important to include an address* (e.g. so you know where to send a reply)*? Why is the date important* (e.g. you know when it was written, there may be more than one letter from that person so you can put them in order)*?* In pairs learners should look at Mrs Sabella's letter to Class 3 and identify the five features. You could ask learners to complete the Focus activity in the Workbook at this point as it provides an opportunity to label the features of a letter.

Say: *Mrs Sabella ended the letter with 'From'. Why did she not write 'Yours faithfully'* (e.g. it would sound too official / formal)*? Why did she not write 'Love'* (e.g. she is their teacher, not a friend or relative)*?*

> **Differentiation ideas:** Support learners by pairing them with a more confident reader.

> **Assessment ideas:** Which features were learners able to identify?

2 What will you say? (10–15 minutes)

Learning intention: To plan a letter.

Resources: Learner's Book, Session 5.4, Activity 2

Description: Direct learners to the introduction for Activity 2. Ask: *What is Mrs Sabella's nephew called?* (Arturo) *What do we know about him?* (lives in England, about 7/8 years old, likes books by Francesca Simon, likes cars, wants to drive a fast car when he grows up) If learners have forgotten details about Arturo, re-read Arturo's email in Session 5.1.

With a partner, learners should talk about the information they could include in a letter to Arturo using the prompts in the Learner's Book. Allow a short time for paired discussion, then ask learners to make notes using the prompts provided.

> **Differentiation ideas:** Support learners in a targeted group, encouraging learners to think about each prompt in turn. You could offer additional prompts, such as: *How will you start your letter? Have you told Arturo where you live?*

Challenge learners to organise their ideas into paragraphs.

3 Write your letter (25–30 minutes)

Learning intention: To write a letter.

Resources: Learner's Book, Session 5.4, Activity 3; Workbook, Session 5.4, Activities 2 and 3; Worksheet 5.2; thesauruses; learners' spelling logs (if used)

Description: Ask learners to look at the letter from Mrs Sabella to Class 3 again. Ask: *Where do you write the address and date* (top right)*?* Show learners how you would write the school address in a letter. Discuss the position of each line of the address. Ask learners to use the school address and current date. Learners can practise writing the address and letter endings using the Practice and Challenge activities in the Workbook.

Direct learners to the position of *Dear* and remind them to use a capital letter for Arturo. Ask: *What does 'in a sensible order' mean* (e.g. grouping things about the same subject together)*?* Direct learners to the character text. Ask them to suggest synonyms for *like* that they could use. Write the suggestions on the board.

When learners have completed their letters, ask them to peer assess using the prompt in the Learner's Book.

> **Differentiation ideas:** Support learners by providing a copy of the school address to stick in their notebooks. Provide Worksheet 5.2 A letter to Arturo as a template.

Challenge learners to find synonyms for ordinary words.

> **Assessment ideas:** Which learners can organise their ideas appropriately? Do any learners jump from topic to topic? Do all learners use the five letter features?

When writing letters, which learners:

- can spell high frequency words accurately
- apply taught spelling patterns (e.g. apostrophes for omission, suffixes, verb endings)
- use a variety of sentence structures in their letters
- ask a question or include a question mark
- structure their letters using paragraphs and/or sentence openings?

Answers:
Learners write their letters.

Plenary idea

Share your letters (5–10 minutes)

Resources: Learners' letters from Activity 3

Description: Ask: *Who thinks their partner wrote an interesting letter to Arturo? What made your partner's letter interesting?*

If there is time, some of the letters could be read aloud.

CROSS-CURRICULAR LINKS

Geography: Ask learners to investigate how non-electronic mail travels around the world.

IT: Explain to learners how to use the layout tools in a word-processing package (e.g. left and right alignment). Learners could use word processing to present their letter to Arturo.

Homework ideas

Ask learners to:

- complete the Workbook activities for this session, if not completed in class
- find out their personal address then practise writing the address as it would appear in a letter heading; learners could be provided with an envelope and asked to write their address on the envelope using their neatest handwriting.

Answers for Workbook

1   heading; greeting; body; ending; signature

2   Learners' own headings.

3   a   first name or nickname
    b   first name (and surname if there is another learner in the class with the same first name)
    c   title and last name / initial and last name

5.5 Looking at homophones

LEARNING PLAN

Learning objectives	Learning intentions	Success criteria
3Rw.01, 3Rw.03, 3Rw.04, 3Rv.01, 3Rs.02, 3Ri.04, 3Ri.07, 3Ri.14, 3Ra.02, 3Ww.04, 3Ww.05, 3Ww.06, 3Wp.02	• Recognise and write homophones. • Explore singular and plural word forms of nouns. • Scan and read texts to locate relevant information to answer questions.	• Learners can recognise and write homophones. • Learners can explore singular and plural word forms of nouns. • Learners can scan and read texts to locate relevant information to answer questions.

LANGUAGE SUPPORT

Learners may want to know more about Argentinian gauchos. A gaucho is a national symbol in Argentina and Uruguay, and they are said to be very skilled and brave horsemen. Explain that *au* in *gaucho* is pronounced *ow* as in *down*. If learners need more help with pronouncing gaucho, you could search online for a pronunciation clip.

Throughout this session, learners will read words with graphemes that can be pronounced in a variety of ways (e.g. lasso, gaucho, people, bench) or have silent letters (e.g. write, knew, would, thought). Learners need to be particularly careful to pronounce the words clearly when working on homophone activities.

Starter idea

A party invitation (10 minutes)

Resources: Learner's Book, Session 5.5: Getting started

Description: Ask: *Can you remember how we invite people to a party?* (send invitations) Explain that learners are going to hear about Arturo's party. Organise learners into pairs and ask them to recall the information needed for a party invitation (e.g. reason for party, who is invited, when and where it will be). Allow learners time to write an invitation, then ask: *Who remembered to ask for a reply? Who remembered the four letters that mean please reply? Who can remember what RSVP stands for* (*répondez s'il vous plaît*)? Encourage learners to refer to Session 2.5 to check they have remembered all the important information.

Main teaching ideas

1 Mrs Sabella's latest letter (15 minutes)

Learning intention: To scan and read texts to locate relevant information to answer questions.

Resources: *Letter to Class 3 (4)* (Learner's Book, Session 5.5, Activity 1); Track 31

Description: Direct learners to Mrs Sabella's letter and ask them to read or listen to the letter and invitation with their partner. Check that learners understand the work a cowboy does. Ask: *What is a lasso* (e.g. a rope with a large loop at one end; a rope cowboys use to catch cattle)? Draw learners' attention to the less common way of pronouncing the *o* at the end of *lasso*.

Remind learners about the methods they can use to find answers to questions in a text (e.g. scan/ read carefully). Encourage learners to answer the questions in their notebooks using neat, joined handwriting.

> **Differentiation ideas:** Challenge learners to find more words that end with a short *o* sound (e.g. gaucho, hello, no, ago, gecko) and a long *o* sound (e.g. lasso, do, to, who, canoe, move).

Answers:
a   A party invitation
b   The village hall
c   A gaucho came (and showed them how to do tricks with a lasso).

2 Singular or plural (20 minutes)

Learning intention: To explore singular and plural forms of nouns.

Resources: Learner's Book, Session 5.5, Activity 2

Description: Ask: *How many cowboys came to Arturo's party? How do you know?* (it says a gaucho) Explain that the plural of gaucho is (*gauchos*). Direct learners to the Writing tip. Ask: *Is the plural spelling of gaucho a regular or irregular spelling?* (regular because we add *s*).

Read aloud the singular words in the table in part a, then allow learners time to copy and complete the table in their notebooks.

Direct learners to the table in part b, then, in pairs, they should discuss what happens to words ending with *x*, *sh*, *s* or *ch* (e.g. add *es*). Allow learners time to copy and complete the table in their notebooks.

Direct learners to the table in part c and ask: *What do you notice about the plural words in the box?* (no *s* or *es* endings; three words have *ee*; three words are animals; five words are about people). Ask learners to match the plurals with the singular words in the table. Explain that words like those in the table are *irregular plurals* because they do not have *s* or *es* in the plural form.

> **Differentiation ideas:** Support learners who work more slowly to draw a single line to create two columns rather than draw the whole table.

Challenge learners by providing additional singular nouns for learners to sort and add to the appropriate table.

> **Assessment ideas:** Do learners select correct plural endings for regular words? You could encourage learners to draw simple pictures of nouns with irregular plural forms and add to class display or working wall. Adding a pictorial dimension may help learners remember the exceptions.

Answers:
a

Singular	Plural
birthday	*birthdays*
trick	tricks
balloon	balloons
cake	cakes

b

Singular	Plural
box	*boxes*
class	classes
brush	brushes
bench	benches

c

Singular	Plural
child	*children*
mouse	mice
person	people
tooth	teeth
sheep	sheep
goose	geese
foot	feet
man	men

3 Sounds right (15–20 minutes)

Learning intention: To recognise and write homophones.

Resources: Learner's Book, Session 5.5, Activity 3; Workbook, Session 5.5

Description: Write the extract from Mrs Sabella's letter on the board. Circle *here* and *write*. Ask learners to read the extract to themselves then ask: *What do you notice about the circled words?* Direct learners to the Language focus box, then explain that *homo/phone* means *same sound*.

Ask learners to answer the two questions. Encourage them to say the words quietly to themselves to help them hear the word. Use the Workbook activities to provide more practice with homophones if there is time in class.

> **Differentiation ideas:** Support learners by allowing them to orally explain the different meanings of each homophone.

Challenge learners to identify more homophone pairs (e.g. know / no, where / wear, too / two, hour / our, heard / herd).

> **Assessment ideas:** Can learners identify the homophones? As with irregular plural nouns, learners may benefit from drawing pictures to illustrate pairs of homophones.

Answers:

a Possible answers include: dear = greeting / deer = animal; here = a place / hear = listen to a voice or noise; write = make a mark on paper / right = being correct / or a direction (turning right).

b new; past; days

Plenary idea

Using homophones (5–10 minutes)

Resources: Learner's Book, Session 5.5

Description: Check that learners have correctly identified the homophones for the three words in Activity 3a. Ask them to use each homophone in a sentence to show what it means.

Homework ideas

Ask learners to:

- complete the Workbook activities for this session, if not completed in class

- choose six nouns with irregular plural forms and draw pictures to illustrate each pair (e.g. one sheep / several sheep; one fish / several fish).

Answers for Workbook

1 great – grate
meet – meat
threw – through
main – mane
know – no
new – knew

2 **a** It is time you went to the party.
b Arturo is eight years old.
c I would love a piece of his birthday cake.
d Can I have a slice of cake too?

3 **a** too, two
b so, sew
c there, their

5.6 A letter of complaint

LEARNING PLAN

Learning objectives	Learning intentions	Success criteria
3Rv.04, 3Rg.05, 3Rg.06, 3Rs.02, 3Ri.04, 3Ri.05, 3Ri.07, 3Ri.12, 3Ri.14, 3Ri.15, 3Ri.16, 3Ri.17, 3Ra.02, 3Ra.03, 3SLm.01, 3SLg.01, 3SLg.04	• Discuss letters of complaint. • Explore multi-clause sentences.	• Learners can discuss letters of complaint. • Learners understand multi-clause sentences.

LANGUAGE SUPPORT

Learners will notice that the type of language used in the letters in this unit differ but may not be able to explain the difference in terms of formal/informal. Learners may describe formal writing as sounding 'grown up' or using 'difficult words'. Learners may describe informal writing as sounding 'friendly', 'easier to understand' or using 'words we use when we speak'.

Be sensitive to the fact that some cultures are unlikely to make a complaint. Some learners may

find it difficult to identify reasons for writing a letter of complaint or find it difficult to write their own letter of complaint. Explain that a formal letter of complaint should never be rude or offend the person receiving it. You may want to choose the topic for your learners to complain about (e.g. an ordered item arrives broken, the wrong size, the wrong colour, or too late).

Starter idea

Formal or informal? (5–10 minutes)

Resources: Learner's Book, Session 5.6: Getting started

Description: Ask learners to look at the letters read so far (e.g. letter from Arturo, postcard, letter of complaint, letters to Class 3, party invitation). Ask: *Do all the letters use the same type of words? How are they different?*

Talk about when we might use formal letters and informal letters. If learners do not understand the terms *formal* and *informal*, explain each term (See Language support).

Allow learners time to sort the letters from the unit into formal and informal groups. Encourage them to add additional letters to each group (e.g. formal: business letters, letters of complaint, invitations, household bills; informal: letters to a friend/person you know, postcards, 'thank you' letters).

Main teaching ideas

1 Mrs Sabella's complaint letter (10–15 minutes)

Learning intention: To discuss letters of complaint.

Resources: *Letter to Class 3 (1)* (Learner's Book, Session 5.6, Activity 1); Track 27; Workbook, Session 5.6

Description: Ask: *What does 'complain' mean?* (something is wrong, not happy about something) *Is 'complain' a noun or a verb?* Explain that *complaint* is a noun that explains whatever is being complained about. Organise learners into small groups, then ask groups to read or listen to Mrs Sabella's letter. Ask groups to choose a scribe and a reporter. Allow time for groups to discuss the four questions then ask the reporter from each group to report answers to the class.

Alternate which group reports their answer first each time to avoid any group responding with 'We think the same as the other groups'. Learners could complete the Focus activity in the Workbook here.

> **Differentiation ideas:** Support learners by dividing your class into groups comprising some learners who would like to be challenged and some learners who would benefit from additional support.

Challenge learners to adopt roles of scribe or reporter.

> **Assessment ideas:** Note how well learners achieved their roles within their groups.

Answers:
a   It says: *I am writing to complain …*
b   Possible answers: greetings and closings, language used in the body of the letter is formal, the signature.
c   Possible answers: includes a heading with address and date, has the five features of letters.
d   Formal

2   Talk about letters of complaint (10 minutes)

Learning intention: To discuss letters of complaint.

Resources: Learner's Book, Session 5.6, Activity 2; Workbook, Session 5.6, Activities 1 and 2

Description: Ask: *What do we call the main section of a letter?* (the body) With a partner, learners should re-read the body of the letter in Activity 1, and then discuss the questions in Activity 2.

Direct learners to the Writing tip then ask: *What evidence did Mrs Sabella use?* (the different lengths of time it took for letters to arrive) *How did Mrs Sabella feel?* (sad because the letters were from people she cared about) *What did Mrs Sabella want to happen?* (someone to explain why the letters took so long) *Which powerful words did Mrs Sabella use?* (particularly important, promptly, grateful for an explanation).

Learners could complete the Practice activity in the Workbook here if there is time in class.

> **Differentiation ideas:** Support learners to think of reasons for writing a letter of complaint.

Challenge learners to support less confident learners.

> **Assessment ideas:** Did learners identify the features of a formal letter? Did they understand why a formal tone is used in some letters?

Answers:
a   Possible answers: when the person feels unhappy about something; when something is broken; when someone has not behaved as we expected.
b   Reason for complaint; why we are unhappy; how we feel; request a letter in return to explain or apologise.
c   Formal: we do not know the person; the person is not a friend.

3   Compound sentences (10 minutes)

Learning intention: To explore multi-clause sentences.

Resources: Learner's Book, Session 5.6, Activity 3; Workbook, Session 5.6, Activity 3

Description: Direct learners to the character and speech bubble, and allow time for them to look back at Unit 4.6. Ask: *What is a multi-clause sentence?* (two ideas joined together) *What type of word do you use to join two ideas?* (a connective, words such as and, but, so).

Ask learners to re-read Mrs Sabella's letter and identify the multi-clause sentences and connectives.

Learners could complete the Challenge activity in the Workbook here.

> **Differentiation ideas:** Challenge learners to support less confident learners.

> **Assessment ideas:** Could learners recall what a multi-clause sentence is? Note which learners identified the multi-clause sentences in Mrs Sabella's letter.

Answers:
A number of letters were written <u>and</u> posted on the same day.
The first arrived within ten days of being posted, <u>but</u> the last of these letters took nearly four times as long.
These letters were very important to me <u>for</u> they were written by people I care about.
I am away from my home at the moment <u>so</u> it is particularly important to me that I receive letters promptly.
I would be grateful for an explanation <u>about</u> why some of these letters took so long.

Plenary idea

All about complaining (5 minutes)

Resources: Thesauruses

Description: Write the verb *complain* on the board. Ask: *Can you think of other words that mean complain* (e.g. grumble, moan, object, protest, criticise, make a fuss, find fault with)?

Homework ideas

Ask learners to:

- complete the Workbook activities for this session, if not completed in class
- write a letter of apology from Correo Argentino to explain why the letters took so long. Direct learners to begin their letters with 'Dear Madam'.

Answers for Workbook

Learners' own answers.

5.7 Beginning and ending letters

LEARNING PLAN

Learning objectives	Learning intentions	Success criteria
3Rw.03, 3Rs.02, 3Rs.03, 3Ri.04, 3Ri.14, 3Ri.15, 3Ri.16, 3Ri.17, 3Wp.02, 3SLm.01, 3SLm.02, 3SLg.02, 3SLg.04	• Explore how letters begin and end.	• Learners understand how letters begin and end.

LANGUAGE SUPPORT

If learners are unfamiliar with sending or receiving letters, you may need to suggest additional letter greetings and endings that may be used for formal and informal letters. Introduce informal letter endings such as: Best wishes; Warmest wishes; Your loving nephew; Love; Goodbye / Bye for now. Introduce formal letter closings such as: Yours respectively; Kind regards; Regards.

Common misconceptions

Misconception	How to identify	How to overcome
Good morning and *Greetings* are formal greetings.	Ask learners to fill out a table of informal and formal greetings. Some learners may insert *Good morning* and *Greetings* in the formal column in the table.	Explain that these are both informal greetings that are sometimes used in formal writing, especially in emails. The rules for writing emails are less clear than rules for letter writing and people are sometimes unsure how to begin an email. Explain that it is best to avoid using these greetings in formal letters.

Starter idea

Formal and informal letters (5 minutes)

Resources: Learner's Book, Session 5.7: Getting started

Description: Ask: *What kind of formal letters have we read so far? What kind of informal letters have we read?* Ask learners to say what all the letters have in common at the beginning and the end (e.g. greeting and closing).

Main teaching ideas

1 Letter greetings (10 minutes)

Learning intention: To explore letter openings.

Resources: Learner's Book, Session 5.7, Activity 1; Workbook, Session 5.7, Activity 2

Description: Invite learners to read aloud the different greetings. With a partner, learners should talk about each greeting and decide whether the greetings are formal or informal. Allow time for learners to complete the table in their notebooks. Refer to Common misconceptions if learners group *Good morning* and *Greetings* under formal greetings.

As a class, discuss what learners notice about all the informal greetings. Use the Practice activity in the Workbook to provide more practice with identifying different types of greeting.

> **Assessment ideas:** Did learners identify the differences in the style of greeting used in formal and informal letters? Could they suggest appropriate greetings for each type of letter?

Answers:
a   Formal greetings: Dear Sir, To Mr Henderson, Dear Madam, Dear Mrs Trainor, To the manager
Informal greetings: Hi Tuhil, Dear Aunty Su, Good morning, Greetings, Dear Cindy, Hello Jake
b   Informal greetings use the person's first name or use no name.

2 Letter closings (15 minutes)

Learning intention: To explore ways of signing off in letters.

Resources: Learner's Book, Session 5.7, Activity 2; Workbook, Session 5.7, Activity 3; thesauruses

Description: Ask: *How did Mrs Sabella end her letter of complaint?* Ask learners to look at the selection of letters and identify other closing words. Write

Yours faithfully and *Yours sincerely* on your board. Encourage learners to segment *sincerely* to help learners read it. Read the Writing tip and make sure learners are clear about when to use each ending.

Ask learners to answer part a in their notebooks and then discuss part b with a partner. Bring the class back together to discuss responses. Use the Challenge activity in the Workbook here to provide more practice with identifying different types of ending.

> **Differentiation ideas:** Challenge learners to support less confident learners with parts a and b.

> **Assessment ideas:** Note which learners needed most support in selecting appropriate closings for letters.

Answers:
a   Possible answers: Love; From; Best wishes; Your good friend; Your loving son/daughter.
b   Learners' own answers.

Plenary idea

Sir Faithful (5–10 minutes)

Resources: Picture of a medieval knight

Description: Say: *Here is a simple way to remember which formal ending to use.* Show learners a picture of a knight. Explain that knights are always given the title *Sir*. Explain that the picture links the words *Sir* and *Faithful*, and helps to remind us to use *Yours faithfully* when using a greeting, such as *Dear Sir* when writing a formal letter to someone we do not know. Explain that a link of this kind is called a mnemonic.

Ask learners to draw their own picture of a knight and write the name *Sir Faithful* underneath.

Homework ideas

Ask learners to:

* find as many words as they can using the letters in *sincerely* (e.g. yes, eye, sin, cry, eel, sir, sly, lie, see, ice, icy, rein, rice, rise, seen, eels, nice, line, cries, since, niece, slice, nieces, screen, scenery, silence, sincere).

Answers for Workbook

1   Formal letters: letters advertising something, invites, complaints, bills, letters from the police

Informal letters: letters from family, 'thank you' letters, letters from friends

2 Possible answers:

Type of letter	Greeting
letters from the police	*Dear Mr Franke*
letters from family	Dear Leila
invites	Leila
letters from friends	Hi Ahmed
bills	Dear Mr Patel
complaints	Dear Sir/Madam
'thank you' letters	Dear Uncle Norman

3 Possible answers:

Type of letter	Greeting
letters from the police	*Yours sincerely*
letters from family	Love, Dad
invites	RSVP
letters from friends	From Mustafa
bills	Yours sincerely
complaints	Yours faithfully
'thank you' letters	From your nephew

5.8 Looking at sentences in a letter

LEARNING PLAN

Learning objectives	Learning intentions	Success criteria
3Rw.02, 3Rw.03, 3Rw.04, 3Rv.01, 3Rg.01, 3Rg.02, 3Rg.05, 3Rg.07, 3Rg.08, 3Rg.10, 3Rg.11, 3Ri.04, 3Ri.06, 3Ri.10, 3Ri.12, 3Ri.14, 3Ri.15, 3Ri.16, 3Ra.02, 3Wg.01, 3Wg.04, 3Wg.06, 3Wg.07, 3Wp.01, 3SLm.02	• Explore, understand and use different types of sentences. • Explore explicit and implicit meanings in a text. • Identify and use appropriate verb tenses.	• Learners can explore, understand and use different types of sentences. • Learners can explore explicit and implicit meanings in a text. • Learners can identify and use appropriate verb tenses.

LANGUAGE SUPPORT

For the final activity of this session, some learners may need to hear both the incorrect sentence and the corrected version in order to identify what is wrong with the sentence. Encourage learners to ask themselves 'Does it sound right?' to help them identify what needs changing.

Starter idea

Different types of sentences (10 minutes)

Resources: Learner's Book, Session 5.8: Getting started

Description: Ask: *What are the different types of punctuation you can use at the end of a sentence? When would you use a question mark (e.g. when you ask a question)? When would you use an exclamation mark* (e.g. when you are surprised or shocked; when you want to warn someone)?

Ask learners to write an example of a statement, exclamation and question in their notebooks. Remind learners to use the appropriate punctuation for each sentence.

When completed, ask learners to peer assess their sentences with a partner.

Main teaching ideas

1 A new letter from Mrs Sabella (15–20 minutes)

Learning intention: To explore explicit and implicit meanings in a text.

Resources: *Letter to Class 3* (5) (Learner's Book, Session 5.8, Activity 1); Track 32; Workbook, Session 5.8, Activities 1 and 2

Description: Explain that learners are going to read a new letter from Mrs Sabella to her class. Ask: *What will you do if you find a word you do not know?* (e.g. segment using syllables, use contextual information, use phonic knowledge, check the meaning in a dictionary) Allow time for learners to read the letter silently. Ask: *Which methods could you use to find answers to questions about the letter?* (e.g. scan, read carefully).

Tell learners that they will need to make sensible guesses (infer) to work out the answer to some questions. Remind them to use complete sentences and correct punctuation when they write answers in their notebooks.

When learners have completed the task, discuss the answers to allow learners to peer mark. You could use the Focus and Practice activities in the Workbook to provide further practice with answering questions about a text.

> **Differentiation ideas:** Support less confident readers by pairing with a more confident partner.

Challenge learners to volunteer to read the letter to the class.

> **Assessment ideas:** Note which learners find it difficult to answer implicit questions. Can learners infer Mrs Sabella's feelings from the information given?

Answers:
a   Mrs Sabella's mother has been in hospital (for a few weeks).
b   Because Mrs Sabella must look after her mother until her mother is completely better.
c   The weather has been terrible.
d   Possible answer: Yes, because she has mentioned it in two letters.
e   Possible answers: She wanted to explain why she had not written; she wanted to tell the class why she had not returned to Argentina.

2 Different sentence types (10–15 minutes)

Learning intention: To explore, understand and use different types of sentence.

Resources: Learner's Book, Session 5.8, Activity 2; Workbook, Session 5.8, Activities 3 and 4

Description: Remind learners of the three sentence types in the Getting started activity, and then ask them to answer the Activity 2 questions in their notebooks.

When learners have finished, ask: *What helped you find a question sentence quickly* (e.g. scanning for a question mark)? *What helped you find an exclamation sentence* (e.g. scanning for an exclamation mark)? Use the Challenge activities in the Workbook to provide practice with identifying and writing each sentence type.

> **Differentiation ideas:** Support learners by discussing possible explanations about the three sentence types in a group.

Challenge learners to think of another question or exclamation sentence Mrs Sabella could have used in her letter (e.g. How are you? Arturo's pictures were incredible!).

> **Assessment ideas:** Are all learners confident in using the three sentence types? Do all learners use basic punctuation correctly?

Answers:
a   Learners' own choice of statement. Possible explanations: to give information or details.
b   *The weather has been terrible!* Possible explanations: to tell you that something is not normal; to tell you how someone feels.
c   Either of the two questions in the text. Possible explanations: to include the reader; when we want to know something about the reader.

3 What is wrong? (20 minutes)

Learning intention: To identify and use appropriate verb tenses.

Resources: Learner's Book, Session 5.8, Activity 3

Description: Write *look, enjoy, draw, come* on the board and ask: *Which word group do these words belong to* (verbs)? Ask learners the read the sentences in the Learner's Book and answer parts a and b. Remind them to look out for *to be* verbs. Ask learners to peer mark their answers.

Ask them to read each sentence quietly with a partner then ask: *What did you notice as you read each sentence?* Try to elicit that the verbs in a sentence should use the same tense (agree). Ask learners to look again at the verbs on the board. Explain that these verbs are in the present tense. Ask: *What are the past tenses of these verbs?* (looked, enjoyed, drew, came) Remind learners that most present tense verbs have *–ed* at the end in the past tense, but some past tense forms are irregular.

Ask: *What is added before the verb when we use the future tense?* (e.g. will: will come, will look) Explain that the sentences in the book may be written in the past, present or future tense. Allow learners time to write the sentences correctly and then mark as a class.

Ask learners to discuss the Reflection question with a partner.

> **Differentiation ideas:** Support learners with selecting the correct verb tense and making changes to irregular verb tenses.

Challenge learners to draw a three-column table with the headings *Past tense*, *Present tense* and *Future tense*. Ask learners to add the verbs in the sentences to the table, then write each verb in its three-verb form.

> **Assessment ideas:** Learners have explored past, present and future verb tenses in previous units and investigated regular and irregular verb endings. How confident are learners with all three tenses? Note which learners are confident in recognising irregular verb forms.

Answers:

a   The verbs in each sentence should use the same tense (agree).

b   We draw pictures all afternoon before we ate tea. Do you enjoyed drawing pictures too?
Watch out, I'll soon be back to made you work hard!
I'll came home as soon as I can.

c   We drew pictures all afternoon before we ate tea. Do you enjoy drawing pictures too?
Watch out, I'll soon be back to make you work hard!
I'll come home as soon as I can.
Most of the past tense verbs in the sentences are irregular.

Plenary idea

Thinking about feelings (5–10 minutes)

Resources: *Letter to Class 3 (5)* (Learner's Book, Session 5.8); Track 32

Description: Ask learners to re-read Mrs Sabella's letter to the class from Activity 1. Learners should discuss with a partner how they think Mrs Sabella's class felt when they read her letter.

Homework ideas

Ask learners to:

•   find three statement sentences, three question sentences and three exclamation sentences in their reading books.

Answers for Workbook

1   a   Padma is staying with her Grandmother.
    b   They went to the beach.
    c   They used the tent so they could change in private and to get out of the sun.

2   a   No, because it says *us* and *we*.
    b   Padma felt the beach was going to be a waste of time.
    c   So she could splash around in the water.
    d   No, because Padma says she is having a good time and she sounds happy about all the things she is doing.

3   Can we get a tent like that? (question)

    We have just come back from a trip to the beach. (statement)

    It was great! (exclamation)

4   Learners' own answers.

5.9 Other written communication

Learning objectives	Learning intentions	Success criteria
3Rw.02, 3Rw.03, 3Rw.04, 3Rg.01, 3Rg.03, 3Rg.05, 3Rg.07, 3Rg.08, 3Rs.02, 3Ri.04, 3Ri.05, 3Ri.06, 3Ri.07, 3Ri.10, 3Ri.16, 3Ri.17, 3Ra.02, 3Ww.05, 3Ww.06, 3Wg.01, 3Wg.02, 3Wg.04, 3Ws.01, 3Ws.02, 3Wc.05, 3Wc.06, 3Wp.03, 3Wp.04, 3SLs.01	• Explore key features of emails and SMS messages. • Identify nouns, pronouns and verbs in texts. • Write different types of sentences.	• Learners can explore key features of emails and SMS messages. • Learners can identify nouns, pronouns and verbs in texts. • Learners can write different types of sentences.

LANGUAGE SUPPORT

When discussing forms of communication, learners may mention a range of messaging programmes (e.g. text messaging, WhatsApp, Instagram, Messenger). Explain that *SMS* is used to cover all forms of text messaging. Learners may also know programmes such as Skype and FaceTime, and video links within other messaging platforms.

Common misconceptions

Misconception	How to identify	How to overcome
A full stop only marks the end of a sentence.	Direct learners to Activity 1c. Learners may identify one or three sentences in the SMS example because they all have capital letters and punctuation at the end.	Suggest learners use a four-point test for sentences: 1 Has it a capital letter? 2 Has it a full stop, question mark or exclamation at the end? 3 Is there a verb? 4 Is the subject in the sentence mentioned? A sentence needs all four features. If there is no verb or subject it is a sentence fragment (part sentence).

Starter idea

Electronic communication (10 minutes)

Resources: Learner's Book, Session 5.9: Getting started

Description: Say to learners: *Mrs Sabella wrote her class a lot of letters while she was in England.* Ask: *What other methods could she have used to communicate with her class?* Elicit from learners that Mrs Sabella could have written emails, sent SMS messages or telephoned her class. Direct learners to the questions in the Learner's Book. Ensure that they understand that SMS stands for Short Message Service and is how messages are sent from a mobile device. Learners may be more familiar with the term *SMS message*. Try to elicit that email and SMS messages do not have home addresses, but they do have the date, greetings, closings, signatures and body text. Learners may comment that SMS messages often include emojis.

Main teaching ideas

 1   Email and SMS messages (10–15 minutes)

Learning intention: To explore key features of emails and SMS messages.

Resources: *Letter to Class 3 (6)* (Learner's Book, Session 5.9, Activity 3); Track 33

Description: Ask learners to read the two messages from Mrs Sabella. How do they know that the two messages from Mrs Sabella did not come by post? (e.g. the address at the top of the email and lack of address in the SMS message.)

Direct learners to the Writing tip. Ask: *Which types of punctuation might you find at the end of a sentence?* (full stop, question mark, exclamation mark) Say: *All sentences start with a capital letter.* Ask: *What else does a sentence need?* Remind learners that all sentences must contain a verb and a subject. Explain that Mrs Sabella is the subject of most of the sentences in these messages.

Ask: *Which pronouns does Mrs Sabella use to talk about herself?* (I, my) In groups, ask learners to discuss the three questions. Try to elicit from learners that the body of an email is structured the same as a letter, but SMS messages do not usually use full sentences.

> **Differentiation ideas:** Support and challenge learners by dividing your class into groups comprising some learners who would like to be challenged and some learners who would benefit from additional support.

> **Assessment ideas:** Do learners understand the difference between a proper sentence and a sentence fragment?

Answers:

a   email verbs:
    I <u>am coming</u> back to Argentina. My mother <u>is</u> better now and she <u>is able</u> to <u>be</u> by herself. I <u>have</u> <u>booked</u> my ticket and I <u>will leave</u>

tomorrow. The flight <u>takes</u> a long time, so I <u>won't be</u> home until Monday morning. I <u>will see</u> you in school on Tuesday.
    SMS verbs: See

b   email pronouns: I, My, she, herself, I you
    SMS pronouns: you

c   email: yes, five sentences.
    SMS: no sentences

2   SMS messages (10–15 minutes)

Learning intention: To identify nouns, pronouns and verbs in texts.

Resources: Learner's Book, Session 5.9, Activity 2

Description: Ask: *What is missing from the three statements in the SMS message?* (e.g. a verb, a subject) Write: *At the airport* on the board, then ask: *How could you change 'At the airport' into a proper sentence?* Write suggestions on the board (e.g. I have arrived at the airport). Invite one learner to underline the verbs (have arrived) and invite another learner to circle the pronoun (I). Ask learners to discuss in pairs other possible sentence ideas using *At the airport*.

Now ask learners to transform the other SMS fragments into sentences, underlining the verbs and circling the pronouns.

> **Differentiation ideas:** Support learners who are uncertain about sentence grammar by encouraging them to use the information in the email to recognise what Mrs Sabella is saying in the SMS message.

Challenge learners to include powerful verbs in their sentences (e.g. I have arrived; My plane has landed; After a long journey, I am home at last!).

> **Assessment ideas:** Do learners understand the difference between a proper sentence and a sentence fragment? Which learners confidently identify verbs and pronouns? Which learners use question sentences but forget to include a question mark?

Can learners expand the SMS sentence fragments? Do learners use appropriate pronouns?

Answers:
(I)<u>am</u> at the airport.
(I)<u>am</u> home at last.
(I)<u>will see</u>(you) tomorrow.

3 Write an email (35–40 minute)

Learning intention: To write different types of sentences.

Resources: *Conversation between Aunty Sonia and Arturo* (Learner's Book, Session 5.9, Activity 3); Track 34; Worksheet 5.3; Differentiated worksheet pack

Description: Explain that learners need to listen carefully to a conversation between Arturo and Aunty Sonia. Direct learners to the character or ask: *Who is Aunty Sonia (Mrs Sabella)?* Play the audio (Track 34), then ask:

- *What did Aunty Sonia receive from Class 3?* (an email)
- *What would Class 3 like Aunty Sonia to bring back from England?* (Arturo)
- *What did Arturo think about that idea?* (he would like Aunty Sonia to be his teacher and meet Class 3)
- *What was Aunty Sonia's good idea?* (they could exchange emails; Arturo could email Pedro)
- *Why did Aunty Sonia think Arturo and Pedro would get on well together?* (they were both good at drawing).

Say: *Talk to your partner about what you could say to Pedro if you were Arturo.* Ask learners to share some of their ideas and write them on the board. You could use Differentiated worksheets 5A–C here to reinforce organising their ideas into paragraphs.

Direct learners to the writing task in the Learner's Book. Remind them to use statements, questions and exclamation sentences in their email. Ask learners to plan their email in their notebooks or use Worksheet 5.3 Plan an email. Allow time for learners to write their emails then direct them to the self-assessment prompt.

> **Differentiation ideas:** Support learners using a word-processing programme to write their letters with the spelling and grammar checking functions enabled.

Challenge learners to use a word-processing programme to write their letters with the spelling and grammar checking functions disabled.

> **Assessment ideas:** Did learners remember to include question and exclamation sentences in their email to Pedro? Did learners use an appropriate greeting, closing and signature in their email?

Audioscript: *Conversation between Aunty Sonia and Arturo*

Arturo: Aunty Sonia, I'm really going to miss you but I know you have to go home. Are you looking forward to going back to see your class? You haven't seen them for a very long time.

Aunty Sonia: Oh Arturo, I am really going to miss you too but it is time for me to go home. I really am looking forward to seeing my class again. In fact this morning I received an email from them. Shall I read it to you?

Arturo: Yes!

Aunty Sonia: Here it is.

Dear Mrs Sabella,

We are so pleased to hear you are coming back. We have been working really hard for Mrs Diaz and have lots of work to show you. We have also looked at lots of pictures of London so we can see where you went with Arturo. We liked Buckingham Palace where the Queen lives.

Will you bring Arturo back with you so we can meet him?

We have really missed you and can't wait for you to be our teacher again. Thank you for all your letters!

See you very soon,

Mateo, Sofia, Catalina and Pedro

(and the rest of Class 3)

Arturo: I wish I could go back with you! It would be really nice if you could be my teacher and I could meet Class 3 [*he laughs*]

Aunty Sonia: It is a shame you can't come back with me but I have a good idea … once I am back in Argentina shall we send each other emails so we can keep in touch? You could also write emails to Pedro in my class, if you'd like? I think you both would really get on. He is a good artist too.

Arturo: Great idea! [*he shouts*]

Plenary idea

An email to Arturo (5 minutes)

Resources: Learners' emails from Activity 3

Description: Invite learners to read their emails to the class. Ask other learners to say what was good about each email and what could be improved.

Homework ideas

Ask learners to:

- complete the Workbook activities for this session, if not completed in class

- talk to family members about the different types of electronic communication they use or know. Make a list.

Answers for Workbook

1 Learners' own messages.

2 Possible answers:

   a Were you at cricket yesterday?

   b I am happy at your news.

c I was / They were with Juanita at playtime.

d Would you like a cup of tea?

e Have you had a good day at school?

3 a Ihave been home for only three hours but I have been very busy! I had to collect my cats from Mrs Menotti. She looked after them while I was with you. She is very kind, but she wanted me to sit down and tell her all about you. The plane I flew home in was very big. It had over 300 seats but they were very close together. Near me was a family. The three children didn't like sitting down for so long and kept running around. Looking at them made me think of you but I think you would have sat more quietly than they did.
   I need to go to bed now. I have to go to school tomorrow and meet all the lovely children in Class 3. I wonder if they have missed me?

b

Noun or noun phrase	Pronouns
Aunty Sonia	I, me, my
Arturo	you
Mrs Menotti	she, her
cats	them
plane	It
seats	they
children on the plane	them, they
children in Class 3	they

5.10 Talking about mail

LEARNING PLAN		
Learning objectives	**Learning intentions**	**Success criteria**
3Ra.03, 3Ws.04, 3Wp.02, 3SLm.01, 3SLm.02, 3SLm.05, 3SLs.01, 3SLs.02, 3SLg.01, 3SLg.04, 3SLr.01	• Talk about and listen to a letter received. • Use a mind map to organise ideas. • Retell a sequence of events fluently and confidently.	• Learners can talk about and listen to a letter received. • Learners can use a mind map to organise ideas. • Learners can retell a sequence of events fluently and confidently.

If learners are unfamiliar with mind maps, you will need to spend some time explaining how to create a mind map. Some learners find mind maps a very useful memory aid.

Starter idea

Talk about mail (5 minutes)

Resources: Learner's Book, Session 5.10: Getting started

Description: Direct learners to the questions in the Learner's Book. Remind them that mail can include postal and electronic mail. Allow learners time to share their experiences of mail.

Main teaching ideas

1 Using a mind map (15–20 minutes)

Learning intention: To use a mind map to organise ideas.

Resources: Learner's Book, Session 5.10, Activity 1; Workbook, Session 5.10, Activity 1; A4 or A3 plain paper; pens; pencils; colouring pencils

Description: You could use the Focus activity in the Workbook before introducing mind maps, to allow learners to explore a different type of mail.

Direct learners to the picture of the mind map, then ask: *Have you ever used a mind map? Why would you use a mind map?* Try to elicit that a mind map is a way of recording many ideas about the same thing. Explain that a mind map begins with the main subject in the centre. Ask: *What is this mind map about?* (mail) Explain that a line is drawn from the centre for each type of mail. Ask learners to talk to a partner about the types of mail shown in the mind map.

Ask: *Why does the 'letters' circle have two lines with two circles coming from it?* (to show there are different types of letters) *Can you think of any other types of letter that could be added to this circle?* (e.g. 'staying in touch' letters) Explain that learners' mind maps should include all the types of mail used in this unit and any other mail they have talked about.

Allow time for learners to complete their mind maps.

> **Differentiation ideas:** Support learners by creating a group mind map and recording learners' ideas onto the mind map for them.

Challenge learners to colour-code their mind maps when they have recorded all the examples of mail (e.g. blue for types of electronic mail, orange for all types of letter).

> **Assessment ideas:** Can learners record all the types of mail in the mind map? Do learners understand how a mind map works?

Answers:
Learners' own mind maps.

2 Speaking and listening (10 minutes)

Learning intention: To talk about and listen to a letter.

Resources: Learner's Book, Session 5.10, Activity 2; a room large enough to allow half the class to be talking at the same time

Description: Explain that learners are going to practise their speaking and listening skills by talking about mail they have received. Remind learners that they can talk about mail they have received by post, by email, as an SMS message or even make their mail story up.

Direct learners to the 'Speaker' and 'Listener' speech bubbles. Ask: *Why is it important to use an interesting voice when you are speaking? Why is it important to look at the person who is speaking?* Check that learners understand the activity, then organise learners into pairs for the speaking and listening activity.

Allow time afterwards for learners to discuss how well they followed the speaking and listening tips.

> **Differentiation ideas:** Support learners by suggesting the more confident speaker in the pair takes the speaking role.

> **Assessment ideas:** Which learners:

- can speak fluently and confidently
- demonstrate good listening skills
- adapt the language they use to help the listener

- use the letters and messages from Mrs Sabella to record a logical sequence of her visit to England
- demonstrate the same level of listening skill in a group as they do in a pair
- ask questions about what they hear to show they understand the main points?

You may want to ask learners to swap roles so that you can assess the speaking and listening skills of both learners in each pair.

3 Postal versus electronic mail (2–3 minutes)

Learning intention: To discuss ideas in small groups.

Resources: Learner's Book, Session 5.10, Activity 3

Description: Ask: *In the last activity, who talked about postal mail? Who talked about electronic mail?* Direct learners to the activity in the Learner's Book, then share learners' ideas (e.g. it is quicker, it is cheaper).

4 Mrs Sabella's story (15–20 minutes)

Learning intention: To retell a sequence of events fluently and confidently.

Resources: Learner's Book, Session 5.10, Activity 4

Description: Organise learners into groups of five, then explain that they are to use all the mail Mrs Sabella has sent to tell the story of her trip to England. Ask learners to number themselves from one to five. Explain that Learner 1 will tell the first part of the story, then Learner 2 will continue the story and so on until all of Mrs Sabella's story has been told. Direct learners to the Reading tip.

Encourage learners to retell the story two or three times, and suggest a different learner starts the story each time.

> **Assessment ideas:** Note which learners were able to recall Mrs Sabella's story. Which learners needed prompts?

Plenary idea

Mrs Sabella's mind map (10-15 minutes)

Resources: Learner's Book, Session 5.10; A4 or A3 plain paper; pens; pencils; colouring crayons

Description: In pairs, ask learners to create a mind map of Mrs Sabella's visit. Explain that learners should include all the places Mrs Sabella visited during her visit and any other events that they think are important about her stay.

CROSS-CURRICULAR LINKS

Mind mapping could be used to map ideas or understanding in many subjects. Mind maps are very useful ways for learners to record links between facts and to demonstrate their understanding of a subject.

Homework ideas

Ask learners to:

- complete the Practice and Challenge activities in the Workbook
- write a chronological story of Mrs Sabella's visit in their own words.

Answers for Workbook

1 True statements: a, e, g, i
2 Possible answers:
   a Milonga means a place where you can learn to dance the tango.
   b Mighty means very high and powerful.
   c Humid means hot and sticky.
   d Cruise means to visit places by boat.
   e Gaucho means Argentine cowboy.
3 Learners' own letters.

5.11 Writing a letter

LEARNING PLAN

Learning objectives	Learning intentions	Success criteria
3Ww.02, 3Ww.03, 3Ww.04, 3Ww.05, 3Ww.06, 3Wv.02, 3Wv.04, 3Wv.05, 3Wv.07, 3Wg.01, 3Wg.02, 3Wg.04, 3Wg.05, 3Wg.06, 3Wg.07, 3Ws.01, 3Ws.02, 3Ws.03, 3Wc.02, 3Wc.05, 3Wc.06, 3Wp.03, 3SLg.02	• Plan a letter. • Write a letter.	• Learners can plan a letter. • Learners can write a letter.

LANGUAGE SUPPORT

When learners plan their letters to Mrs Sabella, their ideas should include things they have done as a class, things about Mrs Sabella and Mrs Diaz, the supply teacher, and things that are just about themselves. Each topic will require learners to use a range of pronouns and you may want to recap pronouns with learners before they begin writing.

Starter ideas

Understanding the past tense (5 minutes)

Resources: Learner's Book, Session 5.11: Getting started

Description: Ask learners to discuss what the past tense is. Do they have the same understanding? Remind learners that most past tense verbs end with –ed. Ask: *What do we call verbs that follow this pattern* (regular verbs)*?* Remind learners that some past tense verbs are irregular, which means they do not follow a spelling pattern. Ask learners to say the past tense form of the verbs in the Learner's Book.

Answers:
helped, carried, showed, ran, smiled

Main teaching ideas

1 Plan a letter (10 minutes)

Learning intention: To plan a letter.

Resources: Learner's Book 5.11, Activity 1

Description: Ask learners to imagine they are one of the learners in Mrs Sabella's class. Direct learners to the activity in the Learner's Book, and the peer assessment prompt. When learners have had a few minutes to discuss, encourage them to share ideas that they want to include in their letter. Note their ideas on the board.

2 Make notes for a letter (10 minutes)

Learning intention: To plan a letter.

Resources: Learner's Book, Session 5.11, Activity 2; Workbook, Session 5.11, Activities 1 and 2; Worksheet 5.4

Description: Ask learners to look back at the features and content of the letter in Session 5.4. Explain that they should think about how they will start the letter, the order of the activities they will include and how they will end their letter. Now direct learners to the activity in the Learner's Book.

Ask: *What could you use to help you choose powerful words?* (e.g. a thesaurus, word lists) Ask: *Which connectives could you use to join simple sentences?* (e.g. and, but, so, because, if) Allow learners time to make notes. You could use the Focus and Practice activities in the Workbook to reinforce vocabulary and multi-clause sentences if there is time in class.

> **Differentiation ideas:** Support learners by providing Worksheet 5.4 Plan a letter to help them structure their planning.

Challenge learners to use a mind map to make their notes.

3 Write a letter (25–30 minutes)

Learning intention: To write a letter.

Resources: Learner's Book, Session 5.11; Worksheet 5.5

Description: Ask learners to write their letters. Learners should:

- include the five features listed in Session 5.4 of the Learner's Book.

- use the address on the postcard in Session 5.1 of the Learner's Book for their letters

- use a date in June for their letters (Mrs Sabella was back in Argentina by 19 July).

Allow time for learners to write their letters using their planning notes.

> **Differentiation ideas:** Support learners by providing Worksheet 5.5 A letter to Mrs Sabella.

Challenge learners to use a word-processing programme to write their letters. Encourage them to use left and right alignment tools. Make sure spelling and grammar checking tools are disabled.

> **Assessment ideas:** Note which learners used five letter-writing features. Which learners chose an appropriate greeting and closing? Did learners make any comment about Mrs Sabella's letters?

Plenary idea

Be proud (5 minutes)

Description: Ask learners to share a multi-clause sentence or powerful word they have used in their letter that they are proud of.

Homework ideas

Ask learners to:

- complete the Workbook activities for this session, if not completed in class

- think of three powerful synonyms for *went*, *best*, and *saw*, and then use each word in a sentence.

Answers for Workbook

1 Learners' own answers.

2 Learners' own sentences.

3 Answers to include learners' synonyms and multi-clause sentences: Thank you for <u>taking</u> me out to London. I had a nice time. I liked it when we went on the big train. The train was big. It was shiny. It was green. I liked it when the train went through the tunnel. It made my eyes feel strange when we came out of the tunnel into the <u>light</u>.

The cat is watching TV with me. Her kittens are playing. <u>They</u> are making a sound. It is a big sound. They are going around the room. The cat is purring.

5.12 Improving your letter

LEARNING PLAN		
Learning objectives	**Learning intentions**	**Success criteria**
3Ww.02, 3Ww.03, 3Ww.04, 3Ww.05, 3Ww.06. 3Wv.02, 3Wv.04, 3Wv.05, 3Wg.01, 3Wg.02, 3Wg.04, 3Wg.05, 3Wg.06, 3Wg.07, 3Ws.01, 3Ws.02, 3Ws.03, 3Ws.04, 3Wc.05, 3Wc.06, 3Wp.01, 3Wp.04, 3Wp.05	• Use neat joined writing to write a letter. • Proofread for grammar, spelling and punctuation errors.	• Learners can use neat joined writing to write a letter. • Learners can proofread for grammar, spelling and punctuation errors.

LANGUAGE SUPPORT

Some learners may have noticed apostrophes used in this way: *Arturo's pictures, Arturo's favourite part of the day*. Avoid discussing apostrophes used for possession when you recap apostrophes for omission during this session. Learners will cover apostrophes for possession in Stage 4.

Starter idea

Letter features (5 minutes)

Resources: Learner's Book, Session 5.12: Getting started; Workbook Session 2.12

Description: Explain that in this session learners should find ways of improving their letter and check their letter for errors. Say: *Tell your partner the word for checking and improving something we have written* (proofreading).

Ask learners to recall the five features they need to include in a letter. Ask: *Will you read your letter carefully to check your letter or will you scan your letter?* Elicit from learners that they can scan their letter for the five features. Allow time for learners to scan their letter with a partner. You can ask learners to complete the Workbook activities for this session now to help develop their proofreading skills if there is time.

Main teaching ideas

1 Focus on grammar (10 minutes)

Learning intention: To proofread for grammar errors.

Resources: Learner's Book, Session 5.12, Activity 1; coloured pencils or pens

Description: Explain that the first time learners re-read their letters they should focus on the grammar. Ask: *What will you do to check the grammar?* Try to elicit from learners that checking the grammar means that the sentences make sense and sound interesting. Direct learners to the activity in the Learner's Book. Explain that they should make grammar changes using a coloured pen or pencil. Tell learners that they must not worry about the letter looking messy as they will have time to re-write it later. Direct learners to the Listening tip. Allow learners time to proofread and improve the grammar in their letter.

> **Differentiation ideas:** Support learners by pairing them with a writing partner.

Challenge learners to find interesting synonyms to replace at least two more ordinary words.

> **Assessment ideas:** Note which learners are willing to make changes to their letters.

2 Focus on punctuation (10-15 minutes)

Learning intention: To proofread for punctuation errors.

Resources: Learner's Book, Session 5.12, Activity 2; coloured pencils or pens

Description: Explain that learners will now check their letter for punctuation errors. Ask them to look at the activity in the Learner's Book and the prompts in the Language focus box.

Remind learners how to use apostrophes. Write *I am* on the board and ask: *How can I shorten these two words?* (remove the *a*) Write *I m* on the board. Ask: *What do I need to show that I have missed a letter out?* (an apostrophe) Invite a learner to add the apostrophe in the correct place (*I'm*).

Tell learners to use a different-coloured pen or pencil to mark punctuation changes. Remind them to re-read their letter once they have made punctuation changes to double check for errors and to ensure that the letter reads well.

> **Differentiation ideas:** Provide support by directing learners to word lists of expanded and contracted words and irregular past tense words.

> **Assessment ideas:** Note which learners used apostrophes for omission correctly.

3 Focus on spelling (10 minutes)

Learning intention: To proofread for spelling errors.

Resources: Learner's Book, Session 5.12, Activity 3; Language worksheet 5B; coloured pencils or pens; learners' or class word lists; dictionaries

Description: Explain that now learners should check for any spelling errors. You could use Language worksheet 5B here. Tell learners to choose a third coloured pencil and to draw a line under any word they think may be incorrect or that they found difficult to spell. Provide access to dictionaries for learners to check these words.

Remind learners that it is easy to choose the wrong spelling of homophones. If learners created homophone lists during Session 5.5, remind them to use these lists as a reference.

When learners have checked their spelling, direct them to the Reflection questions.

> **Differentiation ideas:** Support learners by reminding them of the strategies and tools available for correcting the words they have identified. Tell them that they can also check a spelling with another learner.

Challenge learners to be a spelling aid to other learners.

> **Assessment ideas:** Can learners identify spelling errors of words they should know?

4 Write your final letter (30–40 minutes)

Learning intention: To use neat joined-up writing to write a letter.

Resources: Learner's Book, Session 5.12, Activity 4; Worksheet 5.6; handwriting pens (if available); a copy of the school's handwriting style, if used

Description: Remind learners how to form or join letters that you know they find difficult.

- Draw four parallel lines on the board to represent handwriting lines.
- Write *Dear Mrs Sabella* on the lines so that learners can see where letters are positioned (e.g. capital letters *D*, *M*, *S* and tall letters *b* and *l* sitting on the third line and extending to the top line; lower-case letters *e*, *a*, *r* sitting on the third line and fitting the space up to the second line).

Ask learners to write their letter. Remind them to include all their proofreading corrections. When learners have finished, direct them to the self-assessment prompt. Learners could use Worksheet 5.6 Checklist for writing a letter as they self-assess.

> **Differentiation ideas:** Support learners who write slowly, by allowing them to omit the address and date from their final letter.

> **Assessment ideas:** Do not expect learners to self-assess against all possible writing features. It is more important that learners self-assess against learning taught in this unit. Learners' letters will also allow you to assess their ability to:

- spell words with common suffixes
- use sentence openings

- use noun phrases
- use multi-clause sentences
- ensure verb tenses agree
- organise their writing into paragraphs.

Plenary idea

How did I do? (5 minutes)

Resources: Worksheet 5.6

Description: Ask: *What should I see in your letter?* Try to elicit the success criteria checklist in Worksheet 5.6 from learners. Write their ideas on the board.

Hand out Worksheet 5.6 and ask learners if there were any criteria on the worksheet that they missed. Ask learners to complete the worksheet, adding faces to show how they think they have done.

Homework ideas

Ask learners to:

- complete the Workbook activities for this session, if not completed in class
- draw a picture to illustrate one part of their letter to Mrs Sabella.

Answers for Workbook

1   Dear <u>A</u>rturo,
    <u>I</u> can<u>'</u>t believe that it<u>'</u>s been a week since I last saw you<u>!</u> <u>S</u>o much has happened in the week<u>.</u>
    <u>I</u> was so pleased to get back to school and meet Class 3 again<u>.</u> <u>I</u> knew it would be exciting to hear about their lessons with the other teacher<u>.</u> <u>I</u> asked them to write about what they had been doing since I last saw them<u>.</u> <u>T</u>hey have been very busy<u>.</u>
    <u>W</u>hat have you been doing<u>?</u> I wish I didn<u>'</u>t live so far away<u>.</u> <u>I</u>t would be so good to see you more often<u>.</u>
    <u>L</u>ove from <u>A</u>unty <u>S</u>onia

2

Words in full	Shortened form
is not	*isn't*
<u>can not</u>	can't
would not	<u>wouldn't</u>
was not	<u>wasn't</u>
<u>could not</u>	couldn't
<u>are not</u>	aren't
were not	<u>weren't</u>
will not	<u>won't</u>

Words in full	Shortened form
I am	I'm
he is	he's
it is	it's
we are	we're
they are	they're
I will	I'll
you will	you'll
we will	we'll

3 Learners' own answers.

CHECK YOUR PROGRESS

1 a False
b True
c False

2 a Mrs Sabella wrote to her class while she in England.

b Did you count how many letters she wrote?

c 'We're going to miss her letters when she comes home,' said Sita.

3 big – enormous
little – tiny
good – pleasant
bad – terrible
nice – wonderful

4 a The guards walked past / in front of / by the gates at Buckingham Palace.

b Mrs Sabella did a tour of London in / on a bus.

5 a write
b to / too
c rain / reign
d bye

PROJECT GUIDANCE

Group project: Explain the project to learners and discuss any ideas they may have. Discuss the importance of choosing a realistic idea. Elicit from learners the importance of using formal language and of being polite. Explain that it is important that they explain themselves clearly and give reasons to support their idea. For example, if learners think there is too much litter around school, they could suggest a litter-picking day or having school litter monitors.

Remind learners to be respectful of each other's ideas and to allow everyone to contribute to the discussion.

Within groups, learners could write letters individually or in pairs. Each group then chooses the best letter to send to the headteacher. Who knows, the headteacher may agree to one of the suggestions!

Pair project: Learners will need access to a computer and have a personal email address for this project. You should seek permission from parents and put these arrangements in place before introducing the project to your learners. The paired project would fit well with the Teaching skills challenge if you have been able to make a link with another school.

CONTINUED

Remind learners to write a title for their email in the subject box. You could ask learners to use the reply tool once they have received their first reply. To remind learners to include an email subject, you may want learners to start a new email each time.

If learners do not have computer access or an email address, adapt the task by organising a paper-based messaging task. Ask pairs of learners to decide who is Writer A and who is Writer B. Explain that Writer A writes the first message and passes it to Writer B. Writer B writes a reply and returns the message to Writer A, who then replies. This continues until both A and B have written six messages.

Solo project: Explain the project to learners and talk about who may have sent them a present.

Remind learners of the 'thank you' letter that Arturo wrote to Aunty Sonia. Learners should re-read this letter before they plan their own letter.

If you used the self-assessment checklist with learners at the end of Session 5.12, ask learners to think about each of these points as they plan their letters.

>6 Bringing stories alive

Unit plan

Session	Approximate number of learning hours	Outline of learning content	Resources
6.1 Reading a playscript	1.5	Read and answer questions about a playscript extract. Identify the similarities and differences in playscripts and stories.	Learner's Book Session 6.1 Workbook Session 6.1
6.2 Looking closely at a playscript	1	Explore the layout of playscripts. Read the next part of a playscript and answer questions about it.	Learner's Book Session 6.2 Workbook Session 6.2 ⬇ Language worksheet 6A
6.3 Writing dialogue and performing a play	1.5–2	Rewrite cartoon dialogue as narrative text and as a playscript. Rewrite a narrative extract as a playscript. Act out part of a play.	Learner's Book Session 6.3 Workbook Session 6.3 ⬇ Worksheets 6.1 and 6.2 ⬇ Language worksheet 6B
6.4 What happens next?	1.5–2	Sequence the main events of a playscript, and write the next section of dialogue. Explore words with soft c.	Learner's Book Session 6.4 Workbook Session 6.4 ⬇ Worksheet 6.1
6.5 Writing a playscript	1.5	Choose a traditional story. Plan and write a playscript for it.	Learner's Book Session 6.5 Workbook Session 6.5 ⬇ Worksheets 6.1 and 6.3 ⬇ Differentiated worksheets 6A–C
6.6 Improving a playscript	1.5	Proofread and improve a playscript. Handwrite or type a final copy. Perform playscripts in groups.	Learner's Book Session 6.6 Workbook Session 6.6 ⬇ Worksheet 6.4
Cross-unit resources			
Learner's Book Check your progress			
Learner's Book Projects			
End-of-unit 6 test			

BACKGROUND KNOWLEDGE

It will be helpful to be familiar with the following English subject knowledge:

- structure of playscripts
- language of playscripts (e.g. narrator, stage directions)
- present tense verbs
- punctuation used in playscripts, including colons and brackets
- narrative and direct speech
- words with soft c
- writing descriptions
- writing dialogue.

TEACHING SKILLS FOCUS

Metacognition: Helping your learners learn

During this unit, encourage your learners to think about how they learn to develop their metacognitive ability. Ask: *Do you learn better in a quiet room? Do you like to have background noise or music? Do you learn best when you make notes? Does it help to explain what you have learned to someone else?* Helping learners recognise what works best for them is a first step in developing metacognition.

At the end of a challenging task ask: *What was the most confusing or difficult part of this session?* Learning that it is okay to be confused or find things difficult is another step in the metacognitive process.

You could ask learners to keep a learning journal. Questions might include:

- What did I find it easy to learn this week? Why?
- What did I have difficulty in learning? Why?
- What have I learned this week that I didn't know or understand previously?
- What is the key idea I have learned this session/ week?

Cambridge Reading Adventures

The Mystery of Sol, by Lauri Kubuitsile, could be used to provide additional opportunities for exploring playscripts.

6.1 Reading a playscript

LEARNING PLAN

Learning objectives	Learning intentions	Success criteria
3Rw.03, 3Rw.04, 3Rv.01, 3Rg.01, 3Rg.10, 3Rs.02, 3Rs.03, 3Ri.02, 3Ri.03, 3Ri.06, 3Ri.07, 3Ri.10, 3Ri.12, 3Ri.14, 3Ri.16, 3Ra.01, 3Ra.02, 3Wp.02, 3SLg.02, 3SLg.04, 3SLp.01, 3SLp.02	• Read a playscript. • Answer questions about a playscript. • Compare the features of stories and playscripts.	• Learners can read a playscript. • Learners can answer questions about a playscript. • Learners can compare the features of stories and playscripts.

LANGUAGE SUPPORT

If learners are unfamiliar with plays and performances you may need to explain unfamiliar words to them (e.g. stage, audience, actors, narrator, script, scenery, costume). Begin a display of unfamiliar words so that learners can refer to them during the unit.

Learners may notice the colons after each characters' name in the script. At Stage 3 you should explain that colons are used in playscripts to separate the character's name from what they say.

Starter idea

What is a play? (5 minutes)

Resources: Learner's Book, Session 6.1: Getting started

Description: Direct learners to the picture in the Learner's Book. Ask: *What can you see?* (e.g. a stage, people watching the stage, children dressed up).

Ask: *What do you think is happening?* Try to elicit that children are performing a play. Direct learners to the questions and allow time for discussion. Introduce the words *stage* and *audience*.

Main teaching ideas

 1 Read a play (20 minutes)

Learning intention: To read a playscript.

Resources: *Four Clever Brothers, Part 1* (Learner's Book, Session 6.1, Activity 1); Track 35; Workbook, Session 6.1, Activity 1

Description: Explain that in this unit learners will explore playscripts. Direct learners to the *Four*

Clever Brothers, Part 1 playscript. Before reading the text, ask: *What do you notice about the way a play is set out compared to a story?* (short sections, names at the side, no paragraphs).

Explain that the characters in a play are known as *actors* and that the character list tells the actor a little bit about each character. Read the character list to the class and direct learners to the Key word and Glossary terms.

Invite a learner to read the introductory paragraph. Ask: *Why do you think the play has a section like this?* (to tell you how the story begins) Ask learners to read the playscript in pairs.

When learners have finished reading, explain that *Judge* is a special actor who is also the storyteller. Storytellers are known as *narrators*. You could use the Focus activity in the Workbook to familiarise learners with an understanding of characters.

Invite six learners to read the play out loud to the class. Each of them should read a different character. Ask: *Why is part of the text in brackets?*

(none of the actors say it) *Who do you think that information is for?* (readers, actors) Explain that this type of information is known as a *stage direction* and tells actors how to act and tells the reader that something new is happening. Ask: *Which verb tense is used in stage directions?* (present tense) Can learners explain why they think the present tense is used (e.g. the action is happening at that moment)?

Ask: *Are there any words in the playscript that you do not understand?* (e.g. concerns, recently, hoof, distress) Explain any unfamiliar words.

> **Differentiation ideas:** Support less confident readers by pairing them with more confident partners.

> **Assessment ideas:** Note which learners are familiar with plays or have seen a play.

2 Answer questions about the play (15 minutes)

Learning intention: To answer questions about a playscript.

Resources: Learner's Book, Session 6.1, Activity 2

Description: Explain that like a story, plays tell the reader about the setting and the characters and that learners should look for clues to find information to answer questions. Direct learners to the Reading tip. Talk about any other times when they have re-read a text to help them answer questions. Ask learners to write their answers in their notebooks.

> **Differentiation ideas:** Support learners by re-reading the character list and Judge's words to help them answer questions a–d.

Answers:
a   six
b   eldest: Tazim; youngest: Latif
c   a dry and dusty desert land
d   hunting
e   They saw footprints smaller than a horse's hoof and spaced well apart.
f   Because Gilad was shouting at them; they were worried Gilad thought they had stolen the camel.

3 Answer questions about the characters (15 minutes)

Learning intention: To answer questions about a playscript.

Resources: Learner's Book, Session 6.1, Activity 3; Workbook, Session 6.1, Activity 2

Description: Explain that learners are going to answer questions about the characters in the playscript. Ask: *Where could you find ideas about how a character feels or the kind of person they are?* (e.g. character list, what a character says, stage directions) Ask learners to work in pairs to answer the questions, then share their answers in a small group. You could use the Practice activity in the Workbook to provide further support with answering questions about characters.

> **Differentiation ideas:** Support learners by directing them to different sections of the playscript.

> **Assessment ideas:** During discussions note which learners demonstrate good inference skills when they discuss characters.

Answers:
a   To explain the story; to give extra details about the story or characters.
b   Possible answers: worried, distressed, foolish.
c   Possible answers: surprised, frightened, concerned, worried.
d   Possible answers: Why do you think it was stolen? When did you see it last?
e   Possible answers: What has happened to the camel and who stole the camel.

4 Comparing stories and playscripts (20 minutes)

Learning intention: To compare the features of stories and playscripts.

Resources: Learner's Book, Session 6.1, Activity 4

Description: In groups, ask learners to list what they know about playscripts. Tell them to include what they know about the layout, the punctuation and how the play develops. Then ask groups to make a list of what they know about stories. Ask: *Are some features the same on each list? Which features are different? Have you remembered what we said about verb tenses? Have you thought about how the dialogue is presented?*

Direct learners to the table in the Learner's Book. Explain that they should use their lists to complete the table. When learners are ready to complete the *Differences* column, tell them to first think about how playscripts are different to stories, and then how stories are different to playscripts.

> **Differentiation ideas:** Support learners by suggesting that they highlight the items that are the same in both lists to help them identify the similarities, then use the non-highlighted items for the differences list.

Challenge learners to find at least four similarities and six differences.

> **Assessment ideas:** Note which learners demonstrate a good understanding of a narrative story. Can they use their knowledge to identify differences between stories and playscripts?

Answers:

Playscripts and stories	
Similarities	Differences
Both stories and playscripts have: • characters • a title • the setting is described • have a beginning, middle and end • speech/dialogue • what is happening is usually explained by one of the characters • use capital letters, full stops, question and exclamation marks	Playscripts have: • a list of characters • narrators • subheadings • the speaker's name in bold on the left side of the page • two dots (colon) after the speaker's name • present tense to say what is happening • extra information in brackets. Stories have: • paragraphs • speech marks

Playscripts and stories	
Similarities	Differences
	• characters that are introduced one by one • past tense or present continuous to tell what has happened / is happening.

Plenary idea

How do they compare? (5–10 minutes)

Resources: Learners' similarities and differences table

Description: Ask each group to share the similarities they identified between playscripts and stories. Repeat, with the differences. Discuss any features that learners missed or disagree about. Ask: *Is it easy to recognise a playscript without reading the words* (yes, from the layout)?

Homework ideas

Ask learners to:

• complete the Workbook activities for this session, if not completed in class

• make a list of the characters in their reading book and write a brief description about each character.

Answers for Workbook

1 a Adil the judge

   b Tazim

   c Latif

   d Gilad

   e Adil the judge

2 a Adil

   b Latif

   c Gilad

   d Gilad could have followed the camel's footprints.

   e Learners' own answers could include: No, because they can see the camel's footprints; Yes, because the camel would not go away on its own.

3 Learners' own responses.

6.2 Looking closely at a playscript

LEARNING PLAN

Learning objectives	Learning intentions	Success criteria
3Rw.03, 3Rv.01, 3Rg.01, 3Rs.02, 3Rs.03, 3Ri.02, 3Ri.03, 3Ri.06, 3Ri.07, 3Ri.10, 3Ri.12, 3Ri.14, 3Ri.16, 3Ra.01, 3Ra.02, 3Wv.01, 3SLm.01, 3SLm.03, 3SLm.04, 3SLm.05, 3SLs.02, 3SLg.01, 3SLg.02, 3SLg.04, 3SLp.01, 3SLp.02, 3SLr.01	• Discuss the layout of a playscript. • Answer questions about a playscript. • Listen and respond to other learners' ideas.	• Learners can discuss the layout of a playscript. • Learners can answer questions about a playscript. • Learners can listen and respond to each other's ideas.

LANGUAGE SUPPORT

Learners should be confident in recognising that adjectives are used to describe a noun. In this session learners will be introduced to adverbs as words that describe a verb. To help learners distinguish between adjectives and adverbs, explain that adjectives *add* information to a noun and adverbs *add* information to a verb.

Common misconceptions

Misconception	How to identify	How to overcome
All words in brackets should be spoken aloud when reading or performing a playscript.	Ask learners to take the role of different characters in a playscript and read a script aloud. Some learners may read the words in brackets.	Carry out an action without saying anything (e.g. walk to the back of the class and pick up a book from a learner's desk). Ask: *What have I just done? Did I tell you what I was doing? Why not?* Elicit from learners that they could see what you were doing. Explain that words in brackets tell an actor(s) what to do but do not need saying because they can be seen.

Starter idea

Thinking about text types (5 minutes)

Resources: Learner's Book, Session 6.2: Getting started

Description: Say: *Talk to your partner about the types of fiction and non-fiction texts you know.* Ask learners to list as many as types as they can. Direct them to the montage and prompts in the Learner's Book. Do they want to add any more text types to their list?

Ask: *Which text types are easy to identify from their layout (e.g. playscripts, story, poem)?*

Main teaching ideas

1 Playscript layout (10–15 minutes)

Learning intention: To discuss the layout of a playscript.

Resources: Learner's Book, Session 6.2, Activity 1; Workbook, Session 6.2, Activities 1 and 2

Description: Direct learners to the Language focus box and ask them to place their finger on each feature in the playscript as you read out the prompt. Use the questions in the Learner's Book to lead a discussion about each layout feature. When you ask each question, ask learners to discuss the question with a partner then answer the question in their notebooks.

Invite learners to share their answers with the class. Learners could complete the Focus and Practice activities in the Workbook at this point if there is time.

> **Differentiation ideas:** Support learners by pairing them with a more confident learner.

> **Assessment ideas:** Can learners identify playscript features?

Answers:
a   title, list of characters
b   you know how many actors are involved; you know what each character is like
c   they tell the actors what to do
d   in two columns: character's name on the left in bold; what the character says is separate from the character's name

2   What happens next? (15 minutes)

Learning intention: To answer questions about a playscript.

Resources: *Four Clever Brothers, Part 2* (Learner's Book, Session 6.2, Activity 2); Track 36; Workbook, Session 6.2, Activity 3; Language worksheet 6A

Description: Ask: *What happened at the end of the playscript in the previous session?* (Gilad thought someone had stolen his camel) Direct learners to the playscript. Read out the Key word and Glossary terms. Allow time for learners to read the playscript silently.

Ask: *Are there any stage directions in this extract?* ('to himself') *Does this stage direction mean Gilad thinks the words or does he say them aloud? How will he say them?* Try to elicit that Gilad could turn away from the other actors and say them aloud and use a gesture to show he is thinking.

Explain that stage directions are sometimes verbs or verb phrases (scowling, shaking his fist) and sometimes words that describe the verb (e.g. crossly, angrily).

Explain that words that describe a verb are known as *adverbs*. Learners could complete the Challenge section of the Workbook or Language worksheet 6A at this point.

Invite volunteers to read the five character parts. Direct them to the questions and tell them to write their answers in their notebooks.

> **Assessment ideas:** Do learners understand that stage directions without brackets are for all characters and those with brackets are for one character (e.g. for himself)? Note which learners were able to recognise and use adverbs.

Answers:
a   The character's name is on the left in bold.
b   Sadiq; Sadiq; Latif
c   four
d   It is a stage direction.

3   Sharing ideas (15 minutes)

Learning intention: To listen and respond to each other's ideas.

Resources: Learner's Book, Session 6.2, Activity 3

Description: Direct learners to the activity in the Learner's Book and read the Listening tip. Ask: *How can you show your partner that you are listening to them?* (eye contact, nodding head, questioning looks, encouraging noises or comments, asking questions) Ask: *How will you respond to your partner's ideas and suggestions?* (say which ideas you agree with, explain politely if you disagree).

Ask learners to choose to be Speaker A or Speaker B. Tell learners that Speaker A will have five minutes to speak. Explain that you will say when they should swap roles and that Speaker B will have five minutes to speak.

When learners have shared their ideas, ask them to think about how well they shared their ideas and listened to their partner.

> **Differentiation ideas:** Challenge those learners with many ideas to demonstrate good listening skills by choosing learners who you think will have fewer ideas to speak first.

> **Assessment ideas:** Do learners demonstrate good listening skills during discussions by making eye contact, responding respectfully and responding with relevant comments or questions?

Answers:
Possible answers: to make it easy for actors to see when they should speak; to give actors information about how to speak/behave; to help actors/readers understand what is happening.

Plenary idea

Stage directions (5–10 minutes)

Description: Re-read Gilad's last words. Ask: *How might the brothers feel when Gilad said this?* (worried, angry, embarrassed, shocked) Say: *With your partner, think of stage directions to describe how Gilad might say these words.* Ask: *How might Gilad look? What might he do?* (speak crossly, look angry, shake his fist) Share learners' ideas.

Homework ideas

Ask learners to:

* complete the Workbook activities for this session, if not completed in class

* draw and label a picture of Gilad's camel using the information in the extract (*lame, carrying wheat on one side and honey on the other, bad-tempered, old*).

Answers for Workbook

1   **a** title

   b character list

   c stage direction

   d dialogue

2   Possible answers:
   The *title* tells you what the play is called and what it may be about.
   The *character list* tells you how many actors take part in the play and something about them.
   The *stage directions* tell actors how to say something or what to do. They also set the scene.
   The *dialogue* tells actors what to say.

3   Learners' own answers. Possible answers might include:

   Latif: Tracking animals is what we do best. (*looking at his brothers*)

6.3 Writing dialogue and performing a play

LEARNING PLAN

Learning objectives	Learning intentions	Success criteria
3Rw.03, 3Rv.01, 3Rg.01, 3Rg.04, 3Rg.10, 3Rs.02, 3Rs.03, 3Ri.02, 3Ri.03, 3Ri.12, 3Ra.01, 3Ra.02, 3Wv.01, 3Wv.03, 3Wg.01, 3Wg.03, 3Wg.06, 3Ws.04, 3Wc.01, 3Wc.04, 3Wc.05, 3SLm.01, 3SLm.04, 3SLm.05, 3SLs.02, 3SLg.01, 3SLg.02, 3SLg.04, 3SLp.02, 3SLp.03, 3SLp.04, 3SLr.01, 3SLr.02	• Identify dialogue. • Write dialogue for a play. • Perform a play.	• Learners can identify dialogue. • Learners can write dialogue for a play. • Learners can perform a play.

Starter idea

What is dialogue? (5 minutes)

Resources: Learner's Book, Session 6.3: Getting started; selection of reading books

Description: Ask learners to discuss what dialogue is with a partner. Then provide them with a selection of reading books to find examples of dialogue. Ask learners to think about what they already know about writing dialogue and how dialogue is laid out.

Direct learners to the question prompts in the Learner's Book. Allow a few minutes for discussion, ask them to share their ideas. Try to elicit that, in a story, dialogue is shown using speech marks, and in a play dialogue is next to the characters' names.

Main teaching ideas

1 Using dialogue in cartoons (25–30 minutes)

Learning intention: To identify dialogue.

Resources: Learner's Book, Session 6.3, Activity 1; Workbook, Session 6.3; Worksheet 6.1

Description: Ask: *What do you know about writing dialogue in a story?* (speech marks around the words spoken; other punctuation outside the speech marks except question marks and exclamation marks; name of speaker outside speech marks; different verbs for *said*) Direct learners to the cartoon.

Ask: *How would you write what the girl says in a story?* Write one suggestion on the board without punctuation (e.g. *can I act the part of the judge asked the girl*). Invite individual learners to add the missing punctuation on the board.

Ask learners to write all the speech in the cartoon as dialogue from a story. Direct learners to the Writing tip.

When learners have completed the dialogue, ask: *How would I write the first words the girl says if I was writing a playscript?* Write a learner's suggestion on the board (e.g. **Girl:** *Can I act the part of the judge?*) Point out the gap between '*Girl:*' and what she says.

Direct learners to part b and allow time for them to complete the activity.

Allow time for learners to discuss in pairs the similarities and differences of the three text types (same words spoken; playscripts are similar to cartoons but use character names instead of picture). Ask: *Did you include any stage directions in the playscript? What could you add?* You could use the Workbook activities to provide further practice in using the three dialogue types.

> **Differentiation ideas:** Support learners who may have difficulty with the layout by providing Worksheet 6.1 Playscript template.

Answers:

a Responses similar to:
'Can I act the part of the judge?' asked the girl.
'That is a great idea,' nodded the boy.
'Which character do you want to act?' she asked.
The boy replied, 'I'd like to be Gilad.'

b Responses similar to:
Girl: Can I act the part of the judge?
Boy: (*nodding*) That is a great idea.
Girl: Which character do you want to act?
Boy: I'd like to be Gilad.

2 Turning stories into playscripts (20 minutes)

Learning intention: To write dialogue for a play.

Resources: *Four Clever Brothers, Part 3* (Learner's Book, Session 6.3, Activity 2); Track 37; Worksheet 6.1; Language worksheet 6B

Description: Remind learners of the end of the playscript in the previous session. Then direct them to the next part of the play in the Learner's Book, which is written as a story.

Draw learners' attention to the word *thieves*. Check that learners understand the word and talk about the difference between the singular and plural spellings (*thief / thieves*). You could use Language worksheet 6B here to provide additional practice with plural endings. Check that learners understand the word *arrested*.

Allow time for learners to read the story paragraph silently, then organise them into groups of six. Tell learners to decide who will play each part (the four brothers, Gilad, a narrator). Allow time for learners to read the story again, with each learner taking a role.

Direct learners to the character and the layout example in the Learner's Book. Tell learners that they will now write the story paragraph as a playscript. Direct them to the verbs *laughed* and *shouted* in the story. Ask: *How could you use these verbs in your playscript?* (stage directions) *Which tense would you use?* (present tense)

When learners have completed their scripts, direct learners to the How am I doing? prompt.

> **Differentiation ideas:** Support learners by providing Worksheet 6.1 Playscript template.

Challenge learners to include at least three stage directions.

> **Assessment ideas:** Can learners rewrite the narrative as a playscript? Note which learners included appropriate stage directions.

Answers:

Tazim:	No sir, we have not stolen your camel! Do we look like camel thieves?
Kamran:	We have simply been walking along this path. I think you must have lost your camel somewhere else.
Sadiq:	(*laughing*) How could we have stolen it? A camel is too big to hide in a pocket! Feel free to search for yourself.
Latif:	Believe us, sir. We have never even seen your camel.
Tazim:	We have simply worked out what your camel is like from the many clues it left behind.
Gilad:	(*shouting*) What rubbish! I will have you arrested!

---

3 Act out *Four Clever Brothers* (30–40 minutes)

Learning intention: To perform a play.

Resources: Learner's Book, Session 6.3, Activity 3; Worksheet 6.2; room large enough for groups to perform

Description: Read the introduction to Activity 3 to the class, including the character's speech-bubble text. Ask: *How might you move or react?* Try to elicit that movements and reactions need to be bigger than normal. Say: *Show me a surprised look* (e.g. open mouths with hands raised in surprise). *Show me anger* (e.g. fierce face and shaking fist). *Show me how an old man might walk* (e.g. bent over; small, slow steps). *Show me surprise* (e.g. open mouth, looking around, pointing to themselves in a 'What me' manner). Praise all learners who show exaggerated movements and reactions.

Organise learners into groups of six and ask them to follow the steps in the Learner's Book. If groups are using Worksheet 6.2 *Four Clever Brothers* playscript, suggest to learners that they mark or highlight their parts and add stage-direction notes (remind learners of the stage directions they added when they wrote their script version from the story extract).

Allow time for learners to practise acting out the play. Direct them to the Reflection question.

> **Assessment ideas:** Note which learners demonstrate good speaking. Do learners listen carefully, make eye contact, use gesture, exaggerate movement and reactions and adapt their voice and language for group work/acting?

Plenary idea

Reviewing a performance (15–20 minutes)

Resources: Learner's Book, Session 6.3; Worksheet 6.2 (marked up)

Description: Explain that each group will perform their play and observing groups will comment on how well learners showed their characters' feelings or reactions.

Remind learners to be respectful and considerate of each other's feelings. You could suggest that learners give two positive comments to every improvement comment.

Allow time for each group to perform. Allow up to five comments for each performance.

Homework ideas

Ask learners to:

- complete the Workbook activities for this session, if not completed in class

- find an example of dialogue in a reading book then rewrite it as a playscript.

Answers for Workbook

Learners' own responses.

6.4 What happens next?

LEARNING PLAN

Learning objectives	Learning intentions	Success criteria
3Rw.01, 3Rg.02, 3Ri.11, 3Ri.12, 3Wg.01, 3Wg.04, 3Wg.05, 3Ws.01, 3Ws.04, 3Wc.01, 3Wc.02, 3Wc.04, 3Wc.05, 3Wp.02, 3SLg.02, 3SLg.04, 3SLp.03	• Record main points and ideas before writing. • Explore the use of question marks and exclamation marks. • Identify the different sounds a grapheme can make. • Predict what happens next in the play.	• Learners can record main points and ideas before writing. • Learners can explore the use of question marks and exclamation marks. • Learners can identify the different sounds a grapheme can make. • Learners can predict what happens next in the play.

LANGUAGE SUPPORT

In this session, learners explore the different sounds the grapheme c makes. In Activity 3 in the Learner's Book, they will look at how the sound changes depending upon the letters that follow it and will be introduced to the terms *hard c* and *soft c*. The words learners are asked to sort have c followed by a vowel, apart from *clearly*. The

c sound can have several forms, such as when preceded by s (e.g. science – when it is almost a silent letter) and when followed by an h (e.g. Christmas, church, chips). If learners find it difficult to sort c sounds, you could help them using the suggestion in Common misconceptions.

Common misconceptions

Misconception	How to identify	How to overcome
In words with a c, the c makes a soft c sound when followed by a vowel and a hard c sound when followed by a consonant.	When learners sort the words in Activity 3, they sort c words where c is followed by a consonant into one column and c words where c is followed by a vowel into the other column.	Ask learners to look at the letters that follow the c. When c is immediately followed by e, i or y it has a *soft c* sound (ice, city, cycle). If c is followed by a, o or u or consonant it has a *hard c* sound (cake, coat, cup, clearly).

Starter idea

Play details (5 minutes)

Resources: Learner's Book, Session 6.4: Getting started

Description: In pairs, ask learners to discuss the prompts in the Learner's Book. Can learners recall the names of the four brothers (Tazim, Kamran, Sadiq, Latif)?

Main teaching ideas

1 The story so far (20 minutes)

Learning intention: To record main points and ideas before writing.

Resources: Learner's Book, Session 6.4, Activity 1

Description: Ask: *How did the story* Four Clever Brothers *begin?* (the brothers saw camel footprints) With a partner, learners should talk about what has happened in the story so far. Explain that learners are going to use these events to write an ordered set of sentences about the story. Direct learners to the Writing tip, then allow learners time to write their notes. Before learners write their sentences, ask: *What do we call sentences that have two ideas joined with words such as 'and', 'but', 'so'?* (multi-clause sentences) *What do we call joining words?* (connectives) When learners have completed their sentences, ask: *Are your sentences in the order in which they happen? Are any of your sentences multi-clause sentences? Have you used a capital letter to start your sentence and appropriate punctuation at the end?*

> **Differentiation ideas:** Challenge learners to be note takers during the paired work to support less confident writers.

> **Assessment ideas:** Do learners identify the main events and sequence them appropriately? Note which learners use multi-clause sentences and connectives.

Answers:

Possible sentences:

a Four brothers were walking along a desert path between two villages and saw some animal footprints.

b The brothers were very good hunters and knew they were camel footprints.

c A man ran up to them and said his camel had been stolen.

d The brothers told the man what they knew about the camel, so the man thought they were the thieves.

2 Listen to the play (15–25 minutes)

Learning intention: To explore the use of question marks and exclamation marks.

Resources: *Four Clever Brothers playscript* (Learner's Book, Session 6.4, Activity 2); Track 38

Description: Explain that learners need to listen carefully to two versions of the playscript. The first version you will be reading out from the extract on this page. In order for the learners to be able to hear a difference between the two versions, please read this extract aloud deliberately plain, without following the exclamation or question marks, and with no emotion. Then play Track 38.

Ask learners to talk in pairs about the differences between the two readings and which they preferred. Ask learners to share their opinions with the class, giving their reasons.

Direct learners to part c in the Learner's Book and ask them to share their ideas (e.g. the punctuation gives you clues to change your voice and helps you add expression).

Ask learners to follow the text as they listen to the audio again. Ask them to listen carefully to the way characters add expression.

If there is time, organise learners into groups of five and ask them to choose a role in the play. Encourage learners to read the script, using the punctuation to add expression.

> **Assessment ideas:** Which learners are able to give reasons to support their ideas? If learners read the playscript in groups, note learners who add expression.

Audioscript: *Four Clever Brothers playscript*

Tazim:	No sir, we have not stolen your camel! Do we look like camel thieves?
Kamran:	We have simply been walking along this path. I think you must have lost your camel somewhere else.
Sadiq:	How could we have stolen it? A camel is too big to hide in a pocket! Feel free to search for yourself.
Latif:	Believe us, sir. We have never even seen your camel. We are innocent!
Tazim:	We have simply worked out what your camel is like from the many clues it left behind.
Gilad:	What rubbish! I will have you arrested!

Answers:
Learners' own responses.

3 Hard and soft c (10–15 minutes)

Learning intention: To identify the different sounds a grapheme can make.

Resources: Learner's Book, Session 6.4, Activity 3; Workbook, Session 6.4

Description: Write *camel* on the board and ask: *What sound does this word begin with?* Ask learners to suggest other words where *ch* has the same sound. Tell learners that this is known as a hard *c* sound. Direct learners to the Language focus box and read the information aloud.

Ask learners to suggest other soft *c* words. Read aloud all the words around the table in the Learner's Book, then ask learners to complete the activity.

When learners have completed the table, ask: *Which column did you put 'concerns' in? Why?* Elicit that *concerns* has both hard and soft *c* sounds. You could use the Workbook activities to reinforce soft and hard *c* words if there is time in class.

> **Differentiation ideas:** Support learners by reading the words for them to help them identify the appropriate column.

Challenge learners to add additional words to each column (e.g. city, cost, climb, bicycle, slice, circle, electricity).

> **Assessment ideas:** Can learners identify soft *c* words? Can they apply an appropriate rule (see Language support).

Answers:

a

Soft c words (c sounds like 's')	Hard c words (c sounds like 'c')
justice	*camel*
place	can
concerns	concerns
recently	carrying
spaced	clearly
faces	case

b *Concerns* has a hard *c* and soft *c* sound.

4 What happens next? (30–40 minutes)

Learning intention: To predict what happens next in a play.

Resources: Learner's Book, Session 6.4, Activity 4; Worksheet 6.1

Description: Explain to learners that they are going to write the next part of the playscript. Remind them that Gilad told the brothers that he will have them arrested for stealing his camel. What do they think will happen next?

Give learners the time to discuss their ideas, using the prompts in Learner's Book, then invite learners to share their ideas with the class. Try to elicit that Gilad could seek help from Adil the judge. Ask: *What might Gilad say when he goes to Adil?* Write a learner's suggestion on the board using playscript layout. Use the example in the answer section if learners need support with ideas. Say: *Talk to your partner about what Adil might say.* Invite learners to share their ideas and write one of their suggestions on the board.

Ask learners to write the next five lines of dialogue for the playscript. Remind them that their dialogue is a conversation and that not every character needs to speak. Direct learners to the Writing tip, then ask: *What kind of punctuation will help the actors?*

Give learners time to write their dialogue.

> **Differentiation ideas:** Support learners who find writing more difficult by providing Worksheet 6.1 Playscript template and suggesting learners use the ideas on the board in their dialogue.

Challenge learners to include stage directions.

> **Assessment ideas:** When writing the next section of dialogue, do learners:

- use the correct layout
- include question marks and exclamation marks
- include stage directions
- read their own scripts with expression?

Answers:
a   Possible answers could include: the brothers were worried; Gilad went to look for someone to arrest the brothers; Gilad found Adil the judge.

b   Possible answers could include:

Gilad:	I am taking you to Adil the judge and he will arrest you.
Sadiq:	Very well. We know that Adil is a fair and wise man. He will sort this out. (*Adil sits under a tree. Gilad and the four brothers walk up to Adil.*)
Gilad:	Adil, these four men have stolen my camel. You must arrest them!
Judge:	(*looks at the brothers*) Is this true? What do you know about Gilad's camel?
Tazim:	We are very good hunters and we know all about Gilad's camel because the footprints it left gave us many clues.

Plenary idea

Exploring words (10 minutes)

Resources: Table of *c* words from Activity 3

Description: Ask learners to look at the words in their table of *c* words. Ask: *Which letters follow the c when the c sounds like 's'* (e)? Provide learners with additional words (e.g. city, cycle, cinema, bicycle) or invite learners who completed the challenge for this activity to share words they identified. Can learners identify a rule for when the *c* in a word is a soft *c*? (see Language support and Common misconceptions.)

Homework ideas

Ask learners to:

- complete the Workbook activities for this session, if not completed in class

- make two posters – one showing the soft *c* rule and the other showing the hard *c* rule.

Answers for Workbook

1   ace, bounce, dance, ice, mice, circle, race, fence, sentence

2   Possible answers:
Words ending in–*ice*: dice, twice, nice, slice, price

3   Possible answers:
Words ending in–*ace*: face, place, palace, space

4   Learners' own answers, e.g. Two <u>mice</u> <u>dance</u> and <u>bounce</u> in a <u>circle</u> on the <u>ice</u>.

6.5 Writing a playscript

LEARNING PLAN

Learning objectives	Learning intentions	Success criteria
3Rs.02, 3Ri.03, 3Ri.07, 3Ri.10, 3Ri.12, 3Ww.05, 3Wv.01, 3Wg.01, 3Wg.04, 3Wg.06, 3Ws.01, 3Ws.04, 3Wc.01, 3Wc.02, 3Wc.04, 3Wc.05, 3Wp.01, 3Wp.02, 3Wp.03, 3SLm.01, 3SLg.02, 3SLg.04, 3SLp.01, 3SLp.02, 3SLp.03	• Plan a playscript. • Write a playscript.	• Learners can plan a playscript. • Learners can write a playscript.

LANGUAGE SUPPORT

You many need to remind learners what a traditional story is. Remind them of some well-known stories from their locality. Ask learners to recall stories they have heard or read in Stages 1 and 2. Remind them that traditional stories are stories that were passed by word of mouth and often have similar themes.

Starter idea

Favourite traditional stories (10 minutes)

Resources: Learner's Book, Session 6.5: Getting started; a selection of traditional stories

Description: Ask: *What is a traditional story* (a story that has been told for many years that most people know)*?* Organise the class into groups and provide each group with a selection of traditional stories (if available). Ask groups to list as many traditional stories as they can.

Encourage learners, still in their groups, to say their favourite traditional story, giving reasons for their choice.

Ask groups to share their ideas. Is there a favourite traditional story in the class?

Main teaching ideas

1 Plan your playscript (30–40 minutes)

Learning intention: To plan a playscript.

Resources: Learner's Book, Session 6.5, Activity 1; Workbook, Session 6.5; Worksheet 6.3; Differentiated worksheet pack

Description: Explain that learners are going to write a playscript for a traditional story. This might be a story the class like best, a story you have chosen or the story provided in Differentiated worksheets 6A–C (How Anansi tricked Chameleon).

Organise learners into groups (these might be based on the Differentiated worksheet they are using). In groups, learners should take turns retelling the chosen traditional story. Ask one learner to retell the beginning, then another learner to continue and so on. Invite a learner to say a sentence summarising the beginning of the story. Write this sentence on the board. Explain that this is the first key event of the story. Invite another learner to suggest the next key event. Note this on the board.

Now, in their groups, learners should decide what the key events are in their story. Explain that when they have agreed the events, each learner should write them in their notebooks, Worksheet 6.3 Playscript planning grid or the templates in the Workbook activities.

Ask learners to write down notes about the setting for the story. In their groups, learners should make a list of characters from the story in their notebooks. Explain that they only need to write a few words about each character (e.g. Anansi: a spider with a large farm; Chameleon: lives alone on a small farm).

Ask: *What kind of stage directions could you include* (e.g. what the character should do; how the character says something)*?* Ask learners to share stage direction ideas for characters in the story, before adding these to their notes. Check that they use the present tense.

When learners have completed the questions direct them to the Reflection question.

> **Differentiation ideas:** Support less confident writers by telling them which part of the story to use, then work with them to plan the playscript.

Challenge confident writers to add a twist to the story (e.g. adding a new character or changing the ending).

> **Assessment ideas:** Assess how well learners sequence the story as they retell it in groups. Note which learners take ideas for dialogue and actions from the text.

Answers:
Learners' own answers. Example answers based on Anansi and Chameleon are given in the Unit 6 Differentiated worksheets.

2 Write your playscript (30 minutes)

Learning intention: To write a playscript.

Resources: Learner's Book, Session 6.5, Activity 2; Worksheet 6.1; learners' planning notes from Activity 1; dictionaries

Description: Remind learners that they do not need to write a playscript for the whole story. Explain that you want them to show how well they can use the features of a playscript. Explain that learners will use the notes they have made. If they have used the Differentiated worksheets, they should use the dialogue they used in their answers.

Ask: *Which verb tense will you use for stage directions?* (present tense) Ask learners to talk to a partner about the punctuation they need for sentences. Remind learners to use neat joined handwriting and to use a dictionary to check spellings.

> **Differentiation ideas:** Support learners with setting out their playscript by providing Worksheet 6.1 Playscript template.

> **Assessment ideas:** Do learners understand the features of playscripts? Can learners use these features in their writing?

Plenary idea

Using expression (5 minutes)

Resources: Learners' playscripts

Description: Ask: *Which punctuation marks could you use to help actors add expression?* (question marks, exclamation marks) Invite learners to read an example from their playscript with expression.

Homework ideas

Ask learners to:

- write a new playscript based on the information in Workbook Session 6.5

- choose three traditional stories from their own culture and for each one write: the title, a list of characters and a description of the setting.

Answers for Workbook

1   Possible character profiles using the play information:
   Character name: *Magda*

Age: *70 years old*
Appearance: *has an old, ragged shawl wrapped around her bent shoulders and a begging bowl*
Role in play: *looks poor but is really a very wealthy lady; she has no children and wants to give her house to a kind child.*

Character name: *Zelda*
Age: *8 years old*
Appearance: *long hair, which she is always fussing with. Her mouth looks as though she is always complaining.*
Role in play: *pretends to be kind to Magda but it is a trick.*

Character name: *Pieter*
Age: *8 years old*
Appearance: *is always smiling*
Role in play: *is usually bossed about by Zelda. He helps the old lady.*

2   Learners' own answers.

3   Learners' own answers.

6.6 Improving a playscript

LEARNING PLAN		
Learning objectives	**Learning intentions**	**Success criteria**
3Rg.01, 3Ra.01, 3Ra.02, 3Ww.02, 3Ww.03, 3Ww.04, 3Ww.05, 3Ww.06, 3Wv.02, 3Wv.07, 3Wg.01, 3Wg.04, 3Wg.05, 3Wg.06, 3Ws.01, 3Ws.04, 3Wc.01, 3Wc.04, 3Wc.05, 3Wc.06, 3Wp.01, 3Wp.03, 3Wp.04, 3Wp.05, 3SLm.01, 3SLm.04, 3SLm.05, 3SLg.01, 3SLp.01, 3SLp.02, 3SLp.03, 3SLp.04, 3SLr.01, 3SLr.02	• Improve a play playscript. • Decide how to present a playscript. • Perform a play.	• Learners can improve a playscript. • Learners can decide how to present a playscript. • Learners can perform a play.

Before learners proofread their playscripts, you might want to recap verbs and adverbs. Ask learners to suggest verbs or adverbs to describe how a character might say something (e.g. grumpily, crossly, laughing, sobbing).

Starter idea

1 Review your playscript (5 minutes)

Resources: Learner's Book, Session 6.6: Getting started; learners' playscripts

Description: Ask learners to consider the playscript they wrote in the last session and how it differs from the original traditional story. Direct them to the prompts in the Learner's Book.

As learners re-read their playscript, encourage them to also think about whether it makes sense.

Main teaching ideas

1 Proofreading (15–20 minutes)

Learning intention: To improve a playscript.

Resources: Learner's Book, Session 6.6, Activity 1; Workbook, Session 6.6, Activities 1–3; Worksheet 6.4; dictionaries

Description: Ask learners what they remember about proofreading from previous units. Note suggestions on the board (e.g. checking spelling and punctuation, adding more interesting words, checking for sense), then direct learners to the checklist in the Learner's Book. You could use the Focus and Practice activities in the Workbook here to develop proofreading skills.

Ask learners to re-read their playscripts and correct errors and make improvements. Tell them to check their spellings using a dictionary or word list. Remind them that they should also check that they have used the correct homophone.

Explain that learners can improve their playscripts by adding additional dialogue or stage directions.

When learners have finished proofreading and improving, ask them to complete Worksheet 6.4 Playscript checklist as they re-read the playscripts with a partner.

2 Vocabulary focus (10–15 minutes)

Learning intention: To improve a playscript.

Resources: Learner's Book, Session 6.6, Activity 2; dictionaries; thesauruses

Description: Write an example of dialogue adapted from *Four Clever Brothers* on the board (e.g. *A camel is big. You can't hide it in a small pocket*). Ask: *Have I used interesting words in this dialogue? Which words could I change?* (e.g. big, small).

In pairs, learners should think of synonyms or noun phrases they could use instead. (e.g. large, bigger than a horse, tiny, coat pocket).

Ask learners to improve the vocabulary in their playscript by changing three words for more interesting synonyms or noun phrases.

> **Differentiation ideas:** Support learners by offering a selection of synonyms.

Answers:
Learners' own responses.

3 Written or typed? (20 minutes)

Learning intention: To decide how to present a playscript.

Resources: Learner's Book, Session 6.6, Activity 3; access to a word-processing program (if appropriate)

Description: Explain that learners are now going to choose how to present their final playscript.

Ask: *What are the benefits of typing your playscript?* (e.g. easier to read, easier to correct mistakes, spell checker) *What are the disadvantages?* (e.g. knowing how to set out the layout) Direct learners to the character and speech bubble in the Learner's Book.

Allow time for learners to either handwrite or type their playscript. Encourage them to correct any other errors they find as they work.

> **Assessment ideas:** Note which learners use neat joined handwriting to present their final copy. Which joins do they need to improve? Note which learners use word-processing layout tools effectively.

4 Performance time (20 minutes)

Learning intention: To perform a play.

Resources: Learner's Book, Session 6.6, Activity 4; learners' playscripts

Description: Ask learners to say *Good morning* in different ways (e.g. cheerfully, grumpily, sadly). Then, ask learners to say *Good morning* as different characters (e.g. an old man, Anansi, Chameleon, Adil the judge). Explain that changing their tone or expression helps listeners to understand and recognise different characters. Explain that learners are now going to perform their plays. Direct them to the Speaking tip.

Organise learners into groups. You may wish to make copies of learners' playscripts so that they do not have to share. If working in groups is not possible, challenge learners to play all the characters in their playscript and use different voices.

Allow time for learners to perform each of the plays written by the learners in their group. If time allows, ask each group to choose one of their plays to perform to the class.

Direct them to the How are we doing? prompt. When groups have had time to discuss, share some of their ideas.

⟩ **Assessment ideas:** Do learners include stage directions in their playscripts and use these to add expression, gestures and movement when they perform? Do learners change their tone of voice and expression to match what the characters are saying or feeling?

Plenary idea

Reflection time (10 minutes)

Description: In pairs, learners should discuss the similarities and differences between narratives and playscripts.

Share ideas (e.g. similarities: speech, a plot, different characters; differences: layout, no verbs for *said*, verb tense, stage directions instead of description).

> **CROSS-CURRICULAR LINKS**
>
> IT: Learners could explore features and tools in a word-processing programme, e.g. using bullet points to write a list of characters and tab keys and alignment tools to set out dialogue.

Homework ideas

Ask learners to:

- complete the Workbook activities for this session, if not completed in class
- write eight quiz questions based on their playscript.

Answers for Workbook

1, 2, 3

Judge: So Gilad had the four brothers arrested and brought to me.

Gilad: Adil, you are a man of justice. (Hear) my plea! These (four) men have stolen my camel and they must be punished. Will you help me?

Judge: Very well, Gilad. I will question them. <u>What</u> do you four <u>men</u> have to say for yourselves? How do you (know) so much about the missing camel?

Tazim: It is very <u>simple</u>, sir. I could tell the camel was blind in one eye because the grass was eaten only on one side of the path. Clearly, the camel did not see the grass on the other side.

Gilad: Humph. That is nonsense. How can he tell <u>anything</u> from a bit of grass?

Judge: Be patient, Gilad. We must hear all they have to say before making a judgement. <u>Leave</u> this to me.

4 Learners' own noun phrases.

5 Learners' own answers.

CHECK YOUR PROGRESS

1 title, list of characters, stage directions, dialogue

2 **a** Playscripts don't use speech marks.

   c Playscripts have the dialogue next to the name of each character.

   e Stories are written using paragraphs.

3 Punctuation helps actors use the correct expression when they speak.

4 Stage directions help actors know how to respond or move.

5 To speak clearly, to add different tones and expression to reflect your character, to use gestures and facial expression to reflect your character and to respond to what is being said or is happening.

PROJECT GUIDANCE

These projects develop learners' skills in writing instructions and lists. You will find it helpful to refer to the guidance about *Setting up and assessing the projects* in the Project guidance in Unit 1.

Group project: Learners choose a traditional story playscript and act it out to the rest of the class.

Explain the task to learners and organise them into groups of six. Learners will need playscripts for a traditional story, or each group could choose one of the playscripts they have written.

Once learners have chosen a play, they will need time to learn their lines. This could be done as a homework activity. Before learners finalise props, you should consider the amount of space and time you have available. Will learners make props (e.g. animal masks, scenery)? Where will learners perform their plays?

Pair project: Learners list and describe the scenery and props they would need for a performance of *Four Clever Brothers*.

Encourage learners to re-read playscript extracts of *Four Clever Brothers* in Sessions 6.1–3 in the Learner's Book. Learners should also refer to the pictures in Sessions 6.1, 6.2 and 6.4 for additional information about scenery and props.

Learners may need to refer to Session 2.2 to recap list making.

Solo project: Learners choose one character from their playscript and clearly describe them so that anyone acting that character will know how to act him or her. Remind learners about the character descriptions they wrote in Session 1.5.

Learners should include details about their character's physical appearance, the clothing they wear, their voice and behaviour. Remind learners that their description should form an image of the character in the actor's mind. Learners should also describe how the character might change during the play.

>7 Going on an adventure

Unit plan

Session	Approximate number of learning hours	Outline of learning content	Resources
7.1 Reading an adventure	1	Explore a playscript and answer questions about it. Act out the playscript and predict what might happen next. Revisit contractions.	Learner's Book Session 7.1 Workbook Session 7.1
7.2 Story beginnings	1–1.5	Read the beginning of three adventure stories and answer questions about them. Revisit noun phrases.	Learner's Book Session 7.2 Workbook Session 7.2
7.3 What happens next?	1.5	Read more of Alfie Small's story and answer questions about it. Explore figurative language, including similes. Use clues from the passage to predict what will happen next.	Learner's Book Session 7.3 Workbook Session 7.3 ⬇ Language worksheet 7A
7.4 Character portraits	1	Write a description of themselves. Explore Alfie Small's character. Use multi-clause sentences to write a character portrait.	Learner's Book Session 7.4 Workbook Session 7.4 ⬇ Differentiated worksheets 7A–C
7.5 Looking at chapters	1	Explore why writers use chapters. Revisit sentence openings, then write sentence openings for chapters in an Alfie Small story.	Learner's Book Session 7.5 Workbook Session 7.5 ⬇ Worksheet 7.1
7.6 Looking at verbs	1.5	Compare two Alfie Small stories. Explore irregular past tense verbs. Plan an Alfie Small adventure.	Learner's Book Session 7.6 Workbook Session 7.6 ⬇ Worksheet 7.2

Session	Approximate number of learning hours	Outline of learning content	Resources
7.7 Looking in more detail	1.5	Compare the similarities and differences of two adventure stories. Role play a character from *Dragon Boy*. Discuss ideas about chapters.	Learner's Book Session 7.7 Workbook Session 7.7
7.8 Setting and dialogue	1	Write a setting description for a dragon story. Revisit the rules for setting out dialogue. Add or correct punctuation in a passage.	Learner's Book Session 7.8 Workbook Session 7.8
7.9 More about paragraphs	1	Revisit paragraphs in narrative texts. Deduce the meanings of unfamiliar words and explore sentence openings.	Learner's Book Session 7.9 Workbook Session 7.9 ⬇ Language worksheet 7B
7.10 Looking at stories	1.5	Write a book review. Explore prefixes. Write opening sentences for paragraphs.	Learner's Book Session 7.10 Workbook Session 7.10 ⬇ Worksheets 7.3 and 7.4
7.11 Writing a story	1.5–2	Plan an adventure story using a storyboard. Write an adventure story based on the storyboard.	Learner's Book Session 7.11 Workbook Session 7.11 ⬇ Worksheet 4.1
7.12 Improving your story	1	Proofread and improve the adventure stories.	Learner's Book Session 7.12 Workbook Session 7.12 ⬇ Worksheet 7.5
Cross-unit resources			
Learner's Book Check your progress Learner's Book Projects End-of-unit 7 test			

BACKGROUND KNOWLEDGE

It will be helpful to be familiar with the following English subject knowledge:

- features of adventure stories
- noun phrases
- position of adjectives in sentences
- simple, multi-clause sentences
- connectives
- figurative language, including similes
- why writers use chapters

- paragraphs
- adverbs and sentence openers of time, place and manner
- sentence and paragraph openings
- first- and third-person storytellers
- narrative and direct speech
- prefixes
- present and past tense of verbs
- irregular past tense of verbs.

TEACHING SKILLS FOCUS

Assessment for Learning (AfL)

As this unit revisits several learning intentions from previous units, it would be valuable to use an Assessment for Learning technique before beginning, e.g. **Know – Want (to know) – Learned (KWL)**.

Start by asking learners to draw a three-column table with the headings *What I know, What I want to know* and *What I have learned*. Ask learners to note in column 1 what they <u>know</u> about writing a story and in column 2 what they <u>want</u> to know or want to improve. Finish each session by asking learners to review their table. Did the session cover items in their middle column? At the end of the unit, ask learners to complete the final column to record what they have learned.

You could incorporate a red, orange (amber) and green 'traffic light' system. Explain that the traffic light colours represent:

- red – I do not feel confident with this
- orange/amber – I feel reasonably confident but need more practice
- green – I have achieved this.

As you read learners' tables, consider whether you agree with their traffic light ratings. Have learners been unnecessarily cautious? Have learners overestimated their abilities?

Did you remember to allow time at the end of each session for learners to review their KWL tables? To what extent did you use learners' KWL tables when you taught each session? Did learners' responses change how you organised groups or how much time you spent on particular activities? How do you think asking learners to reflect on their learning affected their approach to learning?

Cambridge Reading Adventures

There are several books in the series that would allow learners to explore adventure stories.

- *Sandstorm* by Peter Millett
- *The Great Escape* by Peter Millett
- *River Rescue* by Peter Millett

7.1 Reading an adventure

LEARNING PLAN

Learning objectives	Learning intentions	Success criteria
3Rw.01, 3Rw.02, 3Rw.03, 3Rg.01, 3Rg.02, 3Rg.03, 3Ri.03, 3Ri.06, 3Ri.10, 3Ri.11, 3Ri.12, 3Ri.15, 3Ri.16, 3Ra.01, 3Ra.02, 3Wg.02, 3Wc.01, 3SLm.01, 3SLp.01, 3SLp.02, 3SLp.03, 3SLp.04	• Explore adventure stories. • Answer questions about an adventure story. • Identify and use apostrophes in contracted words. • Perform a playscript.	• Learners can explore adventure stories. • Learners can answer questions about an adventure story. • Learners can identify and use apostrophes in contracted words. • Learners can perform a playscript.

LANGUAGE SUPPORT

The *ture* sound in *adventure* is formed from two less common digraphs: *tu* sounding *ch*; *re* sounding *ur*. It is worth exploring the word *adventure* at the start of this session.

Encourage learners to identify the spelling and sounds within the word. The plenary activity provides an opportunity to explore other *ture* words.

Common misconceptions

Misconception	How to identify	How to overcome
Contractions have only one possible expansion and never have multiple expansions.	Write the following sentences on the board: • *There's been no rain for three months.* • *It's been a long time since my holiday.* • *She's gone on holiday.* Ask learners to expand the contractions (There has been, It has been, She has gone). Note the expansions they use.	Explain that *when* the event occurs affects how the contraction is expanded. Tell learners to read the whole sentence and identify the tense (present, future, past). Explain that present- and future-tense sentences use *is* (e.g. There is, He is, It is). Past-tense sentences use *has* (e.g. There has, It has, She has). Write more sentences on the board: • *It is my birthday tomorrow.* (It is) • *There's been an accident in the playground.* (There has) • *He's been late every day this week.* (He has) Ask learners to read each sentence and decide when the event takes place before they expand the contractions.

Starter idea

What is an adventure? (10 minutes)

Resources: Learner's Book, Session 7.1: Getting started; Workbook, Session 7.1, Activity 1

Description: Write *adventure* on the board. Ask a learner to read the word. Ask: *How many syllables does the word have?* (three – ad/ven/ture) Explain that *ture* makes a *cher* sound. Ask: *What is an adventure?* Try to elicit that an adventure:

- starts with an everyday event
- involves a frightening or exciting situation
- ends well.

Direct learners to the photographs in the Learner's Book. In pairs, they should discuss the question prompts. If learners are unfamiliar with the word *scary*, explain that it is a synonym for *frightening*. Use the Focus activity in the Workbook as an opportunity for learners to explain which of the adventures they would like to have.

Main teaching ideas

1 Playscript adventure (10–15 minutes)

Learning intention: To explore adventure stories.

Resources: *A day out* (Learner's Book, Session 7.1, Activity 1); Track 39

Description: Explain that you will read a playscript. Ask learners to follow the text as you read it with expression. Then, direct them to the Reading tip and read each point to them. Invite learners to:

- read two sentences, demonstrating a pause between each sentence
- explain what happens to your voice when you ask a question
- identify each exclamation mark and say what the character is feeling
- list the possibilities Fernando gives in his second piece of dialogue.

Check that learners are familiar with the word *coach*. Read the instructions for Activity 1, then allow time for learners to read the playscript.

⟩ **Differentiation ideas:** Challenge three confident readers to read the playscript.

2 Answer questions (20 minutes)

Learning intention: To answer questions about an adventure story.

Resources: Learner's Book, Session 7.1, Activity 2

Description: Explain that learners are going to write answers to the playscript questions in their notebooks. Explain that the last three questions have no right or wrong answers. Tell learners that they should give reasons for their answers using some of the information in the text (e.g. I think Ana is determined because even though Fernando and Lucas said no, she still wanted to go further up the river).

When learners have finished, mark answers as a class. Share examples of learners' answers to questions e–g. Praise answers that include text-based explanations.

⟩ **Assessment ideas:** Note which learners use evidence from the playscript to support answers.

Answers:
a Fernando, Lucas, Ana
b There are too many people.
c He knows Mum and Dad will not like it.
d Snakes and spiders, falling into the river, tripping over a branch, getting stung or bitten, getting lost
e Learners' sentences could include reference to Ana being brave / determined / thoughtless and not thinking about the consequences.
f Yes – one of the things Fernando suggested might happen.
g Learners' own answers.

3 Contractions (10 minutes)

Learning intention: To identify and use apostrophes in contracted words.

Resources: Learner's Book, Session 7.1, Activity 3; Workbook, Session 7.1, Activity 2

Description: Say: *Give me an example of a contraction from the playscript* (e.g. they're, let's). Ask: *What is a contraction?* (two words that are joined and have one or more letters removed) Direct learners to the character and speech-bubble text, if necessary. Ask them to discuss other contractions they know.

Allow time for learners to complete the activity in their notebooks. Use the Practice activity in the Workbook to offer practice with correcting punctuation errors, including missing apostrophes.

> **Differentiation ideas:** Support learners by providing a selection of expanded words to match each contraction.

> **Assessment ideas:** Which learners can recall previous work on contractions? Which contractions do learners find difficult to expand?

Answers:
they're – they are, let's – let us, there's – there is, won't – will not, wouldn't – would not, I'm – I am, can't – can not, we'd – we had, don't – do not

4 Acting time (15 minutes)

Learning intention: To perform a playscript.

Resources: Learner's Book, Session 7.1, Activity 4; a space large enough for groups to perform

Description: Organise learners into groups of three and explain the activity. Remind them to use what they learned about playscripts in Unit 6 (e.g. using gestures, adding expression and movement, using stage directions).

Allow learners time to act out the playscript. Encourage groups to discuss what might happen next, then invite some groups to share their ideas.

Allow time for learners to act out their predictions.

> **Assessment ideas:** Can learners suggest what might happen next in the playscript? Do learners use any of the ideas from the playscript?

Plenary idea

ture words (5 minutes)

Resources: Dictionaries

Description: Remind learners of the *cher* sound at the end of *adventure*. Ask learners to think of other *ture* words (e.g. picture, furniture, future, capture, nature, creature, feature, culture). Remind learners to check the spelling of each word in a dictionary.

Ask learners to write a clue for one of their words and then ask a partner to guess their word from the clue.

Homework ideas

Ask learners to:

- complete the Challenge activity in the Workbook

- make a crossword using six *ture* words and write clues for each word.

Answers for Workbook

1 Learners' own answers.

2 Fernando hurried after his brother and sister. He didn't want to go but he knew they would never forgive him if he didn't. He felt in the pockets of his shorts to see what he could find. He found a piece of string, three coins and his catapult. He pulled out his catapult. Now he felt better. He hurried on after his brother and sister.

3 Possible answers:
concerned, worried, anxious, frightened, practical, relieved, pleased, loyal

7.2 Story beginnings

LEARNING PLAN

Learning objectives	Learning intentions	Success criteria
3Rw.02, 3Rw.03, 3Rv.01, 3Rv.04, 3Rg.01, 3Rg.07, 3Rg.08, 3Rs.02, 3Ri.03, 3Ri.16, 3Ri.17, 3Ra.01, 3Ra.02, 3Ra.03, 3Ra.04, 3Wv.05, 3SLg.02, 3SLg.03, 3SLg.04	• Read and discuss story beginnings. • Explore the use of noun phrases. • Explore adjectives.	• Learners can read and discuss story beginnings. • Learners can explore the use of noun phrases. • Learners can explore adjectives.

LANGUAGE SUPPORT

Much of the vocabulary in this session may be unfamiliar to learners. Make sure that learners understand new words. They may find some of the vocabulary useful when they write their own adventure story. You could encourage learners to make a collection of useful words and phrases (e.g. dangerous band of smugglers, rickety shed).

Common misconceptions

Misconception	How to identify	How to overcome
A noun phrase can be written with the adjective either before or after the noun.	Write the following sentences on the board: • *I found a small boat.* • *The grass is long.* Ask learners to say which sentences use a noun phrase. (*I found a small boat.*) Learners may identify noun phrases in both sentences (e.g. small boat, grass is long).	Write *small boat* and *grass is long* on the board. Ask learners to say which word group all the words belong to (i.e. adjectives: *small, long*; nouns: *boat, grass*; verbs: *is*). Explain that when adjectives are after a noun, you use a verb. Noun phrases are only made using adjective + noun.

Starter idea

Fiction books (5 minutes)

Resources: Learner's Book, Session 7.2: Getting started; selection of fiction books; learners' reading books

Description: Give every learner a fiction book or their reading book. Ask them to take turns to read the first five lines of their book to a partner. Invite learners to share a beginning they would like to read more of. Can learners explain why they want to read more?

Main teaching ideas

1 Story beginnings (15 minutes)

Learning intention: To read and discuss story beginnings.

Resources: Story beginnings 1, 2 and 3 (Learner's Book, Session 7.2, Activity 1); Tracks 40, 41 and 42; Workbook, Session 7.2, Activities 1 and 2

Description: Explain that learners are going to read the beginning of three stories. Before reading each extract, direct learners to the relevant Glossary terms.

After reading each extract ask: *Were there any words you didn't understand? Were you able to work out the meaning using clues in the text and picture? What kind of story could this extract be from?*

Draw learners' attention to the phrases *armed only with a bucket and spade, dangerous band of smugglers* and *sitting on a hump*. Do learners understand the underlined words? Explain each word as: *protected, gang* and *small grassy hill*.

You could use the Focus activity in the Workbook at this point to consolidate learners' recognition of adventure story beginnings.

> **Differentiation ideas:** Challenge learners by asking for volunteers to read the extracts to the class.

2 Questions about story beginnings (20 minutes)

Learning intention: To read and discuss story beginnings.

Resources: Learner's Book, Session 7.2, Activity 2; Workbook, Session 7.2, Activity 1

Description: Ask learners to work in pairs to discuss the answers to the questions in the Learner's Book. Tell them that they should give reasons for their opinions (e.g. 'I would like to read more of Extract 1 because it sounds as though the adventure will not be too frightening'). Allow learners a few minutes to discuss parts a and b. Then explain that they should think about who is telling the story, who the characters are, the language used and the layout of each story to respond to parts c and d.

Allow time for pairs to discuss each question, then invite learners to share their opinions with the class or in small groups. Use the Focus activity in the Workbook if you did not use it at the end of Activity 1.

> **Differentiation ideas:** Support learners by discussing the questions in a group.

> **Assessment ideas:** Note which learners are familiar with the adventure story genre. Note which learners give simple answers (e.g. I liked the last extract because I like stories about dragons).

Answers:
a   Learners' own ideas.
b   Learners' own ideas.
c   Possible answers: In Extract 1 the character tells the story (first person); Extracts 2 and 3 are told by a narrator; in Extracts 1 and 3 the characters have names; Extract 2 tells you it is a story; Extract 3 has dialogue; the extracts are about explorers, pirates, smugglers or dragons.
d   Learners' own answers may include feeling excited, interested, worried.

---

3 Noun phrases (10–15 minutes)

Learning intention: To explore the use of noun phrases.

Resources: Learner's Book, Session 7.2, Activity 3; Workbook, Session 7.2, Activity 3

Description: You could use the Practice activity in the Workbook here, if you think learners would benefit from recapping adjectives. Ask: *What kind of shed is in Alfie Small's garden?* (rickety) *Which word group does* rickety *belong to?* (adjectives) Ask learners to identify more adjectives in the passage (e.g. famous, dangerous, special, long, tall, small). Ask: *Who can remember what a noun phrase is?* (adjective(s) plus a noun) Direct learners to the noun phrases in the Learner's Book and allow them time to complete the activity.

Ask learners to read the Reflection questions and invite them to share their reasons for using noun phrases (e.g. they give you more information; make it sound more interesting). Direct learners to the character.

> **Assessment ideas:** Assess to what extent learners understand what a noun phrase is. Do learners know how to create a noun phrase?

Answers:
a   Following words underlined: famous, real, sleeping, poor, helpless, little
b   Following words circled: explorer, dragons, girl
c   before

---

4 Adjectives in sentences (10–15 minutes)

Learning intention: To explore adjectives.

Resources: Learner's Book, Session 7.2, Activity 4; Workbook, Session 7.2, Activity 4

Description: Read the sentences in the Learner's Book. Ask: *Do any of the sentences use noun phrases?* If learners incorrectly identify a noun phrase, refer to the activity in Common misconceptions.

Allow time for learners to answer the questions in their notebooks. You could use the Challenge activity in the Workbook to provide further practice with using noun phrases.

> **Differentiation ideas:** Support less confident writers by pairing with a confident learner.

> **Assessment ideas:** Do learners understand that adjectives and noun phrases provide more details to keep the reader interested? Can learners confidently identify the word groups: nouns, verbs, adjectives?

Answers:
a   Following words underlined: long, tall, long, scaly, scary, brave
b   Following words circled: grass, weeds, dragons, pirates
c   Adjectives are after the noun
d   When adjectives are after the noun there is a verb between the noun and adjective. In noun phrases adjectives go before the noun and there is no verb.

Plenary idea

Noun phrase hunt (5–10 minutes)

Description: Write five short sentences on the board (e.g. *The grass is long*; *The weeds are tall*; *The table is rickety*; *The bucket is large and blue*; *The spade is red and made of plastic*). Ask learners to write each sentence as a noun phrase in their notebooks (e.g. the long grass; the tall weeds; the rickety table; the large, blue bucket; the red plastic spade).

Homework ideas

Ask learners to:

*   complete the Workbook activities for this session, if not completed in class

*   find examples of five noun phrases in their reading book; learners could then choose a character or an object from their reading book and write three noun phrases of their own.

Answers for Workbook

1 a and d

2 Possible reasons: it sounds as though something is going to happen; there is a problem that needs solving.

3 Learners' own answers. Possible answers include:
a   The <u>long</u> snake <u>twisted</u>.
b   The tree is <u>tall</u>.
c   The roots are <u>old</u> and <u>deep</u>.
d   A <u>cracked</u> branch.
e   The sound was <u>sweet</u> and <u>beautiful</u>.
f   The <u>winding</u> river.
g   The <u>hidden</u> pool.
h   The sand is <u>soft</u> and <u>golden</u>.
i   Some <u>ripe</u> fruit.
j   The children are <u>lost</u> and <u>frightened</u>.

4 a N
b S
c S
d N
e S
f N
g N
h S
i N
j S

5 Learners' own answers.

7.3 What happens next?

LEARNING PLAN		
Learning objectives	**Learning intentions**	**Success criteria**
3Rw.03, 3Rv.02, 3Rv.04, 3Rv.07, 3Rg.01, 3Ri.11, 3Ra.01, 3Ra.02, 3Wv.05, 3Wv.06, 3Wc.03, 3SLg.02, 3SLg.03, 3SLg.04	• Read and answer questions about a text. • Look in more detail at the language used in a passage. • Predict what might happen next.	• Learners can read and answer questions about a text. • Learners can look in more detail at the language used in a passage. • Learners can predict what might happen next.

LANGUAGE SUPPORT

The story extract in this session includes figurative language that uses verbs learners may be unfamiliar with (*flowed* faster, *racing* along, *grinding* noise, *yawning* mouth, smoke *billowing* up, *steered*). You could ask learners to begin a personal word bank and write synonyms for each verb.

Starter idea

Parts of speech (10 minutes)

Resources: Learner's Book, Session 7.3: Getting started

Description: In pairs, ask learners to list the parts of speech (word groups) they know. Ask learners to give you two examples of a noun, adjective, verb and pronoun. Direct learners to the sentences in the Learner's Book. Ask them to write the sentences in their notebooks, then write the four parts of speech as headings beneath.

Ask learners to write the examples they find under each heading (e.g. nouns: *stream, water, speedboat*; verbs: *climbed, paddled, got, flowed, was, racing*; adjectives: *bigger, faster, fast*; pronouns: *I*).

Main teaching ideas

1 Alfie's adventure (15–20 minutes)

Learning intention: To read and answer questions about a text.

Resources: *A Dark Cave* (Learner's Book, Session 7.3, Activity 1); Track 43; dictionary; thesaurus

Description: Explain that you are going to read the next part of Alfie's adventure and that learners should follow the text as you read. Tell them that they are likely to hear several unfamiliar words. Ask learners to note words they do not understand in their notebooks.

When you have read the text, direct learners to the Glossary terms, then discuss any other words they have noted. When learners are familiar with the vocabulary, direct them to the Reading tip.

Ask learners to re-read the text two or three times in their heads. Say: *Talk to your partner about the kind of picture the story created in your mind; what you think Alfie was feeling; and what you think Alfie was thinking.*

Direct learners to the questions. Ask them to discuss each question with a partner, then write their answers in their notebooks.

> **Differentiation ideas:** Support and challenge learners by pairing more confident learners with less confident learners.

> **Assessment ideas:** Note which learners were able to use contextual information to work out the meaning of unfamiliar vocabulary.

Answers:

a   No, the rock was shaped like a dragon's head.

b   The cave opened up *like a yawning mouth*.

c   The rocks were *as sharp as dragon fangs*.

d   Learners' own answers.

e   Learners' own answers.

2   Figurative language (15–20 minutes)

Learning intention: To look in more detail at the language used in a passage.

Resources: Learner's Book, Session 7.3, Activity 2; Workbook, Session 7.3; Language worksheet 7A

Description: Ask: *What did Alfie say the opening of the cave was <u>like</u> (a yawning mouth)? Does this help you picture the cave in your mind?* Explain that writers often describe something as being *like something else* to help create a clearer picture in your mind. This is known as figurative language. Ask learners to read the Language focus text.

In pairs, learners should identify other examples of figurative language in the passage in Activity 1. Now, read the phrases in part a. Ask: *Is it exciting to watch paint dry? Why did the writer use this description?* Try to elicit that the description helps you understand how boring the activity is.

Ask learners to identify the similes in the activity. Remind them to look for the words *like* and *as*. They should then write a sentence using one of the similes.

When completed, invite learners to share the similes and/or sentences they wrote. Use the Workbook activities or Language worksheet 7A to provide further practice with similes.

> **Differentiation ideas:** Support learners by suggesting ideas to use for their sentences with similes (e.g. a frozen pond, an icicle, a television programme, an activity they find boring, a superhero).

Challenge learners to write a sentence for each simile.

> **Assessment ideas:** Note which learners can recall previous learning about similes.

Answers:

a   it sparkled like a diamond; as exciting as watching paint dry; as strong as an ox

b   Learners' own sentences.

3   Time to listen (15 minutes)

Learning intention: To look in more detail at the language used in a passage.

Resources: *Tuhil and Meena 1* and *2* (Learner's Book, Session 7.3, Activity 3); Tracks 44 and 45

Description: Explain that learners are going to listen to two texts telling the same story in different ways. Play Track 44 and ask learners to talk in pairs about the scene. Ask: *Can you picture the scene of Tuhil and Meena riding along the lane? Can you picture the scene with the houses? Will everyone's picture look the same?* Try to elicit that pictures would have differences because the passage only gives some of the details.

Play Track 45, then ask learners to talk in pairs again about how this text is different. Ask: *Has your picture of each scene changed? Why?* Try to elicit that the second text gives us more details, which makes it easier for us to form a clearer picture in our minds and means that learners' pictures will have fewer differences.

Audioscript: *Tuhil and Meena 1*

On a Sunday evening, Tuhil and Meena were riding their horses along a lane. They were chatting about school and about how the spelling tests were getting harder than last year. Suddenly, the horses heard a loud noise and were scared. They galloped off into the woods. Tuhil and Meena had no control of either horse, they were terrified. The horses were getting faster and faster, dodging trees and brambles, jumping small streams, racing each other at great speed.

Suddenly they came to a clearing in the woods and the horses stopped. Tuhil and Meena gasped. There, in front of them, were four houses. The houses were set around a pond with fish and frogs playing in the water. The leaves on the floor around the houses were a different colour to the rest of the leaves in the wood they'd ridden through. Just at that moment, a man walked out of one of the houses, and shouted at them. They didn't understand what he said … were they in a place with a new language?

Audioscript: *Tuhil and Meena 2*

On a Sunday evening, the sun was setting like an orange ball in the sky. Tuhil and Meena were riding their horses along a lane. They were chatting about school and about how the spelling tests were getting harder than last year. Suddenly, the horses heard a loud noise and were scared. They galloped as fast as the wind into the woods. Tuhil and Meena had no control of either horse, they were terrified. The horses were getting faster and faster, dodging trees and the razor-sharp brambles, jumping small streams, racing each other at great speed.

Suddenly they came upon a clearing in the woods. The horses skidded to a halt. Tuhil and Meena gasped. There in front of them were four houses. The houses were small with doll's house doors, a lot smaller than their doors at home! The houses were made out of sticky, toffee-coloured mud, small twigs and soft cushion leaves. They were set around a sparkling glass pond with sapphire blue fish and green and black spotted frogs. The leaves on the floor around the houses were a different colour to the rest of the leaves in the wood they'd ridden through; they were a lighter green, with splashes of pink. Just at that moment, a miniature, grey-bearded man walked out of one of the houses and shouted at them while waving a long black stick. They didn't understand what he said … were they in a place with a new language?

4 What happens next? (20 minutes)

Learning intention: To predict what might happen next.

Resources: Learner's Book, Session 7.3, Activity 4

Description: Ask learners to re-read the passage about Alfie in Activity 1. Now ask learners to read the instructions for Activity 4. Ask: *Which clues could you use?* (sea is a little bit rough; can see an island, trees and smoke) Ask learners to think about: what happened while Alfie was on the choppy sea; whether Alfie reached the island; where the smoke is coming from; and whether anyone lived on the island and if they were good or bad. Remind learners that there are no right or wrong answers.

Before learners draw their pictures, ask them to talk in pairs about their ideas. When learners have finished drawing, explain that they should try to label their picture using figurative language, such as noun phrases and similes. Remind them to use interesting adjectives and verbs.

> **Differentiation ideas:** Support less confident writers by pairing with a more confident writing partner.

> **Assessment ideas:** Were learners able to use the clues to make sensible predictions about what might happen next to Alfie? Note which learners used interesting adjectives and verbs. Which learners used figurative language in their labels?

Answers:
Learners' own answers. Possible labels: a whale; Alfie in the sea monster's mouth; sharp teeth; lots of trees; an old man sitting beside a fire; Alfie hid behind a bush, crouching like a tiger.

Plenary idea

Story ideas (5–10 minutes)

Description: Ask learners to share their ideas about where Alfie was, what he saw and what he did. Discuss the variety of predictions suggested.

Homework ideas

Ask learners to:

- complete the Workbook activities for this session, if not completed in class
- use the labels from their picture to write the next part of Alfie's adventure.

Answers for Workbook

1 Following similes underlined: as fast as a speedboat; like a dragon's head; like a yawning mouth; as sharp as dragon fangs.

2 Possible answers:
   a The man's hair was as black as the night.
   b I am so hungry I could eat like a horse.
   c As Anya walked along the street she felt as free as a bird.
   d He closed his eyes, knowing he would sleep like a dog.

3 Possible answers:
   water: The water was as clear as crystal.
   clouds: The clouds looked like piles of fluffy white cushions.

4 Learners' own answers.

7.4 Character portraits

LEARNING PLAN

Learning objectives	Learning intentions	Success criteria
3Rv.04, 3Ri.02, 3Ri.06, 3Ri.10, 3Ri.12, 3Ri.15, 3Ri.16, 3Wv.05, 3Wv.06, 3Wv.07, 3Wg.01, 3Wg.04, 3Wg.05, 3Wc.01, 3Wc.02, 3Wc.03, 3Wp.01, 3Wp.04, 3SLm.01, 3SLp.01	• Talk about characters. • Write about a story character. • Use multi-clause sentences.	• Learners can talk about characters. • Learners can write about a story character. • Learners can use multi-clause sentences.

LANGUAGE SUPPORT

By Stage 3, learners should be able to use a wide range of connectives (e.g. because, although, even though, while) rather than limiting themselves to *and*, *but* and *so*. If learners need further practice, give them pairs of simple sentences and ask them to suggest connectives that could join them.

Starter idea

Who am I? (15 minutes)

Resources: Learner's Book, Session 7.4: Getting started; writing paper

Description: Ask learners to think about how they would describe themselves to someone else. Say: *Think about what you look like; how you like to dress; what you like/ don't like; and the kind of person you are.* Read the Getting started activity together, then organise learners into small groups. Provide sheets of writing paper for learners to write their descriptions. Remind them not to write their name on the paper. Ask learners to fold up their descriptions and place them in a bowl, box or pile on their table. Allow time for groups to read and match the descriptions to each group member.

Main teaching ideas

1 Talking about Alfie (10 minutes)

Learning intention: To talk about characters.

Resources: Learner's Book, Session 7.4, Activity 1; *Story beginning 1* (Learner's Book, Session 7.2); Track 40; *A Dark Cave* (Learner's Book, Session 7.3); Track 43

Description: Direct learners to the Learner's Book and read the prompts. Tell them to re-read the extracts about Alfie from Sessions 7.2 and 7.3 of the Learner's Book. Ask: *Do you know what Alfie looks like? Where could you find this information* (the pictures)? Ask: *What do you think Alfie might have in his rucksack?* Try to elicit that Alfie will have items that could be useful on his adventures. Give learners time to discuss their ideas with a partner.

⟩ **Differentiation ideas:** Challenge more confident readers by pairing them with less confident readers so that they can read the text to or with their partner.

Answers:
Possible answers:
brown hair, red striped jumper, rucksack; likes exploring and having adventures; thinks an adventure can happen at any time; likes finding new things; brave; frightened

2 Character portrait (25–30 minutes)

Learning intentions: To write about a story character; to use multi-clause sentences.

Resources: Learner's Book, Session 7.4, Activity 2; Workbook, Session 7.4; Differentiated worksheet pack; dictionaries

Description: Tell learners that they are going to use information about Alfie to write a character portrait. Explain that this is a written description of a character. It is called a character portrait because we are creating a picture of a character using words. You could use the Workbook activities here to provide learners with structured support for writing a character portrait before they begin writing their character portraits of Alfie.

Direct learners to the prompts in the Learner's Book. Ask: *Can you give me an example of a noun phrase* (e.g. small boy; brown hair)? Write *Alfie got into his boat* on the board. Ask: *Which interesting verb could I use instead of got* (e.g. climbed, stepped, wobbled)?

Ask: *What sentence types could you use in your writing?* (e.g. question sentences, exclamation sentences) Ask: *Can you think of a simile to describe how brave Alfie is?* (e.g. as brave as a lion).

Read the Writing tip. Ask learners to recall connectives they know (e.g. and, but, so, if, because, although).

Write two simple sentences on the board (e.g. *Alfie was brave. Alfie was a young boy*). Ask: *When I join the sentences do I need to change any other words?* Try to elicit that the second *Alfie* will change to the pronoun *he*. You could use Differentiated worksheets 7A–C to provide practice with using connectives to write multi-clause sentences.

Allow time for learners to complete their character portraits in their notebooks. Remind them to use their ideas about Alfie from Activity 1, to use neat, joined handwriting and to check spellings in a dictionary.

⟩ **Differentiation ideas:** Support learners with creating multi-clause sentences by providing a selection of connectives on cards.

⟩ **Assessment ideas:** Note which learners can recall previous learning about noun phrases, similes, connectives and multi-clause sentences. To assess learning during the session, compare the language and sentence types learners use in their own character portrait with their character portraits of Alfie Small.

Plenary idea

Describing Alfie (5 minutes)

Resources: Learner's Book, Session 7.4

Description: In groups, ask learners to take turns reading their character portraits of Alfie. Ask them to peer assess each learner's use of connectives, noun phrases and inclusion of a simile.

Homework ideas

Ask learners to:

- complete the Workbook activities for this session, if not completed in class
- draw and label all the items they think Alfie might have in his rucksack (e.g. magnifying glass, fold-up periscope to see around corners, string, penknife, balloon).

Answers for Workbook

Learners' own answers.

7.5 Looking at chapters

LEARNING PLAN

Learning objectives	Learning intentions	Success criteria
3Rv.01, 3Rv.04, 3Rv.06, 3Rv.07, 3Rg.06, 3Rs.01, 3Rs.02, 3Rs.03, 3Rs.04, 3Ri.01, 3Ri.10, 3Ri.16, 3Ri.17, 3Ra.03, 3Ra.04, 3Wv.04, 3Wg.01, 3Wg.05, 3Ws.01, 3Ws.03, 3Wp.01	• Explore how chapters are used in books. • Look in more detail at sentence openings.	• Learners can explore how chapters are used in books. • Learners can look in more detail at sentence openings.

LANGUAGE SUPPORT

When less confident learners first use sentence openings, it is best to limit them to using single adverbs (e.g. First, Next, Yesterday, Suddenly). More confident learners will be keen to explore sentence openers (e.g. Later that day, All at once, Slowly and carefully). Encourage learners to recognise that adverbs/sentence openers explain when, where or how something happens. Do not worry about learners using the terms *time*, *place* and *manner* at this stage.

Starter idea

What is a chapter? (10 minutes)

Resources: Learner's Book, Session 7.5: Getting started; selection of fiction books with chapters

Description: Organise learners into pairs. Give each pair a fiction book and ask learners to have a brief look through it. Ask: *Does your book have chapters? How are the chapters shown?* Elicit that some fiction books have chapters, and some do not. Explain that when books have chapters some authors number each chapter and some use a chapter heading. Allow time for pairs to discuss the questions in the Learner's Book.

Main teaching ideas

1 Chapter headings (20–25 minutes)

Learning intention: To explore how chapters are used in books.

Resources: Learner's Book, Session 7.5, Activity 1; Workbook, Session 7.5, Activities 1 and 2; Worksheet 7.1

Description: Direct learners to the activity in the Learner's Book. Ask them to share their ideas about why chapters are used in books. Try to elicit that writers use chapters to break the stories into sections, to separate topics in non-fiction books, to give clues about the content of the chapter using chapter headings and to create interest.

Now read the chapter headings in part b of Activity 1. If appropriate, explain the words *sizzling* (cooking with a hissing sound) and *captured* (grab/trap something that does not want to be grabbed/trapped).

Explain that the chapter heading gives a clue about what might happen next. Ask: *Which chapters have you already read?* (Chapters 1 and 2) Ask learners to use the chapter headings to take turns telling each other a story about what could happen.

When learners have finished, direct them to the character and speech-bubble text. Ask: *Do the chapter headings make you want to read more about Alfie Small? Which chapter do you think will be the most exciting? Do you think Chapter 5 is the last chapter in the story?* You could use the Focus and Practice activities in the Workbook or Worksheet 7.1 Chapter headings here to provide further practice.

⟩ **Differentiation ideas:** Support learners using questions to scaffold ideas for each chapter:

- *Who was cooking the sausages? Was it someone good or bad?*
- *Who was captured? Did they escape?*
- *How did Alfie become Captain Alfie?*
- *What did Alfie do about the shark?*

⟩ **Assessment ideas:** Assess whether learners can recognise *Sizzling sausages* as an example of onomatopoeia? Ask learners to think about how well the word *sizzling* matches the sound sausages make when they are cooking.

Answers:
Learners' own responses.

2 Sentence openings (20 minutes)

Learning intention: To look in more detail at sentence openings.

Resources: Learner's Book, Session 7.5, Activity 2; Workbook, Session 7.5, Activity 2

Description: Direct learners to Activity 2 in the Learner's Book. Read the Language focus text aloud. Can learners recall what these sentence openings are called (sentence openers)? Ask learners to share examples of other sentence openings (e.g. Once upon a time; It was a sunny day; Next; Finally; Suddenly).

Read the words and phrases in the boxes in part a and ask learners to look at the partial sentences beneath. Explain that writers sometimes put a comma after the sentence opening to show that it is extra information that can be separated from the main sentence (e.g. Later that day, Alfie spotted the shark).

Ask learners to use the sentence openers in the boxes to write the complete sentences in their notebooks using neat joined handwriting. Remind learners to use capital letters to start sentences and for proper nouns, and to use the correct punctuation at the end of each sentence. Use the Practice activity in the Workbook, if not already used, to provide further practice with using sentence openings.

> **Differentiation ideas:** Support learners by suggesting that they test whether the sentence opening makes sense by saying the sentence silently before writing it in their notebook.

Challenge learners to use a comma after each sentence opening.

> **Assessment ideas:** Assess whether learners understand each type of adverb/adverbial phrase by asking them to perform these actions as you read the words in the boxes in Activity 2:

- when: look at an imaginary watch on their wrist (all at once; early one morning; when he was ready)

- where: draw an imaginary circle in front of them to indicate the world (at the end; behind his shed)

- how: fingers of one hand walk across the palm of the other hand (joyfully; to his surprise; carefully).

Answers:
Possible answers:
- Early one morning, Alfie left his house and walked down his garden path.
- Behind his shed, he found a stream.
- To his surprise, there was a boat.
- Carefully, he climbed into the boat.
- When he was ready, he started to paddle.

Plenary idea

Silly Consequences game (10 minutes)

Resources: Long strips of paper; pencils

Description: Organise learners into groups of three and label group members as A, B and C. Give each group a strip of paper and a pencil. Explain that learners are going to take turns to write a silly story on the paper strip. Explain that learners will not know what the learner before them has written.

Ask A in each group to write a sentence opener at the top of the strip (e.g. One sunny day). The As fold the paper over hiding their sentence and pass it to the Bs. Ask the Bs to write a sentence (e.g. I went for a walk). They fold the paper over and pass it to the Cs. The Cs write a new sentence opener and the pattern continues.

When the strip is full, ask groups to unfold the strip and read the silly story.

Homework ideas

Ask learners to:

- complete the Workbook activities for this session, if not completed in class

- play the Silly Consequences game, as in the plenary, with friends or family members.

Answers for Workbook

1   Possible order:
    Chapter 1 The morning everything changed
    Chapter 2 A night on a train
    Chapter 3 Surprise meeting
    Chapter 4 Race to the prize
    Chapter 5 Back home at last

2   Learners' own answers. Possible sentence openings:
    Chapter 1: It was an ordinary sunny morning
    Chapter 2: After school
    Chapter 3: Cautiously
    Chapter 4: As quickly as I could
    Chapter 5: Tired and hungry

3   Possible answers:

Sentence openings		
When	**Where**	**How**
Yesterday	Behind the tree	Quickly
Early that morning	As I walked along the street	All at once
At the end of the day	In the middle of the forest	Very slowly

7.6 Looking at verbs

Learning objectives	Learning intentions	Success criteria
3Rw.03, 3Rw.04, 3Rv.01, 3Rg.01, 3Rg.08, 3Rg.10, 3Rg.11, 3Rs.01, 3Rs.02, 3Ri.03, 3Ri.07, 3Ri.16, 3Ri.17, 3Ra.03, 3Wv.05, 3Wv.06, 3Wg.01, 3Wg.04, 3Wg.05, 3Wg.06, 3Wg.07, 3Ws.01, 3Ws.02, 3Ws.03, 3Wc.01, 3Wc.02, 3Wc.03, 3Wc.05, 3SLm.01, 3SLg.02, 3SLg.03, 3SLg.04	• Compare stories by the same author. • Answer questions about a story. • Recognise past tense irregular verbs. • Plan an Alfie Small adventure.	• Learners can compare stories by the same author. • Learners can answer questions about a story. • Learners can recognise past tense irregular verbs. • Learners can plan an Alfie Small adventure.

LANGUAGE SUPPORT

There is no easy way to learn which verbs use the irregular past tense. Unfortunately, the spellings for irregular verbs just have to be learned.

Learners who find inference questions difficult may not realise the character of Jed is a dog and not a person. You may need to direct learners to additional clues in the text (e.g. references to Jed *whining*).

Starter idea

Verbs (5 minutes)

Resources: Learner's Book, Session 7.6: Getting started

Description: Write the verb *jump* on the board. Ask: *Which word group does this word belong to?* Write *jumped* on the board. Ask: *How has the verb changed* (e.g. added *–ed*; it is in the past)*?* In pairs, learners should discuss differences between past and present tense verbs and say three examples of each.

Main teaching ideas

1 and 2   Another story (30 minutes)

Learning intentions: To compare stories by the same author; to answer questions about a story.

Resources: *The Stripy Balloon* (Learner's Book, Session 7.6, Activities 1 and 2); Track 46; Worksheet 7.2

Description: Before reading the passage, direct learners to the picture to help them understand the noun phrase *wicker basket*. When you have read the passage, ask: *What does buffeted mean?* Encourage learners to read the rest of the sentence and use their knowledge of balloons.

Ask learners to re-read the passage, and then think about the initial questions (Activity 1) in the Learner's Book. Elicit that the author is Nick Ward but that the story uses Alfie Small as the storyteller. Then ask: *Which parts of the story were similar to the previous story about Alfie?* You could use Worksheet 7.2 Comparing stories now. Explain that all Alfie Small adventures use the same story structure.

Ask learners to complete the questions in Activity 2 in their notebooks. Remind them to refer to the passage.

> **Differentiation ideas:** Support learners by directing them to the passage to find clues for implicit and open-ended comprehension questions.

> **Assessment ideas:** Did learners recognise that the extract is another Alfie Small adventure?

Answers:

a   A stripy balloon with a wicker basket

b   A dog

c   A monstrous ogre's face

d   Whine

e   Story has similar events; uses similar language and vocabulary

f   Learners' own answers (e.g. Alfie will meet a dragon or a strange beast).

g   Learners' own answers (e.g. Jed because he is a dog and he had not been on an adventure before).

h   Learners' own answers (e.g. a large bird lived on the rocky landscape and they rode on its back).

3 Past and present tense (10 minutes)

Learning intention: To recognise past tense irregular verbs.

Resources: Learner's Book, Session 7.6, Activity 3; Workbook, Session 7.6, Activities 1 and 2

Description: Remind learners of the verb activity at the start of the session. Ask them to talk to their partner about the verbs in the story passage. Ask: *Are the verbs mostly in the simple present tense or the simple past tense?* (simple past).

Invite a learner to read the Language focus text aloud. Explain that irregular past tense verbs do not follow a pattern and can sometimes be very different from the present tense form (e.g. go – went, is –was).

Allow learners time to match the present tense and past tense verbs in their notebooks. You could use the Focus activity in the Workbook to provide further practice with recognising the difference between present tense and irregular past tense verbs.

> **Differentiation ideas:** Challenge learners to write sentences using each past tense verb.

> **Assessment ideas:** Can learners identify the correct pairs of present and irregular past tense verbs?

Answers:
Run – ran, write – wrote, give – gave, draw – drew, come – came

4 Looking for irregular verbs (10 minutes)

Learning intention: To recognise past tense irregular verbs.

Resources: Learner's Book, Session 7.6, Activity 4; Workbook, Session 7.6 Activities 3 and 4

Description: Explain that learners are going to look for irregular verbs in the Alfie Small passage. Read aloud the first sentence in the text. Ask: *Which words are verbs?* (*pushed, found, hanging*) Write the words on the board then ask: *Which words are in the past tense?* (pushed; found) *Which has an irregular spelling?* (found).

Explain that some verbs combine with *to be* or *to have* verbs (e.g. *was* buffeted, *were* thrown, *had* changed). Explain that learners do not have to include the *to be* and *to have* verb forms in their answers. You could use the Practice and Challenge activities in the Workbook to provide practice with *to be* verbs and other irregular past tense verbs.

> **Differentiation ideas:** Support learners by reading every sentence and asking them to identify the verbs each time. Learners can then decide which are in the past tense and whether the spelling is irregular.

> **Assessment ideas:** Are learners able to recognise all past tense forms of the *to be* verb family?

Answers:
Any five of these irregular verbs:
found, rose, swept, began, thrown, went, cried, untied, was.

5 Plan an adventure (30 minutes)

Learning intention: To plan an Alfie Small adventure.

Resources: Learner's Book, Session 7.6, Activity 5; Worksheet 7.2

Description: Ask: *Does Alfie have long or short adventures* (lots of short adventures)? In pairs, learners should recall Alfie's character (brave explorer) and the similarities between stories of Alfie Small adventures (e.g. all begin with finding something, he always travels somewhere). Explain that learners are going to plan an Alfie Small adventure and that their adventure will be in chapters.

Direct learners to the prompts in the Learner's Book. Ask: *How can chapter headings help plan a story?* (e.g. organise Alfie's adventures, gives clues about the adventure) Remind learners of the chapter headings in Session 7.5 of the Learner's Book and the story events of an Alfie Small adventure. You could ask them to look at the table they completed in Worksheet 7.2 if you used it in Activity 1. Allow time for learners to write their chapter headings and talk to their partners. Direct them to the Writing tip. Then allow time for learners to write the start of their story.

> **Differentiation ideas:** Support learners by agreeing chapter headings as a group, then ask learners to refer to the story events table in Worksheet 7.2 to remind them of how the story develops.

> **Assessment ideas:** Use learners' adventure story to assess how well learners can use and spell irregular past tense verbs. Which learners can use all past tense forms of the to be verb family? Can learners match the past tense to the different pronouns?

Plenary idea

Sizzling sausages (10 minutes)

Description: Remind learners of the chapter headings in Session 7.5 of the Learner's Book, then point out the heading 'Sizzling sausages'. In pairs, ask learners to look at their own chapter headings. Ask learners to choose one heading and rewrite it using two or three words that all begin with the same letter (e.g. Dangerous Dragons, Creepy Caves, Soggy Socks). As a further challenge, you could ask learners to use an onomatopoeic word.

Homework ideas

Ask learners to:

*   complete the Workbook activities for this session, if not completed in class

*   identify past tense verbs in their reading book, then sort them into regular and irregular spellings.

Answers for Workbook

1   a   slept

  b   drank

  c   caught

2   a   made / baked / ate

  b   grew

  c   swam

3

Present tense	Past tense
I am	I was
you are	you were
he is	he was
she is	she was
it is	it was
we are	we were
they are	they were

4   a   came: *to come*
  b   bought: to buy
  c   ate: to eat
  d   gave: to give
  e   spoke: to speak
  f   made: to make
  g   grew: to grow
  h   ran: to run

7.7 Looking in more detail

LEARNING PLAN		
Learning objectives	**Learning intentions**	**Success criteria**
3Rw.01, 3Rw.03, 3Rv.01, 3Rv.04, 3Rg.01, 3Rs.01, 3Rs.02, 3Rs.03, 3Ri.03, 3Ri.06, 3Ri.07, 3Ri.10, 3Ri.12, 3Ri.16, 3Ri.17, 3Ra.01, 3Ra.02, 3Ra.03, 3Wp.02, 3SLm.01, 3SLm.02, 3SLm.03, 3SLm.04, 3SLs.01, 3SLs.02, 3SLg.02, 3SLg.03, 3SLg.04, 3SLp.04, 3SLr.02	• Answer questions about *Dragon Boy*. • Discuss similarities and differences in adventure stories. • Role play a story character. • Listen to others and give opinions.	• Learners can answer questions about *Dragon Boy*. • Learners can discuss similarities and differences in adventure stories. • Learners can role play a story character. • Learners can listen and give opinions.

LANGUAGE SUPPORT

You will need to explain the colloquial terms used for family members in *Dragon Boy*:

- Da – Dad
- Ma – Mum
- Granda – Grandad

Starter idea

Looking back (5 minutes)

Resources: Learner's Book, Session 7.7: Getting started

Description: In pairs, learners should recall the first passage they read from *Dragon Boy*. Ask learners to re-read the beginning of *Dragon Boy* by Pippa Goodheart in Session 7.2 to check how well they recalled the passage.

Remind learners of the meaning of unfamiliar words (e.g. *hump, Granda*).

Main teaching ideas

1 *Dragon Boy* (20–25 minutes)

Learning intention: To answer questions about an extract from *Dragon Boy*.

Resources: *Fire Snatcher* (Learner's Book, Session 7.7, Activity 1); Track 47; Workbook, Session 7.7; dictionary

Description: Read the introduction, then ask learners to follow the text as you read the passage from *Dragon Boy* to the class. Ask learners to recall strategies they can use to work out the meaning of unfamiliar words (e.g. contextual clues, reading more of the sentence, phonic knowledge).

Ask learners to re-read the passage silently, then check that they understand unfamiliar words and phrases (e.g. *tiptoe-quiet, jabbed, thrust, flare*). Invite a learner to read the dictionary definition of any unfamiliar words.

You could ask learners to complete the Focus activity in the Workbook now as this asks them to identify all the sentences about the Fire Snatcher. Ask learners to answer the questions in their notebooks and give reasons for their answers to questions e, f and g.

> **Differentiation ideas:** Support learners by working in a small group to help them find answers to the questions, especially those that are implicit.

> **Assessment ideas:** Note which learners find it difficult to answer questions about the text when they have to draw on information that is implicit to the text. Which learners cannot support their ideas with reference to the passage? Focus on inference-style questions during guided reading sessions to build learners confidence and skill with this style of question.

Answers:

a Possible answers: warm their homes, cook their food, make life good.
b They chose the biggest, bravest man in the village.
c He needed the spear to wake the sleeping dragon.
d Possible answers: the dry wood would burn more easily when he caught the dragon's fiery breath.
e Possible answer: he needed to be brave because he had to wake the dragon and get very close to it, which would be dangerous because the dragons breathed fire.
f Possible answers: Fire Snatchers would feel: proud to be chosen; excited about doing something brave; anxious about the dragon catching them; worried about not getting the fire.
g Learners' own answers.

---

2 Discuss and compare (20 minutes)

Learning intention: To discuss similarities and differences in adventure stories.

Resources: Learner's Book, Session 7.7, Activity 2

Description: Organise learners into groups of five or six. Try to ensure that each group has learners with a variety of skills and strengths. Explain the activity to learners, then ask groups some prompt questions to help direct their thinking before they complete the table. Ask: *Who are the storytellers in the stories? Do all the stories have the same types of character? Why do the characters have adventures?*

Allow time for groups to discuss the different stories, and then to complete the table individually. Ask groups to share ideas.

> **Differentiation ideas:** Support and challenge learners by asking groups to complete the table together rather than individually. More confident writers could act as scribes in each group.

> **Assessment ideas:** Can learners identify the similarities and differences of the two adventure stories?

Answers:
Possible answers:

Similarities	Differences
Both adventure stories *Dragon Boy* and Alfie Small story *A dark cave* are about dragons	Alfie tells his own story – first person
	Granda is the storyteller – third person
Fire Snatcher and Alfie are both brave	Alfie Small is a small boy
Fire Snatcher and Alfie do not get hurt	Fire Snatcher is the biggest, bravest man in the village
Manage to beat the monster/dragon	Alfie chooses to explore and have adventures, but the Fire Snatcher is chosen by others

3 Role play (20–25 minutes)

Learning intention: To role play a story character.

Resources: Learner's Book, Session 7.7, Activity 3; Workbook, Session 7.7, Activity 2; a space large enough for role play

Description: You could ask learners to complete the Practice activity in the Workbook to provide practice in identifying a character's responses.

If possible, use a large space where learners can move around for the role play. Begin by asking learners to mime different feelings using facial expressions (e.g. sad, angry, frightened, worried, excited).

Ask: *Does the Fire Snatcher feel the same throughout the story?* In pairs, learners should talk about how the Fire Snatcher might feel: when he is chosen by the villagers; when he looks for and finds the dragon; when he snatches the fire; and when he returns to the village with the fire.

Ask learners to practise miming the different feelings in groups. Invite one learner to demonstrate a feeling, then invite other learners to use interesting adjectives to guess which point in the story is being mimed and what the feeling is.

Ask: *How will the Fire Snatcher's behaviour and actions change during the story?* In pairs, learners should talk about words and phrases that describe how the Fire Snatcher will react to things he sees, hears or smells.

Ask learners to move around the room role playing the Fire Snatcher at different points of the story. Invite learners to share their actions and then describe them using powerful verbs (e.g. waving, tiptoeing, sneaking, creeping, jumping, returning proudly).

> **Differentiation ideas:** Support less confident performers with more confident partners.

> **Assessment ideas:** During the activity, note which learners used interesting adjectives and noun phrases, and powerful verbs to talk about the Fire Snatcher.

4 Sharing ideas (5 minutes)

Learning intention: To listen to others and give opinions.

Resources: Learner's Book, Session 7.7, Activity 4

Description: Direct learners to the activity and read the Listening tip. Do learners agree, or do they have different opinions? Can they give reasons for their opinions? Do they listen and respond politely to alternative viewpoints?

Invite learners to share their partners' opinions with the class.

> **Assessment ideas:** Note which learners demonstrate good listening skills when they explain their partners' opinions.

Answers:
a   The passage is near the beginning of the story.
b   Learners' own answers. Possible answers: Yes, because you are at a cliff-hanger and makes you want to read more; No, because you need more of the story to happen.

Plenary idea

Chapter headings (5 minutes)

Description: Explain that the passage in this session is the second chapter in *Dragon Boy*.

In pairs, learners should discuss what they think the heading for this chapter might be. What about the third chapter heading? What about the first chapter heading?

Homework ideas

Ask learners to:

* complete the Workbook activities for this session, if not completed in class

* compare the similarities and differences of an adventure story they know with either an Alfie Small adventure or *Dragon Boy*.

Answers for Workbook

1 Learners should have underlined the following sentences:
   So they chose the biggest, bravest man in the village.
   They gave him a fine spear and they called him Fire Snatcher.
   My da, your great-granda, Lily, was Fire Snatcher and hero of the village.
   All he had to do was creep, tiptoe-quiet into the hills, then jump, suddenly, on a sleeping dragon and poke it with his spear.
   As it roared, the Fire Snatcher thrust his torch of dry wood into the flare of the dragon's fiery breath to light it.

2 Learners' own answers. Possible words or phrases:

   a See or hear: sleeping dragon, roar fire, fiery breath

   b feel: excited, anxious, happy

3 Learners' own answers.

7.8 Setting and dialogue

LEARNING PLAN

Learning objectives	Learning intentions	Success criteria
3Rv.05, 3Rg.01, 3Rg.04, 3Ri.16, 3Wv.03, 3Wv.05, 3Wv.06, 3Wv.07, 3Wg.01, 3Wg.03, 3Ws.01, 3Ws.02, 3Wc.03, 3Wp.04	• Describe a setting. • Explore dialogue. • Use punctuation correctly within sentences and for dialogue.	• Learners can describe a setting. • Learners can explore dialogue. • Learners can use punctuation correctly within sentences and for dialogue.

LANGUAGE SUPPORT

You may need to recap what a setting is before you begin this session. Check that learners understand that a setting is any place where something takes place. Learners may well limit their description of a setting to what they can see. You will need to prompt them to include things they can hear and smell.

Common misconceptions

Misconception	How to identify	How to overcome
Speech marks go around every sentence spoken by the character rather than around the start and end of a speech.	Ask learners to complete Activity 3. When learners add the correct punctuation to the passage, they may put speech marks at the beginning and end of every sentence in a character's speech (e.g. 'She found one ordinary baby dragon and another baby.' 'He was pink and soft instead of green and scaly.')	Ask learners to look at what Granda says to Lily when she asks how the Fire Snatcher caught the fire (see Session 7.7 of the Learner's Book). Ask learners how many sentences there are in Granda's reply (nine). Then ask learners how many pairs of speech marks they can find in Granda's reply (two). Ask learners to identify where the second pair of speech marks begin and end.

Starter idea

Nouns and adjectives (5–10 minutes)

Resources: Learner's Book, Session 7.8: Getting started

Description: Ask learners to talk to a partner about the word groups they know. Allow learners time to discuss the prompts about nouns and adjectives in the Learner's Book. Invite learners to share ideas (e.g. nouns are naming words; proper nouns start with a capital letter; adjectives are describing words).

Ask learners to make two columns in their notebooks with the headings *Nouns* and *Adjectives*. Explain the activity in the Learner's Book and allow learners a few minutes to complete it.

Main teaching ideas

1 Dragon settings (25 minutes)

Learning intention: To describe a setting.

Resources: Learner's Book, Session 7.8, Activity 1; dictionaries; thesauruses; learners' personal word collections from Session 7.7, if used

Description: Choose two confident readers to re-read the passage from *Dragon Boy* as Lily and Granda. Ask the class to close their eyes. Say: *Think about your role play of the Fire Snatcher. Try to picture what the Dragon Hills look like.* Ask: *Are there trees? What time of day is it? Can you see things clearly or is there a mist? Are you shivering or shaking? Why? Where is the dragon? Is it near rocks? Is it in a cave?*

Re-read the passage (as learners sit with their eyes closed). Ask learners to talk to a partner about their ideas for the setting.

Direct learners to the Writing tip, then ask them to write a paragraph to describe the setting. Remind learners to use available resources to find interesting words and to check spellings.

When learners have finished, ask them to share their paragraph with a partner and talk about the description. Which words do they think describe the setting clearly? Which word choices could be improved?

> **Differentiation ideas:** Support learners by suggesting synonyms for less interesting word choices.

Challenge learners to include a simile.

> **Assessment ideas:** Note which learners found it difficult to select suitable adjectives to describe the setting so that you can provide more support during the next activities.

Answers:
Learners' own answers.

2 Who is speaking? (10 minutes)

Learning intention: To explore dialogue.

Resources: Learner's Book, Session 7.8, Activity 2

Description: Ask: *What is the term we use for speech in a story?* (dialogue) Say: *Tell your partner what you can remember about setting out speech.*

Ask learners to look at Granda's paragraph beginning 'Well, Lily ... ' to '... breath to light it.' Ask: *How many pairs of speech marks can you find* (two)? *Why?* Tell learners that the writer has broken Granda's speech into two parts with the words *said Granda.*

Read the Language focus text, then ask learners to discuss the questions with a partner. Allow time for discussion, then share learners' suggestions for alternatives to *said*.

> **Assessment ideas:** Are learners able to identify alternatives to *said*?

Answers:
a   Two speakers (Lily, Granda)
b   Speech marks at the beginning and end of what is said
c   One time
d   Asked
e   Possible alternatives to *asked*: questioned, queried, enquired, wondered.

3   Missing punctuation (15–20 minutes)

Learning intention: To use punctuation correctly within sentences and for dialogue.

Resources: Learner's Book, Session 7.8, Activity 3; Workbook, Session 7.8; coloured pens or pencils; learners' personal word collections, if used

Description: Direct learners to the passage and explain that the gaps in the passage show places where the speech verb has been missed out. Ask learners to read the passage and to put *said* in each gap. Remind them that when writing dialogue every time a new speaker speaks, you need to start a new line.

When learners have read the passage, ask them how many times Granda spoke (*twice*). Ask them to discuss why the author does not always tell the reader who is speaking (e.g. uses the name of the person they are speaking to; you can tell who the speaker is from what they say).

Ask learners to think about what happens whenever they come to a full stop, exclamation mark or question mark (e.g. take a breath, pause). If there is time in class, ask learners to complete the Workbook activities to provide practice in punctuating dialogue and using synonyms for *said*.

Tell learners to re-read the passage quietly in pairs and to notice when they take a breath. Explain that this may help them identify that some punctuation is missing. Remind learners to use collections or a thesaurus to find alternatives for *said*.

Ask learners to copy out the passage into their notebooks, adding missing punctuation and

correcting errors, and inserting speech verbs using a different-coloured pen or pencil.

Allow learners time to complete the activity then ask them to peer mark with a partner. Ask learners to discuss the Reflection questions.

> **Differentiation ideas:** Support learners by reading the passage so that they hear when you pause to signal the end of a sentence.

> **Assessment ideas:** Note which learners can punctuate their own work but need support adding or correcting punctuation in the passage they copy. Which learners show greater awareness when correcting the passage than they do when producing independent writing?

Answers:
Punctuation answers (Learners' own answers for *said* alternatives):
'Who was Dragon Boy?' <u>said</u> (asked, queried) Lily.
'Well, Lily,' <u>said</u> (replied, answered) Granda. 'There was a big fire and the villagers ran away. A mother dragon went to see if her eggs had hatched. What do you think she saw?'
'I don't know,' <u>said</u> (wondered, whispered) Lily.
'She found one ordinary baby dragon and another baby. He was pink and soft instead of green and scaly.'
'I bet he was Dragon Boy,' <u>said</u> (gasped, suggested, announced) Lily.

Plenary idea

Build-a-Flower (5–10 minutes)

Description: Remind learners of how to play the flower-in-a-pot version of Hangman (see Session 4.6, Plenary idea).

Draw a dash on the board for each letter of a synonym of *said* (e.g. wondered). Ask learners to guess the word before all the petals are on the flower. If there is time, learners could play the game in pairs or small groups.

Homework ideas

Ask learners to:

* complete the Workbook activities for this session, if not completed in class

* write a setting description of an outdoor space close to where they live.

Answers for Workbook

1 a 'I am reading this book on dragons,' said Rupesh.
  b 'It is a good book,' replied Sam.
  c 'I love reading about dragons,' Rupesh explained.
  d 'So do I,' laughed Sam.

2 a 'Do you believe in dragons?' asked Rupesh.
  b 'I'm not sure,' replied Sam.
  c 'What about you?' queried Sam.
  d 'Definitely!' exclaimed Rupesh.

3 'Did Dragon Boy know that he was a human?' asked Lucy.

'No,' smiled Granda. 'He grew up with dragons. They were his brothers and sisters and his friends.'

'Could he do everything that they could do?' wondered Lily.

Granda replied, 'No, he couldn't fly. But most of all he couldn't make fire. That's what he wanted most.'

'What happened to him?' demanded Lily.

'You'll have to wait and find out later,' answered Granda.

7.9 More about paragraphs

LEARNING PLAN

Learning objectives	Learning intentions	Success criteria
3Rw.01, 3Rw.02, 3Rw.03, 3Rw.04, 3Rv.01, 3Rv.04, 3Rv.06, 3Rv.07, 3Rg.01, 3Rg.10, 3Rg.11, 3Rs.01, 3Rs.02, 3Rs.03, 3Rs.04, 3Ri.06, 3Ri.07, 3Ri.10, 3Ri.12, 3Ri.14, 3Ri.15, 3Ri.16, 3Ri.17, 3Ra.01, 3Ra.02, 3SLm.01, 3SLs.01, 3SLg.02, 3SLg.03, 3SLg.04	• Discuss the use of paragraphs and sentence openings. • Work out the meaning of unfamiliar words using the context. • Scan and read texts in detail to answer questions.	• Learners can discuss the use of paragraphs and sentence openings. • Learners can work out the meaning of unfamiliar words using the context. • Learners can scan and read texts in detail to answer questions.

LANGUAGE SUPPORT

Learners may need support to work out the meaning of unfamiliar words. They might find it helpful to link an action or a picture to help them understand the word. For example, to help learners understand *crouching* ask them to go into a crouching position as if they were beside the fire. Explain what *smouldering* means. Help learners understand *the smouldering flowered into flames* by imagining a fire just beginning to burn then bursting into flames like a flower suddenly opening up.

You could explore the different *ou* sounds in the passage (e.g. *u* in *young*; *ow* in *shouted*, *without*, *crouching*; *o* in *smouldered*). You could also explore the different *ow* sounds (e.g. *o* in *own*, *yellow*; *ow* in *flowered*).

Starter idea

Talk about paragraphs (5 minutes)

Resources: Learner's Book, Session 7.9: Getting started; a selection of reading books

Description: Provide pairs of learners with a reading book, then explain that during this session learners will explore how writers use paragraphs. Ask them what they can recall about paragraphs from Unit 4.

Ask learners to look at the paragraphs in the reading books to help them answer the questions in the Learner's Book (e.g. breaks the story up; a new paragraph means a change of idea or event; sometimes indented). Remind learners that dialogue does not count as a new paragraph.

Main teaching ideas

1 *Dragon Boy* (20 minutes)

Learning intention: To work out the meaning of unfamiliar words using context.

Resources: *Fire!* (Learner's Book, Session 7.9, Activity 1); Track 48; Workbook, Session 7.9, Activity 1; Language worksheet 7B

Description: Ask learners to look at the layout of the *Dragon Boy* passage. Ask:

- *How many paragraphs can you find?* (four)

- *Is there any dialogue in the passage?* (yes)

- *Who is speaking?* (Dragon Boy)

- *Why has the writer used capital letters for CLACK?* (to emphasise the sound)

- *What type of word is CLACK?* (onomatopoeic)

Ask learners to talk to a partner about the strategies they know for reading unfamiliar words (e.g. phonic knowledge, segmenting, contextual clues). Ask: *How can you work out the meaning of a new word?* You could use Language worksheet 7B to provide further practice with segmenting unfamiliar vocabulary and finding out what the words mean.

Explain that reading more of the sentence, or using information that we already know, can help us. Check that learners understand that this is known as *the context*.

Read the introduction to the passage, then ask learners to listen to Track 48, before they read the passage themselves. Ask learners to make a list of any unfamiliar words as they read so that you can discuss them later.

Ask learners to talk to a partner about what has happened in the passage, then invite them to share their ideas (e.g. Dragon Boy was very sad because he couldn't make fire and the other dragons laughed at him. By accident Dragon Boy found a way of making fire by striking two stones together and singing a fiery song).

Ask: *Does Dragon Boy know he is not a dragon?* Try to elicit that Dragon Boy feels different. Explore how feeling different might make Dragon Boy feel. Be sensitive to learners who may have experienced these feelings. Learners could complete the Focus activity in the Workbook now to provide further practice with identifying the main events in paragraphs.

> **Differentiation ideas:** Support less confident readers by pairing them with a more confident reading partner.

> **Assessment ideas:** Note which learners can use contextual clues and the knowledge of dragons and fire-making to work out the meaning of unfamiliar words.

2 Questions about the passage (15 minutes)

Learning intention: To scan and read texts in detail to answer questions.

Resources: Learner's Book, Session 7.9, Activity 2

Description: Read the Reading tip aloud. Can learners remember what scanning a text means? Ask learners to answer the questions in their notebooks. Tell them that they should give reasons for their answers.

> **Assessment ideas:** Note which learners can identify implicit and explicit information in a text. Could all learners support their answers with appropriate reasons?

Answers:

a He went off on his own because the dragons laughed at him / because he couldn't make fire.

b He felt sad/angry.

c He kicked at some flint stones.

d He saw: a flash of yellow, a spark flash, smoke, flames. He smelt: smoky flint stones, grass smouldering, smoke. He heard: the stones clack. He felt: the wind on his back, happy, excited.

e He sang a fiery dragon song.

f Learners' own answers supported by a reason.

3 Paragraph openings (10–15 minutes)

Learning intention: To discuss the use of paragraphs and sentence openings.

Resources: Learner's Book, Session 7.9, Activity 3; Workbook, Session 7.9, Activities 2 and 3

Description: Remind learners of the discussion at the start of the session about paragraphs. Ask them to re-read the passage from Activity 1, then direct them to the Language focus box.

As a class, discuss why the writer started a new paragraph when she did (e.g. there was a new event, something different happened). Ask: *Which words or phrases open the paragraphs?* Explain that writers often use words or phrases to start a paragraph to signal that something is changing, such as when, where or how something is happening. Ask learners to identify which of the paragraphs use words or phrases in this way (paragraphs 1, 2 and 3).

Allow time for learners to discuss part b. Share answers so that learners can peer mark.

You could use the Practice and Challenge activities in the Workbook to provide further practice in writing opening sentences and with writing a paragraph.

> **Differentiation ideas:** Challenge learners to identify paragraphs in other *Dragon Boy* passages and to decide whether they begin with adverbs that say when, where or how the event is happening.

> **Assessment ideas:** Can learners explain why writers begin new paragraphs?

Answers:
a   There was a new event; something different happened.
b   Paragraph 1: One day: shows when it happens.
    Paragraph 2: As the sun began to set: shows when it happens.
    Paragraph 3: Quickly: show how it happens.
    Paragraph 4: CLACK! is the sound of how it happens.

Plenary idea

Sentence openings (10 minutes)

Description: Ask learners to re-read the last paragraph in the passage in this session. In pairs, can they think of a how, when or how sentence opener to replace the word *CLACK*?

Ask for volunteers to share their ideas. Then ask learners to think about what the next paragraph could be about (e.g. Dragon Boy runs home; someone hears him singing). Can they suggest a suitable sentence opening for this paragraph?

Homework ideas

Ask learners to:

- complete the Workbook activities for this session, if not completed in class

- use their list of unfamiliar words from the *Dragon Boy* passage, then write a synonym or definition based on what they think the word means.

Answers for Workbook

1, 2

Possible answers:

Paragraph	What the paragraph is about	Opening sentences
1	The children in the playground kick a ball over the school fence.	One day ...
2	The children cannot wait for school to be over for the day.	The afternoon ...
3	The children search for the ball.	Carefully ...
4	They find the ball, but a dragon is sitting next to it.	Before their eyes ... / Suddenly ...
5	The children and the dragon become friends.	Fortunately ... / Thankfully ...
6	The children and the dragon play football over the school fence.	The next day ... / Ever since then ...

3 Learners' own final paragraphs.

7.10 Looking at stories

LEARNING PLAN

Learning objectives	Learning intentions	Success criteria
3Ri.17, 3Ra.01, 3Ra.03, 3Ra.04 3Ww.03, 3Wg.01, 3Wg.04, 3Wg.05, 3Wg.06, 3Wg.07, 3Ws.02, 3Ws.03, 3Wc.02, 3Wc.05, 3SLm.01, 3SLm.02, 3SLs.02, 3SLg.02, 3SLg.03, 3SLg.04	• Write a book review. • Investigate prefixes. • Look closely at sentence openings.	• Learners can write a book review. • Learners can investigate prefixes. • Learners can look closely at sentence openings.

LANGUAGE SUPPORT

When looking at the word *review*, explain to learners that the word *view* means an opinion, an idea, a way of thinking about something. You could introduce learners to the phrases *in my view* and *from my point of view*. Encourage learners to use these phrases instead of *I think, my idea is*, etc.

Learners have looked at suffixes in previous units. Explain that a prefix is something that is fixed before the root word to change its meaning. Explain that the *pre–* is a prefix meaning *before*. Learners may find this helpful in remembering that prefixes are fixed before the root word and suffixes are fixed after the word. You could discuss other words that have the prefix *pre–* (e.g. *preview* = see before, *predict* = guess what may happen, *prehistoric* = before time).

Common misconceptions

Misconception	How to identify	How to overcome
A book review is the same as a book blurb.	Ask learners to read a book review and a blurb. Ask them what these pieces of text are called. Some learners may think they are both blurbs/book reviews.	Ask learners to find the following features in both texts: • information about the story • whether the writer enjoyed the book and why • who would enjoy the book and why. Guide learners to understanding that reviews include opinions and recommendations; blurbs do not.

Starter idea

Book choices (5 minutes)

Resources: Learner's Book, Session 7.10: Getting started

Description: Remind learners of the Alfie Small adventures and *Dragon Boy* texts discussed in this unit, then direct them to the prompts and picture in the Learner's Book. Allow learners time to discuss their preferences.

Main teaching ideas

1 Book review (30–40 minutes)

Learning intention: To write a book review.

Resources: Learner's Book, Session 7.10, Activity 1; Worksheets 7.3 and 7.4

Description: Invite learners to explain their reasons for choosing either the Alfie Small stories or *Dragon Boy*. Then, invite them to say what they did not like about each book. Explain that giving reasons for liking or not liking a book is part of reviewing a book.

Read the review prompts in the Learner's Book. Ask learners to decide which book they will review. Encourage less confident writers to choose a book from the unit, as this will make it easier for you to support their writing.

Explain or remind learners that what happens in a story is known as *the plot*. In pairs, learners should talk about: what they will say about the plot; how they will encourage others to read the book; what age of reader will enjoy the book; and what interests will they have. Before learners begin writing, explain that some book reviews end with a question to make the reader curious about the book.

You can read the review in Worksheet 7.3 Book review example or use Worksheet 7.4 Book review template. Tell learners that their reviews should have at least three paragraphs to cover the three prompts in the Learner's Book. Encourage learners to use interesting adjectives and powerful verbs in their reviews.

When learners have finished their reviews, direct them to the How am I doing? prompt.

> **Differentiation ideas:** Support learners by working with them in a group. Worksheet 7.4 could be used to scaffold their review.

> **Assessment ideas:** Use learners' book reviews to assess writing skills. Note which learners used multi-clause sentences, paragraphs to organise their writing, the correct spelling of regular and irregular past tense verbs and a range of sentence types.

Answers:
Learners' own answers.

2 Prefixes (15–20 minutes)

Learning intention: To investigate prefixes.

Resources: Learner's Book, Session 7.10, Activity 2; Workbook, Session 7.10; dictionaries

Description: Write *Review* on the board and ask: *Which shorter word can you find inside this word?* (view) Invite a learner to read the dictionary definition of *view*. Read the Language focus text. Explain that the prefix *re–* means to go back to something. Can learners use these definitions to work out what *review* means? (Try to elicit that *review* means *to think or talk about something again.*)

Explain that a prefix is something fixed to the front of the root word and that the spelling of the root word does not change. Ask learners to answer the questions in their notebooks, then peer mark answers to check that all learners have understood what a prefix is.

You could use the Workbook activities to provide further practice with prefixes if there is time in class.

Answers:
a   return, inactive, uncover, redo, incorrect, unkind, recycle, inaccurate, unhappy
b   Possible definitions:
    Return: to come back to
    Redo: to do again
    Unhappy: not happy
    Unkind: not kind
    Incorrect: not correct
    Inaccurate: not accurate
c   Possible explanations:
    re–: to do again
    un–: not
    in–: not

3 Dragon adventure (20 minutes)

Learning intention: To look closely at sentence openings.

Resources: Learner's Book, Session 7.10, Activity 3; Worksheet 4.1

Description: Direct learners to the storyboard in the Learner's Book. Read the title, then ask learners to talk to a partner about what they think is happening in each picture. Encourage partners to question each other about whether their ideas makes sense. Are there gaps in the story? Does their plot explain why the dragon flies away or how the boy feels as he waves goodbye?

Explain that each picture in the storyboard can represent a paragraph in a story. Remind learners of the paragraph openers they explored in the previous session. Allow time for learners to write their opening words or phrases.

When learners have finished, ask them to retell their stories in pairs, using their sentence openings as they go through each picture.

> **Differentiation ideas:** Support learners by pairing them with a more confident writer when they discuss the pictures. You could also provide less confident writers with a list of adverbs and sentence openers. They could refer to Worksheet 4.1 Story boxes.

> **Assessment ideas:** Did learners choose sentence openings that would sequence a story? Note which learners used well-chosen sentence openers.

Answers:
Possible sentence openings:
Box 2: One beautiful afternoon
Box 3: That night
Box 4: The next day
Box 5: A few weeks later; When the dragon was much bigger
Box 6: Sadly; At last

Plenary idea

Dragon story review (5–10 minutes)

Resources: Learners' storyboards from Activity 3

Description: In pairs, learners should talk about which readers might like their dragon story. Will the story be for young children or children of their age? Will both girls and boys like it?

Homework ideas

Ask learners to:

* complete the Workbook activities for this session, if not completed in class

* make a list of words with prefixes in their reading book; ask learners to write each word as a word sum (e.g. review = *re–* + view).

Answers for Workbook

1 a *dis–* + appear = <u>disappear</u>

   b *un–* + fair = <u>unfair</u>

   c *re–* + appear = <u>reappear</u>

   d *mis–* + behave = <u>misbehave</u>

   e *re–* + write = <u>rewrite</u>

   f *dis–* + agree = <u>disagree</u>

   g *in–* + correct = <u>incorrect</u>

   h *re–* + view = <u>review</u>

2 Possible words with prefixes:

   a *un–*: unkind, unhappy

   b *re–*: redo, review

   c *dis–*: disappear, dishonest

   d *in–*: incorrect, inaccurate

3 Possible answers:

   a *un–* = not (unkind = not kind; unhappy = not happy)

   b *re–* = again (redo = do again; review = look again)

   c *dis–* = not (disappear = not visible; dishonest = not honest)

   d *in–* = not (incorrect = not correct; inaccurate = not accurate)

7.11 Writing a story

LEARNING PLAN

Learning objectives	Learning intentions	Success criteria
3Ww.02, 3Ww.03, 3Ww.05, 3Wv.02, 3Wv.03, 3Wv.04, 3Wv.05, 3Wv.06, 3Wv.07, 3Wg.01, 3Wg.03, 3Wg.04, 3Wg.05, 3Wg.06, 3Wg.07, 3Wg.08, 3Ws.01, 3Ws.02, 3Ws.03, 3Wc.01, 3Wc.02, 3Wc.03, 3Wp.04, 3SLm.02, 3SLm.03, 3SLm.05, 3SLs.01, 3SLs.02, 3SLg.02, 3SLg.03, 3SLg.04	• Plan a story using a storyboard. • Discuss ways to improve a story plan. • Write an adventure story.	• Learners can plan a story using a storyboard. • Learners can discuss ways to improve their story plan. • Learners can write an adventure story.

LANGUAGE SUPPORT

Make sure learners understand that the most important things about an adventure story are the events or *risky situations* that occur and not the characters. You could spend time brainstorming different *risky situations* that could occur (e.g. becoming lost, becoming trapped, falling, ending up in a dangerous place). You could then brainstorm ideas about what a character may have with them (or find on the journey) that helps them overcome the problem (e.g. a piece of string, a torch, a tool of some kind, a piece of flint).

Starter ideas

A good adventure (5–10 minutes)

Resources: Learner's Book, Session 7.11: Getting started

Description: Talk about what makes a good adventure story. Read the speech bubbles in the Learner's Book and explain that *risky situations* means events when something could go wrong.

Try to elicit that all the statements in the Learner's Book would make a good adventure story. Accept additional statements about exciting events or characters being in danger. Discourage specific suggestions about actual plots.

Main teaching ideas

1 Storyboard planning (20–25 minutes)

Learning intention: To plan a story using a storyboard.

Resources: Learner's Book, Session 7.11, Activity 1; learners' storyboards from Session 7.10

Description: Explain that learners are going to write their own adventure story. Remind them about the chapter headings and story ideas they thought of for an Alfie Small story in Session 7.6 and the storyboard they planned in Session 7.10.

Tell learners that they can choose to write their own Alfie Small adventure or a dragon adventure. Remind them that storyboards only show the main events of a story. Explain that learners should not spend lots of time drawing detailed pictures. Ask them to add their own sentence openings in the box below each picture.

> **Differentiation ideas:** Support less confident writers by suggesting they draw pictures like those in Session 7.10 but make one change (e.g. the

main character, where the egg is found, what the dragon burns).

Challenge confident writers to plan an adventure story using an idea of their own.

Answers:
Learners' own storyboards.

---

2 Making improvements (15 minutes)

Learning intention: To discuss ways to improve story plans.

Resources: Learner's Book, Session 7.11, Activity 2; Workbook, Session 7.11, Activities 1 and 2

Description: Say: *I am going to tell you my adventure story using the storyboard in the Learner's Book.* (e.g. *It is about a boy and a dragon. There is an egg and it has a dragon inside it. When the dragon has grown bigger it starts to breathe fire and it burns things down. The boy found the egg in a box in his house. In the end the dragon flies away and the boy is sad.*)

Ask: *Have I told my story in the right order? Is my story very interesting? How could I make my story more interesting?* (e.g. names of the characters; extra details; adjectives to describe the egg, the dragon and feelings) Use the Focus activities in the Workbook now to provide further practice with improving a story.

Direct learners to the Speaking tip. Explain that they need to think about the details they will include when they tell their story to a partner, and the order in which they introduce these details. Ask learners to practise telling their story quietly to themselves.

Allow time for learners to retell their stories in pairs. Explain that partners should:

• say what they liked about the story

• ask questions about parts of the story they did not understand

• suggest some improvements.

⟩ **Differentiation ideas:** Support less confident writers by assisting them as they retell their stories.

⟩ **Assessment ideas:** Note which learners were able to provide appropriate feedback.

3 Write your story (45 minutes)

Learning intention: To write an adventure story.

Resources: Learner's Book, Session 7.11, Activity 3; dictionaries; learners' personal word collections, if used

Description: Explain to learners that they are now going to write their adventure stories. Ask: *Which types of words do you use to describe a character or a setting?* (adjectives, noun phrases, similes) Ask learners to make notes about their main character. Ask them to write their ideas for describing how the character feels, what the character hears and sees.

Ask: *Which types of words will help to make the characters' actions more interesting* (powerful verbs, adverbs, sentence openers dialogue)? Ask learners to note their ideas of synonyms for *said*.

Ask learners to write the title of their story at the top of their notebook page and tell them that they have 30 minutes to write their story. Remind learners to use the sentence openings from their storyboard.

After 15 minutes, ask learners to re-read their story to check that it matches their storyboard ideas. Have learners used their descriptions? Have they used a dictionary or word collections to check their spelling? Have they used the idea in the Writing tip?

Allow time for learners to make some improvements before they continue writing.

⟩ **Differentiation ideas:** Support less confident writers by helping them identify when they need to start a new paragraph.

Challenge confident writers to include at least one simile in their story.

⟩ **Assessment ideas:** Do learners' stories follow a logical sequence? Note which learners have used adverbs and sentence openers to sequence their paragraphs. Note which learners listened to feedback from partners and were willing to make changes to their writing. Note which learners have used present and past tense appropriately. Have learners remembered which verbs have an irregular past tense?

Note which learners have used:

• paragraphs

• character descriptions

- powerful and interesting words
- figurative language
- interesting sentence openings
- a mixture of simple, compound and complex sentences and a range of connectives
- dialogue.

Plenary idea

Sharing adventures (10 minutes)

Resources: Learners' stories

Description: Invite learners to read a paragraph of their story that they think is particularly exciting.

Homework ideas

Ask learners to:

- complete the Practice and Challenge activities in the Workbook
- design a front cover for their story (remind learners to include the story title and their name).

Answers for Workbook

Learners' own answers.

7.12 Improving your story

LEARNING PLAN

Learning objectives	Learning intentions	Success criteria
3Ww.02, 3Ww.03, 3Ww.05, 3Ww.06, 3Wv.02, 3Wv.03, 3Wv.04, 3Wv.05, 3Wv.06, 3Wv.07, 3Wg.01, 3Wg.02, 3Wg.03, 3Wg.04, 3Wg.05, 3Wg.06, 3Wg.07, 3Wg.08, 3Ws.01, 3Ws.02, 3Ws.03, 3Wc.01, 3Wc.03, 3Wp.04, 3Wp.05	• Proofread an adventure story. • Improve an adventure story.	• Learners can proofread their adventure story. • Learners can improve their adventure story.

LANGUAGE SUPPORT

Before learners proofread their stories, you may want to recap some of the spelling and language structures you have looked at during the unit (e.g. irregular past tense verbs, words with prefixes, synonyms for *said*, similes). When recapping irregular past tense verbs you may want to focus on *to be* and how these change with different pronouns.

Starter idea

Re-read your story (5 minutes)

Resources: Learner's Book, Session 7.12: Getting started

Description: Ask learners to look at their storyboard and to read their story. Are they happy with it?

Encourage learners to identify a part of the story they are not happy with. Suggest that they draw a triangle on the left-hand side of the section they want to change. Then tell them to draw another triangle on the left-hand side of the page below their storyboard and write replacement text for their story there.

Main teaching ideas

1 Checking spelling and punctuation (10 minutes)

Learning intention: To proofread an adventure story.

Resources: Learner's Book, Session 7.12, Activity 1; dictionaries; learners' personal word collections, if used

Description: Remind learners that proofreading means checking that their story makes sense and has no errors. Tell them that they should also check that their story follows their storyboard plan.

Read the instructions in the Learner's Book. Explain that learners will find it easier to spot errors if they read their story quietly to themselves or to a partner, if they are happy to do so. Remind learners that they should use all resources available to check spelling accuracy. Ask them to draw a wobbly line under incorrect spellings, then write the correct spelling above the original.

> **Differentiation ideas:** Support learners who find spelling more difficult by suggesting that they only identify three words that they think are spelled incorrectly.

Challenge confident writers by asking them to check that dialogue is punctuated correctly.

2 Making changes (10 minutes)

Learning intention: To improve an adventure story.

Resources: Learner's Book, Session 7.12, Activity 2; Workbook, Session 7.12, Activities 1 and 2

Description: Use the Focus and Practice activities in the Workbook to develop learners' vocabulary. Explain to learners that they are now going to improve their writing.

Direct them to prompt a in the Learner's Book. Give learners an example of how to improve a noun (e.g. change 'tree' to 'oak tree') or add a noun phrase (e.g. change 'egg' to 'enormous speckled egg').

When learners have made their noun changes, read the remaining questions b and c. *Have learners used powerful verbs? Have they used adverbs?* Remind learners of how *to be* and *to have* verbs change with different pronouns.

Give learners time to make further changes.

> **Differentiation ideas:** Support learners by providing word lists of irregular past tense verbs.

3 Final changes (15 minutes)

Learning intention: To improve an adventure story.

Resources: Learner's Book, Session 7.12, Activity 3; Worksheet 7.5

Description: Direct learners to the list of features they should have used in their writing (Activity 3 in Session 7.11).

Ask learners to write the list in their notebooks and draw a smiley face next to each feature they have used. Alternatively, you could provide Worksheet 7.5 Adventure story checklist. Ask learners to think about which feature they could make even better. Can they find three more things to change? When learners have finished improving their stories, direct them to the How are we doing? prompt.

If any learners are reluctant to share their stories, suggest that they write two things that they like about their story and one thing they think they could improve. Remind learners that points for improvement do not have to be items from the features list (e.g. improvements could be: the story title, handwriting, layout).

> **Assessment ideas:** Use the checklist in the Learner's Book Session 7.11 or Worksheet 7.5 to assess how well learners have applied the skills taught in this unit.

Plenary idea

What have I learned? (5–10 minutes)

Resources: Learners' Know-Want-Learned lists (KWL)

Description: In their notebooks, ask learners to list two or three skills they can do better or can do now that they could not do at the start of the unit.

If learners created KWL lists at the start of the unit, they should use these. Ask them to put a tick next to anything they wanted to learn and think they have learned, In the final column, ask learners to write anything they have learned that they were not expecting to learn.

Homework ideas

Ask learners to:

* complete the Challenge activity in the Workbook

* make a list of three nouns, three verbs and three adverbs that they used in their story that they want to learn to spell; ask learners to practise these spellings by writing them several times in rainbow colours.

Answers for Workbook

1 Possible answers:
Scary words: afraid, startling, creepy, frightening, shadowy, spooky
Night-time words: mysterious, quiet, creepy, shadowy, dark, silent
Happy words: bright, merry, glad, funny, jolly, pleased

2 Learners' own noun phrases.

3 Learners' own responses.

CHECK YOUR PROGRESS

1 Suggestions for a good adventure story might include:

   • a character who goes on a journey

   • a story with risky/dangerous/exciting situations

   • a plot filled with action

   • readers often wonder what will happen next.

2 Possible answers:

   a A noun: dragon, boat, egg, balloon, children, monster

   b An adjective: green, bright, creepy, sad, huge, small

   c A verb: jumped, laughed, cried, climbed

   d A pronoun: he, she, it, you, we, them

   e A connective: and, but, so, if, because, although

3 Possible answers:

   a mountain: enormous, snow-covered mountains

   b rock pool: a cold, murky rock pool

   c boat: a small red fishing boat

4 Possible answer: The dragon's mouth was like a huge, dark cave.

5 a had
   b was
   c made

PROJECT GUIDANCE

These projects develop learners' skills in: writing character descriptions; planning and writing an adventure story; speaking and listening skills; and using speech, gesture and movement to create a character. You will find it helpful to refer to the guidance about *Setting up and assessing the projects* in the Project guidance in Unit 1.

Group project: Explain the project to learners. Discuss the adventure stories learners know well and write three to four titles on the board. Then organise learners into groups of no more than eight. If the story has more than eight characters, learners could play more than one role.

Remind learners of what they learned during the role-play activity in Session 7.7 and allow them the use of small props.

During group discussion, assess learners' ability to speak confidently, ask questions and listen politely to others. During the role play, assess how well learners use gesture and movement to portray their characters.

CONTINUED

Pair project: Before introducing the project, decide how you will organise pairs. You could pair less confident writers with a more confident writer so that they have support to write more complex stories than they would on their own. Alternatively, you could pair less confident writers and ask them to write a story together, taking turns to write sentences so that they share their ideas.

Pairing learners working at a similar level allows you to control the learners' story plan. You could ask less confident writers to base their story on an Alfie Small adventure, restrict their storyboard to six frames or use the Worksheet templates. Ask more confident writers to use eight to ten storyboard frames and to use chapters and chapter headings.

When learners have finished, assess whether their storyboards:

- have an interesting starting point
- show a variety of settings that will lead to risky events
- have a logical ending

- show interesting openings for paragraphs
- have additional notes about words that can be used to describe settings or characters.

Solo project: Explain the project to learners and allow time for them to plan their writing. Ask learners to draw a detailed picture of their character. Ask: *What are they wearing? Do they have anything in a pocket? If they are carrying a bag or ruck sack, what is inside?*

Once learners have finished their drawings, ask them to label their portrait using adjectives and noun phrases to match the prompts in the project.

When learners have finished their character portrait, ask them to proofread and improve their writing. Remind learners to refer to their detailed drawing.

When learners have finished, assess:

- use of interesting adjectives and noun phrases
- use of accurate sentence punctuation
- whether the description includes the character's appearance, attitudes, thoughts and feelings.

> 8 Wonderful world

Unit plan

Session	Approximate number of learning hours	Outline of learning content	Resources
8.1 Holidays	1	Write a description of a holiday setting. Read and answer questions about a holiday fact file.	Learner's Book Session 8.1 Workbook Session 8.1
8.2 In the library	1	Explore how fiction and non-fiction books are organised in a library. Organise authors' names alphabetically.	Learner's Book Session 8.2 Workbook Session 8.2
8.3 Inside a non-fiction book	1	Explore indexes and contents pages. Explore layout and features in non-fiction books.	Learner's Book Session 8.3 Workbook Session 8.3
8.4 Skimming and scanning	1	Revisit skimming and scanning texts, and answer questions about both methods. Ask and answer questions about a text. Chose the correct verb form to complete sentences.	Learner's Book Session 8.4 Workbook Session 8.4 ⤓ Worksheet 8.1
8.5 Using paragraphs	1.5	Write paragraphs about a topic. Write multi-clause and conditional sentences.	Learner's Book Session 8.5 Workbook Session 8.5 ⤓ Language worksheet 8A
8.6 Language features of information texts	1.5	Identify fact and opinion in information texts. Explore verb tenses, adjectives, pronouns and prepositions in information texts.	Learner's Book Session 8.6 Workbook Session 8.6 ⤓ Differentiated worksheets 8A–C
8.7 Non-fiction e-texts	1	Explore a fact file about an e-text. Compare the differences between e-texts and non-fiction books.	Learner's Book Session 8.7 Workbook Session 8.7
8.8 Planning a talk	1.5	Choose a subject for a talk. Plan the different topics to cover in the talk and research them.	Learner's Book Session 8.8 Workbook Session 8.8 ⤓ Worksheets 8.1 and 8.2
8.9 Giving your talk	1	Practise and then give a talk to a group. Identify ways to improve the talk.	Learner's Book Session 8.9 Workbook Session 8.9

Session	Approximate number of learning hours	Outline of learning content	Resources
8.10 Planning an information text	1	Choose a country to write an information text about. Research key questions about the country and plan the text.	Learner's Book Session 8.10 Workbook Session 8.10 📥 Worksheets 8.1 and 8.2 📥 Language worksheet 8B
8.11 Writing an information text	1	Write an information text using the plan from the previous session.	Learner's Book Session 8.11 Workbook Session 8.11 📥 Worksheet 8.3
8.12 Improving your text	1	Proofread and improve the information text. Present the information text for display.	Learner's Book Session 8.12 Workbook Session 8.12 📥 Worksheets 8.3 and 8.4

Cross-unit resources

Learner's Book Check your progress

Learner's Book Projects

End-of-unit 8 test

BACKGROUND KNOWLEDGE

It will be helpful to be familiar with the following English subject knowledge:

- how a library is organised
- alphabetical order
- the Dewey Decimal System of classification
- features of information texts
- pronouns
- prepositions
- verb tenses
- identifying fact and opinion statements
- conditional sentences.

TEACHING SKILLS FOCUS

Active learning

Encouraging your learners to take an active role during sessions helps them recall what has been taught and deepens their learning. One way to do this is to ask open questions so that learners must reason for themselves and thus externalise their thinking.

Try using questions such as: *What do you remember about ...? Why do you think ...? What difference will X make? How can you change / find / solve ...?*

How do these questions change your learners' involvement in the lesson?

Open questions can lead to longer discussions but may also result in learners suggesting inaccurate ideas or answers. It is important that you repeat or summarise the correct information, e.g. you can reaffirm an answer saying *'Well done, X, you are quite right'*, then repeat what the learner said so that everyone has a clear understanding.

TEACHING SKILLS FOCUS CONTINUED

Think about the effect that reaffirming a learner's answer will have on their attitude to learning. You may wish to return to examples on future occasions (e.g. *Can you remember what X said about …?*).

Did your style of asking questions change during the unit? Did your use of open questions increase?

What difference did this make to the way learners responded? Were learners who didn't usually offer answers more willing to get involved when they realised that the answer wasn't a matter of getting it correct or incorrect? Did learners who do not usually offer answers surprise you with their comments and insight?

Cambridge Reading Adventures

There are several books in the series that would allow learners to explore information texts.

- *The Book of World Facts* by Anita Ganeri
- *A World of Deserts* by Kathryn Harper
- *Timbuktu* by Kathryn Harper

8.1 Holidays

LEARNING PLAN

Learning objectives	Learning intentions	Success criteria
3Rw.03, 3Rv.01, 3Rg.01, 3Rs.02, 3Rs.03, 3Ri.01, 3Ri.04, 3Ri.05, 3Ri.06, 3Ri.07, 3Ri.15, 3Ri.16, 3Ra.02, 3Wv.01, 3Wv.05, 3Wg.01, 3Wg.05, 3Wg.06, 3Ws.02, 3SLm.01, 3SLm.02, 3SLm.03	• Write a description of a place. • Read and answer questions about a text. • Use specialised vocabulary.	• Learners can write a description of a place. • Learners can read and answer questions about a text. • Learners can use specialised vocabulary.

LANGUAGE SUPPORT

When discussing the places learners have visited, or would like to visit for holidays, you could introduce the word *destination*. Encourage learners to use the phrases 'my favourite destination' or 'a destination I would like to visit'.

Learners should be familiar with fact files, but you may want to recap what a fact file is. Check that learners understand that fact files are non-fiction texts that record some key facts or information about a subject.

Starter idea

Holidays (5 minutes)

Resources: Learner's Book, Session 8.1: Getting started

Description: Ask learners to work in pairs to discuss and answer the questions in the Learner's Book.

Be sensitive to learners who may not have been on holiday. Explain that learners can talk about places they would like to visit or places they have visited for a day trip. In pairs, learners should discuss the photographs in the Learner's Book. Ask learners to volunteer descriptions and note on the board any interesting vocabulary they use.

Main teaching ideas

1 Holiday description (15–20 minutes)

Learning intention: To write a description of a place.

Resources: Learner's Book, Session 8.1, Activity 1

Description: Explain the activity to learners. Tell them that their descriptions should include:

- the name of the holiday destination
- what it looks like
- what they did there
- why they like it.

Remind learners to use capital letters for proper nouns and at the start of sentences.

Answers:
Learners' own responses.

2 Holiday fact files (20–25 minutes)

Learning intention: To read and answer questions about a text.

Resources: *Holiday fact file* (Learner's Book, Session 8.1, Activity 2); Track 49; Workbook, Session 8.1

Description: Direct learners to the fact file in the Learner's Book.

Read the information in each box. Remind learners to use contextual information to work out the meaning of unfamiliar words (e.g. *stunning* scenery; *cruise* ships; *admire* the views; *barrier* reef; *scuba* dive, *snorkel*).

Allow learners time to answer questions in their notebooks.

If there is time, you could use the Workbook activities here to consolidate learners' understanding of holiday fact files.

> **Differentiation ideas:** Support learners by discussing unfamiliar words with them.

Challenge learners to volunteer to read a fact file aloud.

> **Assessment ideas:** Did learners use contextual information to work out the meaning of unfamiliar vocabulary?

Answers:

a   the Caribbean

b   the Caribbean, Brazil, South Africa, Australia, India

c   the Amazon rainforest

d   Canada, China, India, Scotland and Northern Ireland (accept UK), South Africa

e   South Africa, Brazil, Australia

f   China, India, the UK (accept Wales and England)

3 Where would you like to visit? (10 minutes)

Learning intention: To use specialised vocabulary.

Resources: Learner's Book, Session 8.1, Activity 3

Description: Direct learners to the activity in the Learner's Book. Ask them to first talk to a partner about the countries they would like to visit.

Explain that information texts use vocabulary that is special to the topic (e.g. *safari, snorkel, carnival, monuments*). Tell learners that they should use the specialised vocabulary when writing their answers (e.g. 'I would love to visit Rio de Janeiro in the spring so that I could see its famous carnival').

> **Assessment ideas:** Note which learners organise their ideas in a sensible order when they write their descriptions. Do learners use the past or present tense consistently across a text? Which learners use multi-clause sentences?

Answers:
Learners' own sentences.

Plenary idea

Twenty Questions game (5 minutes)

Description: Play a Twenty Questions game with the class. Tell them that you are thinking of a country from the fact file and they must guess the country by asking questions. Explain that you can only answer *yes* or *no*.

The learner who guesses the right answer in fewer than twenty questions then chooses a country for others to guess. Note which learners use specialised vocabulary in their questions.

CROSS-CURRICULAR LINKS

Geography: Ask learners to locate places they have visited on country maps and/or world maps. Learners could write a label with their name to add to the maps.

Homework ideas

Ask learners to:

- Complete the Workbook activities for this session, if not completed in class.

- Draw a postcard picture of their favourite holiday/day-trip destination. Ask learners to write a message on their postcard about their visit to the destination. Ask them to include the town/city name on their picture. Use learners' pictures to create a class display.

Answers for Workbook

Learners' own answers.

8.2 In the library

LEARNING PLAN

Learning objectives	Learning intentions	Success criteria
3Rv.03, 3Rs.03, 3Ri.01, 3Ri.04, 3Ri.09, 3Ri.16, 3Wv.01, 3Ws.04	• Look at how the books in libraries are organised. • Organise books alphabetically.	• Learners can look at how the books in libraries are organised. • Learners can organise books alphabetically.

LANGUAGE SUPPORT

Explain *classifying* as *grouping things that are the same*. You could remind learners of activities in maths and science, using the suggestions under Cross-curricular links.

You could explain that the Dewey Decimal System was invented in 1876 by an American librarian called Melvil Dewey. Explain that each category is split many times. For example, the category for birds (598) is split into further categories so that

decimal points are necessary (e.g. water birds: 598.4; raptors, birds of prey: 598.9).

When learners sort fiction authors, you may want to explain that the prefix *Mc* means 'son of' as in the author Colin McNaughton. As the use of prefixes and suffixes to names occurs in many cultures, you could explore whether learners can suggest any examples of names from their own cultures.

Starter idea

Alphabetical order (10 minutes)

Resources: Learner's Book, Session 8.2: Getting started

Description: Say a letter of the alphabet and ask a learner to say which letter follows it. That learner then chooses another letter and asks a different learner to say which letter comes next. Continue like this until you feel learners are confident with alphabetical order.

Read the prompt and list of countries in the boxes. Support learners who lack confidence with sorting words alphabetically using the second letter.

When learners have written and shared their lists with a partner, peer mark lists as a class.

Answers:

Mexico, Singapore, Spain, Sri Lanka, Thailand, Tunisia

Main teaching ideas

1 Library books (15–20 minutes)

Learning intention: To look at how the books in libraries are organised.

Resources: Learner's Book, Session 8.2, Activity 1; Workbook, Session 8.2, Activity 1

Description: If you have a class or school library, you could begin by discussing how the books are organised there. Find out whether any learners have visited a library or a bookshop. Ask: *How are the books organised there?* Ask learners to talk to a partner about the two bookshelf pictures in the Learner's Book. Tell them to use the information in the labels in both pictures to answer the questions.

When learners have finished, peer mark answers, then ask: *What other shelves and labels might there be in a library* (e.g. shelves for authors whose names begin with other letters of the alphabet, shelves/labels for other subjects)*?* Use the Focus activity in the Workbook if learners need further practice with identifying fiction and non-fiction books.

> **Differentiation ideas:** Support less confident readers by pairing with more confident partners.

Answers:

a   shelf I – fiction; shelf II – non-fiction

b   Learners' own answers. Possible reasons: the titles on shelf I sound like stories; the label on shelf II says Geography and Travel.

c   Books on shelf I are in alphabetical order using the author's family name; books on shelf II are organised by country and number.

d   on shelf II with books on Africa and number 916

e   on shelf I with authors whose family names begin with B

f   in the Geography and Travel shelf (accept answers indicating shelf II if the learner's country is shown in the picture)

2 The Dewey Decimal System (15 minutes)

Learning intention: To look at how the books in libraries are organised.

Resources: *The Dewey Decimal System* (Learner's Book, Session 8.2, Activity 2); Track 50; Workbook, Session 8.2, Activity 3

Description: Read the information in the Reading tip. Explain that libraries all over the world organise non-fiction books using the Dewey Decimal System. Ask: *Why do you think libraries use this system?* (e.g. it makes it easier to find a book) Direct learners to the Dewey Decimal System poster in the Learner's Book, then read the categories to learners.

Ask: *Where will I find a book about the internet* (section 600–699)*? What about birds* (section 500–599)*?* When learners are familiar with the poster, allow time for them to answer the questions in their notebooks.

You could use the Challenge activity in the Workbook to provide further practice with the Dewey Decimal System. If possible, organise a visit to a library so that learners can look for non-fiction books using the Dewey Decimal System.

> **Differentiation ideas:** Challenge learners to ask each other questions about where different books can be found using the Dewey Decimal System.

> **Assessment ideas:** Do learners understand:

- that fiction and non-fiction books are organised differently

- the value of sorting non-fiction books by category

- how to sort a range of topics into appropriate categories?

Answers:

a   400–499

b   900–999

c   500–599 (accept 590–599 using the Reading tip)

d   200–299

e   700–799

f   500–599

3 Alphabetical authors (15 minutes)

Learning intention: To organise books alphabetically.

Resources: Learner's Book, Session 8.2, Activity 3; Workbook, Session 8.2, Activity 2

Description: Read the list of authors' names. Ask: *Which authors do you recognise* (e.g. Roald Dahl, Francesca Simon, Alfie Smith)? Direct learners to the Writing tip, then allow them time to sort the list of names alphabetically.

Peer mark answers as a class. Learners could complete the Practice activity in the Workbook if they need further practice with sorting alphabetically.

› **Differentiation ideas:** Support learners by giving them each author name on a separate piece of paper so that they can physically sort them before writing the list in their notebooks.

Challenge learners by asking them to think of five more authors to include in the list.

› **Assessment ideas:** Note which learners:

- need support when sorting alphabetically
- use second letters of words when ordering alphabetically.

Answers:
Laurence Anholt, Roald Dahl, Anne Fine, Pippa Goodhart, Rose Impey, Colin McNaughton, A.A. Milne, Michael Morpurgo, Jill Murphy, Jon Scieszka, Francesca Simon, Alfie Smith, Martin Waddell, Jacqueline Wilson

Plenary idea

Sorting non-fiction (5–10 minutes)

Resources: A list of non-fiction titles

Description: Write a list of non-fiction titles on the board (e.g. *Great Pianists, Volcanoes, Looking After Your Pet, The History of Japan, Great Thinkers, Plastics, How Computers Work, Crocodiles of Africa*). In pairs, learners should use the Dewey Decimal System to sort each title into the correct category (e.g. *Great Pianists* (700–799), *Volcanoes* (900–999), *Looking After Your Pet* (000–099), *The History of Japan* (900–999), *Great Thinkers* (100–199), *Plastics* (500–599), *How Computers Work* (600–699), *Crocodiles of Africa* (500–599)).

CROSS-CURRICULAR LINKS

Maths (Numbers): Use the Dewey Decimal System as a starting point for counting on and back in 1s, 10s and 100s from any starting number.

Look for opportunities to use classification techniques in other activities and subjects, e.g. sorting materials by their properties or classifying animals as insects, mammals and reptiles.

Homework ideas

Ask learners to:

- complete the Workbook activities for this session, if not completed in class
- find a variety of food items at home to sort into different categories (e.g. fruit, vegetables, tinned, carbohydrates). Ask learners to list each item alphabetically within each category.

Answers for Workbook

1
- **a** NF
- **b** F
- **c** F
- **d** NF
- **e** NF
- **f** F
- **g** NF
- **h** F

2 1 Helen Cooper, 2 June Crebbin, 3 Thomas Docherty, 4 Julia Donaldson, 5 Allan Drummond, 6 Pippa Goodhart, 7 Julia Jarman, 8 Michael Rosen, 9 Nick Sharratt, 10 Adam Stower

3
- **a** *The Life Cycle of a Frog*: 500–599
- **b** *Religions Around the World*: 200–299
- **c** *The History of America*: 900–999
- **d** *Mobile Phones Today*: 600–699
- **e** *Learning to Draw*: 700–799
- **f** *Great Children's Authors*: 800–899
- **g** *Speaking German on Holiday*: 400–499
- **h** *100 Questions about Space*: 500–599

8.3 Inside a non-fiction book

LEARNING PLAN

Learning objectives	Learning intentions	Success criteria
3Rs.02, 3Rs.03, 3Ri.01, 3Ri.04, 3Ri.05, 3Ri.14, 3Ri.15, 3Ri.16, 3SLm.03, 3SLs.02	• Discuss in detail what is found in a non-fiction book. • Explore the features of non-fiction texts.	• Learners can discuss in detail what is found in a non-fiction book. • Learners can explore the features of non-fiction texts.

LANGUAGE SUPPORT

The use of internet material means many learners may be unfamiliar with the layout of non-fiction texts. Online material follows a standard linear layout, whereas non-fiction books have more varied page layouts (e.g. callout sections, 'Did you know?' boxes, 'Amazing fact' bubbles). Spend some time discussing the different features and layouts of pages to help learners recognise the way text, subheadings and captions are presented in various forms.

Common misconceptions

Misconception	How to identify	How to overcome
The contents page is a better resource than the index when deciding whether a book has the information you need.	Give learners books about a chosen subject (e.g. deserts). Ask learners whether their book has information about an aspect of that subject (e.g. a desert animal such as a snake). Note which learners check the contents page and assume that the item is not listed because it is not in the contents page.	Explain that a contents page would be very long if everything in the book was listed. When deciding whether a book has the information you need. It helps to check the index page for the information you are looking for.

Starter idea

Differences (10 minutes)

Resources: Learner's Book, Session 8.3: Getting started; selection of fiction and non-fiction books

Description: If possible, give learners a fiction and a non-fiction book to compare or direct them to the picture in the Learner's Book. Allow learners time to look at both types of book with a partner before they write a list of differences. For example:

Fiction	Non-fiction
chapters may have headings	contents page
story follows an order: beginning, middle, end	index glossary
dialogue	can be read in any order
paragraphs with narrative text	chapter headings

Fiction	Non-fiction
characters	information arranged in sections on a page
story is not true	facts
may have some pictures	pictures, photographs and diagrams

Main teaching ideas

1 Contents and index pages (5–10 minutes)

Learning intention: To discuss in detail what is found in a non-fiction book.

Resources: Learner's Book, Session 8.3, Activity 1; non-fiction books

Description: Invite a learner to read the Reading tip aloud. Give learners a non-fiction book and ask them to find the contents page. Ask: *Is this page always in the same place in a book? Where?* Ask learners to compare the contents page in their book with the picture in the Learner's Book. Ask: *Is the layout the same in both books?* Ask learners to talk to a partner about the layout.

Ask learners to find the index page in their book. Repeat the questions you asked about contents pages.

Ask learners to talk to a partner about the layout used for the contents page and the index page. How are they different? Discuss the differences learners identified. Make a list of the differences identified for each page. Ask: *Why are there gaps in the page numbers on the contents page?* (the subject is on more than one page).

Answers:
Contents page (found at the beginning of a book): non-alphabetical; two columns with chapter names at one side and page numbers opposite; page numbers are in order but not consecutive.
Index page (found at the end of the book): organised alphabetically; numbers next to the subject; some subjects have more than one number next to them.

2 Checking understanding (10–15 minutes)

Learning intention: To discuss in detail what is found in a non-fiction book.

Resources: Learner's Book, Session 8.3, Activity 2

Description: Ask learners to answer the questions in their notebooks.

› **Differentiation ideas:** Support learners by directing them to the appropriate page to answer each question.

Challenge learners to answer using complete sentences.

Answers:

a   page 6

b   Town and Country

c   Cayman Islands; food; Grenada; Puerto Rico; Saint Lucia; towns and cities

d   cricket; football

e   (Caribbean) food

f   Town and Country; Shopping

3 Features of non-fiction texts (15 minutes)

Learning intention: To explore the features of non-fiction texts.

Resources: Learner's Book, Session 8.3, Activity 3; Workbook, Session 8.3, Activities 1 and 2; non-fiction books

Description: Remind learners of the differences they noted about fiction and non-fiction texts at the start of the session. Read the activity prompt in the Learner's Book. Then give pairs of learners a non-fiction book and ask them to open the book at the start of a topic.

As you read each bullet point in the Language focus box, ask learners to put a finger on the relevant feature in the book. When learners have located each feature, direct them to the Reading tip.

Ask pairs of learners to swap books with another pair and browse and discuss the new book.

Use the Focus and Practice activities in the Workbook to provide further practice with identifying the features of non-fiction texts.

› **Differentiation ideas:** Support learners in a small group by helping them to identify the features listed.

Challenge learners to compare the layout of two information books, then share what they have noticed about the way some subheadings are written (e.g. 'Did you know?' questions; fact files; 'Amazing fact' features).

> **Assessment ideas:** Ask learners to look at a contents page, then ask them *Where will I find …?* and *What will I find …?* questions to assess their understanding. Include questions about information that could be included within a topic heading and pages that are part of a chapter but not listed as page numbers.

Answers:
Learners' own responses.

Plenary idea

Asking questions (5 minutes)

Resources: Learner's Book 8.3; non-fiction books

Description: In pairs, learners should ask their partner *What …?* and *Where will you find …?* questions about the contents and index pages of their book. Learners could use the contents and index pages in the Learner's Book (e.g. *Where will I find information about hurricanes?* (page 9); *What will I find on page 15?* (shopping in Puerto Rico)).

Homework ideas

Ask learners to:

*   complete the Challenge activity in the Workbook

*   make a mind map of what they have learned about the differences between fiction and non-fiction texts.

Answers for Workbook

1. a heading
    b text
    c subheading
    d diagram
    e list
    f glossary
    g caption

2. Learners' own answers.

3. Learners' own answers.

8.4 Skimming and scanning

LEARNING PLAN

Learning objectives	Learning intentions	Success criteria
3Rw.03, 3Rg.01, 3Rg.10, 3Ri.06, 3Ri.10, 3Ri.14, 3Ri.16, 3Wg.01, 3Wg.06, 3Wc.05, 3SLm.01, 3SLm.02, 3SLm.03, 3SLs.02, 3SLg.02, 3SLg.03, 3SLg.04	• Discuss different ways of reading a text. • Answer questions about a non-fiction text. • Identify verbs to match nouns or pronouns.	• Learners can discuss different ways of reading a text. • Learners can answer questions about a non-fiction text. • Learners can identify verbs to match nouns or pronouns.

LANGUAGE SUPPORT

In this session, learners are asked to choose the correct verb to complete a sentence. This involves recognising whether the noun is in the first, second or third person. Learners may find it helpful to change the noun into the appropriate pronoun form (e.g. whales = they; a boat = it).

Starter idea

Browsing books (5–10 minutes)

Resources: Learner's Book, Session 8.4: Getting started; non-fiction books

Description: Give pairs of learners a non-fiction book and ask them to explore the book and discuss what they do and do not like about it. Remind learners to listen politely to their partner's opinion and to ask questions to encourage their partner to explain their reasons for liking or not liking things about the book.

Bring the class back together: how did learners quickly make decisions about what they liked and didn't like? If necessary, re-read the Reading tip about browsing books from Session 8.3.

Main teaching ideas

1 Reading a text (15 minutes)

Learning intention: To discuss different ways of reading a text.

Resources: *Seasons in the Caribbean* (Learner's Book, Session 8.4, Activity 1); Track 51

Description: Direct learners to the Reading tip. Tell them to think about which method they will use to read the text aloud about the Caribbean. Remind learners to use quiet voices as they read.

When learners have read the text, ask them to say which method they used. Ask: *Did any of you read the Glossary term? When did you read it?* (before or after reading the text) *What did you do when you read the Glossary term?* (looked for the word in the text) *Which reading technique did you use if you looked for the Glossary term in the text?* (scanning).

> **Differentiation ideas:** Support and challenge learners by asking more confident readers to read the text with a less confident reader.

> **Assessment ideas:** Which reading methods did learners use to read the text?

Answers:
Learners' own answers.

2 Answering questions (15 minutes)

Learning intention: To answer questions about a non-fiction text.

Resources: Learner's Book, Session 8.4, Activity 2; Workbook, Session 8.4; Worksheet 8.1

Description: Direct learners to the character and speech-bubble text. Ask them to consider this as they answer the questions. Ask learners to write their answers in their notebooks.

When learners have finished, ask them to say which reading technique they used to answer the questions by a show of hands. Most learners should have used scanning, especially for question a. Reinforce the idea that scanning a text for a specific word or piece of information is a good skill to develop, especially when reading information.

Use Worksheet 8.1 Slimy snails fact sheet or the Workbook activities to provide further practice of answering questions about a text.

> **Differentiation ideas:** Support learners when answers involve information that is implicit in the text (e.g. questions d and e).

Answers:

a   season/s = ten times; hurricane/s = three times; Caribbean = three times

b   December to May

c   inland, nearer the mountains

d   during the wet season; eight

e   the wind is very strong; there would be very heavy rain

f   Learners' own answers. Most answers will refer to the dry season.

3 Writing questions (20 minutes)

Learning intention: To discuss different ways of reading a text.

Resources: Learner's Book, Session 8.4, Activity 3; non-fiction books

Description: Pair learners with partners working at a similar reading level. Give each pair a book with text at their reading level. Encourage learners to write questions about the book for their partner. Remind them to end their questions with question marks and use capital letters for the start of sentences and proper nouns. Ask learners to swap questions and try to answer them.

Discuss the techniques learners used. Learners should have skimmed texts initially, then read texts in detail once, then used scanning to find answers to questions.

> **Differentiation ideas:** Support learners by asking them to use a text in a non-fiction book you allocated them. Limit learners to ask no more than five questions.

Challenge learners to ask questions about specific information in the text (explicit information) and questions that mean their partner has to look more carefully (implicit information) or use their own ideas in the answer.

> **Assessment ideas:** Do learners understand that skimming will give them a general understanding of a text and scanning allows them to answer specific questions?

Answers:
Learners' own questions (and answers about reading techniques).

4   Verb choices (15 minutes)

Learning intention: To identify the verb to match the noun or pronoun.

Resources: Learner's Book, Session 8.4, Activity 4

Description: Ask learners to read the sentence in part a, then ask: *Which pronoun could I use instead of* whales? (They) *Which verb should I use with* They? (swim) *Which verb would I use if the sentence was about one whale?* (swims) Explain that verbs change to match the noun or pronoun.

Ask learners to choose the correct verb for each of the sentences in the Learner's Book.

> **Differentiation ideas:** Support learners by helping them to change the noun to a pronoun if they are unsure about which verb to use.

> **Assessment ideas:** Note which learners matched pronouns and verbs appropriately.

Answers

a   swim

b   pass; look

c   takes; want

d   live

e   is; is

f   burrow; lie; get

Plenary idea

Scan for verbs (5 minutes)

Resources: *Seasons in the Caribbean* (Learner's Book, Session 8.4); Track 51

Description: Explain that learners are going to scan for verbs in the text about the Caribbean.

Ask learners to choose two verbs from the text and ask their partner to say what another present tense form of the verb could be (e.g. starts – start; lasts – last; come – comes).

Homework ideas

Ask learners to:

*   complete the Workbook activities for this session, if not completed in class

*   find ten present tense verbs in their reading book and write each verb to match the pronouns *I*, *she*, *you* and *we*.

Answers for Workbook

1   a   Which *types of home* are in the *centre of the cities*?

   b   Why might some families live near the edge of the city?

   c   Which island has chattel houses on it?

   d   Why can chattel houses be moved to different places?

   e   How old are the oldest chattel houses?

2   Cities on Caribbean islands often have new and expensive flats or apartments in the centre. Cheaper houses are normally further out, around the edge of the city.
   In Barbados, wooden houses built on stone blocks are called chattel houses. They can be moved to different places because they are not built into the ground. Chattel houses are often painted in pale colours to help keep them cool. The oldest chattel houses were built more than 200 years ago.

3   a   new and expensive flats and apartments

   b   houses are cheaper

   c   Barbados

   d   they are not built into the ground (accept: they are built on stone blocks)

   e   more than 200 years old

8.5 Using paragraphs

LEARNING PLAN

Learning objectives	Learning intentions	Success criteria
3Rg.05, 3Rg.06, 3Rs.01, 3Rs.03, 3Ri.07, 3Ri.14, 3Ri.15, 3Wg.05, 3Ws.02, 3Wc.06	• Write paragraphs about a known topic. • Discuss and write multi-clause sentences. • Discuss and write conditional sentences.	• Learners can write paragraphs about a known topic. • Learners can discuss and write multi-clause sentences. • Learners can discuss and write conditional sentences.

LANGUAGE SUPPORT

You many need to recap what a paragraph is and the reasons for starting a new paragraph. In narrative writing, paragraphs are often signalled using words that indicate when, where and how an event occurs (e.g. suddenly, one day, in the garden). Make sure that learners understand that words of this type are not used to indicate new paragraphs in non-fiction writing. Remind learners that a new paragraph signals a new idea, new information or a new fact.

Common misconceptions

Misconception	How to identify	How to overcome
Multi-clause sentences are all conditional sentences.	Ask learners to complete Activity 3. Some learners may add extra information to the main clause and not a condition.	Write the following sentence on the board: *You can go out to play and run around.* Explain to learners the actions are not connected. Now write: *You can go out to play if you want to run around.* Explain that learners will only be allowed to run around if they go outside. *Running around* is a condition of the second part of the sentence.

Starter idea

Weather paragraph (10–15 minutes)

Resources: Learner's Book, Session 8.5: Getting started; a selection of non-fiction books

Description: Ask learners to re-read the paragraph about seasons in the Caribbean in Session 8.4. Ask: *How many paragraphs are there in the text* (four)?

Tell learners to discuss the questions in the Learner's Book with a partner. Try to elicit that paragraphs are used to break the text up into sections and that each section is about a different idea (e.g. introduction about the seasons, the wet season, hurricanes, the dry season).

Give learners a non-fiction book to share. Allow learners a few minutes to identify the ideas in paragraphs on one page of the book with a partner.

Main teaching ideas

1 Topic paragraphs (15–20 minutes)

Learning intention: To write some paragraphs about a known topic.

Resources: Learner's Book, Session 8.5, Activity 1

Description: Explain that learners are going to write two paragraphs about a topic they know (e.g. where they live, a hobby, a pet, a place they have visited). Ask them to talk to a partner about their topic to help them identify two ideas they could write about. Encourage learners to ask their partner questions (e.g. *Why do you like …?*; *How often do you …?*; *How long have you …?*).

Direct learners to the character and speech-bubble text. Ask them to make a note of the main idea for their first paragraph and add some key words to include in the paragraph. Then ask learners to repeat this for the second paragraph. Remind them to use the correct sentence punctuation.

> **Assessment ideas:** Note which learners can organise their ideas into separate paragraphs.

Answers:
Learners' own ideas and paragraphs.

2 Multi-clause sentences (15 minutes)

Learning intention: To discuss and write multi-clause sentences.

Resources: Learner's Book, Session 8.5, Activity 2

Description: Ask learners to re-read their topic paragraphs. Ask: *Has anyone used a multi-clause sentence?* Invite two or three volunteers to share their examples. Write each sentence on the board, then read the Language focus text. Ask: *Can you identify the connective in each sentence? Can you identify a main clause?*

Ask learners to add a connective and additional information to each of the sentences a–c in the Learner's Book to turn them into multi-clause sentences.

> **Differentiation ideas:**

Support learners by asking further questions about each sentence (e.g. *Why would you like to visit the Caribbean? Which connective can link this reason?*).

Challenge learners to avoid using *and* and *but*.

> **Assessment ideas:** Note which learners can identify the main clause of a sentence.

Answers:
Learners' own answers.

3 Conditional sentences (15 minutes)

Learning intention: To discuss and write conditional sentences.

Resources: Learner's Book, Session 8.5, Activity 3; Workbook, Session 8.5, Activity 1; Language worksheet 8A

Description: Read the Language focus text. Ask learners to suggest connectives that might introduce a conditional clause (e.g. if, unless, when, even though, as long as, although, otherwise). Allow time for learners to complete the sentences in their notebooks.

Use the Focus activity in the Workbook or Language worksheet 8A if learners need further practice with conditional sentences.

> **Differentiation ideas:** Support learners by providing a list of connectives that can introduce a conditional clause.

> **Assessment ideas:** Can learners use a variety of connectives other than *and* or *but*? Note which learners can add conditional clauses to sentences. Note which learners can re-write sentences with the conditional clause at the start of a sentence.

Answers:
Learners' own answers. Possible conditional sentences:

a I would like to visit the Caribbean unless it is the wet season.

b We can visit the white beaches, if you have finished your homework.

c It is beautiful in the dry season, when the hurricane season ends.

Plenary idea

Turn it around (10 minutes)

Description: Invite volunteers to share their sentences. Re-write one of the sentences on the board, putting the conditional clause at the start of the sentence (e.g. *When you come home from school, we can visit the white beaches*). Ask: *Is this still a conditional sentence (yes)?* Ask learners to choose one of their sentences and re-write it with the conditional clause at the start.

CROSS-CURRICULAR LINKS

Ask learners to write two paragraphs about a history, geography or science topic. Encourage learners to identify the idea that will be included in each paragraph.

Homework ideas

Ask learners to:

• complete the Workbook activities for this session, if not completed in class

• copy three or four short paragraphs from an information book in their neatest joined handwriting, then identify the main idea in each paragraph.

Answers for Workbook

1 Learners' own answers. Possible connectives might be:

   a Some people visit the Caribbean for the holidays but / while other people live there.

   b Tourists enjoy sitting on the beach and / after / as well as swimming in the sea.

   c Hurricanes can be dangerous because the winds are extremely powerful.

   d People sit in storm shelters, if they can find one close-by.

2 Learners' own answers.

3 Learners' own answers. Possible sentences:

   a I will bring my bike if it is a sunny day.

   b I will wear a hat if I go to the wedding.

   c We can finish watching the movie if it is not too late.

   d You get water from ice when it melts.

8.6 Language features of information texts

LEARNING PLAN

Learning objectives	Learning intentions	Success criteria
3Rw.03, 3Rv.01, 3Rv.04, 3Rg.01, 3Rg.08, 3Rg.09, 3Rg.10, 3Rs.02, 3Ri.01, 3Ri.04, 3Ri.05, 3Ri.13, 3Ri.14, 3Ri.15, 3Ri.16, 3Ra.02, 3SLm.01, 3SLm.03, 3SLg.02	• Look in detail at language features of information texts. • Investigate the difference between fact and opinion in information texts.	• Learners can look in detail at language features of information texts. • Learners can investigate the difference between fact and opinion in information texts.

LANGUAGE SUPPORT

Help learners understand the difference between fact and opinion by explaining that:

• facts: are true and can be proved (e.g. There are many canals in Venice).

• opinions: are what someone thinks, feels or believes; they cannot be proved or disproved (e.g. I love pizza).

Common misconceptions

Misconception	How to identify	How to overcome
Learners identify like / love / enjoy statements as facts.	Note learners' answers when asked to identify fact and opinion statements in the Getting started activity.	Ask learners to look at the verb used in a statement of opinion, e.g. *People enjoy visiting Uluru.* Ask learners which other verbs could be used instead of *enjoy* (e.g. love, like, adore). Then ask learners to identify the verb in a statement of fact, e.g. *Uluru is near the Simpson Desert.* Ask which other verbs could be used instead of *is* (none). Explain that learners can identify fact/opinion statements by checking whether the verb can be changed.

Starter idea

Fact or opinion (10 minutes)

Resources: Learner's Book, Session 8.6: Getting started

Description: Write *Fact* and *Opinion* on the board. Ask: *How are facts and opinions different?* Try to elicit that facts are true, and opinions are what someone thinks or feels. Ask learners to discuss the statements in the Learner's Book (fact; opinion; opinion; opinion).

Many learners may identify *I love riding my bike* as fact because it is true for the person saying it. Explain that, because the statement cannot be proved or disproved, the statement is that person's opinion.

Invite learners to suggest other examples of facts and opinions.

Main teaching ideas

1 Questions about Australia (10–15 minutes)

Learning intention: To look in detail at the language features of information texts.

Resources: *Australia fact file* (Learner's Book, Session 8.6, Activity 1); Track 52

Description: Invite a confident reader to read the text aloud. Ask learners to re-read the text quietly before they answer the questions. When learners have completed the activity, peer mark answers.

Answers:

a
- information about the outback / Ayers Rock / Uluru
- Possible headings: The Australian outback; Ayers Rock / Uluru.
- present tense
- Ayers Rock
- Learners' possible answers: Because it is like a mountain in the middle of the desert.

b–c Learners' own answers.

2 Fact or opinion (15–20 minutes)

Learning intention: To investigate the difference between fact and opinion in information texts.

Resources: Learner's Book, Session 8.6, Activity 2; Workbook, Session 8.6; Differentiated worksheet pack

Description: Read the Language focus text, then remind learners about the statements they discussed in the Getting started activity. Use Differentiated worksheets 8A–C to help learners recognise facts and opinions.

In pairs, learners should talk about the information they expect to find in information texts. Will it be fact or opinion?

Ask learners to re-read the text about Australia with a partner. Explain that one learner should keep a tally of facts and the other learner should keep a tally of opinions. Tell learners that they will need to discuss each piece of information then agree which tally to add it to.

Ask learners to complete questions a–d (learners may have slightly different answers but all learners should have identified more facts than opinions). As a class, discuss why information texts have more facts than opinions.

You could use the Workbook activities to provide further practice with identifying fact and opinion.

> **Differentiation ideas:** Support less confident readers with a more confident partner.

> **Assessment ideas:** As many learners find it difficult to distinguish fact from opinion, note which learners have most difficulty. Use the Common misconceptions activity to support them.

Answers:

a 13

b Learners' own answers.

c Possible answers: probably the most dramatic natural feature in the country; a spiritual place for many; most found it a tough climb; stunning time to see Uluru is at sunset.

d Learners' reasons may include: information texts must give you information that should be true; information means it is factual.

3 Verbs and adjectives (5 minutes)

Learning intention: To look in detail at the language features of information texts.

Resources: Learner's Book, Session 8.6, Activity 3

Description: Direct learners to the Listening tip. Allow time for them to discuss the questions, then discuss their answers. Do learners understand that the language of information texts and fiction texts is different?

Answers:
- present tense
- mainly simple verbs (is, are, were, visit, want, can) – not powerful verbs
- simple adjectives for facts (huge, dry, flat, red);

a few powerful adjectives used in opinions (stunning, dramatic)

4 Questions about language (25–30 minutes)

Learning intention: To look in detail at the language features of information texts.

Resources: Learner's Book, Session 8.6, Activity 4

Description: Ask learners to recall the different word groups they know (e.g. nouns, verbs, adjectives, adverbs, pronouns, prepositions). Prompt learners' recall of any groups they omit, e.g. by asking: *What kind of word is 'quickly'? 'down'? 'near'?* Direct learners to the character and speech-bubble text.

Ask learners to answer the questions from the Learner's Book. Peer mark answers.

Direct learners to the Reflection questions. You could ask learners to create a mind map or a differences table to show their understanding of the language in information and fiction texts.

> **Differentiation ideas:** Support less confident learners by asking them to find five verbs and five adjectives. Read sentences that contain a preposition and ask learners to identify the preposition in each sentence.

> **Assessment ideas:** Note which learners show a good understanding of the different word groups.

Answers:

a Verbs: is, called, visit, want, see, given, have, lived, were, allowed, climb, found, are, allowed, can, walk, see. The verb *is* is used most.

b Adjectives: huge, dry, flat, red, mountain-sized, dramatic, natural, traditional, Aboriginal, English, ten, thousand, spiritual, one, sandstone, steep, tough, stunning. Most of the adjectives give more facts.

c Pronouns: it, its, they. The pronouns *I, you, we* are not used.

d Prepositions: centre, middle, near, top, around.

e Punctuation: full stops, commas, a hyphen, a colon. There are no question marks or exclamation marks because the text uses factual statements.

Plenary idea

Spot the Facts game (5 minutes)

Description: In pairs, ask learners to write one factual statement and two opinion statements about themselves or a topic they know well. Learners challenge their partner to 'spot the fact'.

Homework ideas

Ask learners to:

- complete the Workbook activities for this session, if not completed in class
- write six factual statements and four opinion statements about their family or locality.

Answers for Workbook

1 Opinion statements: a, c, e, h

2 Learners' own sentences.

3 Learners' own facts and opinions.

8.7 Non-fiction e-texts

LEARNING PLAN

Learning objectives	Learning intentions	Success criteria
3Rw.03, 3Rv.01, 3Rg.01, 3Rs.02, 3Rs.03, 3Ri.05, 3Wv.01, 3SLm.01, 3SLm.03, 3SLg.02, 3SLg.03, 3SLg.04	• Discuss e-texts and how they are different from books. • Use vocabulary specific to a topic.	• Learners can discuss e-texts and how they are different from books. • Learners can use vocabulary specific to a topic.

LANGUAGE SUPPORT

You may need to introduce and explain vocabulary associated with web pages and e-texts. Learners will explore:

- tabs: These run along the top of a web page and allow learners to move between different web pages. (You can make comparisons with moving between pages in a book or between different books.)
- drop-down menus: Subheadings that provide lists of topics under one heading. They take learners directly to a page. (You can make comparisons with contents pages in books.)
- hyperlinks: Links embedded within a page that can take learners directly to another section of the page, or another associated topic.

Some hyperlinks open to show enlarged pictures, videos or audio.

- search boxes: Used in search engines to find websites, but can also be found in a website to find information on that site. (You can make comparisons with index pages in books.)
- search engines: Web pages that helps you find information anywhere on the World Wide Web. Most learners will have heard of Google, but it is worth explaining that there are other search engines. (You can make comparisons with the Dewey Decimal System.)
- homepages: The opening page of websites. (You can make comparisons with the contents page and blurb of a book.)

Common misconceptions

Misconception	How to identify	How to overcome
All information on all web pages is true.	Ask learners how information is added to the internet. Try to elicit that people upload information.	Explain that anyone can create a web page and upload information to the internet. Explain that, because there is so much information on the internet, not everything can be checked and that this can lead to some information being added that is not correct. Explain that this is why learners should choose the websites they use carefully.

Starter idea

What is an e-text? (5 minutes)

Resources: Learner's Book, Session 8.7: Getting started

Description: Ask learners to work in pairs and discuss the questions in the Learner's Book. Do learners understand that the *e* in *e-text* stands for electronic? Which learners have limited experience of using electronic devices?

Main teaching ideas

 1 Fact file (15 minutes)

Learning intention: To discuss e-texts and how they are different from books.

Resources: *e-text fact file* (Learner's Book, Session 8.7, Activity 1); Track 53; internet access

Description: Ask learners to discuss the similarities and differences of reading information in books and e-texts. Ask: *Which text type do you prefer using?* Some learners may prefer the layout of books and find the presentation less distracting and easier to locate specific information. Other learners may prefer e-texts because they can follow links to related information.

Read the e-text fact file and discuss each feature. If possible, show learners an example of an e-text with these features. Direct learners to the Reading tip, then allow them time to discuss the questions.

> **Differentiation ideas:** Support less confident readers by pairing them with more confident readers.

Answers:
Learners' own answers.

2 Compare e-texts and books (15 minutes)

Learning intention: To discuss e-texts and how they are different from books.

Resources: *Using the internet safely* (Learner's Book, Session 8.7, Activity 2); Track 54; Workbook, Session 8.7; internet access; selection of non-fiction books

Description: To make sure that learners read e-texts that are suitable for their age group, you should select sites or provide web links that you want learners to use and you know are safe. Before learners begin, direct them to the 'Use the internet safely' text. You could discuss with learners why the points in this text are important.

Provide a selection of non-fiction books. Show learners a web page and how to use the search boxes, drop-down menus and hyperlinks to find the information they want. Allow learners time to compare the two text types.

Bring the class back together and discuss answers. You could use the Workbook activities to provide further practice if there is time in class.

> **Differentiation ideas:** Support learners by directing them to a carefully chosen e-text.

> **Assessment ideas:** Note which learners can identify key differences between books and e-texts. Can they support their opinions about each text type with reference to the features?

Answers:

a Yes, paragraphs in both text types are used for each idea.

b Yes, although some learners may find it more difficult to scroll through web pages.

c Yes

d No. In a book you can use the contents page or index to find the page(s) you need. In an e-text, you use a search box and need to know what to search for. In an e-text you use hyperlinks, which link to other pages.

3 Country key words (15–20 minutes)

Learning intention: To use vocabulary specific to a topic.

Resources: Learner's Book, Session 8.7, Activity 3; internet access; non-fiction books

Description: Explain the activity to learners and ask them to choose a country to research with a partner. Ask: *What are the first things you would want to know about a country? Which key things would you want to say about this country/your home country?* Try to elicit that learners should include information about where it is (e.g. which continent, nearby countries, main cities) and what it is known for (e.g. important landmarks/places to visit, special events).

In pairs, learners explore a book or e-text about their country and write a list of words they might like to use when writing about that country.

> **Differentiation ideas:** Support learners by directing them to a text/e-text that matches their current reading level.

> **Assessment ideas:** Can learners find relevant information from different text types? Which learners can use an e-text with confidence?

Answers:
Learners' own answers.

Plenary idea

Sharing information sources (5 minutes)

Description: Ask: *Did you find a book or an e-text more helpful? Why?* Did learners find any features in the e-text that were not listed in the Learner's Book? What were they? How were they helpful when finding information?

Have any learners changed their opinion about the text type they prefer using?

CROSS-CURRICULAR LINKS

IT: Consider linking the work in this session with your wider e-safety teaching.

Homework ideas

Ask learners to:

*   complete the Workbook activities for this session, if not completed in class

*   design a homepage about their country on paper. Learners could add subheadings for drop-down menus, search boxes, pictures and even hyperlinks that take the user to a different page (which could be shown on a separate sheet of paper).

Answers for Workbook

1 Learners' own answers. Possible differences: e-texts are read from a screen, not a paper page; e-texts use hyperlinks; you can go directly to a new section of an e-text without turning pages; e-texts can include videos or audio; you can print the screen of an e-text; you can email the text in an e-text to others.

2

Books	e-texts	Purpose
contents page	drop-down menu	tells you where you can find a topic
heading	heading	tells you what the topic is
main text	main text	gives you information
index	search box	helps you to find a particular word or idea
–	hyperlinks	lets you move to other information linked to the topic
photos	photos or videos	illustrates information so you can see it as well as read about it

3 and **4** Learners' own answers.

8.8 Planning a talk

LEARNING PLAN

Learning objectives	Learning intentions	Success criteria
3Rw.03, 3Rv.01, 3Rg.01, 3Ri.01, 3Ri.04, 3Ri.07, 3Ri.09, 3Ri.10, 3Ri.13, 3Ri.14, 3Ri.15, 3Ri.16, 3Ra.02, 3Wv.01, 3Ws.04, 3Wc.02, 3Wc.05, 3Wc.06, 3Wp.02, 3SLm.01, 3SLm.02, 3SLm.03, 3SLp.05	• Plan a talk in a group. • Use texts and e-texts to research a topic for a talk.	• Learners can plan a talk in a group. • Learners can use texts and e-texts to research a topic for a talk.

LANGUAGE SUPPORT

Depending on the age of your learners, you may want to explain that when they search for information, they should use key words in the search boxes to find information using a search engine. Younger learners or learners at lower reading levels may find it helpful to add 'children', 'kids' or 'Elementary stage' to their search. This will help them find information more suitable to their age or reading level.

Starter idea

Favourite subject (5–10 minutes)

Resources: Learner's Book, Session 8.8: Getting started

Description: Ask learners to think of subjects they find interesting (e.g. cricket, birds, Brazil, cooking). Ask them to choose one of these subjects and think of questions they would like to ask about it.

Remind learners of the key-word lists they wrote in the previous session. Tell learners that their questions should cover different things about their subject.

Main teaching ideas

1 **Explore a topic in groups (5–10 minutes)**

Learning intention: To plan a talk as a group.

Resources: Learner's Book, Session 8.8, Activity 1; Workbook, Session 8.8

Description: Explain that learners are going to give a talk in groups. Discuss what makes group work successful. Direct learners to the table in the Learner's Book. Talk about how the subject has been split into topics.

Split learners into groups of six or eight (learners can then work in pairs when they carry out research). Consider grouping learners with similar interests.

Ask groups to discuss and agree a subject they would like to do a talk about (e.g. countries, animals, festivals). Alternatively, you could allocate a subject to each group or use the Workbook activities and ask learners to give a talk on a hobby.

> **Differentiation ideas:** Challenge more confident learners to support less confident speakers and readers within the group.

Answers:
Learners' own answers.

2 Plan a topic (15–20 minutes)

Learning intention: To plan a talk as a group.

Resources: Learner's Book, Session 8.8, Activity 2; Workbook, Session 8.8

Description: Ask learners to look at the table in the previous activity again, particularly the way that the 'Norway' subject has been split into different topics. Tell learners to copy the table structure into their notebooks or continue using the Workbook activities.

Ask learners to agree on three/four talk topics for their subject and then to complete the first column of the table. In groups, encourage learners to evaluate their topics and questions. Will the topics cover a range of information about their subject?

Prompt groups to allocate pairs to research each topic. How will they do this?

> **Differentiation ideas:** Challenge learners to support less confident speakers and readers within the group.

Answers:
Learners' own answers.

3 Research a topic (40 minutes)

Learning intention: To use texts and e-texts to research a topic for a talk.

Resources: Learner's Book, Session 8.8, Activity 3; Worksheets 8.1 and 8.2; non-fiction books; internet access for e-texts

Description: Encourage learners to select books and e-texts to help them to research their topic. If you have limited non-fiction resources, learners could use the information in Worksheet 8.1 Slimy snails fact sheet.

Direct learners to the Reading tip and check that they can recall the difference between skimming and scanning. In pairs, ask learners to carry out their research. One learner in each pair could make notes as the other learner reads information. Learners should then complete the answer column of their table. Alternatively, you may wish to provide Worksheet 8.2 Planning and recording information for more scaffolded support.

Tell learners that their answers should give them enough information to allow them to prepare their talk.

> **Differentiation ideas:** Support learners who benefit from more structured support and limited choices by asking them to use the information in Worksheet 8.1 rather than find new information.

> **Assessment ideas:** During group discussions assess whether:

- group members work collaboratively to plan a talk
- learners listen politely to each other's ideas
- learners find it difficult to make contributions
- more confident learners are supportive of other group members.

Answers:
Learners' own answers.

Plenary idea

Group work (10 minutes)

Description: Ask each pair to share what they have learned about the topic they researched with the rest of their group. Have all pairs found answers to the questions they were researching?

Ask groups to consider whether they have enough information to talk about the subject they researched.

Homework ideas

Ask learners to:

- complete the Workbook activities for this session, if not completed in class
- create a wordsearch using at least ten words from their topic.

Answers for Workbook

Learners' own answers.

8.9 Giving your talk

LEARNING PLAN

Learning objectives	Learning intentions	Success criteria
3SLm.01, 3SLm.02, 3SLm.03, 3SLm.04, 3SLm.05, 3SLs.02, 3SLg.01, 3SLg.02, 3SLp.01, 3SLp.03, 3SLp.05, 3SLr.01	• Give a talk on a chosen subject. • Consider and develop the skills needed when giving a talk.	• Learners can give a talk on a subject they have chosen. • Learners can consider and develop the skills needed when giving a talk.

LANGUAGE SUPPORT

Although learners will be used to speaking in groups and class discussions, they may not appreciate how different it is to give a talk. Consider introducing the terms *formal language* and *informal language*. You could explain that informal language uses the sort of words we use when talking to a friend. Informal language includes the use of contractions, whereas formal language uses the full forms.

Starter idea

Reading aloud (10 minutes)

Resources: Learner's Book, Session 8.9: Getting started; selection of non-fiction books

Description: Give learners a non-fiction book each. Read the prompts in the Learner's Book to introduce the activity. Tell learners to read their paragraph to themselves and to ask for help if there are any words they need help with reading or understanding. Allow learners a few minutes to practise reading to themselves and then ask pairs to take it in turns to read to one another. Tell learners that their feedback should include one or two things their partner did well and one thing to improve.

Main teaching ideas

1 Listen to a talk (15 minutes)

Learning intention: To consider the skills needed when giving a talk.

Resources: *A Talk on Norway* (Learner's Book, Session 8.9, Activity 1); Track 55

Description: Play Track 55. Ask learners to talk to a partner about which topics the speakers talked about (where Norway is, cities, countryside).

Read the Speaking tip. Ask: *How will you recognise the present tense* (e.g. use of is / are / has)*?* Ask learners to think about the Speaking tip as they listen to the Norway talk again.

Discuss the questions in the Learner's Book. Help learners recognise that each topic is introduced informally rather than with actual headings (e.g. the sentence *Nearly one million people live in the capital city Oslo* introduces cities, rather than a speaker saying *Cities in Norway*). Learners' answers should reflect that the audio achieves the points in the Speaking tip.

Encourage learners to think of questions they would like to ask about the talk.

> **Assessment ideas:** Note which learners demonstrate good listening skills.

Audioscript: *A Talk on Norway*

Speaker 1:	We are going to give a talk on Norway. We hope you will find it interesting.
Speaker 2:	Norway is a country found in northern Europe. The north of the

country is in the very cold Arctic Circle. Other countries close-by are Sweden, Denmark, Finland, Poland, Germany and the United Kingdom.

Speaker 1: Nearly one million people live in the capital city Oslo. It has a beautiful sculpture park and is known for its Viking ship museum. The Vikings first came from Norway.

Speaker 2: However, people don't normally visit Norway for its cities but for the countryside.

Speaker 1: There are stunning fjords where the sea reaches far inland. In the winter people enjoy skiing and climb glaciers which are frozen masses of ice. It is also known as the land with the midnight sun because the sun doesn't set in the summer.

Speaker 2: Norway also has interesting wildlife, including reindeers and opportunities to whale-watch.

Speaker 1: Would anyone like to ask us any questions?

Answers:
Learners' own answers.

2 Prepare your talk (15–20 minutes)

Learning intention: To develop the skills needed when giving a talk.

Resources: Learner's Book, Session 8.9, Activity 2; space for groups to rehearse their talks

Description: Explain that giving a talk is not the same as chatting with a friend. Tell learners that they must think carefully about the words they choose to use and how they will introduce the talk and each topic. Explain that speakers sometimes begin talks by welcoming listeners and end with a time for questions.

Remind learners about the importance of making eye contact. Ask: *What other ways could you communicate without speaking* (e.g. hand gestures, smiling, nodding)*?* Ask learners to work together in their groups to prepare their talks. Consider

setting a time limit for the talks (e.g. no more than five minutes).

When learners have had some time to practise their talks, ask them to re-read the Speaking tip. Have they achieved all the points? Which parts of their talk can they improve?

> **Differentiation ideas:** Support learners by allowing them to give their talk using notes.

Challenge learners to prepare visual aids or a PowerPoint presentation to support their group's talk.

3 Give a talk (20–30 minutes)

Learning intention: To give a talk on a chosen subject.

Resources: Learner's Book, Session 8.9, Activity 3; Workbook, Session 8.9

Description: Decide in which order the groups will give their talks. Ask: *How can you show that you are listening well* (e.g. eye contact, not talking while someone else is talking)*?* Tell learners to make a note of any questions they have during the talks. Listeners could also note things they think the speakers have done well or could improve. Allow time for groups to give their talks. Remind learners of the importance of listening to each other carefully.

After each talk, allow time for feedback. Remind learners of the importance of giving feedback politely and with consideration for others' feelings. When all groups have given their talks, direct learners to the How am I doing? prompt. Learners could use the Workbook activities to record their reflections if there is time in class.

> **Differentiation ideas:** Support learners by allowing them to give their talk using notes.

> **Assessment ideas:** When groups give their talks, assess which learners:

- speak confidently and clearly
- use gestures and other non-verbal communication
- show awareness of their audience (e.g. use different language, expression, dealing with questions)
- work well as a group
- listen carefully
- ask appropriate questions
- ask questions politely.

It is important that you assess learners' speaking and listening skills, not learners' knowledge of the subject they have prepared.

Plenary idea

Review time (5 minutes)

Description: Discuss the similarities and differences between presenting information in a talk and presenting it in written form. Learners may comment that:

- both use present tense and subject specific vocabulary
- talks do not usually include topic headings

- written information does not allow the reader to ask questions.

Ask learners to think about which format they prefer.

Homework ideas

Ask learners to:

- complete the Workbook activities for this session, if not completed in class
- use their subject notes to write a paragraph about each of the topics in their talk.

Answers for Workbook

Learners' own answers.

8.10 Planning an information text

LEARNING PLAN		
Learning objectives	**Learning intentions**	**Success criteria**
3Rw.03, 3Rv.01, 3Rv.02, 3Rv.04, 3Rg.01, 3Rs.02, 3Rs.03, 3Ri.05, 3Ri.07, 3Ri.13, 3Ri.14, 3Ri.15, 3Ri.16, 3Ra.02, 3Wv.01, 3Wg.01, 3Ws.02, 3Ws.04, 3Wc.02, 3Wp.02	• Plan questions to research. • Choose a way of recording information. • Record and research information for an information text.	• Learners can plan questions to research. • Learners can choose a way of recording information. • Learners can record and research information for an information text.

LANGUAGE SUPPORT
You may want to introduce some vocabulary specific to researching countries (e.g. climate, temperature, temperate, tropical, population, historical sites) as learners are likely to come across these words during their research. You could use Language worksheet 8B to support this.

Starter idea

Compare texts (5–10 minutes)

Resources: Learner's Book, Session 8.10: Getting started; Workbook, Session 8.10; Worksheet 8.1

Description: Direct learners to the prompts in the Learner's Book. Ask them to re-read the texts in the unit. You could also refer learners to the text in the

Workbook or Worksheet 8.1 Slimy snails fact sheet as these include the layout features you want learners to use in their own writing.

Try to elicit that all the texts use the present tense and language specific to the topic. Some of the texts use:

- pictures to give extra information
- paragraphs or sections to group related information

- subheadings to make it easier to find information
- glossaries to explain technical words.

Main teaching ideas

1 Choose a country (10–15 minutes)

Learning intention: To plan questions to research.

Resources: Learner's Book, Session 8.10, Activity 1

Description: Explain that learners are going to write their own information text about a country. You could ask them to research India so that they are able to use the Workbook activities later in the session. Alternatively, you could choose another subject for learners to research (e.g. animals, rainforests, transport).

When learners have chosen the subject they will research, ask them to write four questions they want to answer about it in their notebooks (e.g. location; weather; scenery; special events). Remind learners to punctuate their questions correctly.

Tell learners that their research questions will help them plan their paragraphs.

Learners' own writing.

> **Differentiation ideas:** Support learners by providing a subject and suggesting questions they could research in pairs.

Challenge learners to think of additional questions.

> **Assessment ideas:** Note which learners were able to select four appropriate questions to research.

2 Record your research (10 minutes)

Learning intention: To choose a way of recording information.

Resources: Learner's Book, Session 8.10, Activity 2; Worksheet 8.2

Description: Explain the activity to learners. Ask: *How helpful did you find the table you used in the previous session? What other methods could you use to record your notes* (e.g. mind maps)*?* Explain that learners should choose a method they think will be best for them (e.g. table, mind map, key words list).

Allow learners time to draw their plan.

Learners' own plans.

> **Differentiation ideas:** Support learners by providing a template to record their research. Remind them that they could use Worksheet 8.2 Planning and recording information.

3 Research your subject (20–30 minutes)

Learning intention: To record and research information for an information text.

Resources: Learner's Book, Session 8.10, Activity 3; Workbook, Session 8.10; Language worksheet 8B; non-fiction books; internet access

Description: Explain that learners are now going to research their subject. Direct them to the Reflection questions. Ask learners to consider this before they begin their research.

If there is time in class, use the Workbook activities for this session to encourage learners to identify interesting words and useful information when they carry out their research. Use Language worksheet 8B to introduce subject-specific vocabulary about countries. Remind them that they can use books or e-texts to research their subjects. Allow time for learners to research their subject and record their notes.

> **Assessment ideas:** Note which learners were able to make relevant notes and record key vocabulary.

Plenary idea

Recording methods (5 minutes)

Description: In groups, ask learners to discuss:

- the method they used to record their questions and answers
- why they chose that method
- how useful they found that method
- how easy they found it to decide what to record
- how useful they think their notes will be.

> CROSS-CURRICULAR LINKS
>
> Provide opportunities for learners to use the research skills they develop in this session across other subjects such as science, history or geography.

Homework ideas

Ask learners to:

- complete the Workbook activities for this session, if not completed in class
- create a short glossary of words from their research notes.

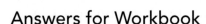
Answers for Workbook

1 Possible words: part of continent of Asia; huge country; population well over a billion; highest mountain range; borders Himalayas, Bay of Bengal, Arabian Sea; land is varied; Thar desert, jungles and Ganges Plain; fertile.

2 Possible questions:

Where is India?

What is its population?

What are its borders?

What is the name of the desert in India?

Where in India can you grow crops?

8.11 Writing an information text

LEARNING PLAN		
Learning objectives	**Learning intentions**	**Success criteria**
3Wv.01, 3Wv.07, 3Wg.01, 3Wg.05, 3Wg.06, 3Wg.08, 3Ws.02, 3Ws.04, 3Wc.02, 3Wc.05, 3Wc.06, 3Wp.01, 3Wp.03, 3SLs.02, 3SLg.02, 3SLg.03	• Consider how well a plan meets the needs of an audience. • Write an information text.	• Learners can consider how well their plan meets the needs of their audience. • Learners can write an information text.

LANGUAGE SUPPORT	
Talk to your learners about who the information text is for. Discuss the word *audience*.	Explain that audience refers to anyone you are presenting something to, either in spoken or written form.

Starter idea

Review your planning (5–10 minutes)

Resources: Learner's Book, Session 8.11: Getting started

Description: Ask learners to read through their planning sheets from the previous session. Ask them to consider whether they have forgotten to include any useful information. Ask: *Do your notes make sense to you?*

Main teaching ideas

1 Is it interesting? (10 minutes)

Learning intention: To consider how well a plan meets the needs of its audience.

Resources: Learner's Book, Session 8.11, Activity 1; Workbook, Session 8.11, Activities 2 and 3

Description: Ask: *Have you included interesting information in your planning sheet? Will other learners find your information interesting?* Ask learners to consider whether they need to check their facts. Have they copied them accurately? You could use the Practice and Challenge activities in the Workbook here.

Allow time for learners to make changes or additions to their notes. Remind them of how they used notes when they prepared their talks.

Ask learners to re-read their notes and practise talking about the information.

⟩ **Differentiation ideas:** Support learners who are less confident with checking their own work by suggesting they share their information with a partner.

2 Time to write (40–45 minutes)

Learning intention: To write an information text.

Resources: Learner's Book, Session 8.11, Activity 2; Worksheet 8.3; non-fiction texts; internet access

Description: In pairs, learners should write a checklist of the features they think their information text should include. Ask them to compare their checklist with the points in the Learner's Book. You could also use Worksheet 8.3 Information-text checklist here.

Did learners include any features in their checklists that are not in the Learner's Book (e.g. prepositions)? If appropriate, revisit conditional sentences. Ask learners to re-read the fact file in Session 8.7 and identify an example of a conditional sentence (e.g. *If you click on a highlighted word or image, you may be shown more information about it*). Ask learners to suggest a multi-clause sentence for their information text. Direct learners to the Writing tip.

Before learners begin writing, consider offering the option of producing handwritten texts or e-texts. Learners choosing to produce e-texts may find it easier to include pictures, diagrams and maps.

Allow learners time to write their information text. After 15 minutes, ask learners to review what they have written using the checklist in the Learner's Book or Worksheet 8.3.

› **Differentiation ideas:** Support less confident writers by pairing them with a confident writer.

Challenge learners to add a glossary to explain subject specific vocabulary.

› **Assessment ideas:** Note which learners can use their notes to write an information text. Which learners:

- organise their topics into paragraphs
- use mainly *to be* / *to have* verbs in the present tense and avoid powerful verbs

- include some adjectives to add interest to their writing
- use subject-specific vocabulary
- use different sentence types
- include pictures, diagrams or maps with captions to provide additional information?

Plenary idea

Interesting facts (5 minutes)

Resources: Learners' information texts

Description: Invite learners to ask pairs of learners questions about the subject they have written about (e.g. *What is the capital city? What sort of climate does your country have?*).

Homework ideas

Ask learners to:

- complete the Workbook activities for this session, if not completed in class
- design a crossword grid and write six crossword clues about information in their texts.

Answers for Workbook

1. a   Yes. India's population is over a billion people.

   b   No. The north of India is bordered by the Himalayas.

   c   The Himalayas.

   d   Himalayas – high; Thar Desert – dry; jungles – hot and wet; Ganges Plain – fertile

2. Learners' own questions.

3. Learners' own answers.

8.12 Improving your text

LEARNING PLAN

Learning objectives	Learning intentions	Success criteria
3Ww.05, 3Ww.06, 3Wv.01, 3Wv.05, 3Wv.07, 3Wg.01, 3Wg.04, 3Wg.05, 3Wg.06, 3Wg.07, 3Wg.08, 3Ws.02, 3Ws.04, 3Wc.05, 3Wc.06, 3Wp.01, 3Wp.03, 3Wp.04, 3Wp.05	• Improve an information text. • Present information text for display.	• Learners can improve an information text they have written. • Learners can present information text for display.

LANGUAGE SUPPORT

You may want to recap verb agreement in sentences. Remind learners about changing a noun to a pronoun in their heads, before they write, as a way of checking which verb they need.

Starter idea

Re-read your writing (5 minutes)

Resources: Learner's Book, Session 8.12: Getting started; learners' information texts from Session 8.11

Description: Ask learners to read and follow the prompts in the Learner's Book. Explain that reading a text aloud can help us notice things that are missing or spot errors. Encourage learners to read their writing quietly to themselves or to a partner.

Main teaching ideas

1 Proofread and improve (20–25 minutes)

Learning intention: To improve an information text.

Resources: Learner's Book, Session 8.12, Activity 1; Workbook, Session 8.12; dictionaries; word lists; coloured pens/pencils; learners' information texts

Description: Direct learners to the proofreading prompts in the Learner's Book. Explain that they will now proofread their writing, either on their own or with a partner. If learners have written e-texts, they could use electronic tools to proofread their work. Use the Workbook activities to provide practice in spotting mistakes if there is time in class.

Ask learners to begin by checking spellings. Remind them of the spelling patterns they know (e.g. common suffix endings, phonic patterns). Encourage learners to underline words they think are misspelled using a coloured pen/pencil, then write the correct spelling above after checking in a dictionary or word list.

Discuss the types of punctuation they could have used (e.g. capital letters for proper nouns, commas in lists, full stops). Ask learners to add or correct punctuation using a different-coloured pen/pencil.

Learners should have mainly used the present tense, with occasional past tense. Remind them to check spellings of irregular past tense verbs.

Ask learners to look at the sentence types they have used.

Can learners:

• re-write some simple sentences as multi-clause sentences

• add additional information to a simple sentence using a connective

• change the order of words in a sentence so that it is more interesting to read?

> **Differentiation ideas:** Support less confident writers and learners who find spelling difficult by asking them to identify a limited number of errors (e.g. five spellings, one sentence to improve).

Challenge confident writers to improve their writing by adding more interesting vocabulary.

> **Assessment ideas:** Note those learners that show improved willingness to make changes to their original writing.

2 Headings and paragraphs (5 minutes)

Learning intention: To improve an information text.

Resources: Learner's Book, Session 8.12, Activity 2

Description: Ask learners to re-read their paragraphs. Ask: *Does your heading give readers a clue about what the paragraph is about? Have you chosen the best word/words for your heading? Have you included any information that would fit better with another paragraph?*

When learners have reviewed their work, direct them to the How are we doing? prompt for further feedback from their partner.

3 Presentation (20 minutes)

Learning intention: To present an information text for display.

Resources: Learner's Book, Session 8.12, Activity 3; Worksheet 8.4; non-fiction books; plain paper; colouring pencils/felt tips

Description: Ask learners to look at how information is presented in non-fiction books. Ask: *Is all the information in one block?* Try to elicit that information may be organised in boxes, as a fact file or overlapping a picture.

Allow learners time to present their work. They could use Worksheet 8.4 Information-text template to present their information. Remind learners to use neat, joined handwriting.

> **Differentiation ideas:** Challenge learners who are confident using a computer to present their information text using a word-processing or desktop publishing programme if available.

> **Assessment ideas:** Note which learners include the key features of information texts in their writing. Which learners use a range of sentence types? Which learners show a good understanding of how the language and layout of non-fiction texts differs from fiction texts?

Plenary idea

Reflection (5 minutes)

Resources: Learners' completed information texts; Worksheet 8.3

Description: Ask learners to look at their information text and identify two things they are pleased with and one thing they think they could improve.

If learners are willing, they could carry out this reflection in pairs using Worksheet 8.3.

Homework ideas

Ask learners to:

*   complete the Workbook activities for this session, if not completed in class
*   design the front cover of the book their information page might belong to; learners should choose a suitable title for the book.

Answers for Workbook

1

Present	Past
have	had
is	was
are	were
come	came
do	did
make	made
say	said
write	wrote
read	read
find	found
buy	brought

2   There is nearly 2000 Bengal tigers in India and about 25 000 Indian elephants. Both these animals were now endangered. That was why many now lived in special protected areas called reserves. Indian culture respect animals. Cows are holy animals and cannot be harmed. Cows wandered freely through the streets of big cities.

3 There ~~is~~ **are** nearly 2000 Bengal tigers in India and about 25 000 Indian elephants. Both these animals ~~were~~ **are** now endangered. That ~~was~~ **is** why many now ~~lived~~ **live** in special protected areas <u>called</u> reserves. Indian culture ~~respect~~ **respects** animals. Cows <u>are</u> holy animals and <u>cannot be</u> harmed. Cows ~~wandered~~ **wander** freely through the streets of big cities.

CHECK YOUR PROGRESS

1 Learners' own answers. Possible differences:
Stories: paragraphs introduce new events; begin with adverbials (e.g. suddenly, the next day)
Information texts: paragraphs introduce new ideas or topics; separate ideas or topics.

2 Learners' own answers. Possible differences in language:
Stories: powerful verbs; interesting adjectives and noun phrases; mainly past tense verbs; uses I, me, you, us adverbs; uses dialogue
Information texts: simple verbs (is / are / has); mainly present tense; some adjectives; uses *it* or *they* pronouns; subject-specific language; no dialogue

3 Learners' own answers. Possible suggestions:
group same ideas into paragraphs; use present tense; use headings and subheadings; add pictures or diagrams to give extra information; choose language linked to the subject.

4 Learners' own answers. Possible sentence additions could include:

a In Australia the cities are near the coast <u>and there are some beautiful beaches</u>.

b Alice Springs is one of the closest towns to Uluru <u>and I would like to go there</u>.

c Hurricanes happen in the Caribbean <u>but only in the wet season</u>.

5 **a** swim

b are

c go

d have

e travel

6 Learners' own answers.

PROJECT GUIDANCE

The solo and paired projects both involve writing information texts. Consider allowing learners to choose whether they will undertake the solo or paired project. The group project provides an opportunity to revisit alphabetical order and the Dewey Decimal System. You will find it helpful to refer to the guidance about *Setting up and assessing the projects* in the Project guidance in Unit 1.

Group project: Explain the project to learners. How you organise your groups will depend upon the number of books you have in your class or school library. If your class or school library has a lot of books, this activity could take a long time so you may want learners to focus on ordering a small section of the library.

Learners will need to use alphabetical order to several letter places when sorting fiction books. Learners could make alphabet labels for the shelving or create alphabetical lists of the available books.

Identifying which category some information books belong to could lead to a lot of interesting discussion (e.g. Do books on space travel belong to science or technology?). Learners could make Dewey classification labels for these non-fiction books.

Note which learners listen to the ideas of others politely. Which learners ask questions to further the discussion?

Pair project: Invite learners to choose their partners as this is likely to make it easier for them to find a common interest. Encourage learners to research the subject independently. One learner could use an information book and the other could use e-texts.

Do learners begin by identifying questions to ask? How do learners record the information they collected? Can learners make effective notes? Does one learner play a greater role during the research phase?

Learners could present their information in handwritten form or electronically. Do learners use the language and layout features of information texts?

Solo project: Explain the project to learners. Before they plan their own fact file, encourage them to spend time brainstorming ideas about what could be included. Ask learners to think about the age of the people they want to encourage to visit their area. Do learners want to encourage visits from people of all ages or focus on young families?

Assess whether learners have used the features of information text in their fact files. Is the fact file written in the present tense?

⟩9 Laughing allowed

Unit plan

Session	Approximate number of learning hours	Outline of learning content	Resources
9.1 Riddles	1	Read riddles and explore puns. Identify homonyms and explore how they are used in puns.	Learner's Book Session 9.1 Workbook Session 9.1 ⬇ Language worksheet 9A
9.2 Wordplay in poetry	1	Explore the use of rhyme and alliteration in poetry. Revisit regular and irregular past tense verbs.	Learner's Book Session 9.2 Workbook Session 9.2 ⬇ Language worksheet 9B
9.3 Funny poems and limericks	1.5	Read and answer questions about funny poems. Explore rhythm and rhyme in limericks. Read and say tongue twisters.	Learner's Book Session 9.3 Workbook Session 9.3 ⬇ Worksheet 9.1 ⬇ Differentiated worksheets 9A–C
9.4 Calligrams and mnemonics	1–1.5	Read a calligram. Explore ways to remember how words are spelled. Write mnemonics for common tricky words.	Learner's Book Session 9.4 Workbook Session 9.4
9.5 Reviewing a poem	1	Review the poems from previous sessions. Record opinions about three poems in a table. Review one of the poems.	Learner's Book Session 9.5 Workbook Session 9.5 ⬇ Worksheet 9.2
9.6 Writing and performing a poem	1–1.5	Plan, write and perform a poem.	Learner's Book Session 9.6 Workbook Session 9.6 ⬇ Worksheet 9.3
Cross-unit resources			
Learner's Book Check your progress			
Learner's Book Projects			
End-of-unit 9 test			
End-of-year test			

BACKGROUND KNOWLEDGE

It will be helpful to be familiar with the following English subject knowledge:

- funny poems (including riddles, limericks and calligrams)
- homophones and homonyms
- alliteration
- anagrams

- rhyme
- nouns, adjectives and verbs
- present and past tense verbs
- irregular past tense
- sentence openers
- rhythm
- performing verse.

TEACHING SKILLS FOCUS

Language awareness

Ensuring that your learners can recognise why something is funny and reach a point where they can enjoy this humour themselves, is a useful skill in learning English. The more learners hear jokes and humorous verse, the more likely they will be to recognise why something is funny.

Consider having a short joke-telling session at the start or end of each session or day. Make sure that you have access to children's jokes online or have a selection of children's joke books. Select the jokes you will use in each session carefully. Share jokes that you find funny so that your learners can see your enjoyment of the joke and so that you can explain the humour to them. Ask learners to talk

to each other about each joke and explain why it is funny as this will aid their language awareness. As learners become more confident in identifying the humour, ask them to take responsibility for selecting and sharing jokes.

By the end of this unit, consider the following questions:

- Have you succeeded in creating a joke-telling culture in your class?
- Are your learners more confident at identifying sound patterns in words?
- Do learners recognise how sound patterns can create humour through puns and wordplay?

9.1 Riddles

LEARNING PLAN

Learning objectives	Learning intentions	Success criteria
3Rw.04, 3Rv.01, 3Rg.07, 3Rg.08, 3Rs.02, 3Ri.02, 3Ri.03, 3Ri.07, 3Ri.16, 3Ra.01, 3Ra.03, 3Ww.04, 3SLr.02	• Explore jokes and riddles. • Explain how the use of words can make things funny. • Identify homonyms.	• Learners understand how the choice of words can make jokes and riddles sound funny. • Learners can explore jokes and riddles. • Learners can identify homonyms.

LANGUAGE SUPPORT

Using words to make things funny is often known as *wordplay*. The Language focus text in the Learner's Book gives several examples of wordplay. You may need to explain some vocabulary to learners (e.g. *honeycomb, snore*).

The term *joke* is often used as a broad term to describe a short narrative or dialogue that is intended to make someone laugh.

A riddle is a type of joke that asks a puzzling question that the listener has to try to solve. A riddle usually involves some wordplay. Many learners will be familiar with the format of a riddle as a joke style, without recognising it as a riddle. Some learners may be familiar with knock-knock jokes. Knock-knock jokes are part-riddle and part-pun.

Common misconceptions

Misconception	How to identify	How to overcome
Homonyms are the same as homophones.	Write a homonym on the board (e.g. bear). Ask learners to explain what the word means (e.g. bear – the animal; bear – to hold up). Ask learners to identify which word group the words belong to. Note learners who identify it as a homophone.	Explain that the word (e.g. bear) has the same sound and the same spelling but homophones have the same sound but a different spelling (e.g. bear / bare).

Starter idea

What makes you laugh? (5–10 minutes)

Resources: Learner's Book, Session 9.1: Getting started

Description: Ask learners to talk about what makes them laugh. Encourage them to name broad topics (e.g. funny incidents, jokes, cartoons) rather than naming specific events or topics.

Do learners know any jokes they can share? Note the range of jokes learners tell (e.g. riddles, knock-knock jokes, narrative jokes) so that you can draw on learners' examples to support their understanding of puns and riddles in later activities.

Ask learners to suggest a definition of a joke (e.g. telling someone something to make them laugh). Direct them to the cartoon in the Learner's Book. Read the text to learners. Do they find it funny? Why? Explain that the cartoon story is an example of a riddle.

Main teaching ideas

1 Read riddles (15 minutes)

Learning intention: To explore jokes and riddles.

Resources: Learner's Book, Session 9.1, Activity 1

Description: Ask learners to read the riddles in the Learner's Book. Ask: *Did the riddles make you smile or laugh? Did any riddles make you groan?*

In pairs, learners should discuss their different reactions to the riddles. Can learners explain which part of the riddle they found funny or made them groan?

Direct learners to the Language focus box. As you read the text, check that learners understand the vocabulary in the examples.

> **Differentiation ideas:** Support less confident readers by pairing with a confident reader.

2 Explain puns (15 minutes)

Learning intention: To explain how the use of words can make things funny.

Resources: Learner's Book, Session 9.1, Activity 2; Workbook, Session 9.1, Activity 1

Description: Explain that to understand a riddle learners should look for the word or words that provide clues (e.g. in the fish joke, fish do not have money, so *keeping their money* are the important words). Explain that when learners have identified the clue words they should think about things or places associated with the clue (e.g. in the fish joke, they should think about purses, wallets or banks).

In pairs, learners should re-read the riddles and discuss possible explanations. Allow time for learners to write their explanations.

Use the Focus activity in the Workbook to provide further practice with understanding puns.

> **Differentiation ideas:** Support learners through class discussion of each riddle to help learners identify the important words each time.

Challenge learners to write a sentence to explain the pun in Getting started (e.g. the clue word is *sides* and you can have a *left* and *right* side and an *inside* and *outside*).

> **Assessment ideas:** Can learners identify the 'clue words'?

Answers:
Learners own explanations. Possible explanations:
Fish riddle: The clue words are *wise* and *keeping your money* so you should think about a safe place to keep money.
Flag riddle: The clue words are *never gets anywhere* so you should think of things that fly but cannot move.
Foot riddle: The clue words are *never make right*. The opposite of *right* is always *left*. Your left foot can never be your right foot.

---

3 Ask a riddle (5–10 minutes)

Learning intention: To explain how the use of words can make things funny.

Resources: Learner's Book, Session 9.1, Activity 3; joke books, if appropriate

Description: Direct learners to the Speaking tip. Tell them to think of other jokes or riddles that use puns. If appropriate, provide joke books for ideas.

Ask learners to work in pairs. Allow time for each learner to say their joke or riddle and for their partner to explain the pun.

> **Assessment ideas:** Note which learners find it difficult to recognise the humour in the jokes.

4 Homonyms (10–15 minutes)

Learning intention: To identify homonyms.

Resources: Learner's Book, Session 9.1, Activity 4; Language worksheet 9A

Description: Ask learners to recall examples of homophones (e.g. write/right, hear/here, see/sea). Direct learners to the title of this unit (*Laughing allowed*). Ask: *What does* allowed *mean in the title* (permission to laugh)? Write *aloud* on the board and elicit the meaning. Remind learners that homophones are words that sound the same but are spelled differently. Direct learners to the Language focus box.

Read each homonym in part a and check that learners are familiar with both meanings. Allow learners time to write their sentences showing the different meanings and then list further homonyms used in Activity 1.

Use Language worksheet 9A to provide further practice with homonyms.

> **Differentiation ideas:** Support learners by providing a dictionary so that they can check the meanings of homophones and homonyms.

> **Assessment ideas:** Do learners understand the difference between homophones and homonyms? Do they understand that these words play an important part in creating puns?

Answers:

a   Learners' own explanations. Possible answers:

bark: Tree trunks are covered in bark. Dogs bark.

bat: You hit a ball with a bat. Bats hang upside down in caves.

light: You switch on a light when it is dark. A feather is light.

sink: A brick will sink if you drop it in water. There is a sink in the kitchen.

watch: A watch tells you the time. I like to watch television.

b   Learners should identify the following homonyms:

bank: land at the side of a river; sloping grassy ground; savings bank

flies: plural of fly (insect); present tense of *to fly* (verb to move through the air with wings)

foot: body part; bottom of a hill/stairs

left: opposite of *right*; what is remaining

Plenary idea

Homonyms (5 minutes)

Description: Remind learners that homonyms are words with the same sound and same spelling as another word. Explain that *bat* is an example of an animal homonym.

In pairs, learners should think of other animal names that are homonyms (e.g. bear – to carry, seal – to close an envelope, duck – to bend down to get out of the way of something, bug – to annoy someone, yak – to talk a lot).

Homework ideas

Ask learners to:

*   complete the Practice and Challenge activities in the Workbook

*   find five homophone pairs and five homonym pairs, then draw pictures or write explanations to show the difference between each pair (e.g. a picture of a whale and a picture of a child crying/wailing).

Answers for Workbook

1   Learners should tick:

a   Fish and <u>ships</u>!

c   In a <u>mooseum</u>!

e   Waiter, waiter – I'm in a hurry. Will my pizza be <u>long</u>?

f   What has four <u>legs</u> but can't walk?

g   It's <u>bean</u> soup, sir.
I don't care what it's <u>been</u> – what is it now?

2   Learners' own sentences. Possible explanations:

a   bank: You keep your money in a bank. I stood on the riverbank looking for fish.

b   can: How fast can you run? I bought a can of paint.

c   kind: My brother is always kind to me. What kind of book do you like?

d   rock: I rock the baby off to sleep. I climbed over the rock.

e   row: The men row the boat. The farmer planted a row of seeds.

f   trip: We took a trip along the river. The boy tripped over in the playground.

3   Learners' own riddles.

9.2 Wordplay in poetry

LEARNING PLAN

Learning objectives	Learning intentions	Success criteria
3Rw.04, 3Rv.01, 3Rg.07, 3Rg.08, 3Rg.10, 3Rg.11, 3Rs.02, 3Ri.02, 3Ri.03, 3Ri.07, 3Ri.16, 3Ri.17, 3Ra.01, 3Ra.02, 3Ww.02, 3Wg.07, 3Wp.02, 3SLm.01, 3SLm.05, 3SLp.01, 3SLp.03, 3SLr.01, 3SLr.02	• Look at the language used in a poem. • Change present tense verbs into their regular or irregular past tense. • Explore alliteration.	• Learners can look at the language used in a poem. • Learners can change present tense verbs into their regular or irregular past tense. • Learners understand alliteration.

LANGUAGE SUPPORT

When learners read *Wordspinning* by John Foster, check that they rhyme *tear* with *dare* and do not pronounce it *tear* as in crying.

You could explain that words like this, with the same spelling but which are pronounced differently and have a different meaning, are known as homographs.

Common misconceptions

Misconception	How to identify	How to overcome
Rhyming words always have the same spelling pattern (e.g. clean / bean).	When learners make their lists of rhyming words, note those learners who only list words with the same spelling pattern.	Write two rhyming words with different spelling patterns on the board (e.g. *green / bean*). Ask learners to say both words. Ask: *Do they end with the same sound? Do they rhyme?* Remind learners that they should focus on the sound of the word and not the spelling pattern when identifying rhyming words.

Starter idea

Rhyming words (10 minutes)

Resources: Learner's Book, Session 9.2: Getting started

Description: Write these two lines of text on the board: *The lazy cat / Lay on the mat.* Ask: *What do you notice about the end of each line?* Elicit that rhyming words have

the same sound at the end. Direct learners to the activity in the Learner's Book.

Learners' lists may include:

• cat: mat, bat, hat, that, flat

• gold: old, hold, told, fold, bold, scold

• clean: lean, green, bean, mean, seen, scene.

Allow time for learners to compare lists.

Main teaching ideas

 1 *Wordspinning* (15–20 minutes)

Learning intention: To look at the language used in a poem.

Resources: *Wordspinning* (Learner's Book, Session 9.2, Activity 1); Track 56; dictionaries

Description: Ask learners to look at the text as you read the poem *Wordspinning*.

Ask: *What do you notice about the words in the first line of the poem?* (*spin, pins, nips* all have the same letters) Explain that words with the same letters in a different order are known as *anagrams*. Ask learners to identify more anagrams in the first verse of the poem (snap, pans, naps; spit, tips; parts, traps).

Ask learners to discuss the words at the start of every line. What do they notice (e.g. all verbs, many of the verbs refer to changing something)? Ask learners to re-read the poem quietly to themselves so that they can hear the rhymes, homophones and homonyms in the poem.

Allow learners time to answer the questions in their notebooks.

> **Differentiation ideas:** Support learners by providing a dictionary so that they can check the meanings of homophones and homonyms.

Challenge learners to think of two more questions about the poem that they could ask a partner.

> **Assessment ideas:** Can learners identify homonyms in the poem? Can learners explain both meanings of each homonym in the poem?

Answers:

a   pins, nips

b   Any three pairs of: nips, tips; naps, traps; stop, shop; dare, tear; mate, state; name, game.

c   a (present tense) verb

d   dare, tear

e   Learners' own answers. Homophone: dear (same sound as 'deer' but different meaning). Possible homonyms: shop – place to buy things / the verb to shop; tear – when someone cries / to open forcibly; post – a letter delivery / a fence post; tame – a domesticated animal or pet / the verb to tame something; mean – to explain something / to be unkind.

2   Identify the past tense (15 minutes)

Learning intention: To change present tense verbs into the regular or irregular past tense.

Resources: Learner's Book 9.2, Activity 2; Workbook, Session 9.2; Language worksheet 9B

Description: Direct learners to the character and speech-bubble text, and then, in pairs, they should discuss other past tense verb spelling rules (e.g. doubling the last letter, dropping the *e* then adding *–ed*).

Ask learners to make two columns in their notebooks – one column for regular past tense verbs and the other for irregular past tense verbs. Ask learners to look at each verb carefully before recording it in the appropriate column. Ask learners to write the present tense and past tense of each verb.

Use the Workbook activities for further practice, or Language worksheet 9B to extend learners' skills with irregular past tense verbs.

> **Differentiation ideas:** Challenge learners to sort verbs into different columns based on the regular rule they follow, plus a column for irregular verbs (see answers above).

> **Assessment ideas:** Can learners identify regular and irregular past tenses of the verbs in the poem? Which learners can sort each verb into a table based on spelling rules, e.g. dropping *e*, doubling last letter, adding *–ed*?

Answers:

Regular past tense verbs			Irregular past tense verbs
(Just add *–ed*)	(Drop e and add *–ed*)	(Double last letter and add *–ed*)	
mix – mixed	carve – carved	snap – snapped	spin – spun
turn – turned	juggle – juggled	rip – ripped	make – made
switch – switched			
whisk – whisked			
twist – twisted			

3 Tongue twisters (10 minutes)

Learning intention: To explore alliteration.

Resources: *Whether the Weather* (Learner's Book, Session 9.2, Activity 3); Track 57

Description: Listen to the audio of *Whether the Weather*, then ask learners to read each tongue twister and then allow them time to repeat them quickly to a partner.

Ask learners to look at the words in *Whether the Weather*. Ask them to explain the homophones (e.g. whether – even if; weather – the temperature, wind, amount of rain or sun on a particular day).

In pairs, learners should discuss the meaning of the poem (e.g. no matter what the weather is like we will not let it bother us). Ask: *Are tongue twisters easy to say?* Discuss the words that caused the most difficulty (e.g. saying *sells* and not *shells*, all the *wh* words).

Read the Reading tip then ask: *What kind of letter is repeated (consonants)? Can you suggest a noun phrase using two or three words that start with the same consonant* (e.g. six sizzling sausages, five fiddling fingers, terrible tongue twisters)? Can learners explain what a tongue twister is (e.g. a phrase or sentence made up of words that begin with the same letter so that it is difficult to say when repeated quickly)?

Ask: *Can you put the noun phrase you thought into a sentence?* Say: *Try to add more words with the same letter* (e.g. Six sizzling sausages in a saucepan; Five fiddling fingers fumbling with forks). Allow learners time to answer the questions in their notebooks.

Answers:

a   Learners' own answers. Possible explanations could refer to the words being difficult to get your tongue around.

b   Learners' own answers. Possible answers could refer to the words being difficult to say and most of the words beginning with the same letter.

4 Play with words (15–20 minutes)

Learning intention: To look in detail at a poem and the words it uses.

Resources: *Wordspinning* and *Whether the Weather* (Learner's Book, Session 9.2); Tracks 56 and 57

Description: Re-read *Whether the Weather* or listen to Track 57 again. Ask learners to identify the text features in both poems (e.g. alliteration, puns, homophones, rhyme).

Ask learners to re-read *Wordspinning*. Ask: *Does Wordspinning use alliteration? Which poem is the easier to say? Which features are used in both poems?* (e.g. puns, homophones).

Read the Speaking tip and explain that reading with rhythm means saying the words so that listeners can hear a pattern to the words and to the lines. Explain that learners are going to choose one of the poems to recite. In pairs, they should discuss the actions that they could add to each of the poems (e.g. snapping their fingers when they recite line 2; mime the verbs *switch, rip, juggle*; spin, turn or twist their bodies; move their hands like a fan to show they are hot; mime shivering with cold).

Allow learners time to practise their poems. Learners could recite their poems to their partner.

⟩ **Differentiation ideas:** Support learners by pairing less confident speakers with a more confident partner and suggesting they choose a poem to recite together.

⟩ **Assessment ideas:** Can learners use the rhythm of the poem when they recite *Wordspinning* or *Whether the Weather*?

Plenary idea

Perform a poem (5–10 minutes)

Description: Invite pairs of learners to volunteer to perform their poem. Ask learners to peer-review each performance, considering strengths and what could be improved. Ask them to consider whether speakers used expression, recited the poem with rhythm and included actions. Remind learners to give feedback politely and with consideration of other learners' feelings.

CROSS-CURRICULAR LINKS

Geography: Use the poem *Whether the Weather* as a starting point for learners to explore weather and climate in a particular country.

Homework ideas

Ask learners to:

- complete the Workbook activities for this session, if not completed in class
- ask family members about tongue twisters they know or find tongue twisters from their own culture.

You could also challenge learners to write a tongue twister of their own.

Answers for Workbook

1   Learners own answers. Possible sentences could be:

   a   Hassan <u>screamed</u> when he was at the top of the roller coaster.

   b   Aunty Sonia <u>reflected</u> on her time in England.

   c   I <u>wrote</u> a long letter to my grandfather.

   d   Min <u>ran</u> to her friend's house as fast as she could.

2

Verb	Present tense	Past tense
to know	they *know*	they <u>knew</u>
to sleep	I <u>sleep</u>	I <u>slept</u>
to drive	she <u>drives</u>	she <u>drove</u>
to give	you <u>give</u>	you <u>gave</u>
to have	it <u>has</u>	it <u>had</u>
to help	we <u>help</u>	we <u>helped</u>
to feed	he <u>feeds</u>	he <u>fed</u>

3   Learners should circle the following words as irregular past tense forms: were, did, ate, thought, bought, went, sight, found, forgot, put, was, said, sank.

9.3 Funny poems and limericks

LEARNING PLAN

Learning objectives	Learning intentions	Success criteria
3Rw.01, 3Rw.02, 3Rw.03, 3Rw.04, 3Rv.01, 3Rv.04, 3Rs.02, 3Ri.02, 3Ri.03, 3Ri.16, 3Ra.01, 3Ra.02, 3Ra.03, 3Ww.04, 3Ww.05, 3Ww.06, 3Wc.01, 3Wc.05, 3Wp.04, 3SLs.01, 3SLg.01, 3SLg.02, 3SLg.03, 3SLg.04, 3SLr.02	• Discuss what makes different poems funny. • Identify the features of limericks. • Write a limerick.	• Learners can discuss what makes different poems funny. • Learners can identify the features of limericks. • Learners can write a limerick.

LANGUAGE SUPPORT

In this session, learners will meet the words *rhythm* and *rhyme*. Draw learners' attention to the fact that the *h* is silent in both words and of the different *y* sound in *rhythm* (a short *i* sound) and *rhyme* (a long *i* sound).

Learners may not understand the use of near rhymes in the second verse (*fast / grass*). If necessary, explain that poets sometimes choose words that almost rhyme, and when this happens it is much easier to hear the pattern of sounds by reading poems aloud, rather than in their head.

Starter idea

What makes it funny? (5 minutes)

Resources: Learner's Book, Session 9.3: Getting started

Description: Ask learners to recall some of the different jokes in previous sessions. Ask: *What did you find funny? Why?* Explain to learners that what people find funny is different for each individual and can vary between cultures. Remind learners to always listen politely to the opinion of others.

Allow learners time to complete the activity in the Learner's Book.

Main teaching ideas

1 Funny poems (15–20 minutes)

Learning intention: To discuss what makes different poems funny.

Resources: *Starter* and *The Monster* (Learner's Book, Session 9.3, Activity 1); Tracks 58 and 59

Description: Organise learners into groups and ask each group to assign the roles of reader, scribe and reporter.

Listen to Track 58, then ask the readers in each group to read *Starter* out loud. Ask groups to discuss parts a–c. The scribes in each group should record the group's answers. Ask the reporters from each group to feed back group answers to the class.

Listen to Track 59, then read *The Monster* as a class and allow learners to complete parts d–f in their notebooks.

In groups, learners should discuss the character's speech-bubble text. Allow time for groups to share the questions they would ask the poets.

> **Differentiation ideas:** Support learners with answering part e by asking: *Did you expect the poem to end as it did?*

Challenge learners to write their own version of *The Monster* (e.g. changing adjectives, changing the last line).

> **Assessment ideas:** During discussions about the poems, do learners comment on how the audio and/or illustrations help their understanding of the text?

Answers:

a   Possible answers: the poem begins with a greeting; the poem is about someone who likes starting things.

b   Possible answers: the poem is unfinished because it is about someone who starts things but does not finish them.

c   say

d   Possible answers: ugly, tall, scary, small.

e   Learners' own answers.

f   Learners' own answers.

2 Crazy days (25–30 minutes)

Learning intention: To discuss what makes different poems funny.

Resources: *Crazy Days* (Learner's Book. Session 9.3, Activity 2); Track 60; Worksheet 9.1

Description: Play Track 60 once, then check that learners understand all of the vocabulary (e.g. '*Twas* – it was; *streetcar* – a vehicle on rails for transporting many passengers; *barefoot* – wearing nothing on the feet).

Read the Listening tip, then play the audio again. Ask learners to discuss part a. Ask learners to share their answers. Did they identify that some of the statements are impossible (e.g. snow cannot rain, you are not barefoot if you are wearing shoes)? Explain that poems of this kind are known as *nonsense poems*. Explain that *Crazy Days* is nonsense because all of the statements are contradictions.

Read parts b–d then play the audio again, and allow time for learners to discuss each question.

Read each of the bullet points in part e. Allow learners time to write an additional verse with their partner.

Use Worksheet 9.1 What makes you laugh? to provide further practice in understanding what makes a poem funny.

> **Differentiation ideas:** Support learners by providing a starting line (e.g. '*Twas lunchtime in the evening*) and the next nonsense line (e.g. *and the stars had gone to bed*). Ask learners to suggest some nonsense ideas for the next two lines. Remind them that the last word of the poem needs to rhyme with *bed*.

> **Assessment ideas:** When learners write an extra verse, do they maintain the rhythm and rhyming pattern heard in the audio?

Audioscript: *Crazy Days*

'Twas midnight on the ocean,
Not a streetcar was in sight;
The sun was shining brightly,
For it rained all day that night.

'Twas a summer day in winter
And snow was raining fast,
As a barefoot boy with shoes on
Stood sitting in the grass.

Answers:

a   Learners' own answers. Possible reasons could refer to the poem sounding sensible until you listen closely to the words and that it uses lots of contradictions.

b   two

c   It begins with the word 'Twas.

d   lines 2 and 4

e   Learners' own answers.

 3   Limericks (10–15 minutes)

Learning intention: To identify the features of limericks.

Resources: *There Was an Old Man with a Beard* (Learner's Book, Session 9.3, Activity 3); Track 61; Workbook, Session 9.3, Activities 1–3

Description: Read the Language focus text, then listen to Track 61 and ask learners to follow the words of the limerick in the Learner's Book. Ask learners to re-read the limerick and use the syllables in the limerick to clap the rhythm. Ask: *Which two lines have the same rhythm?* (lines 3 and 4, and 1, 2 and 5) *What else is the same about lines 3 and 4, and 1, 2 and 3?* (each group rhymes) Explain that all limericks follow this pattern. Ask: *Which word has a silent letter?* (wren).

In groups, learners should re-read the limerick and then discuss what makes it funny. Explain that learners should ask each other questions about what they have said (e.g. ask learners to give reasons for an opinion) or add comments of their own in support or against what has been said (e.g. *Like you, I thought ...*; *That's interesting, but I thought ...*).

Direct learners to the character and speech-bubble text. Are learners surprised that this limerick was written so long ago? Why?

Use the Focus and Practice activities in the Workbook to provide further practice with rhythm and rhyme.

> **Assessment ideas:** Do learners use the visual information in the illustration of the limerick to understand new vocabulary (e.g. *lark*, *wren*)?

Answers:
Learners' own responses.

4   Another limerick (15 minutes)

Learning intention: To write a limerick.

Resources: Learner's Book, Session 9.3, Activity 4; Differentiated worksheet pack

Description: As a class, re-read the limerick from the previous activity. Now ask learners to look at the limerick with gaps and decide which words they could use to complete it. Encourage them to keep the rhythm the same as the original. Allow learners time to choose which words they think are the most important in their limerick.

If there is time, allow pairs to read their limericks and explain their choice of important words.

You could use Differentiated worksheets 9A–C to provide learners with a further opportunity to identify the rhythm of a limerick and to change the words within it.

> **Differentiation ideas:** Support less confident writers using questions as prompts:

- *Who has the beard* (e.g. an old woman, a young boy, an old goat)?

- *What could the animals do apart from build a nest* (e.g. go to sleep, make a mess, lay an egg)?

- *Which other animals live in the beard?*

Challenge confident writers to change other words in the limerick (e.g. change one set of rhyming words).

> **Assessment ideas:** Can learners use their understanding of rhythm to complete the limerick?

Answers:

a   Learners' own limericks.

b   Learners' own choices of words with an appropriate explanation.

Plenary idea

Review limericks (5 minutes)

Resources: Learners' limericks from Activity 4

Description: Ask learners to peer review their limericks. Does the limerick follow the rhyming pattern with lines 1, 2 and 5 rhyming and lines 3 and 4 rhyming? Does it follow the same rhythm as Edward Lear's limerick? Are there any words learners want to change?

Homework ideas

Ask learners to:

• complete the Challenge activity in the Workbook

• write a limerick about a member of their family or a friend.

Answers for Workbook

1   Learners read and clap the rhythm of the limerick.

2   end of lines 1, 2 and 5: Dumbree, tea, Dumbree end of lines 3 and 4: mice, nice

3   Learners' own answers.

4   Learners' own answers.

9.4 Calligrams and mnemonics

LEARNING PLAN

Learning objectives	Learning intentions	Success criteria
3Rw.03, 3Rv.01, 3Rv.02, 3Rs.02, 3Ri.02, 3Ri.03, 3Ri.07, 3Ri.16, 3Ri.17, 3Ra.01, 3Ra.02, 3Ww.01, 3Ww.05, 3Ww.06, 3Wc.05, 3Wp.01, 3Wp.03, 3SLr.02	• Look at different ways to remember how to spell words. • Explore different ways a phoneme can be written. • Use visual prompts as a spelling strategy. • Use mnemonics as a spelling strategy.	• Learners know different ways to remember how to spell words. • Learners understand different ways a phoneme can be written. • Learners can use visual prompts as a spelling strategy. • Learners can use mnemonics as a spelling strategy.

LANGUAGE SUPPORT

For some learners it can be helpful to make connections between words and meaning. A few learners may also notice the word *phone* within *homophone* and *phoneme*. This may help them to link the word *phone* with *sound*.

Starter idea

Spelling aids (10 minutes)

Resources: Learner's Book, Session 9.4: Getting started

Description: Explain that in this session learners are going to think about ways of remembering how to spell difficult words.

In pairs, learners should talk about the activity in the Learner's Book. List learners' suggestions for ways to remember spellings on the board.

Discuss the questions in the Learner's Book. Ask: *What happens when you spell a word incorrectly on a computer?* (e.g. auto-correct, red wiggly line under the word, drop-down menu with list of alternative spellings).

Main teaching ideas

1 *Kite* calligram (20 minutes)

Learning intentions: To look at different ways to remember how to spell words; to use visual prompts as a spelling strategy.

Resources: *Kite* (Learner's Book, Session 9.4, Activity 1); Track 62

Description: Write *calligram* on the board and point out each syllable to support learners with reading and saying the word. Listen to Track 62.

Direct learners to the character and speech-bubble text. Read the information, then explain that calligram poems are often shapes. Ask learners to close their eyes as you read the calligram. Ask: *What is the calligram describing?*

Ask learners to look at the calligram in the Learner's Book. Can learners see the kite shape? Ask them to listen to you re-read the poem as they follow the words. Ask: *Does the calligram have a rhythm? Do any of the words rhyme* (flight, height, night)?

Ask learners to answer the questions in their notebooks, in sentences and using neat joined handwriting.

⟩ **Assessment ideas:** Note which learners can identify the rhyming words.

Answers:

a   The poet used a kite shape because the poem is about a kite.

b   Someone had made the kite as part of a project on flight.

c   *attain a great height* means to go up very high.

d   The kite got stuck in a tree.

e   Learners' own answers. Possible answers: the kite will stay in the tree; someone will climb the tree to get the kite; the wind will blow the kite down; someone will pull on the string until the kite is free.

2 Sounds in words (10 minutes)

Learning intention: To explore different ways a phoneme can be written.

Resources: Learner's Book, Session 9.4, Activity 2

Description: Direct learners to the word *stuck* in the poem. Ask learners which sound they can identify at the end of the word (*ck*). In pairs, learners should re-read the poem quietly and listen for other words with a *ck* sound. Remind them that the word may have a different spelling.

When learners have identified the other word with a *ck* sound, ask them to read the words in part c and answer this question in their notebooks.

⟩ **Differentiation ideas:** Support learners by reading the poem to them so that they can identify the sounds.

Challenge learners to list more words with *f* and *ck* sounds.

⟩ **Assessment ideas:** Can learners find the different ways the phonemes *f* and *ck* can be written?

Answers:

b   Possible words with *ck* sound: *looks, like, kite* (accept *project*).

c   Learners should underline: *f* and *ph*; *c* and *ck*

3 Calligram words (15 minutes)

Learning intention: To use visual prompts as a spelling strategy.

Resources: Learner's Book, Session 9.4, Activity 3; dictionaries

Description: Ask learners to look at the calligram words in the Language focus box (*stretch, gleam* and *drop*). Ask learners to close their eyes. Read the word *stretch*, then ask: *Can you picture the word*

stretch*? Can you picture in your head how the word is spelled?* In pairs, learners should repeat this with the words *gleam* and *drop*.

Discuss part a in the Learner's Book. Ask learners to share their ideas.

Ask learners to think of three words they could use to create calligrams. Remind them to check that they have spelled the words correctly before creating their calligrams.

> **Differentiation ideas:** Support learners by suggesting words they could use (e.g. freeze, ice, fire).

Challenge learners to create calligrams of five words.

> **Assessment ideas:** Note which learners were able to imagine and create calligram words.

Answers:

a   Learners' own answers. Possible answers could refer to calligrams painting a picture in their head which helps them see the letters, or helping them focus on each letter instead of rushing over the word.

b   Learners' own calligrams.

4   Mnemonics (10 minutes)

Learning intention: To use mnemonics as a spelling strategy.

Resources: Learner's Book, Session 9.4; Workbook, Session 9.4; dictionaries; spelling logs

Description: Write *mnemonic* on the board. Explain that the first *m* is silent. Show learners how to break the word into three syllables (*ne-mon-ik*). Can learners explain what a mnemonic is? Direct learners to the Language focus box and read the mnemonics. Ask: *Do all the mnemonics use the letters of the word to create a saying?* (e.g. because, said) *What other methods do they use?* (e.g. uses part of the word in a sentence to emphasise a spelling pattern, for example *end* in fri*end*) Allow learners time to talk to a partner about how useful they think these mnemonics are.

Ask: *Why might it be helpful to have a strategy for remembering these directions and words?* (e.g. they can be difficult to remember, they are tricky

words to spell) *Can you think of any other mnemonics that you would find easier to remember for these words?* (e.g. 'I see my friend on <u>Fri</u>day' because it would remind me to put the *i* before the *e*).

Use the Workbook activities to provide further practice with mnemonics if there is time in class.

> **Assessment ideas:** Note which learners can name a variety of spelling strategies, especially for spelling difficult words. The kind of strategy learners use may depend on how they learn. Note which learners prefer visual prompts, as these learners are more likely to use calligrams.

5   Write a mnemonic (10–15 minutes)

Learning intention: To use mnemonics as a spelling strategy.

Resources: Learner's Book, Session 9.4, Activity 5

Description: Explain that learners are going to write their own mnemonic for two difficult words. Remind them of the points of the compass mnemonic and point out the picture of the naughty elephant squirting water. Explain that linking a visual prompt, such as a picture or calligram, can make the mnemonic easier to remember.

Remind learners that their mnemonic can look at the whole word or part of the word (e.g. The <u>ant</u> w<u>ant</u>s to go home). Remind them to check that they have spelled the words correctly before they write their mnemonic.

When learners have written their mnemonic in their notebooks, direct them to the Writing tip. If learners do not already use a spelling log, you could ask them to begin one in the back of their notebooks, or provide a new book for recording ideas.

> **Differentiation ideas:** Support learners who find spelling difficult by pairing them with a more confident learner.

> **Assessment ideas:** Note the types of mnemonic learners prefer.

Answers:
Learners' own mnemonics.

Plenary idea

Remembering words (5 minutes)

Resources: Spelling logs

Description: In pairs, learners should choose a word they find difficult to spell and create a calligram or mnemonic for that word. Share learners' ideas. Are there any calligrams or mnemonics that the whole class could use?

Encourage learners to add their calligram or mnemonic to their spelling log.

CROSS-CURRICULAR LINKS

Science: Ask learners to create a calligram to help them remember the definition or spelling of some new vocabulary related to a science topic.

Homework ideas

Ask learners to:

- complete the Workbook activities for this session, if not completed in class
- create a colourful poster of calligrams of difficult words.

Answers for Workbook

1 Learners' own responses.

2 Learners' own calligrams.

3 **a** rhythm
  b because
  c ocean
  d necessary

4 Learners' own responses.

9.5 Reviewing a poem

LEARNING PLAN

Learning objectives	Learning intentions	Success criteria
3Rs.02, 3Ri.02, 3Ri.03, 3Ri.07, 3Ri.09, 3Ri.16, 3Ri.17, 3Ra.02, 3Ra.03, 3Ww.02, 3Ww.05, 3Ww.06, 3Wv.01, 3Wv.07, 3Wg.01, 3Wg.06, 3Wg.07, 3Ws.01, 3Ws.02, 3Wc.02, 3Wc.05, 3Wc.06, 3Wp.02, 3Wp.04, 3SLg.02, 3SLg.03, 3SLr.02	• Record information about poems in a table. • Write a review for a poem. • Update and use a spelling log.	• Learners can record information about poems in a table. • Learners can write a review for a poem. • Learners can update and use a spelling log.

LANGUAGE SUPPORT

You many need to recap the terms *wordplay* and *nonsense* as these words will help learners explain their ideas when they talk about the poems and write their reviews.

Starter idea

Re-read poems (5 minutes)

Resources: Learner's Book, Session 9.5: Getting started

Description: Ask learners to re-read the poems listed in the Learner's Book. Ask: *How will the pattern of the words affect how you say the poem* (e.g. follow the rhythm, use the rhyming words)? *How could you make the poem interesting to listen to* (e.g. add expression)?

Main teaching ideas

1 Complete a table (20 minutes)

Learning intention: To record information about poems in a table.

Resources: Learner's Book, Session 9.5, Activity 1; Workbook, Session 9.5, Activity 1

Description: In groups, learners should discuss what they thought about each of the poems. Which poem(s) did most of the group enjoy? Why? Which poem(s) did the group not enjoy?

Why? You could ask learners to use the Focus activity in the Workbook here as prompts to their discussion.

Point to the tables in the Learner's Book. Show learners how you would complete the table using one of the poems as an example. Ask learners to draw the table in their notebooks. Tell them that they should choose poems that they liked and poems they did not like.

Allow learners time to complete the table, then ask for volunteers to share one of their comments about one of the poems.

⟩ **Differentiation ideas:** Support learners by providing copies of the table.

Challenge learners by asking them to add additional rows to the table and review more of the poems.

⟩ **Assessment ideas:** Can learners support their opinions about a poem with reasons that reference the text? Can learners use the correct language to describe each type of poem?

Answers:

Learners' own answers. An example row in the table could be:

Name of poem	Favourite line in poem	What I like about this poem	What I do not like about this poem
Wordspinning	Juggle taste into state	The way the poem jumbles words up to make new ones.	The rhyming words *dare* and *tear* because you have to think about how you say tear.

2 Review a poem (20 minutes)

Learning intention: To review a poem learners have read.

Resources: Learner's Book, Session 9.5, Activity 2; Worksheet 9.2

Description: Ask learners to list the types of poem they have read in this unit (e.g. riddles, tongue twisters, poems with puns, poems that used wordplay, limericks, funny/nonsense poems, calligram/shape poems). Explain that learners are going to write a review of one of the poems. Remind them of the book reviews they have written. Ask learners to talk to a partner about the kind of information that should be included.

Direct learners to the bullet points in the Learner's Book. *How you will organise your writing* (paragraphs)? *What kind of words will you use* (adjectives, noun phrases)?

Encourage learners to use the ideas from the table they completed in Activity 1 in their review and to make notes about some of the words they will use before they start writing. Allow learners time to write their reviews in their notebooks.

⟩ **Differentiation ideas:** Support learners by providing them with Worksheet 9.2 Poem-review template. They could use the template to plan or write their review.

Challenge learners to use sequencing words to start their paragraphs.

> **Assessment ideas:** Use learners' poem reviews to assess their:

- use of different sentence structures (e.g. statement, question and exclamation sentences)
- sentence punctuation
- use of paragraphs
- use of sentence starters to organise paragraphs
- correct use of different past tense verb endings, suggesting they understand the different rules (e.g. doubling consonant, adding *–d* or *–t*)
- recall of spellings of irregular past tense verbs.

Answers:
Learners' own answers.

3 Check your spelling (10 minutes)

Learning intention: To update and use a spelling log.

Resources: Learner's Book, Session 9.5, Activity 3; dictionaries; computers; spelling logs

Description: Ask: *Have you used any words that are tricky to spell in your review? Did you use any spelling mnemonics when you wrote these words? What else can you use to check your spelling?*

Ask learners to check the spellings in their review and update (or create) spelling logs, using the bullet points in the Learner's Book for reference. Remind them to check their spelling in a dictionary or by using a computer.

Which tricky spellings did learners identify? Ask: *Did the mnemonics help you with words you have found tricky in the past?*

Allow time for learners to share their reviews and discuss the How are you doing? questions with a partner.

> **Differentiation ideas:** Challenge learners to create a calligram or mnemonic for some of the words they found tricky to spell.

> **Assessment ideas:** Note any improvement in learners' spelling of difficult words. Ask these learners if they used any of the mnemonics or calligrams they are familiar with.

Plenary idea

Twenty Questions spelling game (10 minutes)

Resources: List of difficult words

Description: Draw a dash on the board for each letter of a difficult word. Tell learners that they start the game with twenty guesses. Explain that they need to guess the letters in your word in order within twenty guesses.

Asking learners to guess the letters in order will encourage them to use the calligrams and mnemonics they have created for these words.

Homework ideas

Ask learners to:

- complete the Workbook activities for this session, if not completed in class
- choose a favourite poem, or one from an anthology, and write a review for it.

Answers for Workbook

Learners' own responses.

9.6 Writing and performing a poem

LEARNING PLAN

Learning objectives	Learning intentions	Success criteria
3Rg.01, 3Ri.03, 3Ri.09, 3Ww.02, 3Ww.04, 3Ww.05, 3Ww.06, 3Wv.01, 3Wv.05, 3Wv.07, 3Wg.01, 3Wg.06, 3Wg.07, 3Ws.01, 3Ws.04, 3Wc.01, 3Wc.02, 3Wc.05, 3Wc.06, 3Wp.04, 3SLm.01, 3SLm.05, 3SLg.01, 3SLg.02, 3SLg.03, 3SLg.04, 3SLp.01, 3SLp.02, 3SLp.03, 3SLp.04, 3SLr.01, 3SLr.02	• Write a poem in a particular style. • Find ways to improve poetry writing. • Perform a poem.	• Learners can write a poem in a particular style. • Learners can find ways to improve their poetry writing. • Learners can perform a poem.

LANGUAGE SUPPORT

Learners may need support in identifying the rhythm of the poem they choose to perform. Some poems, such as limericks, have a very clear rhythm, but the rhythm in other poems is less clear (e.g. *Kite*).

You may want to encourage learners who are less confident performers to choose poems with very clear rhythms.

Common misconceptions

Misconception	How to identify	How to overcome
Rhyming words in poems give a poem its rhythm.	Ask learners to read *Kite* aloud. Note learners who read the poem as if it is a rhyming poem (e.g. pausing at the words *flight* and *height*) to give the poem a rhythm.	Explain that not all poems have rhyming words and that rhyming words can sometimes be within a line, rather than at the end. Ask: *Why do poets start new lines* (e.g. to give the poem a shape, to show us the rhythm)? Explain that the shape of the poem and the way the lines are written are more important than rhyming words and that this is what gives a poem its rhythm.

Starter idea

Types of poem (5–10 minutes)

Resources: Learner's Book, Session 9.6: Getting started

Description: In pairs, learners should discuss the four types of poem in the list in the Learner's Book. Invite learners to share their ideas. For example:

- Wordplay: uses puns and homophones/homonyms; changes the words to make them funny

- Limericks: have five lines; lines 1, 2 and 5 rhyme and lines 3 and 4 rhyme; start with *There was a ...*

- Calligrams: make the shape of what they are about; make the shape that matches the word

- Tongue twisters: words begin with the same letter; they're difficult to say.

Main teaching ideas

1 Choose a type of poem (40 minutes)

Learning intention: To write a poem in a particular style.

Resources: Learner's Book, Session 9.6, Activity 1; Workbook, Session 9.6; dictionaries; thesauruses

Description: Explain the activity to learners. They can use the Workbook activities for this session to help them plan and write their poem. Ask learners to choose a style of poem to write. Organise learners into pairs or small groups made up of learners who have chosen the same poem style.

Ask groups to brainstorm ideas for what the poem could be about. Each group could choose a scribe to record suggestions. Ask individual learners to choose a subject for their poem from the ideas generated. If any group members chose the same subject, suggest that they might work together.

Ask: *What type of words might be useful in your poem* (e.g. rhyming words, nouns, adjectives, present or past tense verbs depending upon the poem type, homophones, alliterative words)? Read the Writing tip, then allow learners time to collect words for their poem. Encourage learners to use dictionaries and a thesaurus to check spellings and gain ideas for words.

Ask learners to re-read a poem from the Learner's Book in the style of the one they will write. Allow them time to write their poems.

Ask learners to read their poems to themselves so that they can hear the rhyming pattern and the rhythm of the poem. Ask: *Do the words sound right? Can you hear the rhymes? Do the words follow the rhythm of your chosen style of poem?*

> **Differentiation ideas:** Support learners by directing them to the Workbook activities for this session.

> **Assessment ideas:** Can learners identify the features of each type of poem found in Unit 9? Can learners use these features as a model for their own writing? Which features are learners most confident in using?

2 Proofread your poem (10–15 minutes)

Learning intention: To find ways to improve poetry writing.

Resources: Learner's Book, Session 9.6, Activity 2; Worksheet 9.3; dictionaries; thesauruses; spelling logs

Description: Explain the activity to learners and organise them into pairs. Read, or ask learners to read, the bulleted checklist in the Learner's Book. You could also provide Worksheet 9.3 Checklist for writing a funy poem for pairs to use as a more detailed poem checklist.

Encourage pairs of learners to read their poems to their partner first, so that their partner hears the poem before seeing the words. If the poem is a calligram, can their partner guess what the shape of the poem will be before they see it?

Ask pairs to discuss way to improve their poems, using the checklist in the Learner's Book or Worksheet 9.3.

Remind learners to check homophone words carefully. Have they used the right spelling in the right place?

Allow learners time to make changes to their poems following feedback.

> **Differentiation ideas:** Support less confident writers by allowing them to adapt an existing poem in their chosen style by changing some of the words.

> **Assessment ideas:** Assess the accuracy of learners' spelling, especially the correct use of homophones, difficult words for which they have written mnemonics and irregular past tense verbs.

3 Performance time (15–20 minutes)

Learning intention: To perform a poem.

Resources: Learner's Book, Session 9.6, Activity 3.

Description: Ask: *What is important when you are performing?* Try to elicit the importance of:

- speaking clearly
- not speaking too quickly
- looking at the audience
- adding expression so that people want to listen
- including gestures.

Read the activity instructions in the Learner's Book. Allow learners time to practise performing.

Explain that learners are going to perform their poems to a small group of learners. You could group learners so that all have written poems in the same style or where each learner has written a poem in a different style.

Allow learners time to perform their poems, then ask them to reflect on their performance using the How am I doing? questions.

⟩ **Assessment ideas:** Can learners perform their poems using a clear voice? Can learners evaluate their performance and identify aspects that they would like to improve?

Plenary idea

What am I? (5 minutes)

Description: Explain that learners are going to play a Twenty Questions-style game about types of poem.

In groups, one learner (Learner A) must think of a type of poem. Other learners try to guess the type of poem by asking no more than five questions. Learner A can only answer 'yes' or 'no'. The learner who guesses correctly thinks of the next poem type. If learners have not guessed after five questions, Learner A gives them the answer and thinks of a new type of poem.

Homework ideas

Ask learners to:

- write clues about words that describe features or types of poem used in this unit (e.g. pun, riddle, calligram, homonym); learners could design a crossword for the answers or use the clues in a group quiz.

Answers for Workbook

Learners' own responses.

CHECK YOUR PROGRESS

1 **a** limericks
   b limericks and funny poems
   c riddles
   d tongue twisters

2 five

3 Learners' own explanations should identify *dear*, meaning a greeting, and *deer*, meaning an animal.

4 Learners' own answers. Words should be written to show the calligram shape, for example:

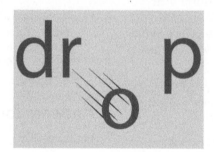

5 Learners' own answers. Possible mnemonics could include: there is a *rat* in *separate*.

PROJECT GUIDANCE

As each of these projects provides a different assessment opportunity, you may decide to use all three projects. The solo project focuses on handwriting. The paired project provides writing and speaking assessment opportunities. The group project focuses on speaking and listening skills.

You will find it helpful to refer to the guidance about *Setting up and assessing the projects* in the Project guidance in Unit 1.

Group project: Explain the project to learners and organise them into groups of five or six. Provide a selection of poems or poetry books from which they can choose their poem.

Discuss what is involved in giving a group performance, for example:

- using a clear voice
- adding expression
- making the rhythm of the poem obvious to the listeners
- keeping in time with each other whenever words or lines are said together
- adding some actions.

Assess how well learners worked as a group. Did they allocate speaking parts fairly? If there was a chorus in the poem, did learners say this together? If so, did learners stay in time with each other? Did speakers make the rhythm of the poem clear? Did they use appropriate actions and expression? Did learners speak clearly and with appropriate volume?

Pair project: Explain the project to learners. Remind them that tongue twisters use alliteration.

You may wish to provide a topic for the tongue twister linked to other curriculum areas. Some learners may find it easier to change words within existing tongue twisters rather than start from scratch.

Provide stopwatches for learners to time how quickly they can recite their tongue twister.

Solo project: Provide a selection of poetry books, or access to online poems, so that learners have a range of poems from which to choose. Explain the project to learners and explain that they can choose any style of poem.

When learners have chosen their poem, ask them to decide whether they will handwrite or type their poem.

Ask learners to look at the illustrations accompanying some of the poems in the Learner's Book, or online. Explain that the illustrations should give readers more information about the text.

Assess learners' joined handwriting or word-processing skills. Have they set their poems using the style of the original poem? Do their illustrations support the text?

> Spelling activities answers

Term 1 Spelling activities

1 Compound words

a anyone anybody anywhere anything anymore

everyone everybody everywhere everything

someone somebody somewhere something

no-one nobody nowhere nothing

b butter + fly = butterfly

earth + worm = earthworm

king + fisher = kingfisher

hammer + head shark = hammerhead shark

grass + hopper = grasshopper

rattle + snake = rattlesnake

jelly + fish = jellyfish

sparrow + hawk = sparrowhawk

2 **Spelling strategies**

a weight

b treasure

c picture

3 Alphabetical order

a a b c d e f g h i j k l m n o p q r s t u v w x y z

b A B C D E F G H I J K L M N O P Q R S T U V W X Y Z

c bear, fish, fox, lion, penguin, seal, tiger, tortoise

4 Spelling rules

Verb	+ –*s*	+ –*ing*	+ –*ed*
push	*pushes*	pushing	pushed
smile	*smiles*	smiling	smiled
knot	knots	knotting	knotted
grin	grins	grinning	*grinned*
circle	circles	*circling*	circled

5 **a** Same letters, different sounds

b glove, move

cough, dough

bruise, guide

weight, height

catalogue, tongue

mallet, wallet

c gl<u>o</u>ve, m<u>o</u>ve

c<u>ough</u>, d<u>ough</u>

br<u>ui</u>se, g<u>ui</u>de

wei<u>ght</u>, hei<u>ght</u>

catalo<u>gue</u>, ton<u>gue</u>

m<u>all</u>et, w<u>all</u>et

Term 2 Spelling activities

1 Spelling strategies

  a crocodile

  b mountain

  c dinosaur

  d computer

2 Contractions

  a he will – he'll

    it is – it's

    they are – they're

  b Learners' own sentences.

3 Homophones

  a one – won

    past – passed

    board – bored

    here – hear

    piece – peace

  b they're – their; there

    too – to; two

4 Suffixes

  a careful – careless

    harmless – harmful

    thankful – thankless

    doubtless – doubtful

    hopeful – hopeless

    painless – painful

    colourless – colourful

    powerless – powerful

  b appointment

    attachment

    awareness

    brightness

    cleverness

    development

    embarrassment

  c busy – <u>busily</u>

    careful – <u>carefully</u>

    caution – (cautious)

    danger – (dangerous)

    easy – <u>easily</u>

    fame – (famous)

    funny – <u>funnily</u>

    fury – (furious)

    kind – <u>kindly</u>

    nerve – (nervous)

5 Spelling rules

    bush – bushes

    book – books

    fox – foxes

    house – houses

    lollipop – lollipops

    wish – wishes

Term 3 Spelling activities

1 Irregular verbs

begin – began

break – broke

bring – brought

buy – bought

catch – caught

come – came

do – did

give – gave

have – had

hear – heard

is – was

make – made

stand – stood

think – thought

throw – threw

2 Prefixes

a *re–* means *again*

b *in–* means *not*

The prefix *in–* becomes *im–* before ... words beginning with *m* or *p*.

The prefix *in–* becomes *il–* before ... words beginning with *l*.

The prefix *in–* become *ir–* before ... words beginning with other letters

c subway – a track, path or road that goes underground

submerge – to put underwater

subheading – under a heading

subtract – to take away

3 Homonyms

a People put their money in a <u>bank</u> to keep it safe.

I like walking along the river <u>bank</u>.

b You <u>wave</u> your hand from side to side when you say goodbye.

The surfer rode to the shore on a huge <u>wave</u>.

c The shepherd put the sheep in a <u>pen</u>.

I wrote a letter with my new <u>pen</u>.

d I'm not feeling very <u>well</u>.

We collected water from the <u>well</u>.

e It was an exciting football <u>match</u>.

He lit a <u>match</u> to light a fire.

4 Different letters, same sound

a <u>g</u>iraffe

b <u>r</u>ain

c <u>m</u>onkey

d <u>d</u>inosaur

e <u>k</u>itten de<u>ck</u>

5 Spelling strategies

a Learners' own caligrams.

b Learners' own mnemonics.

6 Spelling log

Learners' own answers.